Shaping the Surface

Shaping the Surface

*Materiality and the History of
British Architecture 1840–2000*

STEPHEN KITE

BLOOMSBURY VISUAL ARTS
LONDON · NEW YORK · OXFORD · NEW DELHI · SYDNEY

BLOOMSBURY VISUAL ARTS
Bloomsbury Publishing Plc
50 Bedford Square, London, WC1B 3DP, UK
1385 Broadway, New York, NY 10018, USA
29 Earlsfort Terrace, Dublin 2, Ireland

BLOOMSBURY, BLOOMSBURY VISUAL ARTS and the Diana logo are trademarks of Bloomsbury Publishing Plc

First published in Great Britain 2022

Copyright © Stephen Kite, 2022

Stephen Kite has asserted his right under the Copyright, Designs and Patents Act, 1988, to be identified as Author of this work.

For legal purposes the Acknowledgements on p. xiv constitute an extension of this copyright page.

Cover design: Eleanor Rose
Cover image: Polychromatic banding, chancel wall, All Saints, Boyne Hill, Berkshire, George Edmund Street © Geoff Brandwood

All rights reserved. No part of this publication may be reproduced or transmitted in any form or by any means, electronic or mechanical, including photocopying, recording, or any information storage or retrieval system, without prior permission in writing from the publishers.

Bloomsbury Publishing Plc does not have any control over, or responsibility for, any third-party websites referred to or in this book. All internet addresses given in this book were correct at the time of going to press. The author and publisher regret any inconvenience caused if addresses have changed or sites have ceased to exist, but can accept no responsibility for any such changes.

A catalogue record for this book is available from the British Library.

ISBN: HB: 978-1-3503-2066-6
PB: 978-1-3503-2065-9
ePDF: 978-1-3503-2067-3
eBook: 978-1-3503-2068-0

Typeset by RefineCatch Limited, Bungay, Suffolk
Printed and bound in India

To find out more about our authors and books visit www.bloomsbury.com and sign up for our newsletters.

For Alana

CONTENTS

List of Figures viii
Acknowledgements xiv

Introduction 1

1 Reading the Wall-Surface: John Ruskin, William Butterfield, and George Edmund Street 9

2 'Think first of the walls': Surfaces of Romance – Morris, Webb, and the Arts and Crafts Domestic Interior 45

3 Smooth and Rough: George Frederick Bodley and Edward Schröder Prior 69

4 Carving the Surface: Edwardian and Inter-War Architecture and Sculpture 99

5 Surfaces and Sharawaggi: Aspects of the Picturesque c. 1925–55 125

6 As Found: Surfaces of Brutalism 153

7 Pattern, Abstraction, Post-Modernism: Lubetkin – Pasmore – Stirling 179

8 High-Tech, Neo-Vernacular, New Materiality: Richard Rogers – Ralph Erskine – Caruso St John 223

Notes 259
Bibliography 293
Index 311

FIGURES

1.1	Courtyard façade of Casa dell'Angelo, Rio di Canonica, Venice (also called Ca' Soranzo).	14
1.2	Giovanni Mansueti, *Miracle of the Relic of the Holy Cross in Campo San Lio* (1494).	16
1.3	John Ruskin, 'Linear and Surface Gothic' (1853).	18
1.4	Monza, Duomo façade, completed 1396.	21
1.5	John Ruskin, 'Wall-Veil Decoration'.	22
1.6	John Ruskin and Le Cavalier Iller, *Pistoia, Church of San Pietro* (*c.* 1846). Half-plate daguerreotype.	23
1.7	All Saints' Margaret Street, interior looking east (1859).	29
1.8	All Saints' Margaret Street, courtyard elevation of south aisle.	30
1.9	All Saints Boyne Hill, Berkshire, 'Church, No. 5 – Buttresses and Lower Part of Tower', colour ink on paper, original drawing, G. E. Street (1864).	37
1.10	George Edmund Street, All Saints Boyne Hill (1858).	39
1.11	George Edmund Street, All Saints Boyne Hill, nave and chancel.	40
1.12	George Edmund Street, All Saints Boyne Hill, detail of chancel, north wall.	42
2.1	Guillaume de Lorris and Jean de Meun, *Roman de la Rose*, 'Lutenist and singers in a walled garden' (*c.* 1490–1500).	47
2.2	Perspective reconstruction of Philip Webb's 1864 design to extend Red House into a 'Palace of Art'.	49
2.3	*Hortus conclusus* analysis of Red House 'Palace of Art'.	50
2.4	F. H. New, *Long Drawing Room at Kelmscott House*, woodcut.	54
2.5	William Morris and Philip Webb, design for *Trellis* wallpaper (1862), pencil, ink and watercolour on paper.	55
2.6	Design for wall decoration in the Green Room at the Victoria and Albert Museum, London, by Philip Webb (formerly the Green Dining Room, South Kensington Museum, London, 1866).	58
2.7	'A corner of the second drawing-room, decorated by William Morris' (1893).	62
2.8	Frontispiece 'A Drawing Room Corner', Robert W. Edis (1881).	64
2.9	*Vine* wallpaper, original design, William Morris (*c.* 1873), pencil and watercolour.	66

FIGURES

3.1 J. J. Joass, watercolour perspective (1901) of Church of the Holy Trinity, South Kensington, London (1901–6), George Frederick Bodley. 70
3.2 E. S. Prior, St Andrew's, Roker, interior perspective (1905), pencil and sepia washes. 71
3.3 George Frederick Bodley, interior of the Church of the Holy Trinity, South Kensington, London (1901–6). 72
3.4 George Frederick Bodley, interior of St Augustine's, Pendlebury (begun 1869). 74
3.5 Dominican church at Ghent, from James Cubitt, *Church Design for Congregations* (1870). 75
3.6 George Frederick Bodley, studies for St Augustine's, Pendlebury. 76
3.7 George Frederick Bodley, interior of St Mary's, Eccleston, Cheshire. 78
3.8 George Frederick Bodley, exterior of St Mary's, Eccleston, Cheshire. 80
3.9 Bodley and Garner, interior of St German's, Roath, Cardiff. 81
3.10 George Frederick Bodley, All Saints, Cambridge, detail of wall-painting at the south-east corner of the south aisle. 83
3.11 George Frederick Bodley, interior of St John the Baptist, Tue Brook, Liverpool. 84
3.12 E. S. Prior, wax model of butterfly-plan cottage (1895). 89
3.13 E. S. Prior, The Barn, Exmouth, Devon (1896), with thatched roof prior to the fire of 1905. 91
3.14 E. S. Prior, The Barn, Exmouth, Devon, surface textures. 92
3.15 E. S. Prior, Voewood, Holt, Norfolk, viewed from the south-east. 93
3.16 E. S. Prior, Voewood, Holt, Norfolk, detail textures at centre of south terrace. 94
3.17 E. S. Prior, Church of St Osmund, Poole, Dorset, study of West End. 95
3.18 W. R. Lethaby, illustration of Byzantine 'tomb at Shefa Amr, in Galilee' (1891). 95
3.19 Edwin Lutyens, Orangery, Hestercombe, Somerset (1927). 96
4.1 Charles Holden, design of a provincial market hall (1897). 103
4.2 John Belcher with A. Beresford Pite, Institute of Chartered Accountants, City of London. 103
4.3 Charles Holden, Bristol Central Library, centre of the north façade. 104
4.4 Charles Holden, Bristol Central Library, view from south-east. 105
4.5 Charles Holden, Bristol Central Library, study of south-east corner. 106
4.6 Charles Holden, British Medical Association building, detail of current Agar Street façade, with defaced figures. 108

LIST OF FIGURES

4.7	Charles Holden, British Medical Association, The Strand façade photographed 11 July 1908 whilst under construction. Epstein's carvings are, from left to right: *Chemical Research*, *Hygeia*, *Matter*, *Primal Energy*.	109
4.8	Sir Muirhead Bone, perspective view from the north-east of Adams, Holden, and Pearson's New Headquarters of the London Electric Railway Company (later London Underground), 55 Broadway, Westminster. Carbon pencil (c. 1927).	112
4.9	Charles Holden, perspective view from the north-east of Adams, Holden, and Pearson's New Headquarters of the London Electric Railway Company (later London Underground), 55 Broadway, Westminster. Pencil and wash (c. 1927).	113
4.10	Henry Moore, *West Wind*, 55 Broadway, north side of east wing.	115
4.11	Henry Moore carving *West Wind*.	116
4.12	Eric Gill, *East Wind*, north side of west wing, 55 Broadway.	117
4.13	Jacob Epstein with *Night*, carved on site on the north-east façade of 55 Broadway.	119
4.14	Serge Chermayeff, House at Bentley Wood, Halland, East Sussex, the garden front with Henry Moore's *Recumbent Figure* (1938) in the foreground.	122
5.1	Christ in Majesty tympanum, St Peter's, Rowlestone, Herefordshire, England.	127
5.2	Kenneth Rowntree, urban panorama of 'sharawaggi' (1944).	130
5.3	Tecton Architects, Highpoint II, North Hill, Highgate, London: the porte-cochère.	131
5.4	Gordon Cullen, drawing of 'House and garden near Halland, Sussex' (Bentley Wood), garden designed by Christopher Tunnard (1938).	133
5.5	Gordon Cullen, illustration for 'The Wall' (1952).	135
5.6	Gordon Cullen, illustration for 'Bankside Regained' (1949).	137
5.7	Kenneth Rowntree, cover of *The Architectural Review* (1944).	137
5.8	John Piper, 'Church of the Holy Innocents, Knowle, Bristol' (1941).	138
5.9	'Three Oxford Colleges by Nikolaus Pevsner', Tom Quad, Christ Church, Oxford (1949).	141
5.10	'Three Oxford Colleges by Nikolaus Pevsner', passage leading from Tom Quad to Peckwater (1949).	142
5.11	'Three Oxford Colleges by Nikolaus Pevsner', cleft leading to Peckwater (1949).	143
5.12	Frederick Gibberd, Market Square, Harlow New Town.	149
5.13	William Holford, plan for the precinct of St Paul's Cathedral, London (1956).	150

FIGURES

6.1	Frederick Gibberd, clock tower seen from the market place at Lansbury, Poplar, London.	155
6.2	Alison and Peter Smithson, Hunstanton School, Norfolk.	157
6.3	Stirling and Gowan, Housing, Ham Common, Richmond, London.	160
6.4	Colin St John Wilson and Arthur Baker, flats at Hereford Square (1959).	161
6.5	Colin St John Wilson, Peter Carter, Alan Colquhoun, Bentham Road Estate, Hackney, London.	162
6.6	Colin St John Wilson, with Alex Hardy, Cambridge School of Architecture extension, the lecture room.	164
6.7	The bathroom in Limerston Street, Chelsea, with wallpaper by Eduardo Paolozzi (1956).	165
6.8	Nigel Henderson, photograph of graffiti on a door window (c. 1949–54).	166
6.9	Nigel Henderson, photograph of the Eduardo Paolozzi ceiling paper to Ronald Jenkins's office at Ove Arup and Partners.	168
6.10	Group 6 exhibit, 'Patio and Pavilion', 'This is Tomorrow' exhibition (1956), Whitechapel Art Gallery, London.	170
6.11	Group 10 exhibit, 'This is Tomorrow' exhibition (1956), Whitechapel Art Gallery, London.	172
7.1	Cover of *The Architectural Review* (1954), showing part of the access elevation of one of the large blocks of the Hallfield Estate, Paddington, London.	180
7.2	Tecton (with Drake and Lasdun), Hallfield Estate, Paddington, London. North-east elevation of large block seen from Bishop's Bridge Road.	182
7.3	Tecton, Spa Green Estate, Finsbury, London. Drawing of bedroom façade of eight-storey block.	185
7.4	Tecton, Spa Green Estate, Finsbury, London. Drawing of living-room elevation of Sadler House.	185
7.5	Comparative patterns: top left, Palace of Urbino; top right, kelim; middle left, Sadler House, Spa Green Estate; middle right, Spa Green Estate, bedroom side of eight-storey block; bottom left, Hallfield Estate access elevation; bottom right, Hallfield Estate, living accommodation elevation.	186
7.6	Luigi Moretti, Casa del Girasole apartments, Rome.	188
7.7	Lubetkin, Peterlee, 'gables that speak' study.	192
7.8	Lubetkin, Peterlee, 'gables that speak' study.	193
7.9	Victor Pasmore, Peterlee, first sketch for disposition of housing groups of the South West Area (1961).	198
7.10	Peterlee, South West Area, layout plan of the first major housing group (1961).	199
7.11	Peterlee, group of houses, South West Area.	200

7.12 Peterlee, group of houses, South West Area. Inside the courtyard of the group of houses shown in Figure 7.11, with a play sculpture designed by Peter Daniel. 201
7.13 Peterlee, view looking outwards from the courtyard shown in Figures 7.11 and 7.12. 202
7.14 James Frazer Stirling and Alan Cordingley. Photograph of elevations and sections for University of Sheffield, Sheffield, England (1953), gelatin silver print. 205
7.15 James Frazer Stirling and Alan Cordingley. Axonometric sketch for University of Sheffield, Sheffield. England (1953), ink, graphite and gouache on paper. 207
7.16 Stirling and Gowan, Leicester University Engineering Building. 212
7.17 James Stirling, Michael Wilford, and Associates. View of the public footpaths, Staatsgalerie, Stuttgart, Germany, 1983–4. Image from colour transparency. 214
7.18 Stirling and Wilford, Clore Gallery, Tate Britain. 217
7.19 James Stirling, Michael Wilford, and Associates. Perspectives for Clore Gallery, London, England (1980), graphite and coloured pencil on paper. 220
7.20 James Stirling, Michael Wilford, and Associates. Axonometric of façade for Clore Gallery, London, England (1980), graphite and coloured pencil on translucent paper. 221
8.1 North elevation, Furniture Manufacturers Association Headquarters, High Wycombe, England (Furniture Factory), Michael Webb (1957–8). 225
8.2 Warren Chalk, Ron Herron, Dennis Crompton, and John Attenborough for Group Leader Norman Engleback within the Special Works Division of the London County Council, South Bank Arts Centre (1960–7), detail view. 227
8.3 Nottingham Shopping Viaduct sketch. Peter Cook and David Greene (1962). 228
8.4 Elevation of competition design, Centre Georges Pompidou, Paris, France. Piano + Rogers. 230
8.5 Oscar Nitzchke, *Maison de la Publicité* project, Paris, 1934–6, elevation (drawing date 1936), ink, colour, pencil, gouache, and graphite on lithograph on board. 231
8.6 Centre Georges Pompidou, Paris, France. Piano + Rogers. Construction of the gerber beam of 'gerberette'. 233
8.7 Richard Rogers Partnership, Lloyds Building, City of London. 234
8.8 Ralph Erskine, Eaglestone housing Milton Keynes, Buckinghamshire. 237
8.9 Design team: Chris Cross, Jeremy Dixon, Mike Gold, Ed Jones, Jim Muldrew, Don Ritson, Derek Walker, Philip Ware: Netherfield housing, Milton Keynes, Buckinghamshire. 238
8.10 Ralph Erskine, 'Project for an Arctic Town' (1958). 239

8.11 Ralph Erskine, Byker Wall, Newcastle upon Tyne, south side. 242
8.12 Ralph Erskine, Byker Wall, Newcastle upon Tyne, north side. 243
8.13 Tony Fretton Architects, Lisson Gallery, London. 246
8.14 Hardwick Hall, Derbyshire, the west front. 248
8.15 Caruso St John, New Art Gallery Walsall, exterior. 250
8.16 Caruso St John, New Art Gallery Walsall, entrance hall. 251

The author and publisher gratefully acknowledge the permission granted to reproduce the copyright material in this book. Every effort has been made to trace the copyright holders and to obtain their permission for the use of copyright material. The publisher apologizes for any errors or omissions in the above list and would be grateful if notified of any corrections that should be incorporated in future reprints or editions of this book.

ACKNOWLEDGEMENTS

Adrian Stokes (1902–1972) and John Ruskin (1819–1900) are both masters in British evocative criticism, each with a unique genius for capturing the qualities of surface and materiality in architecture. I have written on both of them; so, although the book before you is a work of the past five years, it has been longer in the making as, for some time, I have wanted to draw these surface-strands together into a critical narrative. Although it is not possible to summarize the debts I have incurred in a quarter-century of pondering these matters, here I would wish to thank the following:

Mhairi McVicar and Charles Drozynski, the conference we organized together at the Welsh School of Architecture, Cardiff University, on *Generosity and Architecture* (June 2018), was an early opportunity to air thoughts on the layered surfaces of William Morris and Philip Webb – aspects published in my chapter in our edited book of that conference, *Generosity and Architecture*. Sandra Kemp, Thomas Hughes, and Kelly Freeman for the invitation to contribute to the timely 'Ruskin and Ecology' seminar (The Ruskin, February 2019); in that forum, I tested my thoughts on Ruskin's wall-veil – again in the context of Morris and Webb, with the ensuing publication of a chapter in *Ruskin's Ecologies* (Hughes and Freeman, eds., 2021). Owen Hopkins and Frances Sands who, as Soane curators (June 2019), hosted the Society of Architectural Historians of Great Britain symposium on 'Architecture and Light', allowing me to explore ideas on the 'Savage' shadows, and shadows of 'Refinement', of Street and Bodley. The Welsh School of Architecture, Cardiff University, for personal research grants towards the cost of archive and field work. The many archivists, librarians, and estate-holders, who have assisted in sourcing materials, permissions, and images, especially those of the collections I have used most. The Royal Institute of British Architects Collections, London, The Victoria and Albert Museum, London, The Paul Mellon Centre for Studies in British Art, London. The late Geoff Brandwood for the generous use of his fine photographs of Victorian architecture. At Bloomsbury, James Thompson who embraced the idea of this book from the beginning, and has supported it throughout, the anonymous readers of the manuscript, and all involved in the detail editing, production, and design, including Alexander Highfield, Rosamunde O' Cleirigh, Eleanor Rose, Elle Bloomberg, Merv Honeywood, and Dave Cummings. Owners of private homes who have allowed visits –

Voewood House, Norfolk, and The Barn, Exmouth. Those who care for public buildings and churches, allowing access, or keeping them unlocked. Family, friends, and colleagues, who have shared ideas, visits to places, and have encouraged – and with good humour – tolerated my surface obsessions: foremost among them, my wife Máire.

Introduction

In *The Englishness of English Art* (1956), the art and architectural historian, Nikolaus Pevsner identifies a 'national mania for beautiful surface quality', and an 'English pleasure in the overall decoration of a surface'. This is a tradition of rectangularity – resistant to the plastic moulding of space – where walls meet at right angles and remain as distinct planes, and buildings aggregate as separate spatial compartments and volumes. Pevsner discovers this sensibility to surface throughout Medieval Gothic, in Elizabethan architecture, in the endless terraces of London's Kensington and Bayswater, in Pugin's façades of the Houses of Parliament, in the flat surfaces of William Morris's wallpapers and other designs, and in British Modernism.

This book investigates the shaping of the surface in British architecture – in materiality, pattern, and meaning – from the middle of the nineteenth century up to the turn of the twenty-first century in a broadly chronological approach that periodizes this modernist time frame into themes connected to significant architects, artists, critics, and projects. These topics include: 'Reading the Wall-Surface' (John Ruskin's wall-veil and the work of William Butterfield and George Edmund Street); 'Surfaces of Romance' (William Morris and Philip Webb); 'Smooth and Rough' (George Frederick Bodley and Edward Schröder Prior); 'Carving the Surface' (Charles Holden and Jacob Epstein); 'Surfaces and Sharawaggi' (the Picturesque, Townscape, and Pevsner); 'Surfaces of Brutalism' (Reyner Banham, Alison and Peter Smithson, James Stirling and James Gowan, Eduardo Paolozzi, Adrian Stokes); 'Pattern, Abstraction, Post-Modernism' (Berthold Lubetkin, Victor Pasmore, James Stirling); 'High Tech, Neo-Vernacular, New Materiality' (Richard Rogers, Ralph Erskine, Adam Caruso and Peter St John).

It has been said that 'Nationality is an address, not a consciousness. A lot of things happen at that address'.[1] The boundaries of that address can be problematic enough in the case of the British archipelago, but in art history, for example, there might be reasonable curatorial consensus as to what should go into London's Tate Britain Gallery, and what should go into Tate Modern. In art and architectural history, a geographical framing continues to prove as useful – and as arbitrary – as a chronological one, enabling limits to be placed upon material that might otherwise be overwhelming. Much more problematic are attempts to elide the geographical address with accounts of national architectural consciousness, as in Pevsner's efforts towards an English *Kunstgeographie*. At the same time, architecture *did* develop within these same geographical boundaries; they *do* describe sites where shifting groups of peoples and cultures have consistently made buildings within a vortex of ideas, topography, climate, politics, and manners, that have engendered recognizable patterns and tendencies – as in those affecting the surfaces and materiality of architecture as investigated herein. This inquiry also stresses the value of Britain's continuous importation of theories, models, and people – the crucial émigré contribution, for example. As for exports, it has increasingly been the case that many British architects have sought their best opportunities abroad – James Stirling's masterpiece is in Stuttgart, Germany.

Equally difficult is the question of 'Englishness' and Britishness'; Pevsner's *Englishness of English Art* isolates the significance of The Picturesque; but this was invented on the Welsh-English borders of the Wye Valley and included Welsh artists of the stature of Thomas Jones and Richard Wilson. And the contribution of Scottish architects, thinkers, and engineers is indivisible to understanding the buildings of Britain and its constituent nations. But to simply use 'British' and 'English' interchangeably would also be cultural appropriation; here both descriptions are used, according to context, or to correspond with the voice of the pertinent architect or critic.

This book's contribution to architectural history, and visual culture, is its detailed examination of the surfaces and materiality of British architecture between1840 and 2000. In undertaking this it joins a broader surface discourse. A seminal work is David Leatherbarrow and Mohsen Mostafavi's *Surface Architecture* (2002). This is a wide-ranging examination of the surface in contemporary architecture. Within our topic area it engages with the post-war period in England, through the ideas of the Independent Group, the notion of the 'As Found', and the work of Alison and Peter Smithson, and Stirling and Gowan – subjects discussed here within Chapters 6 and 7. An example of a more focused analysis of architecture as surface is Anuradha Chatterjee's *John Ruskin and the Fabric of Architecture* (2018), which studies Ruskin's wall-veil through the lenses of dress-studies and gender. Ruskin's theory of the wall-veil is foundational to our 1840–2000 period and occupies Chapter 1, with its influence upon Morris and Webb taken forward in Chapter 2. Paul Binski's *Gothic Wonder: Art, Artifice and the Decorated Style 1290–1350* (2014) extends Pevsner in its study of the 'aesthetics of surface' in English Gothic; on these matters see, for example, Chapter 5 of the present book. Joseph A. Amato's *Surfaces: A History* (2013) traces the human relationship with surfaces much more broadly, examining the walls and streets of our homes and cities, but also surfaces as wider experiential and cultural phenomena. Many studies engage with these matters by interrogating a particular material, as does Adrian Forty in *Concrete and Culture: A Material History* (2012). For example, Forty examines the 'Nationality of Concrete', noting how the Smithsons dressed their concrete in Portland stone in their Economist Building, London to accord with the 'sober and specifically English business attire' of most of London's public buildings. He also offers insights into the uses of concrete in London's Hayward Gallery and Queen Elizabeth Hall, and by Caruso St John in The New Art Gallery Walsall. Here, Holden's proto-Modernist use of Portland stone is a prominent aspect of Chapter 4, and interpretations of the latter works will be found in Chapter 8. In a similar vein is Richard Weston's *Materials, Form and Architecture* (2003) with its focus on the tectonic and material aspects of architecture, and Alec Clifton-Taylor's classic *The Pattern of English Building* (1962). Then there is a vast hinterland of works which examine the visual cultures of Britishness and Englishness; in architecture, Sutherland Lyall's *The State of British Architecture* (1980) and Alan Powers' *Britain: Modern Architecture in History* (2007) are significant; more broadly, numerous books can be cited such as David Matless's *Landscape and Englishness* (1998), Kitty Hauser's *Shadow Sites: Photography, Archaeology, and the British Landscape 1927–1955* (2007), Robert Hoozee's edited volume *British Vision: Observation and Imagination in British Art 1750–1950* (2008), Mark A. Cheetham's *Artwriting, Nation, and Cosmopolitanism in Britain* (2012), and Alexandra Harris's *Weatherland: Writers and Artists Under English Skies* (2015).

As noted, the argument of the book unfolds within a broadly chronological framework of eight chapters, structured by themes, linked to architects, artists, critics, and projects of surface significance.

Chapter 1: Reading the Wall-Surface: John Ruskin, William Butterfield, and George Edmund Street

John Ruskin's vigorous prose-poetry awakened the hearts of his readers to read the surfaces of the Gothic buildings of Venice as the leaves of a book, and as a lesson of warning from one – now-fallen – maritime state to another. His forcible readings of these architectural 'pages' of Venice and northern Italy in *The Seven Lamps of Architecture* (1849) and *The Stones of Venice* (1851–3) re-signified the surfaces of British architecture – through the second half of the nineteenth century and deep into the twentieth century – transforming how they were conceived and made. This chapter reads the 'development' of the constructed and 'incrusted' surface in High Victorian architecture through the theories of Ruskin and George Edmund Street, and in the built works of William Butterfield and Street himself. It is owing to Ruskin, together with Street and Butterfield, that a strong feeling for broad surfaces and bold masses became a characteristic trait, both of High Victorian architecture and that of the ensuing Arts and Crafts.

Chapter 2: 'Think first of the walls': Surfaces of Romance – Morris, Webb, and the Arts and Crafts Domestic Interior

This chapter examines the translation of Ruskin's wall-veil, and his readings of the Gothic surfaces of Venice, to the wall-planes of the Arts and Crafts dwellings of William Morris and Philip Webb, both acolytes of Ruskin and products of the Street atelier – albeit a brief tenure in Morris's case. The medieval spirit of Red House – the home Webb designed for Morris in 1858–9 – was encapsulated in the *hortus ludi* of the Garden of Pleasure; a vision fully captured in the unrealized 'Palace of Art' Webb planned for the families of Morris and Edward Burne-Jones as an enlarged U-plan Red House. Here that love of the earth-veil of nature is expressed in the wall-veil as a layered composition akin to the images found in medieval missals. Moving to the interiors of Webb and Morris, the ecologies of Nature are likewise engendered in flat patterns, in generously layered hierarchies of surface, scaled to simplicity or splendour.

Chapter 3: Smooth and Rough: George Frederick Bodley and Edward Schröder Prior

The Morris-ian domestic world of romantically layered surfaces breaks with the muscularity of the High Victorian style. The 'refinement' in the ecclesiastical work of George Frederick Bodley (1827–1907) elides the domestic and public realms; Bodley's church interiors aspire to the same beauties of surface, colour, and furnishing, as would be the intention in the rooms of a fine house. Compare a Bodley church, such as Holy Trinity, South Kensington, London (1901–6) with Edward Schröder Prior's St Andrew's, Roker (1905). In both the space is conceived as one unitary volume for, as John Betjeman has pointed out, such Arts and Crafts architects sought different proportions of 'either height and narrowness, or breadth and length. Their churches either soar or spread'. Their chosen styles of Late Decorated or Perpendicular – no longer 'Middle-Pointed' – respond to the desire for a purer 'Englishness' in architectural language. But, in contrast to Bodley's smoothness, Prior also called for 'Texture as a Quality of Art and a Condition for Architecture' (1890) and his surfaces retain a Savage roughness in their handmade textures of brick, sea-pebbles, and rocky stonework.

Chapter 4: Carving the Surface: Edwardian and Inter-War Architecture and Sculpture

Making a bridge between the Arts and Crafts and inter-war Modernism, this chapter assesses the carved surfaces of the Edwardian and inter-war years in the work of Charles Holden (1875–1960); an architect whom John Summerson described as 'the last of the Edwardians and the first of the

English Moderns'. Holden's 'English Modern' mediates a proto-Modernist abstraction between the white-architecture icons of the neo-Corbusian avant-garde, and the overtly academic classical buildings of a period which also witnessed a high point in architectural sculpture. The need of the new century for large professional, commercial, and governmental headquarters gave scope – to architects and sculptors alike – to define the language for a progressively technocratic future. Many of these buildings – including those of Holden – would now be thought of as conventionally traditional, but their makers all saw themselves as 'modern' to some extent, and the sculpture enlivening their surfaces was integral to these variants of modernity. Both the cladding and sculpture of many of these structures were in stone – often the Portland stone that Holden loved for its weathering qualities. Among the constructions of these confusingly eclectic years, Holden's work stands out in its harnessing of Walt Whitman-esque energies and the sublimity of the USA skyscraper, to an English abstraction of surface derived from Wren and Hawksmoor, and Arts and Crafts traditions. Holden extended his devotion to naked stone to embrace a diversity of sculptors – including Charles Pibworth, Jacob Epstein, Eric Gill, and Henry Moore – each, in their way, 'modern' as representatives of The New Sculpture or of Carving Direct.

Chapter 5: Surfaces and Sharawaggi: Aspects of the Picturesque c. 1925–55

This chapter examines the rediscovery of the British Picturesque in that dialectic between Rationalism and Neo-Romanticism, as it emerged in the period leading up to World War II, evolved through the war itself, and resonated for over a decade thereafter. These movements arose from tensions between Modernism's predisposition to unlocated 'international' abstractions and more located 'national' encounters with histories and places. On the one hand, there are Nikolaus Pevsner's (1902–1983) formalist readings of the Englishness of the English surface – based upon his German academic training in the analysis of style within the *Zeitgeist* – but emplaced insofar as they stress national character. On the other hand, the atmospheric readings of the textures of British architecture and landscape – made by observers such as John Piper and John Betjeman – were labelled as Neo-Romanticism. To characterize these attitudes as necessarily totally opposed – as in Timothy Mowl's *Stylistic Cold Wars: Betjeman versus Pevsner* (2011) – can miss many overlaps of approach, not least in the rekindling of Picturesque ideas in both camps. In its pages, *The Architectural Review* relayed the Picturesque through the notions of 'Sharawaggi' and *Townscape*, popularized in Gordon Cullen's vivid draughtsmanship as ad hoc 'high' and 'low' collages of urban fabric – injected with elements of Surrealism. Pevsner's scholarship also advanced the Picturesque as a Modernist tool in the reconfiguration of the city. Both Rational and Neo-Romantic strands reached their culmination fully a decade after the end of World War II; in Pevsner's case in his BBC Reith Lectures of 1955, on *The Englishness of English Art*, while Basil Spence's winning neo-Gothic design of 1951, for the competition to design a new Cathedral of St Michael at Coventry – in the context of the medieval building blitzed in November 1940 – was the definitive *Gesamtkunstwerk* of Neo-Romanticism.

Chapter 6: As Found: Surfaces of Brutalism

In his essay on the 'Revenge of the Picturesque' (1968), Reyner Banham describes the persistence of this English visual philosophy in the polemics of post-World War II British architecture up to, and beyond, the mid-1960s – notwithstanding its associations with old-guard empiricism in the minds of Corbusian Modernists. The Picturesque would manifestly include Basil Spence's Coventry Cathedral, but Banham also accused the avant-garde leaders themselves as capitulating to 'the genius of the place', citing the *Townscape* informality of Alison and Peter Smithson's *The Economist* cluster (1959–64), and the asymmetries of Stirling and Gowan's Leicester University Engineering Building (1959–63). The most consequential British contribution to these fierce arguments was the ethic and aesthetic of 'The New Brutalism', coined around 1952 and defined in Banham's 'The New Brutalism' essay in *The Architectural Review* of December 1955. A 'Brutalist' building will exhibit three key qualities: first, formal legibility of plan; second, clear exhibition of structure; and third, valuation of materials for their inherent qualities 'as found'. This chapter examines these 'As Found' surfaces of Brutalism beginning with Banham's major point of Brutalist reference, Alison and Peter Smithson's Hunstanton School in Norfolk (1949–54). Banham ponders that 'English architectural psychology' which imports a style – in this case the steel-frame-and-infill of Mies van der Rohe's Illinois Institute of Technology, Chicago (IIT) – and 'corrects' it to local circumstance; as English Palladianism had 'corrected' Palladio, or Ruskin had 'corrected' Venetian Gothic. The parallels in 'bloody-mindedness' between Butterfield and Brutalism are examined, as in Stirling and Gowan's flats at Ham Common, London (1955–8). The Brutalist wallpapers and fabrics of Eduardo Paolozzi and Nigel Henderson are also studied for being, as indicative of their time, as those of William Morris; these works – and other surfaces generated by the *This is Tomorrow* exhibition (1956) – are read through the psychoanalytical lenses of Anton Ehrenzweig and Adrian Stokes.

Chapter 7: Pattern, Abstraction, Post-Modernism: Lubetkin – Pasmore – Stirling

This chapter begins with the issues of facadism-versus-functionalism which Lubetkin and Tecton had first brought to the fore in their Highpoint II of

1936–8. Again, it was Banham who encapsulated the issues at stake in a criticism on 'Façade' he wrote with regard to *The Architectural Review's* publication, in November 1954, of Tecton's Hallfield Estate in Paddington, London. Should the faces of these immense post-war housing blocks arise as the outcome of technical and programmatic needs – as a functionalist would require – or be considered as works of art in their own right? Rejecting both positivist *Sachlichkeit*, or a romantic retreat into *Gemütlichkeit*, Lubetkin argued for an integration of planning, structure, and architectural expressivity. Consequently, the first part of this chapter examines how Lubetkin articulated patterns of living in the façades of Tecton projects such as Priory Green Estate, Finsbury, London (1943–51). Lubetkin continued these experiments in his short-term involvement with Peterlee New Town (designated 1948) in the north-east of England where the extraordinary 'gables that speak' of his housing designs, anticipate the semiotics of Post-Modernism, and echo Ruskin's call for the surfaces of architecture to be readable. Following Lubetkin's disgruntled departure from Peterlee, the story was taken forward in other ways, by the artist Victor Pasmore. For a quarter-century Pasmore worked with the architects of Peterlee, on the experiment of applying Piet Mondrian's principles of 'constructed abstract art' to the interrelations of settlement-pattern and landscape; extending these ideas – at the level of the dwelling-cluster – to the planar-compositions of cross-walls and flat roofs. This neglected constructed abstract avant-garde – that had once been as important a part of the *This is Tomorrow* exhibition (1956) as the Pop of Richard Hamilton or the Brutalism of the Smithsons – occupies the second part of this chapter. Finally, James Stirling – in the role of homo ludens – continues to be a key actor in these post-war surface narratives; firstly, as the author (with James Gowan) of the Engineering Faculty, Leicester University (1959) whose skin-like surfaces collage features of canonic Modernism, Victorian industrialism, Butterfield-ian bloody-mindedness, and Brutalist bombast. Equally significant is his transition from this complicated Late-Modernist stance, to an equally involved Post-Modernist embrace of history, context, and *architecture parlante*; examined here briefly in the Staatsgalerie, Stuttgart (1977–83) and, more closely, in his Clore Gallery extension to Tate Britain, London (1978–86). Even though, Stirling himself, always vehemently tore off any Po-Mo labels attached to his work.

Chapter 8: High-Tech, Neo-Vernacular, New Materiality: Richard Rogers – Ralph Erskine – Caruso St John

In taking this narrative up to the turn of the twenty-first century, this final chapter is also tripartite in its structure, as it investigates the three important strands of: High-Tech, Neo-Vernacular, and New Materiality – languages that are more interrelated in their surface character than might at first appear. These approaches are respectively represented by the practices of

Richard Rogers (initially with Renzo Piano), Ralph Erskine, and Adam Caruso and Peter St John.

The exponents of the exo-skeletons of High-Tech saw themselves as continuing the bravura Victorian traditions of The Crystal Palace and the great railway termini; the Archigram pioneer Peter Cook regarded this Victorian and High-Tech enthusiasm for audacious invention as an intrinsic part of the 'English psychology'. Yet, until this High-Tech outbreak of the 1960s and 1970s, the skeletal had been suppressed in Britain, in part owing to Ruskin's scorn for a 'new style' of iron architecture; the Great Court of the Oxford University Museum (opened 1860) remains an isolated experimentation in what might have evolved as a Ruskinian iron and steel architecture. The first part of this chapter traces the path to Richard Rogers's Lloyds Building (1976–86), via Piano and Rogers's Centre Pompidou in Paris, to the seminal ideas of the English Archigram Group in the 1960s. They may look different, but the flexible infrastructures of High-Tech, or the homely 'sheddery' of Ralph Erskine's Byker Wall in Newcastle-upon-Tyne, both aspire towards a bottom-up *architecture without architects* (cf. Bernard Rudofsky); in the one case by empowering the desires of consumer-culture, in the other by fostering popular participation in the design process. And – whether made of steel, or brick and timber – the surfaces of both Rogers and Erskine deploy an aesthetics of *bricolage*. The second part of this chapter analyses these surfaces of Erskine in the context of approaches that have variously been called: Romantic Functionalism, Romantic Pragmatism, or Neo-Vernacular. By the 1980s, those surveying the eclectic state of British architecture, found a field scattered with the remnants of the countless style-wars of: Brutalism, Empiricism, Post-Modernism, High-Tech, Neo-Vernacular, and so forth. As so often in these pages, the meanings that can be generated through making and material would again provide a *rappel à l'ordre*; a New Materiality visible in the work of Adam Caruso and Peter St John, whose New Art Gallery Walsall (opened in February 2000) takes this enquiry into the shaping of surface, and the materiality of British architecture, up to the turn of the twenty-first century.

CHAPTER ONE

Reading the Wall-Surface

John Ruskin, William Butterfield, and George Edmund Street

John Ruskin called his *St Mark's Rest* (published in parts from 1877) the 'fourth volume' of his celebrated *The Stones of Venice* (1851–3); here the surfaces of the city are both the leaves of a book and a salt-smelling skin – not such opposing metaphors given the vellum leaves of the medieval manuscripts beloved by Ruskin. His preface describes the autobiographies of nations as written 'in three manuscripts;– the book of their deeds, their words, and the book of their art'. The most 'trustworthy one is the last', and 'the history of Venice is chiefly written in such manuscript. It once lay open on the waves, miraculous, like St Cuthbert's book,– a golden legend on countless leaves',[1] but now it has been brutishly cut and singed into fragments of 'blackened scroll' which Ruskin's redeeming work – as in his earlier volumes of *The Stones of Venice* – enables us to *read*. Ruskin lets Venice speak for herself, telling 'her own story, in her own handwriting. . . . Not a word shall *I* have to say in the matter . . . except to deepen the letters for you when [these cut and blackened fragments] are indistinct . . .'.[2] And in compelling imagery Venice's scrolls are skin, it is 'this amphibious city – this Phocaea, or sea-dog of towns, – looking with soft human eyes at you from the sand, Proteus himself latent in the salt-smelling skin of her'.[3] Like the Proteus of Greek legend its surfaces are aspect-changing, it can be both male and female, it 'can add colours to the chameleon / Change shapes with Proteus for advantages'.[4]

And 'Mr Ruskin *was* heard', as his contemporary Charles Eastlake confirms in his *A History of the Gothic Revival* of 1872, for whereas 'previous apologists for the [Gothic] Revival had relied more or less on ecclesiastical sentiment, on historical interest, or on a vague sense of the picturesque for their plea in its favour', Ruskin's vigorous prose-poetry struck 'a chord of human sympathy that vibrated through all hearts . . .'.[5] His forcible readings of the pages and skins of Venice and northern Italy in *The Seven Lamps of Architecture* (1849) and *The Stones of Venice* would re-signify the surfaces of British architecture through the second half of the nineteenth century and deep into the twentieth, transforming how they were conceived, made, and symbolized. This chapter reads the 'development' of the constructed and 'incrusted' surface in High Victorian architecture through the theories of Ruskin and George Edmund Street, and in the built works of William Butterfield and Street himself.

Ruskin closes his pivotal 'Nature of Gothic' chapter in the second volume of *Stones of Venice* with the injunction: 'Lastly, *Read* the sculpture. . . . Thenceforward the criticism of the building is to be conducted precisely on the same principles as that of a book; and it must depend on the knowledge, feeling, and not a little on the industry and perseverance of the reader, whether, even in the case of the best works, he either perceive them to be great, or feel them to be entertaining'.[6] Ruskin's own industry and perseverance in reading the scattered pages of the city that 'once lay open on the waves' is attested by the vast system of diaries, worksheets, and pocketbooks crammed with notes and sketches, that laid the foundations of *The Stones of Venice*.[7] Elizabeth Helsinger claims these three volumes as 'Ruskin's first and his most sustained effort to combine religious and artistic reading in a single critical activity'.[8] In Ruskin's command to '*Read*' she identifies four symbolic languages. First, there is the manifest language of sculpture and pictorial iconography.[9] Then there is the language of the picturesque, that 'golden stain of time'; for Ruskin the 'glory of a building . . . is in its Age, and in that deep sense of voicefulness, of stern watching, of mysterious sympathy . . . which we feel in walls that have long been washed by the passing waves of humanity'.[10] Finally, there are two symbolic languages architecture develops from nature: the inherent geological record of the stones themselves, and their theological message.[11] Opening the final and third volume of *The Stones of Venice*, Ruskin affirms that the preceding two books have 'dwelt . . . on the historical language of stones; let us not forget this, which is their theological language'. As the same passage explains, such stones set 'forth [the] eternity and . . . TRUTH' of the Deity, just as the 'elements of the universe – its air, its water, and its flame. . .'.[12] Such exegesis is rooted in Ruskin's evangelical upbringing and his childhood daily Bible-reading at his mother's side. In practical terms, all these languages will be laid out and contested on the surfaces of High Victorian architecture.

Ruskin was not the first to analogize texts to the surfaces of architecture but, to reiterate Eastlake's point, he made once vague historical or literary sentiments to 'vibrate in human hearts' in synthesizing these iconographical, aesthetic, material, and metaphysical languages. William

Morris, for example, testified to the conversion experience of reading Ruskin's readings – especially the 'Nature of Gothic' chapter of *Stones*. Laugier, Boullée, and others had theorized the face of building as 'architecture parlante' in the second half of the eighteenth century. More galvanizing to nineteenth-century debates was Victor Hugo's *Notre Dame de Paris* of 1831–2 wherein he appealed to architecture as 'the great book of mankind, man's chief form of expression in the various stages of his development, either as force or intelligence'.[13] Ruskin had read Hugo's *The Hunchback of Notre Dame* in the 1830s, and claimed to have hated it, but the novelist's vision of architecture as writing the story of a nation was clearly an influence.[14] An extreme example of Early Victorian building-as-book symbolism in 'ecclesiastical design' is G. F. Lewis's *Illustrations of Kilpeck Church, Herefordshire* of 1842. When Moses builds an altar at God's command – as described in the book of Exodus – for Lewis 'altar and book [are] one and the same when an event was ordered by the Lord to be recorded'. In those days, 'an altar was . . . intended for the same purpose as a book is at present. We have only to consider the material, stone, to be the leaves, and the . . . chisel to be the pen'.[15] Such early churches were designed 'with intelligence, making them books in which the community could read the Law and the Gospel'.[16] Of the robustly carved Norman of Kilpeck, itself, Lewis opines: 'This little Church, through art, is made a book in which information is conveyed to all who are able to read its pages'; the 'power of speech' is given to 'stones, wood, and glass'.[17] The 'textual turn' of making books of a building's surfaces can be located at the very cusp of the Victorian era in the building of the small church of St Mary and St Nicholas at Littlemore, Oxford between 1835 and 1836 by the architect Henry Underwood for his client John Henry Newman.[18] Littlemore was small, but didactically loaded in embodying the Tractarian principles that had made Newman and the Oxford Movement famous. Emerging as a presence in the 1830s, the Tractarians urged a revival of Catholic canons within the Church of England, shortly to be paralleled by the Ecclesiologists of the Cambridge Movement with their particular stress on the role of architecture and art in the revival of Anglican Catholicism. In a sermon given soon after Littlemore's consecration, Newman told his parishioners that they should see their new church as itself a Tract, as 'a book, a holy book, which you may look at and read, and which will suggest to you many good thoughts of God and heaven'.[19] Many revolted against the Anglo-Catholic implications of what was being looked at and read here, the be-candled high altars and so forth – Ruskin prominent among them given his evangelical Christian upbringing. But adumbrated in Littlemore, in the words of Newman, or lesser contributors to the discourse such as Lewis, and no less Ruskin himself, is the idea of the church building as a communicative vessel whose wall-surfaces gather meanings to speak in rich material, symbolic, and spiritual overtones.

Emergence of the Gothic wall-veil

The first surface of Venice, the aforementioned amphibious 'sea-dog of towns', was naturally not that of architecture itself but the protean 'salt-smelling skin' of the sandy earth whereon it arose. Ruskin opens his fifth volume of *Modern Painters* with this preeminent surface 'The Earth-Veil': 'The earth in its depths must remain dead and cold, incapable except of slow crystalline change; but at its surface, which human beings look upon and deal with, it ministers to them through a veil of strange intermediate being . . .'.[20] In the next chapter of this book, we will show William Morris, following Ruskin, writing in *News from Nowhere* of 'the spirit of the new days, of our days' as a 'delight in the life of the world; intense and overweening love of the very skin and surface of the earth, on which man dwells, such as a lover has in the fair flesh of the woman he loves . . .'.[21] Expanding on the imagery of the earth-veil Ruskin depicts it variously as 'a carpet', as 'a fantasy of embroidery' of 'tall spreading of foliage' with the 'unerring uprightness as of temple pillars' all cleaving to the underlying strength of rock or transient sand. Accordingly, Ruskin earlier applied lessons from the 'school of nature' in defining the wall-veil as the main intermediary surface in architecture in his first volume of *Stones of Venice*. In his *John Ruskin and Victorian Architecture*, Michael Brooks calls Ruskin's wall-veil his 'most dramatic contribution to architectural terminology'; 'wall-veil' was soon on the lips of pupils in architectural offices in the 1850s as 'an early sign of the approaching Ruskinian wave'.[22] As Eastlake writing in 1872 recalls, these pupils also 'astonished their masters by talking of the Savageness of Northern Gothic, of the Intemperance of Curves, and the Laws of Foliation . . .'.[23]

What then is this defining surface of the wall-veil? The wall is the first of Ruskin's three divisions of architecture into walls, roofs, and apertures: 'A wall is an even and united fence, whether of wood, earth, stone, or metal'. Statically the wall has to contend with vertical or lateral forces; its strength can be increased 'by some general addition to its thickness; but if the pressure becomes very great, it is gathered up into *piers* to resist vertical pressure, and supported by *buttresses* to resist lateral pressure'.[24] A true wall-veil must retain its breadth of surface between the piers (where these are necessary), neither becoming a line of piers altogether, nor a continuous rampart-like buttress. On the one hand, this membrane-like sheer surface of the wall appears to owe something to the fabric analogies of Gottfried Semper; on the other, it seems to anticipate the modern 'curtain-wall' of frame-and-cladding.[25] These parallels are certainly worth pursuing, but Ruskin's wall-veil never aims at the atectonic dematerialization Semper sought when he argued that 'the annihilation of reality, of the material, is necessary if form is to emerge as a meaningful symbol'.[26] Nor, as is well known, was Ruskin enamoured of the potential of the Crystal Palace's iron-frame and cladding. In truth, Ruskin's wall-veil is always embodied in material substance even if that may be no more than an 'incrustation' of thin sheets of marble, as cortex to a masonry core. In contrast to Semper's desire to annihilate material, read Ruskin on the ornament of the wall-veil:

> But this is to be noted of all good wall ornament, that it retains the expression of *firm and massive substance, and of broad surface*, and that architecture instantly declined when linear design was substituted for massive, and the sense of weight of wall was lost in a wilderness of upright or undulating rods.[27]

In the chapter of *Stones of Venice* on 'Gothic Palaces' (chapter 7, vol. 2), the wall-surfaces of Venice are seen to appear in their full breadth, co-equally with the emergence of Gothic architecture out of the Byzantine-Romanesque of the city. Byzantine palaces, such as the thirteenth-century Ca' Loredan and Ca' Farsetti at the Rialto, have no wall-veils to speak of, characterized as they are by tier on tier of continuous stilted arches on slender columns, making for maximum transparency and 'rapid vertical accents' stayed only by occasional narrow piers.[28] Ruskin notes that 'the first story of a Byzantine palace consists of, perhaps, eighteen or twenty arches, reaching from one side of the house to the other . . .'. Then 'a great change takes place in the Gothic period. These long arcades break, as it were, into pieces, and coagulate into central and lateral windows, and small arched doors, pierced in great surfaces of brick wall'.[29] As one Byzantine family of forms of repeated arcades dies out, another Gothic one is born of surface and aperture. In Ruskin's active prose, architectural styles are urgently animate,[30] the Gothic 'breaks' and 'coagulates' the Byzantine arcades, making its surfaces with the natural energy of geological forces, with that 'Changefulness' of the preceding 'Nature of Gothic' chapter, that can 'expand into a hall, coil into a staircase, or spring into a spire, with undegraded grace and unexhausted energy . . .'.[31] So the typical tripartite Venetian palace emerges with its more solid façade of visible wall-surfaces; the arcade is now restricted to the centre of the *piano-nobile* (lighting the deep *portego* hall behind), while the sea-story now just has its water-gate and a few related openings.

Ruskin's unpublished drafts of this 'Gothic Palaces' chapter detail these changes through the 'Angel House' or Casa dell'Angelo, a complete late example of the pre-Gothic building type on the Calle di Rimedio near Campo Santa Maria Formosa. All these pre-Gothic palaces comprise a long, narrow rectangular block of two or more storeys, which contains a large first-floor hall accessed by an external stair. There are two main layouts; in the Casa dell'Angelo type the *long* side of the block has the main *inward-looking* façade which overlooks a walled court – not the immediate street or canal (the other layout is that of the above-mentioned Loredan and Farsetti palaces, at the Rialto, where the façade is placed *outward-facing* to canal or street, on the *short* side of the rectangular block, transforming thereby the palace's relationship to the urban fabric).[32] The austere windows of the upper two storeys of the Casa dell'Angelo are 'one of the most extensive and perfect

FIGURE 1.1 *Courtyard façade of Casa dell'Angelo, Rio di Canonica, Venice (also called Ca' Soranzo). Photograph © Cameraphoto Arte, Venezia.*

examples' of Ruskin's transitional 'second order' of Venetian arches in their fully established form.[33] Here the *inner* part of the arch is still of the stilted round-arched Byzantine form of the 'first order', but in the ogee contour of the pointed *outer* arch the Gothic spirit begins to show itself.

Ruskin's unpublished drafts on the Casa dell'Angelo deserve extended quotation for showing the moment when the Gothic wall surface emerges. Ruskin closes 'an argument by offering an experience'[34] – most obviously in celebrated passages such as the approach to St Mark's of this second volume of *Stones* – but even the following, more everyday notes, draw readers into 'watching' the life of a building as active participants:

Fronting the bridge which crosses the Rio de Palazzo and leads into the Calle di Rimedio, is a square door, surrounded by an architrave of red marble.... The wall in which this occurs has been restored; but passing beneath it, we enter a courtyard fenced from the Calle di Rimedio by a wall with parapets, and, on the other side by a most picturesque mass of buildings. The ground floor has been much altered, but three shafts are still left, ... which instead of carrying arches, as hitherto we have been accustomed to find them, sustain a massy horizontal wooden beam, on which rests the first floor of the house above.... In the first storey above these shafts is a group of four windows sustained by three shafts and two pilasters. Both shafts and pilasters stand *without any base*, on a low continuous plinth....

... [Previously] the whole width of the house is considered as one arcade with intervals more or less wide. But [now] the idea of the continuous arcade is lost. The groups of its arches contract themselves only *windows*.... The windows as they shrink in width, shrink in height also, draw up their feet, as it were, and instead of falling to the general foundation of the building, receive ... a narrow plinth ... for a foundation of their own. At the same time the great arch of the entrance sinks into a mere door, and the building, *instead of the appearance of a great court or public space surrounded by arcades, assumes that of a very closely veiled private house, with doors and windows of ordinary size* ....[35]

As the openings shrink and sink, a last echo of Byzantine arcaded feeling – in the now 'closely-veiled' Gothic palace – survives in the typically 'connected group of central windows' of their upper storeys. In the third volume of *Stones of Venice*, Ruskin sums up these great changes: 'the principal difference in general form and treatment between the Byzantine and Gothic palaces was the contraction of the marble facing into the narrow spaces between the windows, leaving large fields of brick wall perfectly bare'.[36] On the aforementioned reading analogy, this 'whole wall of the palace was considered as the page of a book to be illuminated'.[37] How the Venetians illuminated the pages offered by these large new surface-fields can be seen in such late fifteenth-century pictures of the city as Giovanni Mansueti's *Miracle of the Relic of the Holy Cross* (1494) or Vittore Carpaccio's *Healing of the Possessed Man* (1494), in the Venice Accademia. Ruskin believes such paintings to be 'the perfectly true representation of what the Architecture of Venice was in her glorious time; trim, dainty,– red and white like the blossom of a carnation,– touched with gold like a peacock's plume, and frescoed, even to its chimney pots, with fairest arabesque ...'.[38] On the left of Mansueti's *Miracle*, the illuminated urban wall-veil recedes steeply, heads pop out to watch the events taking place below and oriental textiles, hung down from the windows, layer further arabesques. Here says Ruskin is 'one harmony of work and life,– all of a piece, you see them, in the wonderful palace-perspective on the left ... with everybody looking out of their windows'.[39] Enough traces of these

FIGURE 1.2 *Giovanni Mansueti*, Miracle of the Relic of the Holy Cross in Campo San Lio *(1494). Gallerie dell'Accademia di Venezia.* © G.A.VE Archivio fotografico 'su concessione del MIC'.

polychromatic façades survive to prove that these Quattrocento artists were not painting fantasies, but the material evidence of the city in front of them.[40]

In his studies of Italian Renaissance architecture of 1867, Jacob Burckhardt famously called Venice the 'city of incrustation' for its commitment to 'uncompromising splendour', as compared to Florence 'the city of rustication',[41] echoing Ruskin's own notable incrusted characterization of the city as a substance of brick overlaid with a wealth of colour and marble.[42] The planar appearance of these architectural surfaces is reinforced by these platings of marble or the skins of colour overlaid on plaster.[43] Certainly Venice realizes much of this wealth of colour, not in marble, but in humble paint on plaster; and Ruskin reads in the common chequer patterns (as those visible in pink and white in Mansueti's *Miracle*) the symbolic message of the 'true chivalric and Gothic spirit' of Christian service, where the diapers possibly echo the 'quarterings of the knights' shields'.[44] Again it will be seen in Mansueti's picture that the chequers are the '*grounds* of design rather than designs themselves'.[45] They make an autonomous field in which windows and doors are cut regardless; consequently, Ruskin is critical of 'modern architects, in such minor imitations as they are beginning to attempt' of these kinds of polychromy, to dispose the patterns symmetrically in relation to the openings. Ruskin mourns 'that the sea winds are bad librarians' and virtually all these painted pages of chivalric spirit have perished. Yet the façade of the Doge's Palace still emblazons the chequered principle in its imperishable diaperings of Istrian stone and pink Verona marble, applied as an atectonic 'veil that disregards architectural members but begins and ends seemingly at random, like a cut from a huge roll of textile'.[46] The Ducal Palace also encompasses the preceding narrative, in dramatically juxtaposing the Byzantine ethos of its arcaded sea-storeys, with the broad Gothic surfaces of its upper stage.

To Ruskin's vivid input of the 'wall-veil' to architectural language, must be added his related concept of 'Surface Gothic'. That planar quality, so conspicuous in the Gothic and Early Renaissance architecture of Venice, is part of a broader feeling for the wall-plane in Italian building. A plate in *Stones of Venice* – comparing 'Linear and Surface Gothic' – puts a filigree Flamboyant canopy from Abbeville in northern France, side by side with a sturdy one from a Scala tomb in Verona, northern Italy. The Abbeville canopy 'is so cut through and through that it is hardly stronger than a piece of lace'; whereas the Verona canopy has 'its surface of stone . . . unpierced, and the mass of it is thick and strong . . .'. The latter attracts 'the eye to broad sculptured *surfaces*, the other to involution of intricate *lines*'.[47] Accepting that both have their beauties, Ruskin insists the 'Italian [Surface] Gothic is the nobler style'. Something very similar to this Linear / Surface distinction had been expressed before Ruskin's exhaustive Venetian research in his 'Lamp of Power' chapter of *The Seven Lamps of Architecture*. As Nature has 'her woods and thickets' and 'her plains, and cliffs', so 'of the many broad divisions under which architecture may be considered, none [are] more significant that those into buildings, whose interest is in their walls, and those whose interest is in the lines dividing their walls'.[48] Ruskin's corporeal instinct is to the sensual skins of wall-architecture: 'Whatever infinity of fair form there may be in the maze of the forest, there is a fairer, as I think, in the surface of the quiet lake; and I hardly know that association of shaft or tracery, for which I would exchange the warm sleep of sunshine on some smooth, broad, human-like front of marble'.[49] In this privileging of wall-architecture, one major 'association' that appears to be contradicted here is that *Association with Natural Scenery and National Character* Ruskin had examined in his first architectural publication *The Poetry of Architecture* (1873–8). So, in his *The Englishness of English Art*, Nikolaus Pevsner examined an English 'national mania for beautiful surface quality', but not for wall-architecture *as such*, rather for 'the lines dividing their walls' as visible in the English Gothic love of over-all linear patterns of every kind.[50] One question that therefore needs to be addressed, is how Ruskin's influential surface theories – conceived among the alleys and canals of Venice – intersected with existent English predilections to surface pattern. Part of the answer lies in interpreting the last two languages ascertained by Helsinger, those geological ones inherent in the materiality of stones themselves, and in their symbolic message.

FIGURE 1.3 *John Ruskin, 'Linear and Surface Gothic' (1853),* The Stones of Venice, *vol. 2, plate 12.*

Reading the geological wall-veil

If the Protean shape-shifting sand is one geological given at Venice, the other is the rampart of the Alps; often veiled in summer, they can be an immediate snow-clad presence on clear cold winter days like those of Ruskin's first *Stones of Venice* fieldwork from November to March 1849–50. From the campanile of Torcello Ruskin saw, to north and west the 'misty band of mountains, touched with snow',[51] or on his approach to Murano recorded 'the linked conclave of the Alps [which] know no decline from their old pre-eminence, nor stoop from their golden thrones in the circle of the horizon'.[52] Ruskin regarded Venice – at the eastern end of the Alps – as one of his spiritual homes upon earth; the other – at the western end of the Alps – was Chamonix, in Switzerland. And when in November 1849 Ruskin descended from the Alps into the plains of Lombardy and the Veneto to begin his work for *The Stones of Venice*, he did so with a mind full of memories of mountain precipices, from the previous summer of geological research, centred at Chamonix, towards the *Of Mountain Beauty* fourth volume of *Modern Painters* – written in defence of the mountain forms in the art of J. M. W. Turner.

As Ruskin acidly remarks at the outset of 'The Wall Veil' chapter of *The Stones of Venice*, 'there are sometimes more valuable lessons to be learned in the school of nature than in that of Vitruvius . . .'.[53] In this mostly geological chapter, the lesson is to be read from the 'coursed masses of precipice' of the eastern front of Mont Cervin (The Matterhorn) – 'the most noble cliff in Europe'.[54] And the message is this: that these mighty, unyielding mountain faces are in fact largely built of frail materials that 'few architects would like to build with', namely a 'loose and slaty shale, of a dull brick-red colour, which yields beneath the foot like ashes . . .'.[55] So it seems 'as if the mountain were upheld by miracle', but the 'great Builder' has bound these loose shales at intervals with 'a course of living rock, of quartz as white as the snow that encircles it, and harder than a band of steel'.[56] Drawing from these observations a key and influential principle of *architectural* stratification, Ruskin concludes 'with great certainty that it is better and easier to strengthen a wall necessarily of imperfect substance, as of brick, by introducing carefully laid courses of stone, than by adding to its thickness . . .'.[57] Moreover, there are weighty 'decorative reasons for adopting the coursed arrangement'.[58] Among the pages of analysis and exquisite drawings given to the Cervin in *Modern Painters* Ruskin ponders, 'is it not a strange type of the things which "out of weakness are made strong"' that out of these feeble materials 'the axe of God should hew that Alpine tower'.[59] Ruskin's use of 'type' here, and the quoting of St Paul's 'Letter to the Hebrews', explicitly invokes his 'typological' evangelical reading of both the Bible and creation itself as divine manuscript. Ruskin declared his first sight of the Alps as 'not only the revelation of the beauty of the earth, but the opening of the first page of its volume'.[60] Read symbolically, the miraculous might of the Cervin is a 'type' of what the 'great Builder' can make out of humanity's frailty; just as well conceived architectural wall-faces of 'imperfect substance' encode the same human drama. It is often assumed that a symbol in architecture, while representing some ideal, is as appliqué as a postmodern sign. This is not borne out here; for his evangelical readers Moses is a real historical figure *and* is also a 'type' of Christ, whose person and actions symbolically foreshadow the events of the New Testament. Ruskin brings into view the cliff of the Cervin as existent *and* metaphorically a manuscript written by God; the surfaces of architecture as substance *and* emblematic text. Chamonix and Venice, mountains and architecture, landscape and building, *Modern Painters* and *Stones of Venice*; out of his strained effort of geologizing, sampling, drawing, measuring, Ruskin erects his 'superstructure in progress' where the eight volumes of both texts make one vast reciprocal whole. Ruskin said that 'all *Modern Painters* together will be the explanation of a parenthesis in *The Stones of Venice*', but he also saw it the other way round, whereby the whole of *Stones of Venice* explains a point in *Modern Painters*.[61]

Appropriately, after a few days in Milan, one of Ruskin's first subjects of analysis was the 'richly striped' cathedral of Monza to the north-east. On 1 November 1849, his diary describes 'a glorious drive from Milan – view of Monte Rosa the finest I have ever seen, some five miles beyond Monza . . .'.[62] In proximity to this – the second highest massif in the Alps – the façade of Monza (completed 1396) is itself a broad striated cliff of stone, divided into five bays by shallow buttresses. Ruskin records 'the stripes of serpentine with which the whole façade is barred horizontally',[63] noting how these courses slope to become voussoirs that integrate the 'two remarkable windows', of three lights and Gothic geometric tracery, to each side of the entrance porch. The banded façade soars sheer as a precipice to a delicate 'roof cornice' of the most elaborate of the four cornice forms classified in *Stones of Venice*, where the upper projecting stone bracket receives support from a shaft borne on another jutting bracket below. Ruskin considered this type as 'evidently adapted' for the character of stone buildings and 'susceptible of the richest decoration, and superbly employed in the cornice of the cathedral of Monza'.[64] His field notes record 'the cornice running up each side of the broad gable pediment is very beautiful, though quaint', and a pocket-book drawing captures with precision the rich 'shadows taken at one in the afternoon' cast by its intricate brackets, shafts, and linking cusped arches.[65] Here is the same geologizing eye that tracked the shadows of the crests of the Cervin and marked the 'silver cornices glittering along the edge of each' of its iron bands.[66] So near the Alps, it is not fanciful to see precipice strength, and glittering crest, in the Gothic imaginations of the builders of this wall-face of green serpentine and pale pink marble mounting to its crystalline cornice. Gothic yes, but of a conservative Romanesque kind; and it was to the Romanesque itself of the northern Italy mainland that Ruskin looked for models of the constructed wall-veil, as compared to the marble-sheeted or stuccoed surfaces of Venetian Gothic incrustation.

Consequently, in the important plate in *Stones of Venice* of 'Wall-Veil Decoration' in which Ruskin compares two surfaces – a living Romanesque

FIGURE 1.4 *Monza, Duomo façade, completed 1396. Photograph Stephen Kite.*

FIGURE 1.5 *John Ruskin, 'Wall-Veil Decoration',* The Stones of Venice, *vol. 1, plate 13.*

wall-detail, with the mechanical Renaissance rustication of the Arthur Club House in St James's Street, London (Thomas Hopper, 1811) – the Romanesque example is taken from the church of San Pietro in Pistoia, a Tuscany city rich in similarly banded structures. Ruskin offers multiple readings to argue the merits of the constructed, polychromatic wall-veil:

> It is perfectly natural that the different kinds of stone used in its successive courses should be of different colours; and there are many associations and analogies which metaphysically justify the introduction of horizontal bands of colour, or of light and shade. They are, in the first place, a kind of expression of the growth or age of the wall, like the rings in the wood of a tree; then they are a farther symbol of the alternation of light and darkness, which was above noted as the source of charm of many inferior mouldings: again, they are valuable as an expression of horizontal space to the imagination, space of which the conception is opposed, and gives more effect by its opposition, to the enclosing power of the wall itself (… probably the great charm of these horizontal bars to the Arabian mind): and again they are valuable in their suggestion of the natural courses of rocks, and beds of the earth itself. And to all these powerful imaginative reasons we have to add the merely ocular charm of interlineal opposition of colour.[67]

Layered here are the key languages examined earlier: the picturesque agemark registered in the wall's growth, the symbolic messages embodied in the stones themselves and their typological import, and the pictorial and iconographic magic latent in pattern, colour, and ornament. The San Pietro detail derives from a daguerreotype. Ruskin was an early enthusiast for this photographic process invented by Louis-Jacques-Mandé Daguerre (made public in 1839) whereby a silver-coated copper plate is sensitized with iodine fumes and exposed to sunlight in a *camera obscura*. Ruskin called them 'sundrawings', delighting in the suggestive chiaroscuro and minutiae of texture of their elusive mirrored images, which intensified his innate immersion in the architectural surface. He bought his first daguerreotypes when in Venice in 1845, went on to commission many others, and had acquired his own equipment by 1849 (producing images with his manservant 'George' Hobbs). As he enthused in a letter to his father of 7 October 1845 from Venice: 'Daguerreotypes taken by this vivid sunlight are glorious things. It is very nearly the same thing as carrying off the palace itself – every chip of stone & stain is there . . .'.[68] They enabled further rich transactions in Ruskin's visual economy as he drew from them as subjects and used them as sources for his published plates; they in turn intensified and extended his established modes of surface representation.

Many of the Tuscany daguerreotypes are of a high professional standard and were probably produced under Ruskin's direction; 'the group of Pistoia scenes, in particular, contains some tours de force – demonstrating bold composition, startling detail and stunning tonalities'.[69] The *c.* 1846 daguerreotype of San Pietro's façade (completed 1263) – on which the

FIGURE 1.6 *John Ruskin and Le Cavalier Iller*, Pistoia, Church of San Pietro, c. 1846. Half-plate daguerreotype. © *The Ruskin, Lancaster University.*

Stones of Venice detail is based (the cast shadows are identical) – is cropped to bring us into the immediate presence of the five shallowly recessed arches with their banded tympana and spandrels of white and green marble; the plate in *Stones* crops much further still, to little more than the spandrel of the right-hand arches. Repudiating generalized topography, the camera's cropping techniques encouraged Ruskin's oral and haptic appetite for the surfaces of architecture, as in the notorious letter to his father from Verona of 2 June 1852: 'I should like to draw all St Mark's and all this Verona stone by stone, to eat it all up into my mind, touch by touch'.[70] *The Stones of Venice* is entirely illustrated by hard-looking at such fragments of surface and detail, and in the Tuscany and Venetian daguerreotypes close-ups predominate.

Banding the British surface

But what did all these Italian wanderings portend for a British architecture of greater surface tension than the classical clubhouses of London's St James? Returning to Eastlake's point that Ruskin was able to strike a vibrant 'chord of human sympathy' beyond ecclesiastical feelings, historicism, and a vague picturesque; he was able to do this because many of the elements that fused to create Ruskinian Gothic were already in debate. Says Eastlake: 'All that had been argued – all that had been preached on the subject previously, was cast into the shade by the vigour of [Ruskin's] protest'.[71] Ruskin's insights synthesized the extant factors that worked towards a more intense reading of the wall-surface. Factors that included: speculations around the new science of geology and its relations to architecture; questions concerning architecture, symbolism, and meaning; interests in architectural polychromy and a fascination with broader sources in Greece, Byzantium, and Arabia; arguments as to how to make architecture 'new', avoiding the 'copyism' of history; and – interweaving all these notions – the idea of architecture as an ethical practice of making. Aware of these surface architecture experiments, Ruskin ruminated:

> No subject has been more open ground of dispute among architects than the decoration of the wall-veil, because no decoration appeared naturally to grow out of its construction. . . . It has become, therefore, a kind of general field for experiments of various effects of surface ornament, or has been abandoned altogether to the mosaicist and fresco painter.[72]

One such experiment is singled out in *Stones of Venice* for qualified praise: 'The church of Christchurch, Streatham, lately built, though spoiled by many grievous errors (the ironwork in the campanile being the grossest), yet affords the inhabitants of the district a means of obtaining some idea of the variety of effects which are possible with no other material than brick'.[73] In this south London church (1840–2), the architect James Wild brought together the growing interests in Byzantine and Islamic architecture as evident, for example, in the ornament and colour theories of his brother-in-law Owen Jones.[74] Restrained in terms of what was to come, the passages of constructed polychromy in Christ Church's broad plain surfaces of ochre brick are striking enough; there is the zig-zag pyramidal roof of the campanile, the accented cornice, and most of all the voussoirs of the clerestory windows, and the major and minor pointed arches of the west front which are picked out in syncopated alternations of red bricks and glazed yellow bricks, evenly separated by yellow stock bricks.[75] The overall aspect of the church is broadly 'Byzantine' in its simple cubic masses and plain soaring campanile, but the pointed western arches are definitely Islamic with their inner and outer curves characteristically struck from different centres. The colouration of these voussoirs derives from images like the coloured plates of the mosques of Cairo in Pascal Coste's *Architecture Arabe ou Monuments du Kaire* of 1839. Ruskin's point on the spatial appeal of 'horizontal bars [of colour] to the Arabian mind' has been quoted. Earlier in *Stones of Venice* he opines how the Arab school only employs its intricate Arabesque ornament for 'features of interest', but bars its larger 'surfaces with horizontal lines of colour, the expression of the level of the Desert',[76] thus he makes another geophysical parallel, equal to that of Venice's mutable sands, and the natural courses of Alpine rocks. For Ruskin the Venetians 'were the only people who had thoroughly sympathized with the Arabs . . . intense love of colour'.[77] His racializing orientalism is most famously summed up in the image of the Ducal Palace, Venice as the 'central building of the world', for its exact fusion of the Roman, Lombard, and Arab, the fluxes of North and South – 'the glacier torrent and the lava stream'.[78] Influenced by the milieu of Owen Jones, Wild himself travelled to Egypt in 1842 where he designed the Anglican church of St Mark in Alexandria. In turn, he supplied Jones with the material on 'Arabian Ornament' of his hugely influential *The Grammar of Ornament* of 1856.[79] Of no interest to Ruskin – given his loathing of surface-less iron architecture – was Jones's success in applying his colour theories to the vast structure of the Crystal Palace at the Great Exhibition of 1851. In terms of the constructed ornamental *brick* surface, the much publicized Christ Church was a significant staging post in making brick acceptable as a material, along with stone, for church architecture. The potential of brick in Britain was further advanced by the repeal of the brick tax in 1850, by rapid advances in manufacturing techniques such as tunnel-kilns, and by a growing railway distribution network.

Butterfield: All Saints', Margaret Street and the Savage Surface

Wild's tentative experiments in brickwork pale beside the great manifesto for constructional colour of William Butterfield's All Saints', Margaret

Street, London which was designed, constructed and ornamented over a long period from 1849. The cornerstone was laid on 9 November 1850 and it was not consecrated until 28 May 1859, although it was *structurally* complete by late 1852. Setting aside their earlier prejudice against such an ostensibly humble material, the ecclesiastic party of the Church of England expressed the following hopes for Butterfield's church plans, in their own journal *The Ecclesiologist*:

> The founders and the architect of this church are anxious to make it a practical example of what we are very anxious to see tested, viz., constructional polychrome. The material of the building, and of the appended clergy and chorister-houses is to be red and black brick, arranged in patterns, with stone windows and bonding in the church. Internally there is to be a use of coloured marble, which was of course impossible in the middle ages.[80]

The church has sometimes been thought to be antecedent to Ruskin's influence, but within its extended construction period there is evidence 'that the decision to make All Saints' a gorgeous display of coloured stones and tiles rather than a plastered frescoed interior was taken after Ruskin's publication of *The Seven Lamps of Architecture* in May 1849'.[81] A letter of 6 August 1849, written by the principal patron, Alexander Beresford-Hope, confirms the change in the original 1849 plans. The original cost estimate

> was on the supposition of [the church] being merely built of common materials. Since then the aesthetic possibilities of different materials have become more and more clear, and the present scheme is that of a church whose character and beauty and effect of colour shall arise from *construction* and not from *superaddition*, namely that the pillars shall be *made of granite* ... the diaper be an encrustation of tiles, and not the track of a paintbrush, and so on.[82]

In 'The Lamp of Beauty' of *The Seven Lamps*, Ruskin cannot 'consider architecture as in anywise perfect without colour', and these 'colours of architecture should be those of natural stones' with their 'lovely and mellow hues'.[83] The other key naturalistic colour principle enunciated here is that shown earlier by the diaperings of the Ducal Palace of Venice, that is to say how colour in nature 'never follows form, but is arranged on an entirely separate system.... The stripes of a zebra do not follow the lines of its body or limbs, still less the spots of a leopard'.[84] Correspondingly, 'we are to consider our building as a kind of organized creature; in colouring we must look to the single and separate organized creatures of Nature' – such as zebras and leopards.

Since its splay-footed spire first soared above Margaret Street – bracketed by the fiercely black-and-red chequered gables of its choir-school, gateway, and clergy-house – All Saints' has been recognized as a masterpiece of High Victorian Gothic, its 'savage' surfaces spawning a far-reaching critical heritage. The choir-school and clergy-house grip a constricted entrance court on this tight urban site. Placing the church to the north of the small plot, Butterfield wedged its entrance porch into the north-west corner of his court, between the east wall of the choir-school, and the south wall of the nave. The worshipper enters the aisle directly passing a baptistery, formed under the tower, immediately on the left. The nave has just three broad bays which lead quite directly into the deep and high chancel; although there is an arch and a change of level between nave and chancel, the effect is of a unitary space. The east-end is a solid party-wall, so this sombrely glowing church is lit only from its high clerestories and the west window. Weighing all the evidence, Paul Thompson concludes that the choice of brick *in itself* probably belongs to the first stage of All Saints' design, but that 'the external patterning of the brick, the theoretical idea of internal mosaics, and the internal use of granite and alabaster may be definitely attributed to Ruskin'.[85] Butterfield's polychromatic *exteriors* also draw on such experiments as have been seen in Wild's work and precedents he knew of in English Tudor building and in German brickwork. But the interior is quite another matter, and further evidence of Ruskin's stimulus as Butterfield's 'only experiment in "encrustation", that is a mere skin of brick and tile mosaic rather than structural colour'.[86] Says Thompson: 'No other architect so consistently explored both the *material expressiveness* of wall architecture, and its *discipline* through wall planes; and, at the same time, through colour, the triumphant joy of *faith*, and through line and pattern, the *insecurity* of an age of doubt and change'.[87] The extent of constructional colour in British Victorian architecture from the 1850s is owing to this collective influence of text and building, to Ruskin's *Seven Lamps* and *Stones of Venice, and* Butterfield's bold manifestation of polychromy's potential in wall-surface architecture. To which must be added George Edmund Street's texts and buildings as examined later.

Remembering the ecclesiastics' ambition for All Saints' that the ornament should 'arise from *construction* and not from *superaddition* . . . the diaper be an encrustation of tiles, and not the track of a paintbrush', terms in use at the time included 'constructional colouration' to describe the combination of building materials of several intrinsic hues; also the phrase 'permanent polychrome' to distinguish lasting techniques from the fugitive 'track of a paintbrush' where ornament is stencilled or brushed in on plaster.[88] The means of representation thus encompass a spectrum; from the paint-on-plaster of much Venetian diapering, to the thin incrusted 'construction' of mosaic and sheets of marble, to a more solid banded construction, as in the church façades of Pistoia or All Saints' own external brickwork.

Given the insurmountable task of building a school of living sculpture in the mid-nineteenth century, Ruskin was driven to conclude that 'the only manner of rich ornament that is open to us is the geometrical colour-mosaic, and that much might result from our strenuously taking up this mode of design'.[89] That is stated in the 'Lamp of Life' of *Seven Lamps*, while the 'Lamp of Beauty' calls for 'breadth of flat surface' and 'vivid colour introduced in flat geometrical panels'.[90] Butterfield's bold response to such Ruskin challenges can be seen, in all its vigour of pattern and scintillating tonality, in the black-and-white perspective of All Saints' interior published by *The Builder* of 4 June 1859. The rich English Decorated Gothic mouldings of the nave-arches dramatize the 'breadth of flat surface' of the spandrels, where great shield-like discs turn on chequered fields of brick and tile. Ruskin categorizes the spandrel as the first of three wall-veil zones 'fitted for surface decoration of the most elaborate kind'[91] (the others are the tympanum and the space between an arch and its gable) and firstly recommends circle-forms. *The Seven Lamps* illustrates a sculpted spandrel from the cathedral of Lisieux where discs roll around a central rosette (the All Saints' principle), and the first volume of *Stones of Venice* gives a detailed plate of the noble spandrel decoration of the Ducal Palace incrusted with red Verona, white, and grey marbles enfolding a central disc of green serpentine. Ruskin stresses 'this decoration by discs, or shield-like ornaments [as] a marked characteristic of Venetian architecture in its earliest ages'.[92] The dates allow for this Ruskin influence on the polychromatic shield-forms of All Saints' decoration, but a more likely source for the actual mosaicist patterns are the boldly coloured plates of Matthew Digby Wyatt's *Specimens of the Geometrical Mosaics of the Middle Ages* of 1849. Wyatt published *Specimens* as the outcome of a European tour commissioned by the mosaic producer John Marriott Blashfield. Technological progress in manufacture, such as that of 'encaustic' tiles around 1839, furthered the aforementioned desire for permanent colouration inspired by such Italian and Oriental exemplars.[93]

The Ruskinian colour-model was then crucial to the development of All Saints', but to what extent is it a zebra or a Ducal Palace – that 'kind of organized creature' where the colour surfaces work on an independent system to the form? For Henry-Russell Hitchcock, it is entirely a zebra where 'the lack of coordination at All Saints' between window arrangement and surface pattern exceeds that to be seen on the Venetian palace which was Ruskin's chief exemplar of over-all polychrome wall treatment . . .'.[94] Whereas Paul Thompson holds that 'the colour patterns at All Saints' are in fact clearly defined by the architectural surfaces, as may be seen from the placing of circular motifs' as just discussed.[95] In arbitration, between these critics, let us take the elevation of the south aisle to the courtyard where the polychromy is made from combinations of red and black brickwork and ochre stone. Butterfield bands these materials to the springing of the arch, and chequers the arch-zone – following structural logic. This constricted wall has complicated rhythms with one wide and a pair of narrow arches divided by a pinnacled buttress; but in all cases Butterfield centres his chequer-patterns to the intervals, and the ochre squares at the centres of the

FIGURE 1.7 *All Saints' Margaret Street. Interior looking east,* The Builder *(4 June 1859), p. 377.*

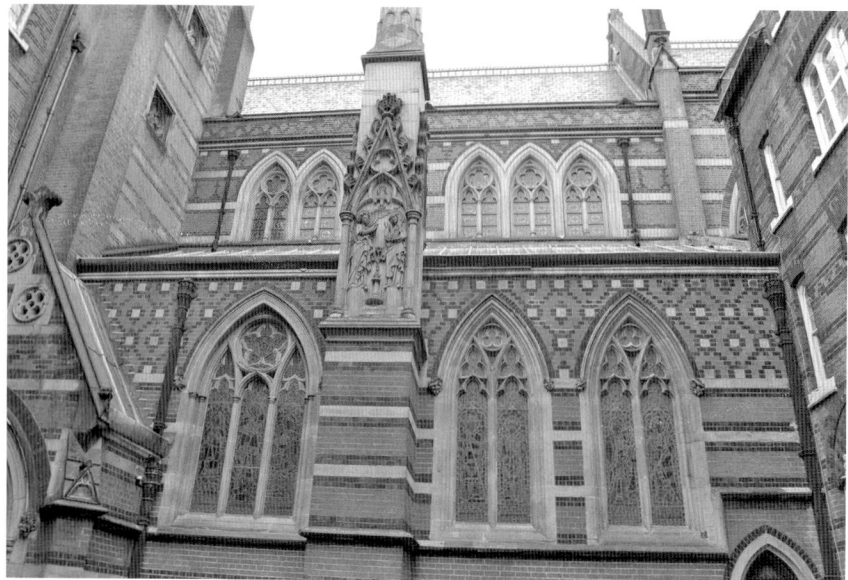

FIGURE 1.8 *All Saints' Margaret Street, courtyard elevation of south aisle. Photograph Stephen Kite.*

diapers *exactly* touch the voussoirs of black brick, framing the stone arches – not at all like the Ducal Palace. It would have taken exact setting-out to achieve this across these varied divisions – Ruskin would have allowed free-pattern. Yet it is also possible to agree that the *impression*, outside and in, of the assault to the eye of these dense fields of patterned brick and mosaic is of sovereignly extended wall-veils following laws of their own. Never again would Butterfield deploy mosaic incrustation to the level of All Saints'. His last masterpiece, St Paul's Cathedral in Melbourne, Australia, designed in 1878, has an interior that is pure Siena, its stripes of grey basalt alternating with cream limestone make it 'his noblest tribute to the Italian masters of constructional colour'.[96]

Butterfield's hauntingly refractory wall-planes resonate through the whole period of this enquiry, interlacing an extensive critical legacy, and the minds and works of many architects whether Modernist, Brutalist, Postmodern, or Late-Modern; they can be said to have engendered a cult of the Savage or Grotesque surface. The well-known first characteristic of Ruskin's 'Nature of Gothic' (*The Stones of Venice*, vol. 2) is 'Savageness' where he contrasts the earth-veils between 'Northern and Southern countries': 'Syria and Greece, Italy and Spain, laid like pieces of a golden pavement into the sea-blue' against the 'masses of leaden rock and heathy moor' of northern lands. Then the coats of creatures, those 'striped zebras' again, and the 'spotted leopards' of warmer climates, as compared to the 'shaggy covering, and dusky plumage' of northern fauna. So we will watch 'with reverence' the Mediterranean builder of surfaces 'as he sets side by side the burning gems, and smooths with soft sculpture the jasper pillars, that are to reflect a ceaseless sunshine', but must not despise his northern brother when 'with rough strength and hurried stroke, he ... heaves into the darkened air the pile of iron buttress and rugged wall ...'.[97] In Ruskin's Savage, ostensibly negative qualities such as 'ignorance', 'ugliness', 'formlessness' can be read as 'signs of the life and liberty of every workman who struck the stone' as when we 'gaze upon the old cathedral front' to enjoy 'the fantastic ignorance of the old sculptors', their 'ugly goblins, and formless monsters'.[98] Closely allied to the Savage is the fourth 'mental characteristic' of Gothic – the Grotesque. In *Stones of Venice*, the 'Grotesque' category is briefly alluded to in the 'Nature of Gothic' chapter, but then deferred to the chapter on 'Grotesque Renaissance' where it is presented in its negative capacity as a symbol of 'The Fall' of Venice, as in Ruskin's revulsion at the deformed 'huge, inhuman, and monstrous' keystone head to the doorway to the Baroque campanile (1611) of the church of Santa Maria Formosa.[99] The first plate of volume three of *Modern Painters* contrasts 'True and False Griffins'. The Lombard-Gothic griffin is a living synthesis of the lion and eagle's predatory power, as it bears upon its back the whole weight of the porch of Verona's Duomo, while nonchalantly seizing a winged dragon in its fierce claws. Whereas, in Ruskin's analysis, the 'false' Classical griffin (from the Temple of Antoninus and Faustina, Rome) is an implausible assemblage of the two creatures' body-parts, barely able to bend the tendril on which its limply extended paw rests. Correspondingly, in painting or literature, true 'grotesque is the expression, in a moment, by a series of symbols thrown together in bold and fearless connection, of truths which it would have taken a long time to express in any verbal way, and of which the connection is left for the beholder to work out for himself; the gaps, left or overleaped by the haste of the imagination, forming the grotesque character'.[100] In *The Stones of Venice*, Ruskin argues that 'there is very little architecture in the world which is, in the full sense of the words, good and noble' – some Gothic and Romanesque, two or three Greek temples perhaps – the remainder depends for its 'power on some development of the grotesque spirit'. In domestic architecture of the Middle Ages it is felt in 'fantastic gables', in 'pinnacled roofs', in 'the blackened timbers, crossed and carved into every conceivable waywardness of imagination, of Normandy and old England', in 'rude hewing' of material, and the like.[101] For Ruskin, it is important to discriminate between Grotesque effects – produced 'exclusively by the fancy of man' – from those of the Picturesque with its associated age-marks 'produced by the working of nature and of time'.[102] Putting all this together, Grotesque architecture expresses itself in strange, or terrible amalgamations, or in jarring juxtapositions of form and symbol, playing its fancies out in waywardly restless surfaces, somewhat roughly wrought.

John Summerson revisited Ruskin's Savage and Grotesque theme in an article in *The Architectural Review* in December 1945, where he included his own photographs of the bombed-out shells of two of Butterfield's major churches – St Matthias, Stoke Newington and St Alban's, Holborn – thrusting into the dark post-Blitz London skies the bare silhouettes and 'rugged walls' of their great saddle-back towers.[103] For Summerson, Butterfield's 'hard red brick' in which 'he set those multiple black bands and innocently crude diapers' oppose vigorous 'workmanship to sensibility ... they are the "noble grotesque" as against the "ignoble grotesque" of rustication and of the kind of architecture which grew out of the drawing board and T-square'.[104] Butterfield, he continues, 'loved the *awkwardness* inseparable from most early Gothic; he loved its strength and adolescence, its coltish negligence. He loved that his porch at All Saints' should collide grotesquely with the wall of the Clergy House ...'.[105] In architectural composition, this is Ruskin's Grotesque definition of 'bold and fearless connection' where the 'connection is left for the beholder to work out for himself'. 'All Butterfield's churches are to a greater or less degree ugly', asserts Summerson, a Savage quality seen in the All Saints' interior where 'he loved to clash the variableness of the pointed arch and to interrupt a rhythmical pattern in an agony of discord'.[106] As Summerson rightly points out, the 'ugliness' theme goes back to the earliest responses to the building, even the mostly sympathetic *Ecclesiologist* praised All Saints' 'force and power', but found here 'the germ of the same dread of beauty, not to say the same preference of ugliness, which so characterizes in fuller development the later paintings of Mr Millais and his followers'.[107] Here the reviewer refers to Millais's *Christ in the House of his Parents* (derisively called 'The Carpenter's Shop') exhibited at the Royal Academy in 1850 and attacked by *The Times* as 'revolting ... with no conceivable omission of misery, of dirt, of even disease'.[108] From very different world-views, Butterfield and Millais are exploring authentic surfaces, communicating life's workaday realism, and non-hierarchical in their evenness of handling; while in terms such as 'ugliness', 'abruptness', 'uncouthness', their critics unwittingly invoke the Savage and Grotesque. Butterfield's visual pugnacity of congested, over-scaled 'zig-zags and stripes' is, for H. S. Goodhart-Rendel, a 'wincing ... blow between the eyes delivered to them by the master's violence ...'[109] – this was published in 1953 in a text based on lectures of 1934. And both Summerson and Ian Nairn (in *Nairn's London*, 1966) associate Butterfield with the 'Gothic' of Emily Bronte's *Wuthering Heights* allying his surfaces by association with Ruskin's Savage Northern 'masses of leaden rock and heathy moor'; on All Saints' Nairn writes: 'Here is the force of *Wuthering Heights* translated into dusky red and black bricks.... The proportions and transfigured gilded violence of this unexpected Heathcliff burn through any artificiality'.[110] Looking forward, many links can be found between Butterfield and later Brutalist, and British Modernist, ethics and aesthetics. For example, Elain Harwood points to the *Architectural Review* of November 1972 where Mark Girouard – reviewing James Stirling's Florey Building in Oxford – pairs an image of this student accommodation with

The Builder interior of All Saints' of 1853: 'Previous to Stirling the only group of architects I know of to work out a consistent prismatic style of hard shiny surfaces were the hard-line Gothicists of the mid-nineteenth century, with Butterfield as their leader'.[111]

'Natural horizontal courses': Street's All Saints, Boyne Hill

One rather earlier project took Ruskin's idea of constructional architectural colour, and stratified flat wall-surfaces, to its logical extreme – the closely banded chancel walls of George Edmund Street's All Saints, Boyne Hill, Berkshire of 1854–7, his earliest masterwork in polychromy, and a church actually consecrated before Butterfield's long-gestated All Saints'. A theorist, as well as a major architect, Street was the most influential critic after Ruskin associated with the formation of High Victorian Gothic; the 'development' of this style of architecture intriguingly progressed – not along the ostensibly 'obvious line of the ferrovitreous architecture of the Crystal Palace' – but took the path of mass and surface of Street's 'highly sophisticated neo-medievalism', and that of his many pupils, Philip Webb, William Morris, John D. Sedding, and Richard Norman Shaw, among them.[112]

When, in the debates of the time, architects and critics spoke of 'development', it was a highly loaded term – posited often against 'copyism' – in the belief that the new Gothic architecture had no need to be archaeological, in its capacity for growth and expression tuned to its age. Theological in its conception, 'development' describes the belief that whereas divine revelation is complete, it is always open to new manifestations of human understanding. Thus one of Street's earliest critical papers (read to the Oxford Architectural Society on 18 February 1852, and published in the *Ecclesiologist*) was on 'The True Principles of Architecture, and the Possibility of Development'; this followed his important 1850 paper 'On the Proper Characteristics of a Town Church'. In his 'True Principles' lecture, Street was anxious to put before his audience 'some observations on true principles in architecture, and of the possibilities of development consequent on their adoption';[113] many of these observations were highly pertinent to the development of the British surface. Straightaway he dismisses the potential for any development in what 'many, I believe, look for most, viz., to [skeletal] construction in iron', this is not 'architecture at all. It is simply engineering'.[114] Then, an important passage attacks the untruthful use of 'uneven surfaces' of Kentish ragstone:

> I hold that in a brick-making and brick-producing district – like London for instance – it is quite absurd to go about hunting in the country in all directions, to find a material which will look antique! and so to bring up

from the middle of Kent a rough, intractable, and picturesque stone, which with its uneven surfaces, serves . . . most efficiently as a collector of soot. It certainly never looks truthful, because it shows that the man who used it thought that in *it* lay the merits of the old buildings in which he had seen it used, and not in the designs themselves of those buildings. Brick would have been his natural material – unless indeed he had funds wherewith to get a better – (which ragstone is not) – and if he had worked truthfully brick must have looked well.[115]

The historian of English building materials, Alec Clifton-Taylor, describes the long history of this 'coarse-textured and brittle' ragstone, worked by the Romans, one that 'unfortunately, because of its relative cheapness, was much patronised by Victorian church architects in the London area. We say unfortunately because Kentish rag is an unaccommodating stone, difficult to dress, and even to square at all precisely, so its uneven surface is all too prone to harbour dirt'.[116] Street's ire is pointedly aimed at virtually all the ragstone town churches previously approved by the Ecclesiologists such as Richard Cromwell Carpenter's model St Mary Magdalene, Munster Square, London (1849–52), praised by the *Ecclesiologist* in 1852 as 'the most artistically correct new church in London'.[117] 'On the Proper Characteristics of a Town Church' (1850) also argues forcefully for *smooth surfaces* and 'to avoid rusticity in any way, whether in material, design, or execution' in the urbane context of a town or city. Street continues:

> I should condemn *in toto* the use of rough walling stones in a town. The sentiment they convey is one different from that which the polished and smooth surfaces of the neighbouring buildings demand, and, I think, inferior by reason of its apparent rudeness. In such a town as London I would much rather use brick than rough stone, simply on account of its superior smoothness and evenness of surface.[118]

Eastlake places rag-surfaced St Mary Magdalene as 'the last church of any note erected in London' before Butterfield revolutionized the Ecclesiological model.[119] Indeed, Street has early praise for 'my friend Mr Butterfield [who] has shown in Margaret Street what can be done in brick'. His 'noble work' shows 'the extent to which brick may be used, and the variety of colour of which it is susceptible point to it as our most available material'.[120] Here Street opposes emphasis on 'the vertical principle of Pointed architecture', on 'the upward tendency of spires, of pinnacles, of buttresses, and of arches', instead stressing the fact 'that all construction is necessarily horizontal, and that if you ornament construction by colour . . . your ornament must necessarily be in horizontal, and not in vertical lines'.[121] He would not travel to northern Italy himself until 1853 (in an itinerary following Ruskin's footsteps) and here in this 1850 talk – undoubtedly inspired by Ruskin's *Seven Lamps* – he praises the Italian parallelism of 'courses of variously coloured stone or marble, laid in natural horizontal courses throughout their buildings, and certainly most lovely in their effect'.[122] He also draws on English examples, such as the tower and steeple at Irchester, Northamptonshire, a superlative example of 'medieval polychromy, in which bands of ironstone alternate with grey Northamptonshire limestone';[123] Italy and England together demonstrating that 'where men had variously coloured stones to use, they wisely used them in distinct horizontal lines'.[124] Street's polychromatically banded chancel walls at All Saints, Boyne Hill have been recognized as 'strikingly similar to contemporary geological sectional drawings'[125] such as those in Robert Bakewell's *Introduction to Geology* of 1833. Along with the fascinating metaphorical suggestions, architects were acutely interested in what the geological sciences could tell them about the characteristics of their raw materials. For the Christian believer, geological discoveries could be both a challenge to faith and a 'development' of it. Ruskin himself was a committed amateur geologist whom, in certain nightmares, held his ears against 'those dreadful Hammers! I hear the clink of them at the end of every cadence of the Bible verses . . .'.[126] Positively, science could demonstrate a God immanent in the development of divine creation as when Robert Chambers, in his hugely popular *Vestiges of Creation* of 1844, writes: 'The organic, the other great department of mundane things, rests in like manner on one law, and that is Development'.[127] By the time that Charles Lyell published his *Principles of Geology* in 1830–3, many had already come to accept the earth's enormous age, in accord with the revelations of *Genesis*. While the notable geologist William Buckland, in *Geology and Mineralogy Considered with Reference to Natural Theology* (1836), showed how fossil evidence could reinforce arguments of the Almighty's ongoing design of Creation.

The church at Boyne Hill forms the north side of a quadrangle of picturesque changefulness, the *Ecclesiologist* of 1854 praising how Street, 'with more than ordinary success', treated the 'various buildings' required by a new parish, not 'as so many separate units' but rather 'as component parts of a quasi-collegiate group'.[128] A gabled vestry extension (A. E. Street, 1910–11) connects the church to the vicarage (1855–7) on the east side of the court, with the school to the south (1855–7), and the clergy house (1859) to the west, completing the court which was centred on a stone Calvary cross (removed 1960s). The 1858 *Ecclesiologist* also complimented Street 'upon a great success at All Saints', but found the 'first impression . . . rather startling, from the overpowering redness of the entire pile. Not only are the walls red brick, but the roof is of red tiles'.[129] The later reviewer thought Street could 'more wisely have toned down the predominant hue by some material of contrasting colour, such as the flints which are so abundant on the neighbouring chalk hills . . .'.[130] There *is* contrast at Boyne Hill, but it is designed to accent the orange-red brick not to mute it, and Street would not have wanted to adulterate Boyne Hill's smooth and even surfaces with the roughness of flint. So it is that the orange-red brick is accented externally with blue-black brick courses and dressings of yellow Bath stone.[131] Boyne Hill benefits from the more intense sensibilities to surface and colour Street gained from his visit to Italy in the autumn of 1853, and as published in his *Brick and Marble in the Middle Ages: Notes of a Tour in the North of Italy* of 1855; there is also his related lecture paper of 26 September 1855 'On Colour as applied to Architecture'. How Street constructed his exterior colour, and what sort of architecture it made possible, may be seen in the outstanding example of All Saints' tower, with its red and off-white banded belfry stage and tall broach spire of pale Bath stone. It is English in its spire-form, and Italian in its proportions; the strong belfry-banding derives from buildings Street had sketched and admired such as the 'really beautiful' Palazzo Pubblico of Udine (banded in red and white marble) and the 'magnificent campanile of the Scaligeri Palace in Verona'.[132] Although the body of the church had been built from 1854–7, this tower was not added until 1865. It originally stood as a soaring, almost free-standing campanile, with arches to an open vaulted porch, lightly joined to the modestly-scaled church at the north-west corner, and anchored by a bold circular stair-turret on the west side. However, in 1910–11 the nave was extended westwards by Street's son Arthur Edmund Street; although sympathetic, this extension absorbed the tower to the serious loss of its free-standing drama at the climax of the ascending curve of Boyn Hill Road. In his *Memoir* of his father, A. E. Street opines that his best towers, such as SS Philip and James, Oxford and Boyne Hill:

> all have a marked beauty of outline, and exhibit great skill in the treatment of the junction of the tower and spire . . . so that there is no sense of any abruptness in the change from the perpendicular line of the tower to the slope of the spire, but the whole mass seems to spring to the sky from the ground itself in one great sweep.[133]

A tower in its sheerness of surface can approach the majesty of nature insisted Ruskin: 'There are few rocks, even among the Alps, that have a clear vertical fall as high as the choir of Beauvais; and if we secure a good precipice of wall, or a sheer unbroken flank of tower . . . we shall feel in them no want of sublimity of size'.[134] Among the materials from Street's office, collected by Paul Joyce (Paul Joyce Archive, The Paul Mellon Centre for Studies in British Art, London), are a number of key drawings for this tower, and the detailed twelve-page 'Specification' (September 1864) for 'the erection of a New Steeple at . . . All Saints Boyne Hill'.[135] A large sheet (655mm × 530mm) of the 'Buttresses and Lower Part of Tower' shows the carefully studied polychromy of this important arched threshold.[136] An intrados and drip-moulding of Bath stone frame bold chamfer and roll-mouldings in the orange-red brick, broken by voussoirs of blue-black courses. Outer blue-black voussoirs carry the arch upwards into a gable-zone – outlined in stone on the wall – pierced by a hexafoil encircled in red-brick and stone, with its

FIGURE 1.9 *All Saints Boyne Hill, Berkshire, 'Church, No. 5 – Buttresses and Lower Part of Tower', colour ink on paper original drawing, G. E. Street, September 1864. PRJ/4/1/2 Paul Joyce Archive, The Paul Mellon Centre for Studies in British Art.*

own upper arc of blue-black voussoirs; all the strong detail here is delightfully calibrated in colour and profile. Street on 'Development' in 1852 had over-argued the principle of constructional truth:

> colour in arches should be kept as much as possible in distinct rims, the same as those natural to the construction; and should on no account, run

across the arch ... and then be continued on in horizontal lines ... like much of the Italian medieval work. And arches should be carefully defined and kept away and distinct in colour from the wall, their office being quite distinct from its office, and therefore not to be confounded with it in decoration.[137]

But now – as is everywhere evident at Boyne Hill – he had seen 'Italian medieval work' with his own eyes, and this Boyne Hill drawing has both the coloured voussoirs running *across* the arch, and the arch bands infusing their energies out into the wall-plane. For instance, a coloured plate on 'Italian Brickwork' in *Brick and Marble in the Middle Ages* has examples of moulded brickwork and 'alternate voussoirs of brick and stone' from 'Windows at Verona'.[138] The 'Specification Sept 1864' stresses the care in workmanship Street demanded: 'The bricks shewn with a moulding or Chamfer or other ornament to be moulded in the most accurate manner. The arch bricks to be all det[ailed] in the most careful manner and wherever so shewn to be black and red. The bricks for arches to be of the size shewn on detail drawing i.e. not more than 2 [inches] at the widest part'.[139]

The recently consecrated church (12 December 1857) can be entered and seen in its full contemporary Tractarian magnificence in an interior from *The Illustrated News of the World* of 2 October 1858.[140] The surpliced choir precede the clergy on their progression into the glowing chancel at the end of a nave packed with a finely dressed congregation. As in *The Builder* interior view of Butterfield's All Saints', a black-and-white image registers the tonal essentials of a richly polychromatic interior. The *Ecclesiologist* of the same year enjoyed 'the first impression, upon entering ... of spaciousness – an effect, which we attribute in considerable measure to the honest boldness with which colour is given by the use of red brick as the material of the internal walls, spandrels, &c'.[141] Between mouldings of pale stone, the nave arcades are expressed as two bands of nail-headed voussoirs in stone, and black and red brick patterns, run in contrapuntal rhythms. The proper climax is the elevated chancel with – to our late-modern eyes – its extraordinarily abstract irregular bands incrusting the tall brick walls, of yellow, turquoise, ochre, and sienna vitreous tiles, edged in black bricks, and interposed by deeper bands of veined polished Derbyshire alabaster. Together with the aforementioned fascination with the geological strata shown by Lyell, Buckland, and Ruskin's researches, one important Italian precedent was the Romanesque basilica of San Zeno Maggiore in Verona. Street admired this 'noble church', built outside and in, 'in *alternate and very irregularly divided courses* of brick and stone':[142]

It is in this use of red brick, and in the bold and successful way in which brick and stone are shown in the interior, that this church is so full of instruction to an English eye; and I could not see such a work without regretting bitterly the insane prejudice which some people indulge against

FIGURE 1.10 *George Edmund Street, All Saints Boyne Hill*, The Illustrated News of the World *(2 October 1858)*.

FIGURE 1.11 *George Edmund Street, All Saints Boyne Hill, nave and chancel. Photograph Geoff Brandwood.*

anything but the cold, dreary, chilling respectability of our English plastered walls, which to me seems to be fit only for occupation by savages.[143]

Boyne Hill's chancel is Street's response to his impassioned appeal in the final pages of *Brick and Marble in the Middle Ages* for 'Colour in

Construction': 'The task and duty of architects at the present day is mainly that of awakening and then satisfying this feeling [for colour]'.[144] As for available materials 'we have not this excuse; we not only know what materials we may obtain, but we have at the same time marvellous facilities for their conveyance between all parts of the country . . .':[145]

> We have alabaster . . .; large fields of marbles, of which those of Devonshire and Ireland are particularly valuable for architectural decoration, and those of Derbyshire and Purbeck for the formation of shafts and columns: we have, moreover, an exhaustless supply of granites of various colours . . . of building-stones of many tints, many of which may be very effective when contrasted. In addition to these natural materials we have every facility for making the most perfect bricks.[146]

In its entirety Boyne Hill celebrates this rich British material sampling, while the chancel closely adheres to another rule from Street's lecture 'On Colour', namely 'to separate all colours by lines, either of metal or black. This will give distinctness, and prevent confusion. . . . How very bad the effect invariably is of blue and red side by side in any kind of work: and it is this juxtaposition of primary colours which in all cases must be ruinous to the effect of any work in which they are introduced . . .'.[147] As has been seen, the boldly coloured chancel tile-bands are edged by lines of black bricks.

* * *

Given the 'developments' as outlined here, it might seem strange in retrospect that the surfaces of British architecture would be re-signified with the density of readings we have seen in the theories of Ruskin and Street, and in the buildings of both Butterfield and Street himself. Certainly there is nothing in the 'luminous volumes of space within brittle envelopes of structure'[148] of some of Pugin's churches, or the rational iron-framing logic of the Crystal Palace, to have expected such surfaces as a probable trajectory of High Victorian architecture. The Ruskin of the 'Lamp of Power' of *The Seven Lamps of Architecture* was crucial to the fact that 'the feeling for broad surfaces and angular masses . . . became characteristic of many areas of mid-Victorian architecture'[149] as again has been examined in the churches of Butterfield and Street. And it might seem stranger still that this 'feeling for broad surfaces' would be predicated upon a synthesis of specific readings of the Romanesque and Gothic buildings of northern Italy allied to more native precedents and instincts, and to the evolving science of geology. Particularly in church architecture, the proliferation of this feeling for broad surfaces gave rise to brick and stone building that is 'compact, angular and assertive [whose] high, broad walls reprove the dappled textures and broken outlines beloved of the ecclesiologists';[150] at any rate, 'beloved of the ecclesiologists' up to the point of Carpenter's Kentish ragstone St Mary Magdalene, London

FIGURE 1.12 George Edmund Street, All Saints Boyne Hill, detail of chancel, north wall. Photograph Geoff Brandwood.

(1849–52). It is the kind of sturdy and massive architecture illustrated in George Truefitt's exactly mid-century *Designs for Country Churches* of 1850.[151] Truefitt prefaces his plates with an attack on how '"Authority" has taken the place of "Originality"' so that 'Church Architecture and "Copyism" [has] become synonymous', offering his muscular, abstractly planar, examples as '*attempts to think* in "Gothic" exclusive of actual authority . . .'.[152] Without disavowing Ruskin's centrality to all the above, only afterwards were these principles disseminated via the contribution of Street's own important practice-based theory (he designed some 260 churches and secular buildings) and the vast schooling of his office; some forty architects have been identified who received part of their training as student or assistant therein.[153] To this point surface awareness has been examined in the public sphere of High Victorian ecclesiastical architecture. Through two of the protégé's of Street's fecund atelier – Philip Webb and William Morris – we shall now turn to the working out of the feeling for surface in the more private realm of the Arts and Crafts domestic interior.

CHAPTER TWO

'Think first of the walls': Surfaces of Romance

Morris, Webb, and the Arts and Crafts Domestic Interior

Red House as *hortus ludi*

In William Morris's utopian socialist vision, *News from Nowhere* (1892) – against the cold 'so-called science of the nineteenth century' – he presents 'the spirit of the new days, of our days' as a 'delight in the life of the world; intense and overweening love of the very skin and surface of the earth, on which man dwells, such as a lover has in the fair flesh of the woman he loves . . .'.[1] He ascribes this sensual passion for the living surface of the earth as the first characteristic of Gothic Art – 'Love of Nature'; joined to this, as the second characteristic, is the epical, story-telling, quality; and joined to both of these is the 'ornamental quality'.[2] Morris sees the aspect that fuses the Gothic love of nature, story-telling, and ornament, as 'the *romantic* quality'. In Percy Lubbock's memories as a schoolboy at Eton College in the 1890s (*Shades of Eton*, 1929), he also pinpoints 'romance' as the atmosphere Morris engenders out of the surfaces of his domestic interiors, relating this 'strange new presence' which 'allows you to work and live as usual, as before, but with romance: the breathable air'.[3] Here he draws a scene of Eton Vice-Provost, Francis Warre Cornish's 'room of pomegranates':

> And first the room in which we sat: the long room, with its two high windows at the end that looked through trees to the river, was such as I had never seen or known before. . . . Dimly and softly hued, yet full of

colour, blue like a mist and green like a forest, the drawing-room of the Cornishes wore distinction with no effort, as if it were everyday wear. It seemed to me a place in which beauty was somehow assumed and taken for granted; it appeared to pass as a matter of course that life has need of beauty, a natural and workaday need. It isn't paraded or shown off, in this manner of being; it is around you, behind you, wherever it happens, noticed or unnoticed, while you talk and think and work. Did I know the name of William Morris when I first entered that soft-shaded room? I forget – perhaps I first heard it there. Anyhow the pomegranates of Morris were on the walls, his glowing tulips were on the chairs or in the hangings; and however little I understood, I knew that it was an air and mood of beauty fresh to my experience. I can't describe, I couldn't exaggerate the romance of the discovery. Say what you will, there remains this magic in the touch of the genius of Morris, that it brings you strangeness and rarity into your own life, the life that *you* lead; and you aren't called to stop and stare and exclaim, you haven't to adapt your ways by force to a strange new presence. It allows you to live and work as usual, as before, but with romance in the breathable air.[4]

Yet on the face of it, in its raw red expression of local English-bond brickwork, Red House, Bexleyheath, Kent – Morris's first married home conceived with Philip Webb in 1858–9 – shows little evident romance. Its solidly 'independent character' and honest lack of pretension – i.e. no mask of stucco – made it an icon of modernity, notably in Nikolaus Pevsner's *Pioneers of Modern Design: from William Morris to Walter Gropius*;[5] these Modernist narratives are invariably yoked to the open-ended plan, whose one-room-and-a-corridor chain is bent into an L of Ruskinian Changefulness.[6] However, it is known that these insistent red brick planes, and the open L-plan, are literally only half the intended story of Red House; a story whose telling discloses richer narratives of romantic surface.

In his first authorized biography of Morris of 1899, J. W. Mackail confirms that while the 'rooms on both limbs of the house faced outward on to the garden. The two other sides of this half-quadrangle were masked by rose-trellises, inclosing a square inner court, in the middle of which rose the most striking architectural feature of the building, a well-house of brickwork and oak timber, with a steep conical tiled roof'.[7] Thus the limbs of the L-plan guarded an outdoor room, a *hortus conclusus* in its specific manifestation of the *hortus ludi* – a garden full of flowers as a setting for delight and courtly love.[8] Known, in the medieval sense as a 'herber'—from the Latin 'herba' (grass or aromatic plant)—to mean a small garden, or an ornamental enclosed flowery mead set within a larger garden.[9] Look at the Garden of Pleasure delicately illuminated in the Flemish fifteenth-century *Roman de la Rose*, a manuscript beloved by both Morris and the Pre-Raphaelite artist Edward Burne-Jones, both of whom studied it in the British Museum; a garden wherein courting and philosophizing takes place around water-fountains – akin to Webb's well-house – against a framework of rose-grown trellises,[10] forerunners of Morris's own trellis enclosures which inspired his first wallpaper design in 1862. In the first 'Medieval Tale' (for March) of Morris's *Earthly Paradise* (1868–70), Cecily discovers the sleeping Michael in a 'pleasance sweet' equipped with old walls blessed 'with wealth of fruit', a glittering fountain and basin, and 'tree and bower and high pleached fence'.[11]

FIGURE 2.1 *Guillaume de Lorris and Jean de Meun*, Roman de la Rose, *'Lutenist and singers in a walled garden' (c. 1490–1500), Harley 4425 f.12v. British Library, London. © The British Library Board. All Rights Reserved / Bridgeman Images.*

Owing to Morris, the garden, and its relations to the house, becomes more architectural, while the domestic interior grows more natural – though without ever losing its firm architectonic basis in the layered wall-plane. In his lecture 'Making the Best of It' (1879), he summed up the garden as a Middle Ages paradise:

> Large or small, [the garden] should look both orderly and rich. It should be well fenced from the outside world. It should by no means imitate either the wilfulness or the wildness of Nature, but should look like a thing never to be seen except near a house. It should in fact, look like a part of the house.[12]

The interaction of the ordered rooms of the evolving Arts and Crafts garden, with the changefulness of the dwelling, are associated with these early ideas of Morris.[13] In the full Red House project, surfaces of varied materiality would have embraced a *hortus ludi* at the heart of Morris's romantic ideal of an art-community, involving his family and that of Burne-Jones. According to Burne-Jones, Webb's design to complete the Red House quadrangle and to make a 'Palace of Art' was 'so beautiful that life seemed to have no more in it to desire...'.[14] But the promised utopia foundered in the unhappy circumstances surrounding the death in 1864, three weeks after his birth, of Burne-Jones and his wife Georgiana's prematurely born second son, Christopher.

Along with the contract drawings of Red House as-built, the Victoria and Albert Museum has Webb's 1864 drawings for this 'Palace of Art' for the Burne-Jones's, and a cheaper reduced scheme. Webb stitched the new wing into the eastern L of Red House, devising a new hipped roof projection on the north side which gave the Burne-Jones's a separate entrance, in balance with the old, and niftily also a seat-bay – with a great swinging shutter – to their new dining room, shaped from the former bachelors' bedroom of Red House. The great gable of a first-floor studio marks out the east elevation, but the courtyard aspect is the most striking as shown in my perspective reconstruction, based on Webb's plans and elevations, a result 'extraordinarily skilful in the way it responds to the original [Red House] while making a new statement on its own'.[15] The existing red brick continues only as a plinth, tying old and new together, and supports a jettied upper storey of half-timber and plaster, punctuated by a semi-circular bay-window; this marks a pause, on the cross-axis of the well-house, to the new wing's upper passage. A bold timber and plaster cove crowns the half-timbering as often found in Kent's medieval Wealden houses. Add in the tile-hanging to the south and east elevations and it will be seen that Webb has drawn upon the full regional material palette. Architect George Devey (1820–1886) anticipated Webb's love for the vernacular, though was more literal in his adoption of local forms and materials, and it is likely that Webb knew of Devey's 1850 cottages at Penshurst, Kent which are also jettied out, half-timbered and rendered above a masonry ground-storey of plain ragstone.[16]

FIGURE 2.2 *Perspective reconstruction of Philip Webb's 1864 design to extend Red House into a 'Palace of Art'. Drawing Stephen Kite.*

Ray Watkinson praises Morris as 'a master in the art of enriching a surface',[17] this sensibility proceeding in part from pondering the outdoor room of the *hortus ludens* as represented in medieval illuminated manuscripts of this kind. As friend and close-reader of Ruskin he imbibed his principles of the architectonic subordination of ornament as laid out in the chapter on 'Treatment of Ornament' in the first volume of *The Stones of Venice* (1851) where Ruskin urges the reader to consider 'the effect of the illuminations of an old missal. In their bold rejection of all principles of perspective, light and shade, and drawing, they are infinitely more ornamental to the page, owing to the vivid opposition of their bright colours and quaint lines . . .'.[18]

In their study of the outdoor room of the *hortus conclusus*, Rob Aben and Saskia de Wit deconstruct such tableaux of the *hortus ludi* as isotropic spaces lacking 'a sense of alignment or a principle element to be discerned, let alone a link between ground plane, enclosure and built mass'.[19] The spatially disconnected components of the *Roman de la Rose* garden – ordered by the plane of the lawn – are itemized in my analytical diagram as: wall and gate, flowery mead, fruit trees, fountain, and trellis enclosure.[20] Especially in its complete U-plan vision, Red House romantically imbricates similar elements. Its architectural language also makes the setting in one of Morris's pencil and ink studies for the painted doors of the St George Cabinet, designed by Philip Webb, for the 1862 Great Exhibition.[21] Soldiers lead away the

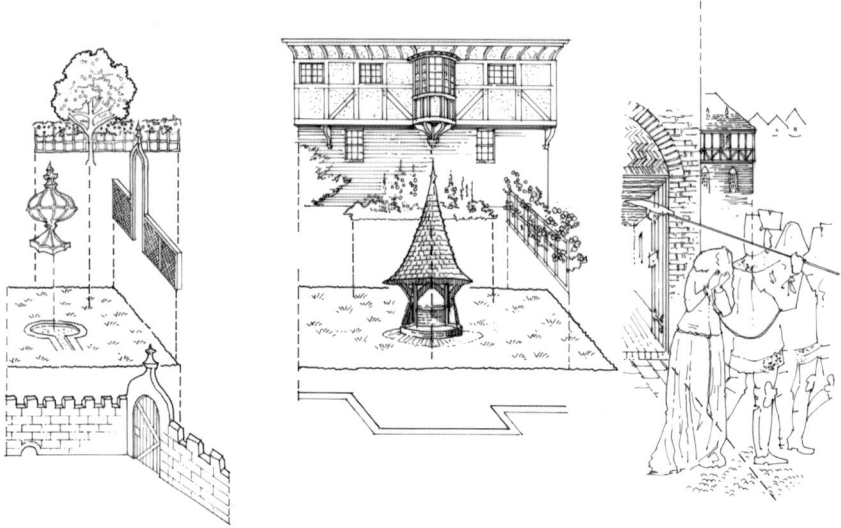

FIGURE 2.3 Hortus conclusus *analysis of Red House 'Palace of Art'*. Drawing Stephen Kite.

anguished daughter of the king, intended to be the dragon's next victim, from before an arched doorway with a tympanum of herringbone brickwork – as outlined on the right in the diagram. A sturdy planked door with wrought-iron strap hinges opens onto a dark beamed and tiled passage drawn in steep perspective. The distant building, locked into the compressed space above the daughter's tresses, remarkably adumbrates the jettied half-timber and brick plinth of the 1864 extensions. Dante Gabriel Rossetti modelled for some of the figures on this cabinet, and his paintings similarly show the influence of the medieval missal 'in their use of a crowded picture plane, the diverse and dense ornamental areas, the slightly unclear spatial treatment within the paintings, the narrow and low spatial boxes . . .'.[22] His 1855 watercolour *Arthur's Tomb*, commissioned by John Ruskin, is one of his remarkable and influential early series of watercolours, 'small, highly-coloured and two-dimensional, they glow with jewel-like colours, and project an intensely romantic vision of the Middle Ages'.[23] In this image the compressed, low spatial box layers the figures of Lancelot and Guinevere at their last meeting, the effigy and frieze of Arthur's tomb itself, and the trunk of a tree whose canopying bower ambiguously elides fore, middle, and back-grounds. The tales of romance, and courtly love in Sir Thomas Malory's *Le Morte d'Arthur* (completed 1471) became a cult in the second phase of the Pre-Raphaelite movement. Morris and Edward Burne-Jones had discovered the book in around 1855 and it was the source for the Arthurian murals painted for the Oxford Union Society in 1857 by the group of seven artists gathered together by Rossetti – including Morris and Burne-Jones.

In his renowned praise of *The English House* (1904–5) of the 1860–1900 period, Hermann Muthesius enlarges on these origins, on how 'artistically speaking it has been important for the treatment of walls . . . that the artistic movement was instigated by painters. Their first move was to look at the wall as a surface. They immediately felt the urge to treat the wall in the noblest way a flat surface can be treated, by covering it with paintings'.[24] So in his lecture in 1889 on *Gothic Architecture*, Morris praises 'Gothic building' for 'it has walls that it is not ashamed of', as compared to the columnar Greek Temple.[25] It is important to emphasize this architectonic basis of Morris's design as in these unashamed surfaces of the Gothic wall-plane. Thus Watkinson points out how it was Morris's 'architectural concept of design, rather than his mastery as a craftsman, that made him so powerful an influence. . . . It is Morris's firm root in architecture that gives long-term sense and coherence to his craft activities'.[26] For Morris saw the adornment of the 'lesser arts' under the umbrella of the 'art of building' as 'the true democratic art, the child of the man-inhabited earth, the expression of the life of man thereon'. He understood architecture as 'guarding the very springs of all art, of all cultivation'.[27]

From the basis of the bare wall the romantic interior is animated in a defined hierarchy: best of all is the story-telling that wall-painting can provide as at the Oxford Union; if no wall-painting, then have the textures of tapestry to represent 'the skin and surface of the earth'; if you cannot afford tapestry, wallpaper can be a weak substitute for its richer effects. As May Morris remembered, 'it has always been amusing to me . . . that my Father, known so generally as a designer of wall-papers, considered that form of wall-covering a makeshift'.[28] In his 1881 lecture, *Some Hints on Pattern-Designing*, Morris sums up this hierarchy from first principles by asking his listeners to imagine themselves in a room 'quite bare of ornament' in which they will have to spend a good part of their lives, and what they might do to 'make the bare walls pleasant and helpful' to them.[29] 'Pattern-designing', he says, 'is the clothing of the walls of a room'. He supposes the 'best art' to clothe these walls 'to be the pictured representation of men's imaginings; what they have thought has happened to the world before their time . . .'.[30] A 'lesser (I will not say worse) art with which to surround our common workaday or restful times' will be 'to clothe our daily and domestic walls with ornament that reminds us of the outward face of the earth, of the innocent love of animals, or of man passing his days between work and rest as he does'.[31] As to the crafts in which surface-patterns are used, after wall-painting, there is the humble 'art of paper-staining'[32] or cotton-printing, but a 'nobler [craft] than paper-staining or cotton-printing' is the textile one of 'figured woven stuffs', 'one of the most important branches' of the pattern-designing art.[33] In 'The Watching of the Falcon' tale of *The Earthly Paradise*, a certain king 'found at last a goodly hall / With glorious hangings on the wall, / Inwrought with trees of every clime, / And stories of the ancient time'.[34] But better than any 'makeshift expedient for covering a wall with something or other' he urged the choice of 'honest whitewash instead, on which sun and shadow play so pleasantly'.[35] He himself often eschewed richness for plain surfaces of pale distemper in his own homes of Red House and Kelmscott Manor.

The architectural coherence of Morris's design stands out as a yet greater achievement in the context of the disrupting forces of the time. In her *From Ornament to Object*, Alina Payne examines how – as a consequence of the nineteenth-century foregrounding of the anonymous crafts of the weaver, potter, and so forth – ornament slipped its architectural moorings and tectonic origins to migrate autonomously across the surfaces of walls, ceilings, and objects. Hence the juxtapositions of miscellaneous architectural details, textile, metalwork, jewellery, etc. in that doyen of English nineteenth-century ornament books, Henry Shaw's *Encyclopaedia of Ornament* (1842), which typically place architectural ornament and objects of daily use within one field and discourse. At one extreme this produced the kind of over-draped Victorian interior that provoked Merton Densher's disgust in Henry James's *The Wings of the Dove* (1902):

> It was the language of the house itself that spoke to him. . . . Never . . . had he seen anything so gregariously ugly. . . . He couldn't . . . call them either Mid-Victorian or Early. . . . He had never dreamed of anything so fringed and scalloped, so buttoned and corded, drawn everywhere so tight, and curled everywhere so thick. He had never dreamed of so much gilt and glass, so much satin and plush, so much rosewood and marble and malachite.[36]

But as Payne argues:

> For Ruskin and Morris architectural ornament was the location of artistic expression for the craftsman. With this move they associated ornament with its anonymous artisan-maker and in so doing operated a similar dislocation that we find in Semper: artistic content moved from the monument and its genius artist to the humble object. . . . Since the architect does not directly handle the materials of his art, this also meant driving a wedge between architecture and ornament. The creative independence that Ruskin attributed to the artisan allowed architectural ornament to float away from architecture and be included in the domain of crafted things.[37]

As we have seen, Medievalist romance inspired this new domain of craft. At the same time, it is Morris's great achievement to contain these potentially dislocating forces, this 'centripetal diffusion of ornament away from its architectural core',[38] within an architectonic unity of ornamental patterns, resonant between the surfaces of wall, textile, paper, furniture, and carpet. *Some Hints on Pattern-Designing* embodies this craft-wisdom, as when Morris says that a carpet-design 'should be quite flat, that it should give no more at least than the merest hint of one plane behind another' for we would not feel comfortable 'walking over what simulates high relief'[39] – a plastic fault in much nineteenth-century pattern design. The art is 'to get the [carpet] design flat' while achieving the aim that 'every little bit of surface must have its own individual beauty of material and colour'.[40]

As in the aforementioned painted surfaces of the St George Cabinet, such object-pieces of architectural furniture mediate between the wall-plane itself and the space of the room. Whether actually built-in, or freestanding against the wall, they have the capacity to project the atmosphere of the wall-pattern outwards *and* to be objects in their own right. Pieces such as the hooded settle Webb designed for Red House in 1860, can also sit out in the space to make a room within a room. Summarizing his theories on the design and making of furniture in his 1878 lecture 'The Lesser Arts of Life', Morris distinguished between this 'state-furniture' of 'sideboards, cabinets, and the like' and 'necessary work-a-day furniture' such as 'chairs, dining and working tables'.[41] Both must be 'well-made and well proportioned', but in the state-furniture 'we need not spare ornament . . . but may make them as elegant and elaborate as we can with carving, inlaying, or painting; these are the blossoms of the art of furniture'.[42] Such sumptuous elements should only be used 'architecturally to dignify important chambers and important places in them', and in conclusion Morris again prioritizes the architectural surface: 'Whatever you have in your rooms think first of the walls, for they are that which makes your house and home . . . however rich and handsome your movables may be'.[43] William Burges (1827–1881) was yet earlier than Morris, Webb, and Burne-Jones in designing painted architectural furniture; his boldly composed 'Wine and Beers' sideboard likely inspired Morris's St George cabinet of the following year.[44]

Muthesius made Morris's injunction to 'think first of the walls' the epigraph to his chapter in *The English House* on the achievements of the English 'Contemporary Interior' Morris had instigated. Expanding on the 'concept of the wall' Muthesius affirms:

> The interior is a whole, the essence of which lies, in fact, in its totality, in its quality as space. In conceiving the interior as a work of art, therefore, the artist must first think of it as a space, that is, as the overall form and the interrelationship of the space-enclosing surfaces.[45]

Notwithstanding his Germanic tendency to essentialize the spatial aspect of architecture, what is noteworthy here is how Muthesius highlights these English interiors as generated from the 'space-enclosing surfaces', and on how 'when it comes to give the room artistic form the wall is the determining factor among the enclosing surfaces'. All these surface experiments were notably essayed in Red House, as we move from the outdoor room of its *hortus ludi* to the interior proper. Tantalizing bits of evidence, given by Mackail, contextualize the little that survives, or was never realized. Such as the wall-painting scheme of scenes from the War of Troy for the walls of the staircase, or the 'magnificent embroidered hangings' that were to cover the walls of the drawing-room together with murals of scenes from the fifteenth-century English romance of 'Sir Degrevaunt'[46] – Burne-Jones only completed three of these. There was none of that makeshift wallpaper, and 'even the ceilings were decorated with bold simple patterns in distemper, the design being pricked into plaster',[47] as remains today in the bold repeating patterns above the staircase. Although the interior intentions were never to be fully realized, recent investigations of the drawing room of Red House, for example, have revealed (beneath later repainting) how much of the original polychromatic scheme was, in fact, completed.[48] These included a painted *simulation* of embroidered 'wall-hangings' around the drawing room of Red House, where formalized plants bear a scroll on which is written: 'Qui bien aime tard oublie' ('Who loves well forgets slowly').[49]

Red House's atmosphere can also be recovered from images of the later interior Morris created for the long drawing room in his home at Kelmscott House, Hammersmith. As Mackail wrote:

> The painted settle and cabinet, which were its chief ornaments, belonged to the earliest days of Red House; the rest of the furniture and decoration was all in the same spirit, and had all the effect of making the room a mass of subdued yet glowing colour, into which the eye sank with a sort of active sense of rest.[50]

A layering of overlapping patterns makes this 'active sense of rest' as shown on Mackail's accompanying woodcut by F. H. New. In succession

FIGURE 2.4 *F. H. New,* Long Drawing Room at Kelmscott House. *Woodcut. From J. W. Mackail,* The Life of William Morris, *vol. 1, facing p. 372.*

there is first the floral embossed and painted leather panels of the 'state-furniture' of Webb's settle; then the dividing 'Peacock and Dragon' woollen curtains are drawn back to show the furthest plane of blue 'Bird' tapestry whose gentle folds background the whole room. At this endpoint a long sturdy table, draped in carpet, holds the space before a fireplace and between a pair of glazed in-built cabinets. The lustre of pots and plates arranged here, and on the mantelpiece beyond, accent the visual field.[51]

Architectural paper-hanging

If Morris abjured wallpaper at home, it was admitted at the Hammersmith Kelmscott House – his main home from 1879–96 – as an extension to his firm's decorating business, where he would entertain existing and potential clients; the dining room had the *Pimpernel* design, and even his own study was papered, although otherwise austere in its absence of carpet or curtains. To understand the basic principles of spatial layering as seen in the Kelmscott drawing room, as applied to the flatness of paper itself, one need look no further than Morris's very first 'Trellis' wallpaper design of 1862. Again the *hortus ludi* is clearly the wellspring once the 'Trellis' design is compared to the actual Red House garden trellis, as shown in Burne-Jones's *The Backgammon Players* (1862) – a study for a painted cabinet panel inspired by this garden of delights.[52] While 'within the bounds of that sweet close' – of the pleasance of the July medieval tale of *Earthly Paradise* – 'Was

FIGURE 2.5 *William Morris and Philip Webb, Design for* Trellis *wallpaper (1862). Pencil, ink and watercolour on paper, 66 × 61 cm. © William Morris Gallery, London Borough of Waltham Forest.*

trellised the bewildering rose'.[53] Going back to that bare wall of *Some Hints on Pattern-Designing*, Morris jokes that if we want nature we could literally nail a 'few cut flowers or bits of boughs' to it. But he asks, 'is it not better to be reminded, however simply, of the close vine-trellis . . .; or of the wild woods and their streams; or of the swallows sweeping above the garden boughs . . .'.[54] 'Trellis' makes analogous memories of nature with its own close rose-trellis, its sprays of foliage and flowers, and its flying birds.

Direct advice on how to use the patterns is given in a guide for visitors, produced by Morris and Company, for their exhibit at the Boston international trade fair of 1883–4. 'Pattern-making is an architectural art' the pamphlet declares, giving 'Trellis' as an example for the customer who rejects a quiet wall and goes for a paper of 'decided patterning' in its 'direction or set' – for 'architectural effect depends upon a nice balance of horizontal, vertical, and oblique'.[55] Morris often disguised his construction lines, but in 'Trellis' the rose-stems entwine the boldly stated architectural lattice. What was Morris's secret in design asks his daughter May?; by what 'instinctive procedure' came he to design 'his first wallpaper with ease as though he had been at the trick for years?' She responds 'that he thought *in mass*, as it were, not *in line*', with a craftsman's instinct for the bold process of block-cutting and printing, he avoided fussy forms and sought expression in a 'breaking . . . juxtaposition of colours'.[56] Look at how Morris lays his leaves and flowers flatly against blocks of crimson and green, in his original 'Trellis' design; now the dominant figure becomes the negative spaces of the squares – *not* the lines of the timber armature – more like the tessellated tiles of a medieval pavement. For Morris, in paper-hangings it was important to frankly accept its 'mechanical nature', to recognize that it 'has to be painted flat on a wall', but within this flatness 'to mysteriously . . . interweave your sprays and stems'.[57] This method would favour the shallow three-layer space of 'Trellis', entwining foreground blossoms, the trellis-grid, and the flitting birds drawn by Webb. Already here is Morris's 'bag of tricks' as Watkinson puts it:[58] a constructing grid (disclosed or concealed), strong flowing lines on which to build interlocking colour-masses of leaf and flower forms, with secondary accents of fauna or flora. Proof of Morris's fondness for this first paper design is its use on the curtains to his beloved Jacobean four-poster bed at Kelmscott Manor – made by May Morris.

What does this tell us about Morris's achievement in this area of design? First of all, there is none of this flatness or subtle layering to be found in the eclectic mid-century papers popular with the confident Victorian bourgeoisie, with their bulbous Rococo curves and floridly naturalistic cabbage roses.[59] Better, and flatter, were the heraldic designs A. W. N. Pugin had advocated in the 1840s, based on the stylized forms of foliage found in medieval work. But these are *excessively* stiff and flat, with no mysterious interweaving, and are more suited to churches or public buildings than domestic interiors. In truth Morris's second design of 'decided patterning' has *some* heraldic stiffness; 'Daisy' – inspired by a fifteenth-century version of Froissart's

Chronicles – was imagined after 'Trellis' but published first. But then again there is a new meadow-freshness in its frank repeat of field-flowers on a grassy ground.

Dividing the wall – The Green Dining Room

'Fruit' (or 'Pomegranate') is the third and most complex of these early designs; here woody stems make a diagonal, not rectilinear, order and wayward leaves disguise the repeats. Affinities to the painted panels in the Green Dining Room at the South Kensington Museum of 1866 make a link to this, the first important commission for Morris, Marshall, Faulkner & Co. in non-ecclesiastical decoration.[60]

Along with the layering of the surface *in depth* as examined, arises the related, and equally fraught, architectural question of the *vertical division* of the wall; Webb's design for what is now the Victoria and Albert Museum was a forerunner in its painted woodwork and threefold vertical splitting up of the wall-plane into dado, filling, and frieze – a division that became very popular in domestic interiors from the mid-1870s to the early 1890s, and a hallmark of the 'artistic' fashion.[61] The high five foot base of panelled oak is stained deep green, and is itself topped by an upper one and a half foot zone of painted panels of the months by Burne-Jones, alternating with herbals similar to the 'Fruit' paper. They resemble the woodcuts in John Gerard's *Herball or Generall Historie of Plantes* (1597) which Morris had loved as a child. The main intermediary zone is made up of cast-plaster slabs each bearing a large olive branch in relief, above comes a frieze of dogs chasing hares which, as Webb told his biographer William Lethaby, was derived from the fifteenth-century font in Newcastle-upon-Tyne Cathedral.[62] As can be seen in Webb's exquisitely detailed 1866 drawing, two large panels of a single olive branch make up the height of the zone. Variety is introduced by simply offsetting the upper panel halfway across the one below. The repeat panels are plain to spot if searched for, but the offset – together with the judiciously scaled pattern-texture of lanceolate leaves – creates the hushing ambience of an olive canopy, heightened by complementary red star-like flowers (not their natural cream) and deep green olive clusters. As Morris's close collaborator, Webb also founded his 'higher decoration . . . directly on fresh study of nature – flowers, foliage, and living creatures'. Flat or low relief ornament he pointed out should 'be a pattern which turns the white ground into a mosaic-like pattern effective at a distance'.[63] The even distribution of pattern in the Dining Room is akin to Morris's early wallpapers, though with less interweaving in the design, as depth is given here by the low relief and texture of the plaster. Lethaby writes that in 'designing patterns . . . [Webb] had not the passionate directness of Morris, but he had what reached as high – a sure visual notion of the thing he wanted and untiring patience in finding his way to it'.[64] Here the romantic

FIGURE 2.6 *Design for wall decoration in the Green Room at the Victoria and Albert Museum, London, by Philip Webb (formerly the Green Dining Room, South Kensington Museum, London, 1866).* © *Victoria and Albert Museum, London.*

atmosphere, evoked by the modelled surfaces of shimmering olive fronds, is that of a Classical Arcadia, mediated through the English Elizabethan pastoral tradition invoked by the *Herball* panels.[65]

Described as the first 'Aesthetic interior', and as the fashionable artistic meeting place it rapidly became, the Green Dining Room was very influential. Its tripartite division of the wall was also soon codified by Charles Eastlake in his key text, linked to the domestic revolution of Morris and Webb, *Hints on Household Taste in Furniture, Upholstery and other Details* of 1868. Such was Eastlake's impact in America that a home furnished in the 'improved taste' was said to have been 'Eastlaked'.[66] He advised that 'paperhangings should in no case be allowed to cover the whole space of a wall from skirting to ceiling', that there should be 'a "dado", or plinth space' and 'a second space, of frieze, just below the ceiling . . .'.[67] It is very unlikely that the medievalist Morris would have admired the Classical basis underlying the three-part wall division – derived from the base, shaft, and capital of the Greek column. For the most part, he thought that unless 'we have a very elaborate scheme of decoration' (as in the case of South Kensington) 'dividing [the wall] once, making it into two spaces', was enough for most interiors.[68] So for textiles he advised having a 'narrow frieze below the cornice, and hang the wall thence to the floor' – as we have seen in his drawing room at Kelmscott House; whereas a single division with a moderate dado of some four and a half feet high was 'fittest for a wall which is to be covered with painted decoration, or its makeshift, paperhangings'.[69] All this ties in with the foregoing analysis; Morris is not interested in the surface as a static *vertically* elaborated plane on which the gaze stops. His surfaces – themselves as naturalistically energized as 'the very skin and surface of the earth' itself – partake in the romantic atmosphere of a visual field that is essentially layered *in depth*.

Morris only worked briefly as an architect – with the great George Edmund Street in 1856 – but his more recent biographer, Fiona MacCarthy (1994), suggests that it was from Street that he grasped the two fundamental design principles we have been exploring: 'Street's sense of architecture as the centre and the ruling force of all design activity' and 'his technique in creating grand effects from myriad components', so that 'a Morris interior is a disciplined amalgam of patterns, colours, textures: wallpapers, friezes, curtain fabrics, wallhangings, painted ceilings, *layer upon layer*'.[70]

'Simplicity or splendour': 1 Holland Park

So, there is the Morris of surfaces of whitewashed simplicity, the Morris who told his friend Edward Carpenter that although 'I have spent . . . a vast amount of time designing furniture and wall-papers, carpets and curtains; . . . after all I am inclined to think that sort of thing is mostly rubbish, and I would prefer for my part to live with the plainest whitewashed walls and wooden chairs and tables'.⁷¹ But as has been shown, even his own homes of Red House and Kelmscott House are a lot richer than this. The easiest way to explain the apparent contradiction is to accept both ends of the scale; for the leading Aesthetic Movement decorator Walter Crane 'the great advantage and charm of the Morrisian method is that it lends itself to either simplicity or splendour. You might be almost as plain as [Henry David] Thoreau, with a rush-bottomed chair; a piece of matting, an oaken trestle table; or you might have gold and lustre . . . jewelled light in the windows, and the walls hung with arras tapestry'.⁷²

An interior of undeniable splendour is the one Morris and Webb created for Alexander (Alecco) Ionides (1840–1898) at 1 Holland Park, London, working for almost a decade between 1879 and 1888. Alecco was then Greek-Consul and had succeeded to the house in 1875, when his father, Alexander Constantine Ionides (born 1810), retired to Hastings. Alecco was one of three children of this wealthy trader in textiles and head of the Anglo-Greek community. Alexander had bought the newly-built house in 1864, as part of the development created by Lady Holland of Holland House, with houses designed by Francis Radford (constructed between 1860 and 1879) in an area that rapidly became popular in artistic circles.⁷³ The house was badly damaged by bombing in World War II and subsequently demolished in 1953, but some key artefacts survive from a celebrated interior which was also well documented, both in contemporary articles and photographs by the eminent architectural photographer Harry Bedford Lemere. Writing in *Studio* towards the end of the century on 'An Epoch-Making House' (1898), Gleeson White already saw the house as of seminal significance:

> A generation which accepts 'Morris' papers and woven fabrics, Mr Philip Webb's fireplaces, and Mr Walter Crane's gesso-work as normal evidence of good taste in furnishing, that finds Mr Whistler's paintings held in honour, and is accustomed to the reverence due to 'blue-and-white' and 'Tanagra' figures, may possibly forget that but a few years ago all these things were appreciated by a comparatively small number, and that it required no little courage for a rich man to include them in his scheme for a House Beautiful.⁷⁴

Externally it was certainly no 'House Beautiful', though well-built Radford's houses were of a typical stuccoed Bayswater character. Webb grumbled that the house he was given to deal with 'was like a feather-bed – shapeless, and when you pushed it in one direction it stuck out in another'.⁷⁵ Its ill-defined external volumes rose above a blank wall that offered nothing to the street. Penetrating this wall visitors found themselves straightaway in a bright lobby decorated with ironwork and William De Morgan tiles. They then ascended at once to the reception rooms via Webb's green-panelled staircase, ingeniously designed with 'a series of higher steps, forming, as it were, pedestals for a collection of bronzes . . .' – as Lewis F. Day points out in his piece on 'A Kensington Interior' in *The Art Journal* of 1893.[76] From the first floor hall, tiled in mosaic to a Webb design, the guest then approached a sequence of three of the finest spaces; two interconnected drawing rooms, divisible by curtains, leading to the dining room, entered at right angles from the second drawing room. The first drawing room was the richest, and was also called the antiquities room owing to its striking display of Alecco's Tanagra statuettes, assembled in a pedimented overmantel of black marble designed by Walter Crane. The walls were richly clothed in 'Chrysanthemum', a paper of Morris's 'decided patterning', here 'laquered in transparent colour over silver'.[77] In the next drawing room the surface properties travel into two striking objects, a grand Broadwood piano (1884–5) with a case decorated in gold and silver gesso to designs by Burne-Jones and Kate Faulkner, and Morris's 'Holland Park' Hammersmith carpet on the floor (1883). Webb's architectural hand predominates in the dining room, firmly structured by his facing fireplace on entering, and elaborate curvaceous sideboard; over the Purbeck marble fire-surround Webb designed an 'unusually elaborate cornice and shelf, carried by six brackets, with small flat arches between'.[78]

Returning, that part of the space illustrated in *The Art Journal* by the Bernard Lemere photograph as 'A corner of the second drawing-room, decorated by William Morris'[79] merits pause, with its intensely cumulative layering of 'Flower Garden' woven silk wall-covering, curtain fabric, pictures such as Burne-Jones's *Pan and Psyche* (1872–4), and Iznik tiles, radiating out into the object-surfaces of the piano-case and the Hammersmith carpet. Day emphasizes the prevailing tonal harmony of all this abundance:

> The walls . . . are hung with a sober textile material, in which the pattern merges itself into a general tint of greenish or greyish blue, according to the angle at which the light happens to fall upon it; the window curtains are of the same, and the woodwork is painted a quite green, which is really a lower tone of the prevailing tint.[80]

As Day adds, brighter colour accents are given by the ceiling and the carpet, with its blue ground bearing, in Gleeson White's words, 'features which Morris made his own – robust generous curves blossoming into flower-like patterns, and with a sense of space unlike the "tight" effect of most modern carpets'.[81] As Linda Parry opines, this was 'one of Morris's most original and popular carpet designs, showing elements of his greatest influences: medievalism, floral realism and eastern precision'.[82] But where Day found harmony, *The Architectural Review* of 1897 was troubled by 'the eclecticism that pervades' 1 Holland Park, preferring the parts where Webb's hand of 'severe simplicity' was strongest to the 'Jeckyll and Dr Hyde "Gothic" work' of Morris.[83] But 'eclecticism' misses the synthesis of the medieval, of the natural world, and of the East, achieved by Morris, whom Gleeson White regards as 'the soul of some thirteenth-century master-

FIGURE 2.7 *'A corner of the second drawing-room, decorated by William Morris'*, The Art Journal *(May 1893), p. 141. Photograph Bernard Lemere.*

craftsman ... re-incarnated.... In the drawing-room, especially full of Morris handiwork, you find Persian influence in rugs and embroideries as strongly evident as is that of the monastery and the trades-guilds of Europe'.[84] Biographer Mackail also stresses Morris's 'catholicity' and his 'carelessness to distinguish among forms of art which from his central and unentangled outlook he perceived to be threaded from one centre thought they might lie on widely-severed arcs ...'.[85] Morris himself said: 'I by nature turn to

Romance rather than classicism' and 'am fairly steeped in medievalism generally';[86] yet his Romance ranges wide, encompassing the classical world (as in the alternating medieval-classical poems of his *Earthly Paradise*, 1868–70), Icelandic saga, and the Orient of the Arabian Nights.

The Architectural Review analyses 1 Holland Park in the context of 'Webb's Town Work'. As houses in 'London Town' such dwellings were particularly refuges of Romance – the *Earthly Paradises* of Morris's poem. As in the poem's Prologue they were settings wherein to 'Forget six counties overhung with smoke / Forget the smoking steam and piston stroke / Forget the spreading of the hideous town'.[87] In the 1870s, Hippolyte Taine found a horrible darkness in London's smoky murk, looking at houses that appeared to him as 'ink stains on blotting paper'.[88] Artists in the Holland Park circle repeatedly complained about smoggy winters when it was too dim to paint, and Henry James described the weather as 'hideous, the heaven being perpetually instained with a sort of dirty fog-paste, like Thames-mud in solution. At 11 a.m. I have to light my candles to read'.[89] Morris also sought to banish the characteristically fashionable gloom produced by many over-draped, over-stuffed, and cluttered late Victorian interiors.[90]

Two Morris letters of this period, to different correspondents, will serve to show the scales of simplicity or splendour. In March 1883 he wrote that he had 'spoken to Mr. A. Ionides about his piano & he will have one of the same make of (green) stained oak: I shall be glad to help as to the tint . . .'.[91] This is the aforementioned Broadwood of gold and silver gesso that set the sumptuous decorative pitch of Alecco's drawing room. Yet in an earlier letter of February 1881 he wrote, in agreement with Ruskin's ideas, that the middle class home should 'do with as little furniture, as little ornament, as you possibly can: my gloss on that is have what you do have good: but look upon it as unmanly to have a luxurious home. I say with utmost seriousness, that it seems as if luxury were going to stifle civilisation: and I protest against it from my soul'.[92]

Robert W. Edis's *The Decoration and Furnishing of Town Houses* of 1881 aims at a mean by giving 'practical hints' to dwellers in Town Houses 'who were anxious to get rid of the utter commonplaceness and vulgarity' of most decoration.[93] As his epigraph he took the Ruskin of *The Two Paths*: 'There is no existing highest-order art but is decorative. . . . Beautiful art can only be produced by people who have beautiful things about them . . .'.[94] The frontispiece 'A Drawing Room Corner' shows Edis's own drawing room at Upper Berkeley Street, and if hardly of whitewashed austerity it is modest as compared to Alecco's opulence. The walls have the two-part division we know Morris recommended for most interiors, above is a nostalgic rural frieze of peacock and flowers to remind the fraught town-dweller of country life, below Morris's 'Fruit' ('Pomegranate') wallpaper – that third of his earliest designs. The glazed cabinet may be to the design of Edis's friend, E. W. Godwin and is flanked by chairs also of a popular Godwin design. The frontality of the image reinforces the layering principles familiar from

FIGURE 2.8 *Frontispiece 'A Drawing Room Corner'*, Robert W. Edis, The Decoration and Furnishing of Town Houses *(1881)*.

Kelmscott House and 1 Holland Park, pictures animate the 'Fruit' background, the cabinet and table are populated with aesthetic object-assemblages of ceramics and books-of-the-day – all adheres to the wall-plane. Edis quotes Owen Jones's insistence – similar to Morris – that in paper-hangings 'nothing should disturb their flatness', that 'the paper should serve as a background' and 'avoid all direct representations of natural objects', consequently it should 'not be advancing to the eyes' as it is only the backdrop to the next layer of 'pictures, engravings, or other ornamental works'.[95] While there is much modernity in these Artistic interiors, their surface-layering is unlike the interiors of Le Corbusier of the 1920s and his conception of the objects of daily life as 'loose, scattered, small-scale sculptural elements that articulated an experience of space and movement'.[96]

But Morris's 'flatness' is equally alive. He got into his stride in wallpaper design in the 1870s producing patterns such as 'Vine' (1873), as used in Alecco Ionides' morning room at 1 Holland Park – patterns which are 'sufficiently interwoven to provide a complex all-over pattern with a shallow depth'.[97] Although much richer than 'Trellis', Morris brackets 'Vine' with that first wallpaper as an example of 'decided' or 'positive' pattern. In his original design drawing, the parallels to 'Trellis' come out strongly in the quartered structure, wherein a vertically meandering vine stem is counterpoised by scrolling shoots bearing massed bunches of grapes, on a background of stylized willow fronds. Note how one willow stem threads through the vine-scrolls as a clear perpendicular axis. In this work of a now practised craftsman, May Morris distinguishes between those of her father's patterns that have a 'simple plan with closely-filled background', and those organized as 'plane upon plane'. 'Vine' she describes as 'a triumphantly rich interweaving of grape-vine and willow, the transparency of the grapes rendered with much enjoyment' – it is 'among the typically Morrisian of the patterns'.[98]

In the Ionides Morning Room the hoops of 'Vine' found echo in the bold acanthus scrolls of Morris's 'The Forest' tapestry which made a frieze to the length of one wall – with Webb's peacock, hare, lion, fox, and raven caught motionless among the leaves.[99] Alecco resorted to this forest-glade as an especially paradisical retreat, writes Day: 'It is one of the cosiest and most reposeful rooms in the house. It is here that Mr. Ionides finds place for his bookcases, his bureau, and suchlike furniture necessary to personal comfort . . .'.[100]

* * *

In a letter of September 1883 to Andreas Scheu (the Viennese refugee anarchist and furniture designer), Morris supplied a 'sketch of my very uneventful life' in which he told the story of Red House very simply:

> At this time [of the 1850s] the revival of Gothic architecture was making great progress in England and naturally touched the Preraphaelite movement also; I threw myself into these movements with all my heart:

FIGURE 2.9 Vine *wallpaper, original design, William Morris, c. 1873, pencil and watercolour.* © *Victoria and Albert Museum, London.*

got a friend [Philip Webb] to build me a house very medieval in spirit in which I lived for 5 years, and set myself to decorating it ...[101]

As argued here, Red House's medieval spirit was encapsulated in the *hortus ludi* of the gardens of pleasure, brought to life in the verses of Morris's *Earthly Paradise*, and most fully envisioned in the unrealized 'Palace of Art' Webb designed for the Morris and Burne-Jones families. In the *hortus conclusus* of this outdoor room, the primary 'love of the very skin and surface of the earth' is made architectonically as spatially compressed layers, of matter and nature, akin to those in the pages of a medieval missal: wall and gate, flowery mead, fruit trees, fountain, and trellis enclosure.

Moving from the outdoor room to the interior proper, Morris's injunction to 'think first of the walls' was seen to also be founded on the 'revival of Gothic architecture' which 'has walls that it is not ashamed of'; here Romance is engendered in a layered hierarchy of surfaces that can be scaled to simplicity or splendour: bare white-washed wall / wall-painting / tapestry / wall-paper, then moving out into the object-surfaces of 'state-furniture', 'work-a-day' pieces, and carpets – all architectonically conceived. The *hortus ludi* was also the root of the 'Trellis' wallpaper design, and the principles of pattern-designing as a mysterious interweaving of sprays and stems, making flat surfaces of shallow depth allied to the same architectural order. From the splendour of Alecco's 1 Holland Park to the relative simplicity of Kelmscott House, or Robert W. Edis's drawing room, beauty becomes a taken-for-granted backdrop to life – wall-surfaces clothed with ornament to remind us 'of the outward face of the earth' and to evoke 'romance in the breathable air'.

CHAPTER THREE

Smooth and Rough

George Frederick Bodley and Edward Schröder Prior

Morris's domestic world of romantically layered surfaces marks an early change in direction from the 'muscular' High Victorian passion for strident polychromy. As George Frederick Bodley (1827–1907) wrote in 1878: 'The interior of an old Church was [now] treated with the same intention, so to speak, as we treat the rooms in our houses. They were made as beautiful in colour and furniture as possible' – thus suggesting a merging between the public arena of the church, and the private space of the home.[1]

Let us compare two contemporary churches of this later Victorian, early twentieth-century era, in their perspective visions: George Frederick Bodley's Holy Trinity, South Kensington, London (1901–6) and Edward Schröder Prior's St Andrew's, Roker (1905). The differences will emerge, but both these images show immediately how much has changed from the earnest High Victorian 'Middle-Pointed' churches of Butterfield and Street. Style is even less important overall, and not an ethical imperative; Prior, for example, readily adopted Queen Anne, Baroque, or Byzantine guises in his work. There is also a call to a purer 'Englishness' – in opposition to native Gothic, mixed with French and Italian motifs. This is manifested in a revival of the later Decorated, and that most English version of Gothic, the Perpendicular – long thought 'debased' – in these advanced late Victorian and early twentieth-century 'artistic' churches. Nave, aisles, and chancel are conceived as one unitary volume for, as John Betjeman has pointed out, such Arts and Crafts architects sought different proportions of 'either height and narrowness, or breadth and length. Their churches either soar or spread'.[2]

FIGURE 3.1 *J. J. Joass, watercolour perspective (1901) of Church of the Holy Trinity, South Kensington, London (1901–6), George Frederick Bodley. RIBA Collections.*

FIGURE 3.2 *E. S. Prior, St Andrew's, Roker, interior perspective 1905, pencil and sepia washes. RIBA Collections.*

'Englishness' in 'breadth of surface'

J. J. Joass represents the breadth and spread of surfaces of Bodley's Holy Trinity in the watercolour perspective he painted for exhibition at The Royal Academy in 1901; a breadth Bodley achieved, despite the constricted triangular site near The Albert Hall, which only allowed a north-south orientation. Apart from showing an unrealized chancel-screen the watercolour accords with the church as built, and Bodley's aim that its 'character will be that of a town Church in the style and manner of the fourteenth century. It will be strictly English in conception and in detail, treated in a broad and somewhat original manner.... The edifice will be an example of our beautiful English Gothic architecture when it was at its best'.³ Slender quatrefoil-plan columns carry the pointed arches of the five-bay nave which immediately supports a pointed timber roof running directly into the chancel. The impression of 'breadth', and spatial delight in the cross-vistas, is heightened by the addition of a four-bay arcade on the liturgical 'north' side of the church. Important also to the transverse rhythms are the deep arcing internal flying-buttresses which tie together all these slender piers and arches, and whose broad surfaces act as baffles, evenly distributing the light from the windows with their curvilinear tracery.

FIGURE 3.3 *George Frederick Bodley, interior of the Church of the Holy Trinity, South Kensington, London (1901–6). Photograph Geoff Brandwood.*

In his major study on G. F. Bodley, Michael Hall isolates 'Bodley's emphasis on the wall plane' as key to his desired characteristic of 'breadth'.[4] In architectural composition he seeks continuity of the wall, never allowing 'buttresses or windows to undermine the sense of a continuous wall surface'.[5] Bodley often internalized his buttresses to maintain the sheerness and continuity of the exterior, enhancing the depth of the wall internally and the reveal itself as a surface, emphasizing the power of his wall-surfaces by unity of material. Joass's watercolour also emphasizes Bodley's feeling for breadth of surface in the floor-plane, rendered here as a shimmeringly wide expanse; he preferred chairs to cumbrous pews, and subtle changes of level between nave and chancel, arguing that 'the long sweep of the almost continuous floor level is effective and adds much look of continuous length and dignity [*sic*]'.[6] The internal buttress idea is forcefully applied in Bodley's gaunt brick vessel of St Augustine, Pendlebury, designed in 1870, and described by Pevsner as 'one of the English churches of all time. Its sheer brick interior and the majestic *sursum* of its interior have never been surpassed in Victorian church building'.[7] A key inspiration was the Dominican church at Ghent published in James Cubitt's influential *Church Design for Congregations* of 1870 as a model of how to achieve a large central congregational area by reducing the aisles so that they 'become merely the necessary passages to the seats' pierced through the depth of these internal buttresses.[8] Bodley lays down the essentials of this masterpiece, quickly and surely, in a small sketch study of Pendlebury's west end. Bodley had no interest in draughtsmanship in itself, as his former pupil Edward Warren remembered, 'for neat and finished drawings he had small regard', but 'his little explanatory sketches, rough though they were, were always vividly graphic. . . . [They] were made anyhow and anywhere . . . on anything handy . . .'.[9] His sketch-section and wall-bay elevations shows the steep roof profile, the simple proportions he liked based on the square, the powerful vaulted volumetric wall-bays – with the plan of deep internal buttresses and passage overlaid – the shallow external buttresses and their stumpy saddle-back pinnacles, and the delicate traceried windows contained between them, drawn below shallow arches upon the smooth flanks of brickwork.

Bodley's surfaces are in no way savage; in a talk to the students of The Royal Academy in 1886 on 'English Architecture in the Middle Ages', he stressed the smooth surfaces of the finest English Gothic:

> For an interior there was no thought of any rude roughness of surface. It was either of smooth ashlar or of smooth plaster, and either case and in all ages such surfaces received colour . . . rich and magnificent diapers in the later fourteenth and fifteenth centuries. . . . An architect has perhaps the most interesting and delightful profession a man can have. In England he has the finest Gothic to study. It will be our own fault if we are not the best Gothic architects in the world.[10]

FIGURE 3.4 George Frederick Bodley, interior of St Augustine's, Pendlebury (begun 1869). Photograph Geoff Brandwood.

FIGURE 3.5 *Dominican church at Ghent, from James Cubitt,* Church Design for Congregations *(1870).*

FIGURE 3.6 *George Frederick Bodley, studies for St Augustine's, Pendlebury. RIBA Collections.*

Together with this turn to Englishness – first expressed in his church of All Saints, Jesus Lane, Cambridge (designed 1861–2) – Bodley led the rejection of High Victorian 'muscularity' and constructional polychromy, towards these ideals of 'breadth' and 'refinement' that characterize the later churches of the 1880s. Domestic architecture underwent a similar transformation from the 'Old English' Vernacular Revival of the 1870s and 1880s – inspired by English cottages, farmhouses, and manor-houses – to the Arts and Crafts of the 1890s and 1900s. Arts and Crafts architects also spoke of the 'breadth' and 'reserve' of their work to distinguish the reticence of their strong simple surface-planes, and calm horizontals, from the picturesque silhouettes and busy material palette of Old English.[11]

Bodley's earliest published statement of his principles was in *The Builder* of 1885, but they had been formulated in essence by 1870, and are again consistent with those published nearly twenty years later, in 1903 – at the time of Holy Trinity, South Kensington – as 'Some Principles that may be Guides for the Applied Arts'. While many of Bodley's precepts align with the Ruskin of *The Seven Lamps of Architecture* and 'The Nature of Gothic', notably absent is any empathy with the license latent in Ruskin's Savageness, Changefulness, or Grotesque.

The 'primary rule and principle for all art [is] the following of Nature . . . in giving to all things we make the very spirit of nature'. 'Closely allied to that of truth to Nature' is 'to endow everything we make with the expression of Life'.[12] And thirdly 'our work should be Beautiful'.[13] Much more distinctively Bodley-an is the fourth 'principle of art' as already outlined – 'breadth of effect'. For Bodley this 'is this grand quality of breadth of effect' allied to Nature's 'grassy hills, . . . broad in colour, in their vast expanse of green' and to the 'great dome' of the sky.[14] He then attacks the cacophonies of muscular architecture:

> What is it that makes the difference between many new buildings and good old examples of architecture? It is not the charm of age, for that chiefly affects the colour. Is it not that the old work has a noble breadth of effect and a unity of idea, restraint, and an avoidance of all discordant elements? While of much modern work must we not say that vulgar confusion, and useless variety and display, take the place of suavity of manner and a dignified and noble breadth of effect? For there is in old buildings a nice economy, not only of material, but of ornament, and there is a satisfying charm about most of them, of almost any period. The old architecture had stately manners. Too many of our new buildings have pretentious ways. I think it is from the lack of the principle of refinement and especially of a delightful breadth of effect that many things suffer now-a-days.[15]

Bodley's distinction between pretension and 'vulgar confusion', and 'stately manners', the 'dignified and noble', and 'refinement', patently reflects social-class, as much as aesthetic, difference. Associated with another principle of 'Delicacy', 'Refinement' is an important principle of its own. In his published Slade Lectures, given at Oxford in 1934, Goodhart-Rendel illustrates this value of Refinement with a watercolour perspective of the nave of Bodley's St Mary's, Eccleston, Cheshire, as a representative example of his 'sensitive and fastidious manner of design' and acutely lays out the pluses and minuses of his style and its socio-religious context:

> The particular style of Bodley . . . was very faithfully mimicked, both by his many pupils and by others with whom he had no personal encounter. It satisfied completely the aspirations of those who believed that the road to national sanctity lay through the older public schools and universities, guarded by Anglican scholarship from the intruding errors of Geneva or of Rome. It was not exactly what the Ecclesiologists had hoped would emerge from their campaign; they had intended something a little more popular, a little more at home in the slums, a little less aloof from the 'progressive' temper of the day. But it was they who were responsible for it, it was they who had long-drawn the aisles, had storied the windows, had segregated the surplice clergy and choir in screened enclosure . . . and had turned the eyes of architects back to a style that had proved harder to develop than to imitate. Things might not have turned out quite as they expected, but in the result there was much more to rejoice over than there was to deplore.[16]

FIGURE 3.7 *George Frederick Bodley, interior of St Mary's, Eccleston, Cheshire. Photograph Geoff Brandwood.*

Obviously Bodley would never have won admission to Goodhart-Rendel's notorious gallery of 'Rogue Architects of the Victorian Era': 'Ruskin's theories, Butterfield's reforms, and Street's sketching holidays had thrown into the Gothic pot much strong seasoning.... The dominant [High Victorian] Gothic party insisted that architecture must above all be "vigorous" and in contemporary office slang the highest praise for a design was to say that it had plenty of "go"'.[17] Bodley worked against both High Victorianism's 'Development' and rejected 'go', fulminating in 1885 against 'that shallow, conceited, and futile attempt to outdo the works of the past by coarseness and what is vulgarly called "go" in design'.[18] In conclusion, Goodhart-Rendel does not rejoice overmuch in Bodley's 'good taste':

> With its masonry finely designed and sympathetically executed, with its sober colouring, its graceful proportions, and its careful avoidance of all vulgarity and violence, [it] is an excellent sort [of building that] cannot be denied.... Nevertheless, the material they handled always is old, correctly medieval, and unadventurous, and we cannot look back from it with anything but regret to the days when Butterfield and Street, their heads full of adventurous fancies, eagerly took toward novelty and development their successors made a point of re-tracing. All that these successors could teach to their disciples was good taste, and the history of art has shown, here as always, that in the not very long run, the wages of good taste is death.[19]

But the story of adventure and novelty of Goodhart-Rendel's reading does not end here, as numbered among his 'Rogue Architects' is Edward Prior (1852–1932) – born a generation later than Bodley. Goodhart-Rendel points out the paradox of how a movement that had once sought to build its 'muscular' monuments in the slums, had now become associated with 'refined' upper-class and aristocratic piety. These changes in audience, and from 'go' to 'refinement', or from boldly constructed surfaces to smoothly plastered or painted ones, invoked masculine-and-feminine subtexts. Gilbert Scott, writing in 1850, preferred Geometrical Decorated as 'its merits as compared with the flowing style, consist chiefly in its retention of the masculine and vigorous character of earlier days. The flowing tracery, though to some eyes more perfect, is too soft and feminine in its beauty to be admitted as the main characteristics of a perfect style'.[20] As evidenced, Bodley admired this very attenuated delicacy of perfection of the late Decorated on the cusp of the Perpendicular.

St Mary, Eccleston – Goodhart-Rendel's aforementioned example of Bodley's refinement – was completed at the turn of the twentieth century to a commission by the most elevated and wealthy of patrons, the 1st Duke of Westminster. Externally it looks hewn from one block of its deep red sandstone, with its rectilinear masses of tower and nave elided into a single plane. Internally the church is vaulted (a rare instance in Bodley's

FIGURE 3.8 *George Frederick Bodley, exterior of St Mary's, Eccleston, Cheshire. Photograph Geoff Brandwood.*

work) above sheer surfaces of sandstone, accentuated by a grid of slender shafts and a string course at the base of the clerestory. Not this unified breadth, but stylistic disparity, lay behind the criticism of St Mary, Eccleston and the contemporary Holy Trinity, Prince Consort Road, in *The Builder* of 1901:

> Both these churches are, in the arcade design, of Early Decorated character . . . in both of them the east window represents a late period of Gothic, verging on Perpendicular. We presume that Mr Bodley thinks it allowable to play with and mix the details of past styles in this manner. It is open to question . . .[21]

But the stylistic hybridity, such as it is, allowed Bodley in each case to exactly tune the qualities of Breadth, Refinement, and Delicacy he sought, fusing the powerful cubic masses of late English Gothic, in its transition to Perpendicular, with the Delicacy of Curvilinear Decorated. Holy Trinity also drew criticism from Bodley's former pupil, Edward Warren – otherwise a devoted admirer of his old master – for what he saw as an 'extreme slimness' and 'attenuation of detail . . . symptomatic of his final manner, and . . . carried to excess in much of his late work'.[22]

Breadth of smooth off-white surfaces, attenuation *without* thinness, and delicacy of moulding and tracery, are found in exhilarating equipoise in

St German, Roath, Cardiff. This, one of the greatest of Bodley's urban churches, was designed in 1881 and completed in 1884, in the period when Bodley was in partnership with Thomas Garner from 1869 to 1898. Goodhart-Rendel caught the feel of the interior as 'a sort of greyhound

FIGURE 3.9 *Bodley and Garner, interior of St German's, Roath, Cardiff. Photograph Geoff Brandwood.*

church – strong, lithe and thin'.[23] Like Holy Trinity, the nave is conceived on the hall-church scheme, with extremely high aisle arcades supporting a wagon vault, with no clerestory. Apart from the aspirations to Englishness in the Late Gothic surfaces and detail, the spatiality of the hall-church model itself in fact derives from German precedents such as the thirteenth-century Franciscan church in Cologne. The interior buttress idea is powerfully explored in the aisles shaping deep cream-plastered and vaulted embrasures to each Decorated window – akin to side-chapels. In his 1885 statement of 'Principles and Characteristics', Bodley spoke for 'due breadth of surface, contrasted with delicate detail' whose

> best effects of Gothic work are obtained by the use of thick walls and small detail, as in windows where the broad splay is finished by a slender shaft, giving a fine line of light and a delicate shadow, contrasting with the uniform light on the wide breadth of surface of the splayed jamb.[24]

Applying the same device in the chancel, the luminous splayed reveals meet just such a 'slender shaft' and are deep enough to allow a passage at the base of the tall windows which penetrates each buttress through an ogee-arched opening. Like the hall-churches of the mendicant orders on which it is modelled, St German was intended as a missionary church in a strongly nonconformist district – most unlike rural ducal Eccleston.

This account of surface-values in Bodley's work has underscored his reflective planes of smooth plaster, or his areas of stone, and St German's light openness certainly marks a break with the richly painted interiors Bodley had preferred in the 1870s. But it should not be forgotten that 'his love of colour and his fine instinct for its employment and distribution were almost phenomenal' as Warren recalls.[25] What Bodley called his 'boyish effort, even antagonistic',[26] his early St Michael and All Angels, Brighton (1860–2) had internal walls of red brickwork. But, as Warren also says, 'Bodley, while delighting in the fine colour of dressed stone, cared little, and ever increasingly less, for exposed brickwork in interiors, and, prompted by his acute instinctive colour sense, revelled from the first in the use of paint and of gilding upon roofs, walls and woodwork, and was never content with a church until he had bought the whole interior into harmony as he conceived it . . .'.[27] At the previously mentioned All Saints, Cambridge, Bodley rejected constructional polychromy and, together with the return to English styles, adopted a scheme of large-scale decorative painting of flowing diaper patterns designed by himself and C. E. Kempe, and carried out by F. R. Leach; here there is not a surface which is not painted, stencilled, or gilded, in what has been seen as something of a Pugin-esque revival.

FIGURE 3.10 *George Frederick Bodley, All Saints, Cambridge, detail of wall-painting at the south-east corner of the south aisle. Photograph Geoff Brandwood.*

In 1899 Bodley published a volume of verse; it is not great poetry, but 'Architecture: The Minster' embodies the harmony of space and surface he aspired to in his work:

How many hands have wrought, one mind conceived!
Yet seems it as one great harmonious chord,
Full and complete, that soundeth lastingly
Through all the massive time it shall endure.[28]

* * *

Charles Eastlake's *A History of the Gothic Revival* is inescapably curtailed as he finished writing it late in the transitional year of 1870 (published 1872), as the 'go' of High Victorianism mutated to the refined breadth of Late Victorian, and Arts and Crafts. Musing on the 'Future Prospect of the [Gothic] Revival', he contrasts the arch 'Rogue-Architect', Samuel Smiles Teulon's St Stephen's, Hampstead (begun 1869), with Bodley's St John the Baptist, Tue Brook, Liverpool (completed 1871). The massive St Stephens was developed, in Teulon's highly personal muscular manner, as a free synthesis of French thirteenth-century Gothic and native English motifs; a polygonal apse, and transepts of widely different heights, engage with a mighty pyramidal tower. For Eastlake 'it represents a sufficiently wide departure from English tradition to be fairly contrasted with works in which respect for that tradition is conspicuous'.[29] Bodley's Liverpool church is 'an admirable model' of that latter respect for native tradition. One particular 'element of beauty which pervades the whole building from its primary construction to the last touch of its embellishment ... is the charm of

FIGURE 3.11 *George Frederick Bodley, interior of St John the Baptist, Tue Brook, Liverpool. Photograph Geoff Brandwood.*

colour'.[30] Bodley's work, in his mature Decorated manner, is dazzling in the varied surface patterns which cover every plane with flowing diapers, stencilled medallions, and gilding. The planarity extends even to the actual ochre and pink stone which seems two-dimensional as the window reveals tellingly demonstrate: 'window reveals are stone surfaces, yet the stone does not turn the corner as mouldings on the face of the adjacent wall. Instead, the patterns painted on the plaster wall surfaces continue to the arris of the intersection of the wall plane and the plane of the window reveal . . .'.[31] Eastlake praises C. E. Kempe's Tree of Life crucifixion over the chancel arch, it is a work that may belong to the 'order of conventionalism', but 'in this truly admirable work the genuine grace of Medieval art seems at length to have been reached. [And] in the architecture which it decorates no appreciable inferiority, whether of design or execution, to the type selected for imitation, can be discerned'.[32]

Looking forward – in comparing these two approaches – the Eastlake of 1870 wrestles with similar issues to those that exercised Goodhart-Rendel looking back in 1934. Between architecture that allows the scope for the 'rich instincts of inventive genius' of a Teulon, or one that sustains a Bodley-an call to a social 'order of conventionalism' – 'to the simplicity of popular faith, nay, the very social conditions which would render a return to Medieval principles universally acceptable'.[33]

Prior: 'Texture as a . . . Condition for Architecture'

That other rendering of St Andrew's Church Roker, made in pencil and sepia by Prior in 1905, is a forceful reminder of the persistence of the Savage surface within the received discourse of Refinement; as Trevor Garnham writes: 'Arts and Crafts architecture can be either soft or hard – either comforting and familiar, with small-scale spaces and refined detailing . . . or a sterner architecture, such as Lethaby's and Prior's, responding to the rationalism of the age'.[34] Prior was responding also to the raw energy of St Andrew's north-eastern industrial context and to the moving primitivity of the nearby Anglo-Saxon monasteries at Monkwearmouth and Jarrow. Bodley's broad hall-churches are proof that 'refined detailing' need not be confined to 'small-scale spaces' and St Andrew's also achieves an expansive spatial unity of congregation, chancel, and altar that invokes later English Gothic. Bodley does not match the breathtaking daring of Prior's structure of near-parabolic arches spanning fifty-two feet, but Prior would have known Bodley's St Augustine's, Pendlebury (1874)[35] and he uses Bodley's same device of a passage driven through deep internal buttresses to serve the pews, bearing *his* arches and massive inner piers upon coupled columns inspired by those in the tower and porch of the Anglo-Saxon Church of

St Peter, Monkwearmouth. At Pendlebury light traverses the smooth plastered surfaces of the thick walls, to meet the line of light and subtle shadow of slender shafts of ashlar sandstone; in contrast at Roker it dramatizes the roughly random uncoursed grey magnesium limestone from nearby Marsden, where it was still traditionally hand-quarried. Only the quoins and arch-voussoirs are dressed stone and the emollient plastered upper areas outlining the voussoirs, as shown in the perspective, were not carried out; the stone clads an innovative hidden structure of concrete and iron rods – only the concrete purlins are directly expressed.

Prior's small built output is outstanding in the material vitality of its expressive – even Expressionist – surfaces realized in allegiance to Ruskin's ideal of the builder-artist-architect. And it is noteworthy that the first of his many publications was on 'Texture as a Quality of Art and a Condition for Architecture' (1890), originating in a lecture given in 1889 to *The National Association for the Advancement of Art in Relation to Industry* – formed in 1888 with William Morris as its President. Key themes in Prior's very Ruskinian paper are: a primary appeal to the lessons of Nature and the surface of the earth; to the qualities of the everyday; to rough Changefulness and Savageness over smooth perfection; and to the hierarchy of the textural wall-veil.

As Morris also felt strongly, the first given of Nature is the 'surface of this earth' and architecture is 'everything that man erects for his use; every product of his labour whereby he alters the surface of this earth in which he lives; and in the humblest of these erections, no less than in the most ambitious, would ask you to reckon man an architect'.[36] So Prior is more interested in the everyday, than in domes or palaces, believing that 'the beauty of an English landscape has its highest expression in the beauty of our old English wayside architecture'.[37] To learn of texture Prior takes us 'to the common roadside building, to village church and shop and cottage, to farm sheds and garden walls . . .'.[38] Prior defines texture as 'a condition of material surface, and as such is of necessity as a condition of the arts', but hints enigmatically at a symbolic and evocative aspect to texture that is more than solely material: 'I shall use the term elastically for something more than material Texture: but it will be readily perceived that the quality, or group of qualities, to which I give the name, are really the material Texture under varying degrees of magnitude, as if presented under lenses of enlarging or diminishing power'.[39] He writes poetically of the textures of nature's surfaces, of 'ribbed and rippled sands' made by the passing tide, and of 'veined, or blotched, or mottled' leaves, and stalks 'ribbed, or hairy, or shaggy with scales'.[40] Of the ostensibly 'most steadfast' rocks and metals available to the architect, he celebrates how nature rapidly reclaims smoothness and polishing through weathering – quoting Horace's 'tamen usque recurret'[41] ('Naturam expellas furca, tamen usque recurret'; 'Drive Nature out with a pitchfork, she'll come right back'). The smooth stone soon becomes 'creased and curdled – fretted with lichen, scrolled with moss', and polished metal rapidly 'crystallizes afresh, shows a tarnish or a still more subtle patina'.[42] And as expected, along with his Association companions, he condemns the industrial 'spirit of the age' which is inimical to 'this infinite grace of Texture' where 'our materials must be commercial materials, made at the cheapest rate, and for the best sale . . .'.[43] In the centenary year of Prior's birth (1952), Edward Grillet reflected in *The Architectural Review* on Prior's achievements, noting how 'unusually violently' Prior had expressed the Arts and Crafts principles for an architecture grown organically from the labour of the craftsmen, pugnaciously opposing drawing-board architecture and the professionalization of the art.[44] 'Architectural Texture' is particularly elusive to the dead drawing-board for it 'cannot be so drawn and dictated' insists Prior:[45] 'For this Texture is a magical garment when well woven. It can throw over bricks and stone a veil which softens their outline, half concealing and adding mystery to beauty, giving our puny heaps something of the effect of Nature's monuments'.[46] An important passage, exploring the principle of textual gradation, is clearly based on the 'marvellous system of adaptation' to viewing distance which Ruskin had discovered in the 'treatment of ornament' of medieval architecture's 'wall-veil', as analysed in *The Stones of Venice*. Prior writes:

> Then of great value are our jointings of brick and stone, the piecing of our woodwork, the coursing of our slates and tiles. With these we may weave a lace-work over roof and wall and floor. More deliberate are rustications, diapers, and pattern-work, our enrichments, flutings, egg and tongue and dentil courses. These, though designed, become merely Texture, when the particularity of their form is obliterated by distance, or fused by the imagination. At a still further distance the larger architecture features themselves – such as windows and piers, pinnacles and buttresses – merge into an undistinguished variation of surface. Herein lie boundless opportunities for achieving the harmonies of Texture; and so we may provide, that from the first view of even the humblest building, this pleasant Texture should lead on by nearer approach to pleasant detail – itself well textured, – and so step by step to the last limits of sight, each step revealing a further veil to be lifted, a further mystery of beauty to be solved. This is the right use of Texture, in its most material sense; the Texture which Nature exhibits in such perfection, and which it has been the aim of all architectures to reproduce.[47]

Ruskin posits four great 'arborescent' orders of ornament in viewing a cathedral tower – as we might a mountain massif – at increasingly closer distances. First, 'the great masses' of 'buttresses and stories and black windows and broad cornices of the tower' as seen 'half a score of miles away'; second, a richer order of 'traceries and shafts and pinnacles . . . as we approach'; third, 'the niches and statues and knobs and flowers, which we can only see when we stand beneath it'; and finally, a 'fourth order of ornament, as delicate as the eye can follow, when any of these [individual] features may be approached'.[48] In *The Dynamics of Architectural Form* (1977), Rudolf Arnheim calls this compositional principle – one so important to the reading of architectural surfaces – 'hierarchic subordination'; a building *acquires* size perceptually insofar as it allows the viewer to grasp it, and to scale from whole to part and back again.[49] As Prior foresaw, too many buildings of the industrial age are wanting scale owing to their un-evocative wall-veils and lack of graspable texture. In Prior's account, Texture is neither entirely matter nor fully symbol; Texture *is* matter certainly, but it is only *through* practical material engagement that matter might be transcended, lifting veils to wider horizons of Poetry and Art. For the last twenty-five years of his life Prior built little, becoming more noted as a scholar; in his 1905 work on *The Cathedral Builders of England* he insists that 'both system and learning were foreign' to the medieval builders. Nor was theirs a craft based on 'the observation and tabulation of . . . styles and ornaments, of mouldings and arch-shapes' that produced the archaeological deadness of so much Gothic Revival work. No, the medieval cathedral arose as 'the elementary shaping of a natural romance, the direct satisfaction of simple ideals – such as height, breadth and extension; solid mass and slender grace; solemn shade and brilliant colour'.[50] Like Ruskin's characterization of Savageness, Prior extols the fact that:

> the very imperfections of [the medieval builder's] processes – as we judge them by our science, the inexactness of his calculations, the hand-to-mouth necessities, were of the substance of his art. The stress of inadequate resources, the constant effort after the impossible, were just the hindrances and disabilities, whose friction stimulated and made the power to rise above them. They give in medieval building to this day the atmosphere that transfigures it, because they express the life of it.[51]

Veils of surface-texture: Voewood House

Sea-mists often bring further mysterious veilings to the textures of Voewood House, the home Prior built for the Reverend Percy Robert Lloyd in 1903–5 on the coastal heathlands near Holt in north-eastern Norfolk. This extended butterfly-plan dwelling was one of Prior's most ambitious experiments to match the medieval art-builder's 'elementary shaping of a natural romance', and to weave transfiguring veils of Texture. To this end he employed the architect Randall Wells as on-site clerk of works, omitting a general contractor, and ensuring a direct link between himself and the craftsmen; Randall Wells came directly from working in a similar role for William Lethaby at the church of All Saints, Brockhampton. The material of flint and gravel came, as-found, from one acre of the seven-acre turnip-field site which Prior dug to a depth of six feet, thence turning his 'quarry' into a sunken garden. In a *Country Life* article of 1909, Lawrence Weaver positions Prior as 'a staunch propagandist in the demand that a building shall be racy of the soil it stands on' and details how 'the materials so obtained were graded and used to build the house, the larger flints for the external facing of the walls, the smaller for the mass concrete [core construction], and the fine sand for mortar . . .'.[52] For dressing the intractable flint a 'fine golden brown' sandstone had to be brought from the west of the county, near Sandringham, with thin tile-bricks also used for other dressings; the pantiles for the roofs are also of East Anglian tradition.

Prior was articled to Richard Norman Shaw, from 1874 up to the forming of his own practice in 1880, and to Shaw is generally attributed the invention of the butterfly-plan in Britain with his virtuoso extension of three huge diagonal wings to the country house of Chesters, Northumberland in 1891.[53] But the next butterfly, devised by his pupil, is totally different in scale and expression to its vast neo-Baroque original, and is the true seed of its many Arts and Crafts offspring. This was a design for a butterfly-plan cottage Prior exhibited as a model at the Royal Academy in 1895; on the back of this he received the commission for the very similar The Barn in Exmouth of 1896–7. As compared to the polish of a professional modelmaker's work, *The Building News* praised Prior's cottage model for being 'comparatively rough in appearance, and revolutionary in its tendencies'.[54] Prior explained his

FIGURE 3.12 *E. S. Prior, wax model of butterfly-plan cottage, 1895. RIBA Collections.*

revolutionary intent in an article on 'Architectural Modelling' in *The Builder* of June 1895. *His* models are not made as a 'device for client-getting', but as an integral part of the design process, so that – against the 'habit of the tee-square' – the architect grasps through his own hands 'that an architectural design is a sculpture in the round', and explores its tactile and textural potential in ways drawing cannot;[55] of course one benefit of the sprawling butterfly-plan is the extensive surfaces it offers for textural play. Juhani Pallasmaa writes how that 'even in the age of computer-aided design and virtual modelling, physical models are incomparable aids in the design process of the architect. . . . The three-dimensional model speaks to the hand and the body as powerfully as to the eye, and the very process of constructing a model simulates the process of construction'.[56] At the same time, these architectural office models tend to be generic in their surfaces, and averse to literal textural simulation – to accusations of train-set modelling. Prior, however, urges the architect to get stuck into textural play:

> For sketch models the French putty . . . is extremely easy of use; it can be coloured to a certain extent by powders, and, when smeared on cardboard, readily takes the form of architectural surfaces. Rough-surfaced cardboard and the corrugated paper used for wrapping bottles have very closely the relative 'values' of wall and roof respectively, and watercolour can give them suggestive tints; but, of course, anything of real texture in these materials is impossible, though they make very pleasant sketchy models. For real interpretative work wax seems indispensable, as taking and keeping both colour and texture with permanence. . . . Powdered colour will give any tint, and any required texture is got by the mixture of suitable ingredients – sands, dusts, or powders. I have used all kinds . . .[57]

But while a 'model brings the architect a step nearer his work than the drawing did', for Prior it 'still does not ground him on the building where he should be placed'.[58]

Hermann Muthesius spread the fame of The Barn by illustrating 'Prior's house with the remarkable plan' in *The English House* (*Das Englische Haus*, 1904, 1905) as among 'attempts to find a better form' of layout for the smaller English house.[59] Along with the remarkable plans, Muthesius showed a photograph of the striking entrance front with its great slate-hung gable locked into the cranked wings and a tumbling bonnet of thatch.[60] The axial arched entrance opens into a hexagonal hall (part double-height originally) as the nucleus of the plan; towards the sea the Dining-Room and Drawing-Room embrace a veranda and terrace. On the approach side the servant elements – of stairs, scullery, and bathrooms – generate a playful scattering of small windows, embedded in the rich textures found through the modelling. For Grillet, 'the effect in The Barn is more like Gaudi in Barcelona than one can see anywhere else in England. It makes even the naughtiest Lutyens appear tame'.[61] Runs of large red boulders sort abstractly with dottings of

FIGURE 3.13 *E. S. Prior, The Barn, Exmouth, Devon, 1896, with thatched roof prior to the fire of 1905. RIBA Collections.*

smaller sea-pebbles, and with lintels, quoins, and stretches of roughly-squared local sandstone. Prior also introduces Dartmoor granite, in the monolithic columns of the veranda, and the capstones to the tapering chimneys.

Returning from its idiosyncratic precedent to the greater scaled Voewood, Prior's first spatial trick is to *disguise* the house's scale by placing the small hexagonal entrance hall at the centre of the north-western butterfly-wing – not on the central axis as in The Barn. The extent of the house is therefore hidden – both by this wing itself and the flanking garden-walls – so that we might be approaching the entrance to a modestly quirky, five-bay medieval manor-house, complete with proudly spiral Tudor-esque chimneys, fabricated 'by laying tile-bricks in lime mortar round a fireclay flue-pipe without any cutting'.[62] The hexagonal concrete-vaulted vestibule is at the lower forecourt level, so it is only on ascending the nine steps of Hopton-Wood stone that the main staircase, and the long corridor – linking library, double-height hall, dining room, and garden loggias – is revealed, and with it the true size of the house. Externally, its full sun-catching spread is best seen from the far southern end of the sunken garden where it is possible to begin to attend to those 'harmonies of texture' Prior outlined in his 1889 lecture.[63] At this distance 'the larger architecture features' as a highly

FIGURE 3.14 E. S. Prior, The Barn, Exmouth, Devon, surface textures. Drawing Stephen Kite.

complex composition whereby a central three-bay central loggia – marking the hall behind – is flanked by three-storey gable elements; off these, half-gables introduce the butterfly-wings, then step abruptly down to the west and east cloisters of library and dining-room; swan-neck curves then swoop up to the gabled polygonal end-bays of these principal rooms. The soaring chimney of the library fireplace marks an emphatic full-stop to these restless contours at the dwelling's south-west corner – breaking the general symmetry. For Weaver in *Country Life* (1909) 'it will readily be admitted that the broken lines of the mass, the almost riotous variety of roof-line, dormer, gable and texture, raise in the mind images most diverse; but there is yet an over-veiling unity that prevents any sense of confusion'.[64] The key to this 'over-veiling unity' is the binding textural scintillation of 'the cool pearly grey of the facing of unbroken flints'[65] held in distantly readable rectilinear armatures of golden sandstone dressings, and decorative pink tile coursings. Rough sandstone diapers stitch together these various components – embodying the ancient pattern-making heraldic 'chequered principle' (as seen in the Doge's Palace, Venice) – and drawing on nearby vernacular models, such as Waxham Great Barn of *c.* 1570.[66] On 'nearer approach to [this] pleasant detail – itself well textured'[67] – equivalent to Ruskin's delicate third and fourth orders of ornament – Prior unveils a mysterious codex of further symbolic motifs, of zig-zags, lozenges, sun-rays, and spirals. This symbolism was undoubtedly influenced by Lethaby's first publication, *Architecture, Mysticism and Myth* (1891), a book which, as J. B. Bullen explains, was 'concerned with the irrational in architecture and building. It rode on the contemporary fashion for mythography, typology and mysticism, and was an attempt to understand architecture in terms of prevailing ideologies and as the expression of psychological symbols'.[68] Lethaby's very chapter titles mythologize the making of surfaces and apertures: 'The World Fabric', 'The Golden Gate of the Sun', 'Pavements Like the Sea', 'Ceilings Like the Sky', 'The Windows of Heaven'. He marshals legends, together with the timeless motifs of mandalas, labyrinths, sunrises, ziggurats, waves, and stars – many of which can be found within the spirited textures of Voewood.

Surface textures, pattern, and symbolism achieve a rich climax in Prior's last work, the Byzantine church of St Osmund in Parkstone, Poole of

FIGURE 3.15 *E. S. Prior, Voewood, Holt, Norfolk, viewed from the south-east. Photograph Stephen Kite.*

FIGURE 3.16 E. S. Prior, *Voewood, Holt, Norfolk*, detail textures at centre of south terrace. Photograph Stephen Kite.

1913–16 (fittingly now St Dunstan's Orthodox Church) where Prior worked outwards from an earlier Byzantine chancel designed by G. A. Bligh Livesay. Pevsner was enthused by the 'riot of colour and texture' of the west front which he found 'prophetic of the Expressionism of the 1920s', and by the 'flickering texture' of 'the brick, mottled from red to brown to yellow'.[69] This variety in colour was obtained by transferring the clay, dug from local beds at Wareham, directly to the moulds.[70] Stocky octagonal brick turrets frame the church's west front, enlivened by engaged half-round shafts at the centre of each face. Pevsner describes the portal spanning between these towers as 'a superbly decisive segmental arch of terracotta, broad and low, spanning from turret to turret and moulded with a trailing vine'.[71] Above this shadowy gateway Prior planted a great wheel window – rimmed in discs of pale pink-ochre terracotta – in a grid of diamond-patterned tilework; these, and the triangular-arched balustrade and windows to the north stair-turret, probably derive from the primitive diagonal pilaster-strip patterns and triangular openings of Anglo-Saxon work, as found in the tenth-century tower of Earls Barton Church, Northamptonshire.[72] In the chapter on 'The Golden Gate of the Sun' in *Architecture, Mysticism and Myth*, Lethaby illustrates the arch to the Byzantine 'tomb at Shefa Amr, in Galilee' where a trailing vine is 'charged with a circular sun-disc' at its head.[73] Prior places a Greek-cross at this point (as also found over the tomb door at Shefa Amr) but his great wheel-window above also invites sun-disc symbolism.

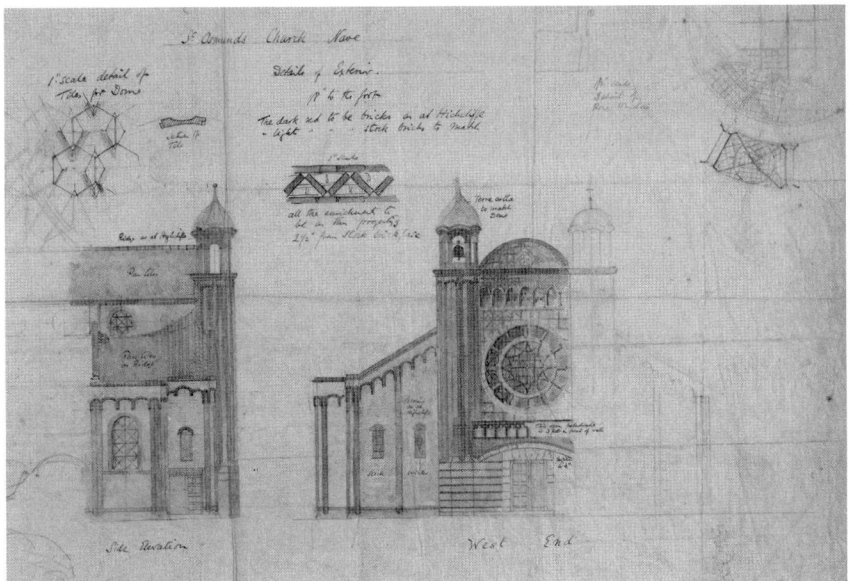

FIGURE 3.17 E. S. Prior, *Church of St Osmund, Poole, Dorset, study of West End*. RIBA Collections.

FIGURE 3.18 W. R. Lethaby, illustration of Byzantine 'tomb at Shefa Amr, in Galilee', from Architecture, Mysticism and Myth *(1891)*.

* * *

Reginald Blomfield – his successful Classical architect contemporary – obliquely praised Prior as the 'strongest personality' to have emerged from Shaw's office, but with the regret that 'his real ability should have taken him further than it did; perhaps he was too unyielding, constitutionally incapable of accepting the *via media*'.[74] But the *via media* of Edwardian and inter-war Britain was often the pompous Imperialist Classicism that Shaw, himself, had inaugurated with his Piccadilly Hotel, London of 1905–8; Blomfield followed his master's grandiose manner when designing The Quadrant, Regent Street, London of 1920–3. As Peter Davey conjectures: 'Yet in the end, which went further? Every one of Prior's buildings repays study with delight and interest. Can anyone say that of the endless acres of Blomfield's work?'[75]

One architect who managed the change to the 'High-Game' of Classicism, while retaining the Arts and Crafts feeling for surface 'texture as a quality of art', was Edwin Lutyens. His garden at Hestercombe, Somerset (1906) imbricates his roots in English vernacular and Classicism's own liaisons with satiric rusticity. An intense moment in the composition of this garden, is the Rotunda, which – with its reflecting pool and pedimented niche – hinges the original Victorian Terrace (*c.* 1877) to the rills and Great Plat of the main formal garden, and to an Orangery echoing Nicholas Hawksmoor's Baroque one at Kensington Palace, London. In both Rotunda and Orangery Lutyens interchanges smooth and rough, refinement and savagery, in a

FIGURE 3.19 *Edwin Lutyens, Orangery, Hestercombe, Somerset.* Country Life *(23 April 1927), p. 639. © Country Life.*

reciprocity of the roughest of split rocks and the smoothest precision of Somerset Ham Hill ashlar. From a base of split stone, the Orangery rises through paired end pilasters – rusticated in unwrought coursed stone and ashlar – to the precisely dressed main cornice, and to the Mannerist arches and intermediate doors; 'there is in the very design of the detail and in the sharp jutting of those ridges above the intervening single doors the faintest suggestion of natural cliff formations . . .'.[76]

CHAPTER FOUR

Carving the Surface

Edwardian and Inter-War Architecture and Sculpture

In his *Age of the Masters* (1975), architectural historian Reyner Banham (1922–1988) presents an aerial photograph of the cubic white dwellings of Walter Gropius, J. P. Oud, Mies van der Rohe, and Le Corbusier – glistening in their wooded background, at the 1927 Weissenhof Exhibition, Stuttgart – as representing a 'stirring moment' of Internationalism when these productions 'stood before the world united in forms and intentions':[1] 'Poised for world conquest, the new architecture discovered that it had a uniform by which friend could be distinguished from foe, a uniform whose adoption indicated that its wearer wanted to be considered as one of the gang'.[2] For Mark Wigley,

> photographs of the idyllic [Weissenhof] collection seemed to capture the look of an imminent future, a coherent environment defined by white walls. . . . The identity of [modern architecture] had finally been located in its white surfaces, surfaces that assumed an unparalleled force, so much so that they continue to define modern architecture long after architects started to remove the layer of paint in favour of the look of exposed concrete or metal.[3]

But Banham questions this hegemony of the white surface, for 'already in the early thirties, Le Corbusier was adjusting his dress, and incorporating sporting or tweedy elements not accepted by the rest of the gang'.[4] Le Corbusier's 'tweedy elements' – as in the holiday house at Mathés (1935) Banham illustrates, with its pitched roofs, rough timberwork, and walls of random masonry – draws on the same vernacular qualities that had also inspired his proselytization of the moral virtues of whitewashed surfaces in his *L'art décoratif d'aujourd'hui* (The Decorative Art of Today) of 1925. Travelling in Bulgaria, in his 1911 *Journey to the East*, the young Le Corbusier (Charles-Edouard Jeanneret) despises the picturesque sentimentalism of painters who admire villages 'just because dung invades the alleys and mud has splattered as high as the roofs'. Arriving at the traditional Bulgarian town of Tŭrnovo, he celebrates its rejection of the 'base negligence' of 'such filth'; here 'each spring, the house that one loves receives its new coat: sparkling white . . .', while inside 'they whitewash each room before Easter and Christmas, and in that way the house is always bright'.[5]

If the High Priest of the international white surface himself exhibits 'tweedy elements' by the 1930s, then inspection of British architecture in the inter-war period yields yet more extremes of 'tweediness', given both the country's climatic and cultural distance from the Mediterranean roots of the white surface, and the fascination with evocative surfaces as explored in the previous chapters. On the climatic challenges of whiteness, take *An Introduction to Modern Architecture*, first published in 1940 by J. M. Richards (then assistant editor of *The Architectural Review*):

> The cleanness and glitter of white walls are satisfying to the modern architect's eye, but in damp or dirty climates few white surfaces survive. They soon become dingy. White walls are not foreign to Britain, which has the successful precedent of Regency stucco buildings. But the smartness of these depends on regular re-painting with expensive oil paint, and in times of financial instability we cannot afford to build in a way that commits us to so much future expenditure on upkeep. Modern architects have made many sad mistakes in using white surfaces that have not lasted, and many now believe that concrete is more satisfactory as a structural material than as a finishing material.[6]

Earlier, in his *The Modern House* of 1934, F. R. S. Yorke had also worried that 'smooth stucco has desirable qualities as a surfacing material, but it is subject to crazing and discolouration, and though much experimental work has been done to produce a non-crazing rendering, the perfect cement surface has yet to be found'.[7] Yorke was a founding member of the MARS (Modern Architectural Research Group) group – started in 1933 to promote Modernist architects in Britain – and *The Modern House* had been commissioned by *The Architectural Review* as part of its own endorsement of the new white architecture. For Wigley, Yorke's argument for Modernism ultimately 'turns on the status of the surface'.[8] Yorke points to Holland 'where painting had, through cubism and expressionism, already given impetus to revolt against copyism in architecture. Mondrian, using clean rectangles of colour and straight lines, influenced men like Dudok and Rietveld. . . . . It also showed the value of straight lines, plane surfaces, a new sense of space and a new sense of proportion'.⁹ Now 'the wall has changed; it is a thin skin, hung on a framework ... The wall surface is regarded, aesthetically, as a continuous plane; as a skin enveloping and expressing the surface of a volume'.¹⁰ Among many celebrated continental examples – for example, Le Corbusier's Villa de Monzie, Garches (1927) – even in later editions of *The Modern House*, Yorke illustrates only a handful of British examples of the 'continuous enveloping membrane' such as Walter Gropius and Maxwell Fry's house in Church Street, Chelsea, of 1936. In truth, such icons of the white-surface were isolated in Britain, and the bulk of architectural production in the inter-war years remained invested in 'traditional' materials of brick and stone, albeit often cloaking a steel or concrete frame, and expressed in a confusion of styles including: free-style Arts and Crafts; neo-Baroque Classicism; variously stripped variants of Classicism approaching abstraction; and a streamlined Moderne or Art-Deco.¹¹

In interpreting British surfaces among this welter, Charles Holden's (1875–1960) work is of great significance; for John Summerson 'it could be said that he was the last of the Edwardians and the first of the English Moderns'.¹² Between 1901 and 1910 this still-young 'last of the Edwardians' realized a series of outstanding buildings distinguished by their 'care for surface treatments' and materiality,¹³ by their massing and planar clarity, and by their ambition to integrate sculptural relief decoration; among them the free-style Bristol Central Reference Library (1902–6), and the Cubist Mannerist, British Medical Association (1906–8) on London's Strand, with its controversial sculptures by the young Jacob Epstein. After the First World War, and some eminent work for the War Graves Commission, Holden emerges as a mature architect retaining the firm belief, as here stated in 1931, that architecture was not based on style, but on 'a firm determination on the part of all designers to keep fitness for purpose always before them as the common basis, and to insist on the severe elimination of the non-essentials'.¹⁴ His 'English Modern' creed reaches its culmination in his stations for the London Underground and its skyscraper headquarters (1926–29) towering over 55 Broadway, London. Both as 'Edwardian' and as 'English Modern' his work – and his efforts to collaborate with sculptors – exposes debates about sculpture's relationship to the architectonic surface, and related tensions between 'carving and modelling' – to the point that carving itself becomes 'clean, moral and closely bound to the English Landscape. As carving becomes English, so modelling becomes foreign'.¹⁵

Whitman-esque Elementalism

Already in Holden's 1897 RIBA Soane Medallion competition entry for a provincial market hall (awarded a Certificate of Merit), *The Architectural Review*, in its very first issue, recognized 'a considerable latent ability', although critical of a design that 'looks more like a church than a market hall',[16] owing to its blocky brick entrance tower – the first among Holden's series of massive strongholds. Beginning at the tower's entrance arch, a frieze of figures threads between the over-scaled buttresses to the upper hall and the arched loggia below. In his obituary to Holden (1960), Nikolaus Pevsner praised this 'extremely bright student's design' and its 'nicely asymmetrical composition [with] no immediate precedent', pointing out that 'the frieze of figures in relief was certainly fashionable at the moment'.[17] Later Holden would acknowledge his debt to John Belcher's Institute of Chartered Accountants (1888–93) in the City of London,[18] where Belcher deployed Baroque motifs in a freestyle Arts and Crafts spirit, introducing a continuous frieze of standing figures, in high-relief, below the sills of the second-storey windows. This highly influential design marks the culmination of a period of increasingly confident collaboration between architects and sculptors to the point that, from 1893, decorative figure sculpture, allied to architecture, became equal in importance to independent figure sculpture; moreover, its architectural setting played an effective public role, as compared to *objets de vertu* hidden away in private collections or in galleries.[19] The Institute's lively friezes were carved by William Hamo Thorneycroft (1850–1923), a key mover in the modernizing movement of the 'New Sculpture' that vitalized the surfaces of late Victorian and Edwardian architecture.[20] For the historian of *The New Sculpture* (1983), Susan Beattie, Thorneycroft's reliefs are 'magnificent in general effect as an element in [Belcher's] architectural design', in their heroic representations of Victorian labour – Education, Commerce, Manufactures, Agriculture, and so forth; yet they also show Thorneycroft's 'unease in the role of architectural sculptor'.[21] For Thorneycroft lacked that instinct for *carving* the stone that is vital to the architectonic conception, 'he was essentially a modeller, interested in the process of building up three-dimensional form in the malleable, fluid substances of clay and bronze to create an effect of movement and spontaneity'.[22] Frederick Pomeroy (1856–1924) – another sculptor in the vanguard of the New Sculpture – explains how the carver works constantly in terms of the final material, such as stone, from the *front or surface plane*, 'this being the true plane of all glyptic art, the opposite to the building up, or back plane of plastic decoration'[23] – namely, that of the modeller. Adumbrated here are tensions that resonate deep into the twentieth century, between the practices of carving and modelling, and between sculpture made in the public sphere in alliance to the 'mother-art' of architecture, or worked independently as a studio and gallery based practice. No one, at the time, would better capture these carving–modelling distinctions than the art-writer Adrian Stokes (1902–1972) whom, in *The Stones of Rimini* (1934), writes how 'a figure carved in stone is fine carving when one feels that not the figure, but the stone through the medium of the figure, has come to life. Plastic conception [modelling], on the other hand, is uppermost when the material [from

FIGURE 4.1 *Charles Holden, design of a provincial market hall.* The Architectural Review *(March 1897)*.

FIGURE 4.2 JOHN BELCHER WITH A. BERESFORD PITE, INSTITUTE OF CHARTERED ACCOUNTANTS, CITY OF LONDON. MARTIN CHARLES / RIBA COLLECTIONS.

which] a figure has been made appears no more than so much suitable stuff for this creation'.[24]

If Thorneycroft's modelling belied the stoniness of the stone-façade, then the architectural sculptor Charles Pibworth (1878–1958) – who often worked for Holden in the first decade of the twentieth century – arguably goes to the other extreme in 'his harsh simplifications and concern to echo the geometry of the masonry block'.[25] Beattie finds in these aspects of Pibworth's work – for Holden at Bristol Central Library (1902–6), and the Law Society, Chancery Lane (1904) – another threat to the aspirations of New Sculpture; for the stone carved 'through the medium of the figure' has here come, not to life, but to an almost Neo-Classical stiffness, explaining why Holden would soon turn to the more vital carving of Jacob Epstein and Eric Gill.[26] Nonetheless, Bristol-born Pibworth's reliefs for his own city's Central Library make up one of his most impressive works; his twenty-one figures, representing characters from early English literature, occupy the lunettes over the three delicate high-waisted oriels at the centre of the library's north façade;[27] for example, the easternmost lunette has Chaucer at the centre, flanked by characters from *The Canterbury Tales*. Broad shallow buttresses frame these small oriels and lunettes and sustain the surface tension of a Bath stone façade terminated by cubic bays; each has a tall glazed oriel in deference to the adjoining mid-twelfth-century Abbey

FIGURE 4.3 *Charles Holden, Bristol Central Library, centre of the north façade. Photograph Stephen Kite.*

Gatehouse on the east, with its Norman arch and double-height late-Perpendicular oriel. Original as it is, Holden's north front is decorous in contrast to the dramatic composition disclosed on passing through the Norman arch to the back of his library. As the land slopes steeply down, the building rears up demonstrating its full height and mass, a fact dissembled by the adroit scaling of the north façade. The way the naked hemicycle of the main stair engages with the Library's sheer east end – with its blocky soaring chimney, recessed planes, and bare gable – has invited comparison with Charles Rennie Mackintosh's junction of angle-turret and abstract volumes at the south-east of Hill House, Helensburgh, also designed in 1902.[28] Influences either way cannot be proven, but vernacular dwellings and castle architecture inspired both architects. In one small study, for instance, Holden's bold pencil marks explore the library's collision of cubes and cylinders, as viewed from the south-east, capturing the essentials of volume and surface.

Holden's ideology of a nakedly expressive architecture was inspired by the sensual verse of the American transcendentalist Walt Whitman, whose *Leaves of Grass* (1855) was published in England in 1868. Holden was galvanized on being introduced to *Leaves of Grass* while in pupillage in Manchester (1892–6); Margaret Holden, his partner from 1899, said it led

FIGURE 4.4 *Charles Holden, Bristol Central Library, view from south-east. Photograph Stephen Kite.*

FIGURE 4.5 *Charles Holden, Bristol Central Library, study of south-east corner. RIBA Collections.*

him 'to an awakening consciousness of Life and an expanding spirit'.[29] Holden sings his praise of Whitman in 'If Whitman Had Been an Architect', a piece that appeared anonymously in *The Architectural Review* of June 1905.[30] In this Whitman-esque prose-poem he ends 'You [Architecture] shall be as naked as you choose', urging 'Modern Buildings' to 'Throw off your mantle of deceits: your cornices, pilasters, mouldings . . . your arts and crafty prettinesses and exaggerated techniques: behind and beyond them all hides the one I love'. And like Whitman, he hymns the heroic labour of free and democratic Man, the 'exquisite music' of 'the bricklayer laying his bricks' in tandem with the machinery of the 'derrick and steam crane'.[31] 'Thoughts For the Strong' – a follow-up text of July 1905 – also ardently argues 'that only the aboriginal force in any building may be called architecture', it praises the 'modern express locomotive [as] incomparably finer than the best work of the best architect of to-day' and again ends with a call not to be 'ashamed of our nakedness – it is in the frank confession of our nakedness that our regeneration lies'.[32] The surprising thing is that the naked surface and blocky massing is already powerfully developed at the back of Bristol Central Library, where it bears the briefest references to Medieval or Classical 'mantles'. Brian Hanson infers that around 1901, early on in his work with Percy Adams, Holden realized that his mission was to inject Adams's elegant plans with three-dimensional 'aboriginal' energy and to this end 'he constructed a design machine. Quite simply the "machine" consisted of a square of about a hundred wooden building blocks, clamped together with two clamps and all free to move up and down. In 1931 he still had this design and was still using it'.[33] Holden's 'machine' might be compared to Frank Lloyd Wright's childhood Froebel Blocks, and the configurations they also inspired of elemental planar relationships, as in Wright's blocky Unity Temple (1906) in Oak Park, Chicago – Wright was also a Whitman devotee.

Virile character – the BMA Building

Holden and Pibworth, together, were incapable of realizing such 'aboriginal force'. But Holden's encounter with the young Jacob Epstein (1880–1959), and their collaboration on the British Medical Association (BMA) Building (1906–8), created a truly Whitman-esque manifestation of the modern struggle into Life; for Nikolaus Pevsner it was 'a building with a more virile character than almost anything of that date in London'.[34] Under the name of Percy Adams, Holden's design won the competition in April 1906 for the new BMA headquarters at the western end of London's Strand (as a result Holden was promoted to a partner in 1907). As he had deferred to the Abbey Gatehouse at Bristol, so here Holden's façades acknowledge the memory of C. R. Cockerell's fine Greek Classical, Westminster Insurance Company's Offices (1832), demolished in the BMA's clearance of the site. Echoing Cockerell's proportions the façade begins as a progression of tall arched openings, divided by broad pilasters, corresponding both to Cockerell's Greek members and to the flat bands Holden had used at the Bristol Library. These lower two stories are of granite, as is the stage above where the rhythms intensify in Cubist complexity as the material segues from granite to Portland stone. The Cockerell-inspired calm ruptures, as Holden's block-machine goes into overdrive; the pilasters extend for one more level in Portland stone, then abruptly terminate; at the same point the window architraves return momentarily, only to be snapped off, permitting the surface planes to ascend unadorned. Hence, the uppermost storey can be read as both a dying echo of the classical language of shaft and support, and as a 'naked' manifesto of Whitman-esque modernity – freed from the 'mantle of deceits' of cornices, pilasters, and mouldings. At the second floor zone of material interchange, Holden described how 'a series of white sculptural figures [in Portland stone], on each side of the windows and set in a framework of dark granite, would serve to weave the two materials together like a white stitching joining a dark to a light material'.[35] Holden's design drawings show upright figures compressed between the granite architrave blades of the second floor windows and the pilasters; but what carver could be found for them, equal to the boldness of this design?

In his *Autobiography* (1940, 1955), Epstein recalls how 'one day in the spring of 1907 Mr Francis Dodd asked me if I could accept a commission from an architect he knew, and decorate a building'.[36] Dodd was an artist friend of Holden (he had painted Holden's portrait in 1917) who befriended Epstein when the young Jewish New Yorker settled in London following his studies in Paris. Growing up in the 'teeming East Side' New York of his birth, Epstein had had a picaresque boyhood of Whitman-esque vitality, as

FIGURE 4.6 Charles Holden, British Medical Association building, detail of current Agar Street façade, with defaced figures. Photograph Stephen Kite.

FIGURE 4.7 *Charles Holden, British Medical Association, The Strand façade photographed 11 July 1908 whilst under construction. Epstein's carvings are, from left to right:* Chemical Research, Hygeia, Matter, Primal Energy. *Historic England Archive.*

he writes: 'The New York of the pre-skyscraper period was my formation ground. I knew all its streets and the water-side, I made excursions into the suburbs; Harlem, Yonkers, Long Island, and Coney Island I knew well, and Rockaway where I bathed in the surf'.[37] Epstein invokes 'the city of ships of which Whitman wrote' where he avidly drew the milling immigrant races;

he was also a ' tremendous reader' consuming 'Whitman's *Leaves of Grass*, all read out of doors, amongst the rocks and lakes of the [Central] Park'.[38]

At the interface, where the façade transitions from dark granite to London's characteristic monumental material of Portland stone, Epstein carved his Portland figures out of respect to its close-grained character. Holden equally prized the weathering qualities of this limestone, maximally exploited in the city's Baroque buildings he admired by Sir Christopher Wren and Nicholas Hawksmoor. He noted how London's rain and air bleached the exposed parts of the building surface, contrasting with the sooty recesses in dramatic chiaroscuro, and he recorded how 'the surface gradually whitens to the ashen colour that is the beauty of London'.[39] Epstein's approach to carving was still evolving in 1907, and the method he adopted for this massive commission was 'impure' in view of the modernist creed of 'carving direct'; first he modelled the figures in clay (using live models), they were then cast in plaster, and only then did Epstein carve them in stone, partly in situ and partly with the help of assistants.[40] At the same time Epstein's deep respect for the architectural sculpture of the past – foremost the Elgin marbles he had studied in the British Museum – equipped him well for Holden's task. One BMA member opined that 'the decoration should consist of their historically famous medical men', but Epstein 'was determined to do a series of nude figures, and surgeons with side-whiskers, no matter how eminent, could have served my purpose as models'.[41] Epstein's scheme was better suited to the drama of life-and-death in which the medical profession was engaged, 'it consisted, for the most part, of nudes in such narrow niches that I was forced to give simple movements to all the figures. In symbolism I tried to represent man and woman, in their various stages from birth to old age – a primitive, but in no way a bizarre programme'.[42]

Epstein's naked parade of figures provoked a furore, notorious in the history of sculpture in Britain. This, together with some decay – due to the large stones being installed upright against their bedding plane – led to their ensuing mutilation as visible to this day.[43] On 27 June 1908 a *British Medical Journal* leading article mocked the ridiculous spectacle of 'the British Public in one of its periodical fits of morality' and praised the figures as 'pre-Adamite'.[44] Epstein responded warmly to this characterization and wrote to the *BMJ* on 4 July 1908 in defence of his aims:

> Apart from my desire to decorate a beautiful building, I have wished to create noble and heroic forms to express in sculpture the great primal facts of man and woman. The first figure starting on the Strand side presents Primal Energy, a symbolic male figure who, with outstretched arm in a forceful gesture as if pressing its way through mists and vapours, blows the breath of life into the atom. Next 'Matter', a figure of rude and primitive aspect, who folds in his arms a mass of rock in which is vaguely infolded the form of a child; thus form and life emerge from the inchoate and lifeless.[45]

Then, to complete this, the shorter Strand façade of the building, come the female and male forms of Hygeia (symbolic Goddess of Medicine and Health) and Chemical Research. The archaic figures express the stoniness of stone and, like Michelangelo's captives, their imprisonment in Holden's confined embrasures. Epstein sums up his statement with the desire 'to give a presentation of figures joyous, energetic, and mystical. That the figures should have an ideal aspect, be possessed of an inner life, is a requirement of sculpture, and also they should adhere to the forms of Nature, the divine aspect of bodies . . .'.[46] Epstein's men and women created a slow pulsing movement along the short (Strand) and long (Agar Street) façades alternating the forceful gestures he describes, with the still frontality of antique tomb-figures. So Primal Energy blows the 'breath of life' across the window interval to the forward-facing Matter, whose upheld 'mass of rock' symbolizes both the quarry beginnings of architecture and – in its fossil-like inscribed foetus – the inception of human-life.

The play of surface against surface: 55 Broadway (1926–9)

Twenty years later, Holden boldly approached Epstein again, tasking him with the key gateway sculptures for the headquarters for the London Underground at 55 Broadway, near St James's Park (1926–9); Adams, Holden, and Pearson had won this commission on the back of their successful series of stations for the Underground's Morden line extension (opened September 1926). In contrast to the early BMA work, here Epstein would rigorously take forward the logic of his carving principles, and Holden yet further his aspirations to a naked Modernism, while embodying his 'visions of an architecture as catholic as life itself'.[47] Brian Hanson describes 55 Broadway as the 'zenith of this catholicity' which 'comes out in the way that sculpture is used. It is a return to sculpture for the architect after what had been a long period of aesthetic sanitation, but it is so wholehearted as to reaffirm its pretty-near-central role in the whole of Holden's philosophy of architecture'.[48] Epstein's figures of Day and Night oversee the entrances at the centre of the two main façades of 55 Broadway at podium level. Much higher up the building – on the parapet of its significant sixth-floor setback – Holden called in the talents of six other sculptors, among them Eric Gill and the young Henry Moore. As we shall see, Henry Moore's anti-architect view of the sculptor's role, brings out the tension in Modernism between the idea of sculpture as a larger-scale public practice, allied to architecture, or as a more autonomous art.

As Holden explains the genesis of the building: 'The shortest way from Victoria Street to St James's Park Station was the basic factor of design and implied a cruciform plan'.[49] That cross configuration, and the set-backs for light and air required by the London Building Acts, generated the ziggurat massing of a building that rose in set-backs to a tower 175 feet high, presiding over its four spurs. It thus broke through the 80-foot building limit of the London County Council on condition that the tower was used for storage only, so for its date it was the nearest thing to a skyscraper in London, one moreover visible from Westminster Abbey. The carbon pencil perspective of *c.* 1927 – by his close friend, the great artist-etcher David Muirhead Bone – represents Broadway's sheer Portland stone surfaces, from a high viewpoint, as already grimy and weathered, as they loom over the wet pavements of a gloomy late London afternoon.[50] As an experienced hospital designer (viz. Bristol Royal Infirmary 1908–11) Holden certainly knew the sanitary logic of Alfred Waterhouse's X-plan University College Hospital

FIGURE 4.8 *Sir Muirhead Bone, perspective view from the north-east of Adams, Holden, and Pearson's New Headquarters of the London Electric Railway Company (later London Underground), 55 Broadway, Westminster. Carbon pencil, c. 1927. RIBA Collections.*

(1897–1906), which introduced light and air, and perspectival complexity to the depths of the urban block. He would also have known Arthur Beresford Pite's fantastic vision for a cruciform St Bartholomew's Hospital – published in the *Builder* of 1904 – which rears its New York-inspired 'great bluff cliffs of masonry' even above the dome of St Paul's Cathedral.[51] But in contrast to Waterhouse's turreted red terracotta façades, *Building* magazine (1931) describes how at Broadway 'plain bands have everywhere taken the place of cornices, and nothing, not even the sculpture, is allowed to interfere with the play of surface against surface or mass against mass'.[52] It is 'a bold building for its date and for London' says Pevsner, 'but still keeping a retreat open to the broad Georgian road'.[53] Despite its drama, Muirhead Bone's perspective does not indicate Holden's evolving sculptural ambitions for the building, showing merely a predictable vertical figure in a corner-niche, and tame winged logos at the set-backs.

In the perspective Holden himself drew from street-level (*c.* 1927) all is now resolved close to the executed project with energetic wind-figures at the set-backs, and Epstein's figures commanding the centres of the plinths. For Gavin Stamp this is very much 'the architect's drawing, concentrating on

FIGURE 4.9 *Charles Holden, perspective view from the north-east of Adams, Holden, and Pearson's New Headquarters of the London Electric Railway Company (later London Underground), 55 Broadway, Westminster. Pencil and wash, c. 1927. RIBA Collections.*

the massing of the design and using shadow to emphasize the pattern of recessed wall-planes building up the central tower', and showing how Holden 'conceived of all his designs in terms of cubic volumes and their outlines'.[54] Holden's sending to Gill a photograph of this drawing, with its unity of sculpture and architecture, was persuasive to that sculptor's acceptance of a key role in the building's sculptural programme.[55]

Holden's proto-Modernism mediates boldness and tradition through his humanistic embrace of the sculptor's art, and the traditional use of Portland stone surfaces pierced by apertures – disguising the steel frame. Indeed, *The Architects' Journal* of October 1929 praised the 'numerous small windows placed in horizontal tiers', in gratitude for 'a building so truly expressive of the twentieth-century spirit, which, however, does not exemplify the monstrous affectations of Modernist design which assume the form of vertical groups of windows enclosed in long slits of reveals deliberately ignoring the floor levels'. 'In spite of its great height [the building] has a pleasant human quality that does not aggressively dissociate itself from the unassuming buildings by which it is surrounded'.[56]

Henry Moore recalls Holden's fatherly approach, in 1928, when persuading him to contribute to 55 Broadway – by then Holden was fifty-three, and Moore just thirty. Holden explained that the tower of the building was inspired by the classical 'Tower of the Winds' in Athens, that it was therefore fitting that the upper reliefs should represent the winds of each quarter, and that he wanted Moore to carve the *West Wind*.[57] Although as committed as Holden to the creed of direct carving, Moore was reluctant to accept the job, for he repudiated the values of architectonic low-relief, often associated with carving, which 'symbolized for [him] the humiliating subservience of the sculptor to the architect, for in ninety-nine cases out of a hundred, the architect only thought of sculpture as a surface decoration, and ordered a relief as a matter of course'.[58] With his instinct to archaic repose, Moore was also troubled by the representation of movement implied by the 'Winds' commission, but Holden insisted that he was 'not asking [Moore] to do a sculpture which is being blown away by the wind'. So, Moore was slowly drawn to the possibilities of the project, and he 'hit on the idea of a figure suggesting a floating movement . . . [the] West, a rainier and softer wind . . .'.[59]

Tension between truth to material, and full sculptural autonomy, comes out in Moore's first important early statement in this inter-war period, his contribution to *Unit One* in 1934, the group founded by eleven avant-garde painters, sculptors, and architects formed in 1933 – Barbara Hepworth and Ben Nicholson among them. First is '*Truth to material*. . . . It is only when the sculptor works direct, when there is an active relationship with his material, that the material can take part in the shaping of an idea. Stone, for example, is hard and concentrated and should not be falsified to look like soft flesh. . . . It should keep its hard tense stoniness'.[60] But he also seeks '*Full three-dimensional realisation.* Complete sculptural expression is form in its full spatial reality. Only to make relief shapes on the surface of the block is to forego the full power of expression of sculpture'.[61] These very tensions go to make Moore's *West Wind* 'far and away the finest of all the flying figures on Holden's building'[62] in the opinion of Richard Cork. Cork closely analyses Moore's sketchbook for *West Wind* as, in page after page, the sculptor responds to the challenges set by this eight feet long figure – by far his largest to date. Multiple studies show Moore grappling between his instinct to weighty recumbent figures, the need for *West Wind* to appear airborne, and the architectonic constraints of Holden's setting. In the determining sheets the figure becomes more Cubistically angular, as it emerges from blocky marks, in overt homage to Holden's language – Holden may even have shown Moore his design 'machine'.[63] Reference can also be made to the Toltec-Maya (900–1000 CE) *Chacmool* limestone figure which Moore admired for its 'stillness and alertness . . . and the legs coming down like columns'.[64] The final figure remains massive, yet commands the moving air with the imperious gesture of its raised right hand, held against a squared countenance of moon-like melancholy. The key contours are deeply-cut to read from seven levels down, but the broad stretches of flesh defer to

FIGURE 4.10 *Henry Moore,* West Wind, *55 Broadway, north side of east wing. © TfL from the London Transport Museum. © Reproduced by permission of The Henry Moore Foundation. All Rights Reserved, DACS / www.henry-moore.org 2021.*

Holden's naked planes, as do the strong horizontals of the left arm and elevated feet and legs, faired to the air-currents. Moore roughed-out *West Wind* in his studio and completed the sculpture, in the heroic tradition of carving, 'on a scaffolding platform [in situ] where there was a space of only about three feet to stand on, and at first [he] was alarmed. It was so high up'.[65]

In the context of a Britishness of surface, Penelope Curtis argues that 'in Britain, by around 1930, there was really only one way of being modern. To be modern was to carve, and to carve abstracted forms derived from but not dependent on the human figure'.[66] Moore's rise to pre-eminence would only serve to emphasize the carving conception over that of modelling; at the same time, as noted, Moore resisted notions of carving predicated on the architectural relief. But – as with Epstein, both here and at the BMA – there was an earlier generation of sculptors, including Eric Gill (1882–1940), 'who were best known as direct carvers [and] were largely those who worked on monumental projects on the surface of the building'.[67] Gill took a leading role at Broadway, over the team of younger sculptors, where he carved a *North*, a *South*, and an *East* wind; architectural relief carving came naturally

FIGURE 4.11 *Henry Moore carving* West Wind. © *TfL from the London Transport Museum.* © *Reproduced by permission of The Henry Moore Foundation. All Rights Reserved, DACS / www.henry-moore.org 2021.*

FIGURE 4.12 *Eric Gill,* East Wind, *north side of west wing, 55 Broadway.* © TfL *from the London Transport Museum.*

to him, and his contribution was to respect Holden's 'Cathedral of Modernity'[68] while emolliating its severity with the 'organic, rounded rhythms' of his crouching impish *Winds*.[69] Gill's practice started with a William Morris, Arts and Crafts identification with medieval guilds where, as he continued to argue in a lecture on 'The Future of Sculpture' of December 1927, 'architecture must always offer the best opportunity for sculpture and the collaboration of architect and sculptor must always be the dream of both';[70] this despite his despondency as he carved at Broadway among the un-medieval furore of modern steel-frame and stone-cladding construction.

Significantly, some critics deployed Gill's Englishness of style to artfully contrive an Anglo-Saxon identity against the 'tribal' sources of Modernism, or the 'foreign' Assyrian or Mayan aspects evident in some of Epstein's work. In such theming Modelling could be viewed as a foreign Expressionism against an English carving made 'clean, moral and closely bound to the English landscape'.[71] Such critical strands are summated in Eric Underwood's *Short History of English Sculpture* of 1933:

> Gill is almost certainly the greatest carver in the world today; his work is in the purest English tradition; in it can be seen again the dramatic quality

of Saxon sculpture, the grace of Nottingham alabasters, the austere formalization of the Romanesque – this especially, the simplicity of the best Gothic and even something of these earlier and better times which still lingers in the Tudor and Stuart tombs.[72]

Some of the prejudices underlying these English–Foreign critical distinctions were laid bare in the commotion that, as at the BMA, followed the exposure to the public of Epstein's *Night* and *Day* groups. Thus the establishment Classicist Sir Reginald Blomfield protested in a letter to *The Manchester Guardian* about 'The Cult of Ugliness', deploring Epstein's 'expressionism which has ended in the grotesque' and bemoaning this parade of 'bestiality [which] still lurks below the surface of our civilization'.[73] The more understanding critic of *The Architectural Review*, Walter Bayes, thought it 'a wise provision which places the two Epstein groups on the two stretches of wall which are built on . . . a curve of an immense radius', finding 'the harshness which in these carvings shocks the tender, modern philistine is nowise excessive'.[74] As basic architectural responses Bayes found reposeful *Night* 'in touch with the main horizontal of the base of the building', while *Day*, a work of 'dominant uprights', respects Broadway's verticality if calling 'attention to the columns below which are not the happiest feature of the design' given, in his view, their over-abstracted capitals.[75] Within this horizontal and vertical contrast, Epstein pointed out that both 'the groups were pyramidal in form, just as the building is',[76] and explained that he simply 'proposed groups of *Day* and *Night* as appropriate to a building that housed offices for transport and for speed'.[77] He wrote vividly of the physical experience of their production:

> I began a six-months' work, which took me through the entire bitter winter months of 1928, working out of doors and in a draught of wind that whistled on one side down the narrow canyon of the street. I invariably began work with a terrible stomach-ache brought on by the cold. After I got over this I was all right and remained on the building until nightfall, having my lunch there, out of doors, so as not to lose time. The carvings were direct in stone, and the building was being put up at the same time. I had to be oblivious to the fact that for some time tons of stone were being hauled up above my head, on a chain, and if this chain broke . . .[78]

Truly a Carving Direct, especially as compared to his earlier hybrid processes at the BMA. Another critic sympathetic to Epstein's 'conception of architectural sculpture' – James Bone in *The Manchester Guardian* – nevertheless constantly invokes foreign metaphors, so '*Night* is a mother figure of heavy Eastern type with a male figure lying on her lap, whom she is stilling to sleep with a gesture of a mighty hand'. He concludes:

FIGURE 4.13 *Jacob Epstein with* Night, *carved on site on the north-east façade of 55 Broadway. © TfL from the London Transport Museum.*

Learned men tell us that there is nothing Assyrian or African about his art and no resemblance to Archaic rock-carving! In short they deny the art pedigree that many writers would force upon him. But if Epstein has taken his studies of these works so deeply into the body of art that they cannot be identified it only increases the suspicion that there is something new as well as something alien to our habits of thought in his sculpture.[79]

Through all this flak, Frank Pick (1878–1941) – as director of London Underground – courageously supported Holden and Epstein. Pick argued that 'we were living in a kind of robot world' as signalled by the repetitive and stark aspects of Holden's design; the work of Epstein and the other sculptors was never intended to be alien to the man- and woman-in-the-street, but to humanize this age of efficiency.[80]

Suckers for reliefs

The 1930s also saw the emergence of important art-writers such as Herbert Read (1893–1968), and the aforementioned Adrian Stokes (1902–1972); the latter's evocative prose proselytized the discipline of direct carving and, from different perspectives, supported the sculpture of both Barbara Hepworth and Henry Moore.[81] Stokes's theory of art is unabashedly founded on architecture as the mother-art. Notably, the sculptures that were the touchstone of his carving thesis, were the low-reliefs Agostino di Duccio (1418–1481) carried out in the 1440s, at the command of Sigismondo Malatesta, to adorn the chapels of his Tempio Malatestiano, in Rimini – magnificently encased by the architect Leon Battista Alberti (1404–1472). Stokes wrote out his obsessions with architectural low-relief, and carving, in his *The Stones of Rimini* of 1934, appearing at a key point in the formation of English Modernism. Enough has been said to make it clear that Moore would bridle at many of Stokes's assumptions, while accepting the 'love of stone' as fundamental to the carver's motives. In Moore we have an artist sympathetic to the ideals of carving, and a careful reader of Stokes, who rejects any architectonic basis for sculpture and the practice of carving – tensions evident in his *West Wind* at 55 Broadway. In 1961, John Russell, the art critic of *The Sunday Times* – together with his wife, Vera Russell – interviewed Henry Moore at the time of the publication of Stokes's *Three Essays on The Painting of Our Time* (1961), wherein Stokes once again expressed his long-held view of 'the primacy of architecture, mother of the arts', and its capacity – impaired, in his view, by industrialization – 'to envelop and feed us without ceremony by means of clamant textures, to enwrap us with a surface . . . .'.[82] Moore complains to Russell: 'I disagree with a lot of that making architecture the kind of touchstone . . . that sort of . . . real mother of the arts. I don't believe it'.[83] Moore argues, if this were so then Paleolithic works would have been impossible at a time when people utilized any available surface, they 'drew on sand, or drew on anywhere' – so why privilege the architectural wall over any other surface? Looking back to the 1920s and 1930s Moore remembers:

I carved because I liked it better. And in that sense I'd call myself a 'carver' rather than a 'modeller' up till a few years ago. Now I think there's no difference in whether one is better than the other, of course not – but at one time I thought there was an actual virtue in carving alone, that carving – that carved sculpture was a better kind of sculpture than modelled sculpture – for me it was.[84]

Then it had been necessary to assert truth to material, and the values of direct carving, against academic art and the use of 'pointing' technicians, but for Moore this had finally become fetishized to the point that 'a snowman made by a child would have to be praised at the expense of a Rodin or a Bernini'.[85] In November 1933 Stokes had reviewed Moore's work sympathetically in *The Spectator*, claiming his exhibition at the Leicester Galleries as 'an artistic event of the first importance' and pointing out 'several objects of a great and novel loveliness' carved in dark African wood, steatite, and even concrete (*Composition*, 1933).[86] Yet he also sensed the three-dimensional pressure in his work, realizing 'how intense has been the plastic aim behind his conception of carving'.[87] Even at this period, when most forceful in his espousal of carving, Moore could only see the relief view of sculpture of Stokes – and others carvers such as Gill – as a timid limitation, as merely a kind of 'drawing' on the architect's prescribed wall. In a statement in the *New English Weekly* of 1932, Moore complained about the 'limitation of relief' of how 'too much direct carving follows the line of least resistance, and, from too great a respect, amounting to fear of the material, remains only relief carving, a smoothed up mass with forms stuck on in relief. By expressing only lines or surfaces it loses sculptural power . . .'.[88] Speaking to the Russells he says the demand for relief is only because the architect 'always wanted an empty blank space on a building filling with decoration, and so they called in the sculptor'.[89] Moore vehemently refutes Stokes's conception of relief:

> I know it's a book on painting and I would be the first to think that Adrian is one of the most original [writers on art] – but the whole approach is through painting and quite naturally the majority of people who write about art have seen a hundred paintings for every piece of sculpture – they've been produced on a painting basis and the majority of writers on art approach sculpture from a painting point of view – Adrian certainly does – and that's what makes so many critics or writers on art suckers for reliefs, which they are. . . . Where Adrian likes his compressed reliefs and the Renaissance reliefs – it really is a painter's kind of sculpture. It's not a sculptor's sculpture in the sense of absolute full three-dimensional existence . . .[90]

In *The Stones of Rimini*, Stokes had already anticipated this criticism of low-relief from the opposite perspective; of Duccio's *Madonna and Child with Angels* in the Victoria and Albert Museum he writes: 'Consider the child of the Virgin and child piece, consider how much of his body is shown by this low relief. You say it is like painting. This as criticism means nothing to me. For I can see here and touch all the values I love in stone. Painting is an offshoot of such carving'.[91]

While Holden's architecture had offered Moore an early opportunity to work at large scale in the public realm, in the sculptor's view it had made his art subservient. A happier outcome came later in the 1930s when the architect Serge Chermayeff (1900–1996) invited Moore to carve a sculpture for the modular timber house he had designed at Bentley Wood overlooking the Sussex South Downs. As Moore stated in 1955:

> The best architects of my own generation began to think seriously about sculpture in relation to their buildings in the late thirties. And when they came round to it, some were persuaded not to have sculpture *on* a building, but *outside* it, in a spatial relation to it. And the beauty of this idea of a spatial relationship is that the sculpture must have its own strong separate identity'.[92]

Moore's describes how his *Recumbent Figure* (1938), carved in green Hornton stone, responds to Chemayeff's' 'long, low-lying building [with its] open view of the long sinuous lines of the Downs. There seemed no point in

FIGURE 4.14 *Serge Chermayeff, House at Bentley Wood, Halland, East Sussex; the garden front with Henry Moore's* Recumbent Figure *(1938) in the foreground. Architectural Press Archive / RIBA Collections. © Reproduced by permission of The Henry Moore Foundation. All Rights Reserved, DACS / www.henry-moore.org 2021.*

opposing all these horizontals. . . . So I carved a reclining figure for him, intending it to be a kind of focal point of all the horizontals . . .'.[93]

* * *

The 'English Modern' of Holden's architecture realized a proto-Modernist abstraction, between the white-architecture icons of the neo-Corbusian avant-garde, and the more overtly Classical buildings of a period which, in London, witnessed a diverse 'high point in architectural sculpture'.[94] The needs of the new century for large professional, commercial, and governmental headquarters gave architects and sculptors alike scope to define the language for an increasingly technocratic future. If many of these buildings – including those of Holden – look traditional nowadays, their architects all saw themselves as, somehow, 'Modern', and the sculpture enlivening their surfaces was integral to their variant conceptions of Modernity. Even the giant-order ionic columns of the unmitigatedly Classical Unilever House of 1930–1 (designed by house-architect J. Lomax Simpson) cloaks advanced spaces designed for cutting-edge accounting and managerial systems. Closer to Holden's proto-Modern manner was Adelaide House (completed 1924), one of the first buildings in the City of London to break from Classical precedent; designed by John Burnet and Thomas Tait, the close-set mullions of its directly expressed façades are capped by giant neo-Egyptian coves. For the main entrance William Reid Dick sculpted a figure which 'matches the stark modernity of the building, an expressionless woman holding a globe, whose body emerges from a plain stone pillar'.[95] A lot of these surfaces – both cladding and sculpture – were in stone, often the Portland stone, Holden admired, for its weathering qualities. New material combinations might be introduced by variations on Art Deco or jazz *moderne*, as in Goodhart-Rendel's St Olave's House on Hay's Wharf (1931–2). Here, the steel-frame is again clad in Portland stone, but the centrepiece of the River Thames façade has gilded faience panels, sculpted by Frank Dobson (1886–1963), and framed in black granite. Gavin Stamp gloomily concludes his rich survey of the final decade of this highly eclectic era as 'confused, tortured, depressed, vulgar, naïve and ultimately, rather unattractive'.[96] Among the confusion, however, the highpoints must include the sustained integrity of Holden's achievements. In his harnessing of Whitman-esque energies, and an appreciation for the sublimity of the USA skyscraper, to an English abstraction of surface that draws on Wren and Hawksmoor, and the Arts and Crafts traditions; he extended this love of naked stone to embrace a diversity of sculptors, each 'Modern' in representing the 'New Sculpture' and carving approaches of successive generations: Pibworth, Epstein, Gill, Moore, and others beside.

CHAPTER FIVE

Surfaces and Sharawaggi
Aspects of the Picturesque
c. 1925–55

In the Modernist and proto-Modernist examples of the last chapter – in contrast to modelling – carving signified an 'English Modern' materiality. This chapter turns to another important dialectic – that of the Rational versus the Neo-Romantic – which shaped debates in the inter-war period, through World War II itself, and for over a decade thereafter. It has been characterized as a tension between *form* and *meaning*, where *form* defines Modernism's instinct to unlocated 'international' abstraction, whereas *meaning* delimits evocative encounters with history and place.[1] Thus Nikolaus Pevsner's (1902–1983) rationalist analysis of the Englishness of the English surface, originated in his German academic training in the analysis of style relative to the *zeitgeist* – yet was located in its emphasis upon national character. Whereas atmospheric readings of the textures of British architecture and landscape – made by observers such as John Piper and John Betjeman – became labelled as Neo-Romanticism. Such rational-romantic mindsets are never unavoidably opposed, as Timothy Mowl suggests in *Stylistic Cold Wars: Betjeman versus Pevsner* (2000); among the many intersections of ideas, came a rediscovery of the powers of the British Picturesque. In the pages of *The Architectural Review*, the Picturesque was popularized as 'Sharawaggi' and *Townscape*, and vividly illustrated in Gordon Cullen's urban bricolages. While Pevsner's scholarship promulgated the Picturesque, as a Modernist tool, in the reconfiguration of the city. Both Rational and Neo-Romantic strands reached their culmination a decade after the end of World War II; Pevsner's BBC Reith Lectures of 1955, on *The Englishness of English Art*, were the culmination of musings on English art dating back to the 1920s, when he was a lecturer at Göttingen University. While Basil Spence's winning neo-Gothic design of 1951, for the competition to design a new Cathedral of St Michael at Coventry – in the context of the medieval building blitzed in November 1940 – has been read as the apotheosis of Neo-Romanticism; certainly as compared to the radical Modernist competition entries, like those designed by Alison and Peter Smithson, and Colin St John Wilson and Peter Carter.

As we saw with Ruskin and Morris, the foremost surface was that of the land itself – explicitly, in this inter-war period, the face of the British landscape. The journal *Antiquity*, founded by the field archaeologist O. G. S. Crawford (1886–1957) in 1927, was inspirational to many writers, artists, and designers in describing that land surface. As H. J. Randall wrote in *Antiquity* in March 1934, 'the face of the country is the most important historical document that we possess. Upon the map of England – "that marvellous palimpsest" – is written much of English history: written in letters of earth and stone, of bank and ditch, of foliage and crop'.[2] In her perceptive study of *Photography, Archaeology, and the British Landscape 1925–1955*, Kitty Hauser contends: 'If modernity flattened out the local and historic with its obliterating surfaces, what counter-image could be more appropriate than archaeological excavation (real or metaphorical) restoring the dimension of depth besides and beneath those surfaces?'[3] The pages of *Antiquity* would open up these surface-depths, to inspire artists such as Paul Nash and John Piper.

Crawford is also credited with the promotion of aerial archaeology in the 1920s and 1930s; from its first issue, *Antiquity* presented these new discoveries made from the air. In the *Antiquity* of March 1931, Crawford tells how aerial photography revealed the outlines of history: 'Only from an altitude of five feet or so can the pattern of a carpet be seen. . . . In just the same way crop-markings on an ancient site can only be seen properly from above'. The aerial view allows us 'to see the sweep of history rather than its details' upon the 'surface of the earth', it allows us to 'stand back and view it from a height of detachment'.[4]

John Piper never flew, but the artist was excited by such images in *Antiquity* as Wiltshire's Silbury Hill, seen from the air, in just the carpet-pattern Crawford describes. Piper's 'Prehistory from the Air', published in the final 1937 issue of the Modernist art journal *Axis*, extols such earthwork images as 'among the most beautiful photographs ever taken'.[5] Frances Spalding shows how Crawford's *Antiquity* 'convinced John [Piper] that flying served the new consciousness, and that the horizonless views offered by aerial photography echoed the flattened use of space in modernist painting'.[6] Piper's *Axis* article makes a present-ness of the past, in connecting Miró and Picasso to prehistory, and to the layered surfaces of the British Landscape. Piper's own Neo-Romanticist trajectory would see him turn sharply away from pure abstraction in 1936 – back to the object, to topography, and to intense depictions of the surfaces of architecture. Influenced by Christopher Hussey's *The Picturesque: Studies in a Point of View* (1927), the paintings he then produced of the great landscapes of the English Picturesque tradition, such as Stourhead and Hafod, retained the flatness and pattern of Cubist and Surrealist experiment.[7] So too, in 'England's Early Sculptors' (*The Architectural Review*, 1 October 1936), Piper casts the Romanesque carvers of churches, such as Kilpeck, as 'forebears of the pure abstractionists of today'.[8] This 'figure sculpture grew out of abstract pattern, and retired back into it at intervals'; for Piper, it is an art 'that shows a specially English character [that] was nourished from many sources. Celtic, Norse and Byzantine . . .'.[9] This is an 'obviously linear art', and this idea of an English fondness for 'unrelenting line', and indulgence in surface pattern, is one that Nikolaus Pevsner would develop as a key aspect of his *The Englishness of English Art* (1956). From the celebrated Herefordshire school of early sculptors – of which Kilpeck Church is the outstanding example – comes the Christ-in Majesty tympanum at Rowlestone where, writes Piper, 'a sustained line is used in a most subtle way to charge a design which is at once rhythmical and rigid . . .'. In *The Englishness of English Art*, Pevsner includes a chapter on William 'Blake and the Flaming Line' as a culmination of these linear qualities. And – in the context of Rowlestone's tympanum – Piper quotes Blake as an exemplar of this 'specially English genius . . . for making a line at once create a shape and enrich it with meaning as part of a whole design . . .'. In Blake's own words:

> Firm and determinate lineaments unbroken by shadows, which ought to display and not hide the form. . . . Leave out this line and you leave out life itself; all is chaos again, and the line of the Almighty must be drawn out upon it before man or beast can exist.[10]

FIGURE 5.1 *Christ in Majesty tympanum, St Peter's, Rowlestone, Herefordshire, England. Photograph Stephen Kite.*

Sharawaggi and Townscape

The *Architectural Review* was central to architectural discourse in the 1930s and 1940s, as its owner-editor Hubert de Cronin Hastings strove to popularize architectural Modernism in Britain, through a diverse cast of contributors including Paul Nash and John Piper, J. M. Richards, John Betjeman, Nikolaus Pevsner, and Gordon Cullen. He drew together these potentially inchoate strands of landscape-readings, Surrealism, Abstraction, Neo-Romanticism, and Rationalism, under the native umbrella of the Picturesque, to produce the urban design creed of 'Townscape'. Writing as 'the Editor' – and later, under the pseudonym of Ivor de Wolfe – Hastings's first foray into print was in January 1944: 'Exterior Furnishing or Sharawaggi: The Art of Making Urban Landscape'.[11] In this essay Hastings sought to 'find a picture' of the Modernist urban landscape acceptable to 'my non-technical fellow-countrymen', one that would give 'a vivid impression of the good [Modernist] things coming to them ....'.[12] Strongly influenced by the 'principles which have been described in a masterly way in Christopher Hussey's *The Picturesque*' (1927),[13] Hastings invoked '*Picturesque Theory*' as 'a national picture-making aptitude', which could be translated as a tool – from its origins in the eighteenth-century landscape – to the understanding and acceptance of the Modernist city. In *The Picturesque* Hussey had reasoned that 'now that town and village planning has received the attention it demands [Uvedale] Price's [1747–1829] observations on the subject are, historically, of considerable interest. No branch of architecture is so closely connected with the picturesque ...'.[14] In his observations 'On Architecture and Buildings', Uvedale Price contends that architects and town-planners could learn much from 'the best old masters of landscape painting, particularly of Poussin' in composing a varied topography:

> In situations of that kind, were an architect with a painter's eye, *to have the planning of the whole*, he would have the opportunity of producing the richest effects, by combining his art with that of painting – by varying the characters of the buildings, and particularly of their summits, according to the place which they were to occupy.[15]

Hussey cites Price's favourable view of Tivoli where 'the general outline of the town appears to yield and vary according to the shape of its foundations with now and then a counteracting line that gives a zest and spirit to the composition ...'.[16] In contrast, on his approach to Bath, Price was disappointed by the city's failure to exploit the opportunities of its varied topography to produce similar painterly effects.

Turning to the conception of 'Sharawaggi', Hastings credits the landscape architect Christopher Tunnard for 'bringing this noble word back into circulation' in his study of Modernist garden-making, *Gardens in the*

Modern Landscape of 1938. Tunnard's book gathered together a series of articles that he had published in *The Architectural Review* between October 1937 and September 1938, such as 'Colour and the Cottage Garden' of January 1938, where he praises 'the more important of the eighteenth-century contributors to the art of garden design – the theorists of Sharawadgi'.[17] These were designers 'who had no faith in mathematics and defied irregularity; who found beauty in infinite variety and treated natural material according to that material's own potential organic pattern'.[18] Sharawadgi, as a term in English landscape writing, can be tracked back to 1685 when Sir William Temple, writing on the 'Gardens of Epicurus', finds most beauty in gardens that are formal and regular while admitting that 'there may be other Forms wholly irregular, that may, for ought I know, have more Beauty than any of the others . . .'.[19] Temple had heard of the buildings and plantings of the Chinese:

> Their greatest Reach of Imagination, is employed in contriving Figures, where the Beauty shall be great, and strike the Eye, but without any Order or Disposition of Parts, that shall be commonly or easily observed. And though we have hardly any Notion of this Sort of Beauty, yet they have a particular Word to express it; and where they find it hit their Eye at first Sight, they say the *Sharawadgi* is fine or admirable . . .[20]

Temple has provoked much discussion on the etymology of this term; one theory points to a possible source in the Japanese word *sawaraji*, meaning 'Let's not touch', or 'Leave things as they are'.[21] The concept was taken up by the great eighteenth-century arbiter of taste, Horace Walpole, who claimed to be 'almost as fond of the Sharawaggi, or Chinese want of symmetry in buildings, as in grounds or gardens'[22] – as is confirmed by the sharawaggi of his own villa at Strawberry Hill, Twickenham (1753–76).

The Architectural Review used lively visualizations to advance its Picturesque-Modernist agenda, notably through the dazzling draughtsmanship of Gordon Cullen. In Hastings's 'Exterior Furnishing' article (January 1944), the painter Kenneth Rowntree illustrated sharawaggi in vignettes, and in a striking half-page urban panorama that sweeps from the interior of a decorator's shop to take in High-Modernist flats, a cottage-ornée, a Victorian pub, and industrial artefacts, including a railway signal and a gasometer; they all pop up above a garden wall, collaged from bricks, random stonework, timber planks, cast-iron railings, and shrubbery. Hastings's caption to this image enjoins us to match 'the variety of shape, pattern and texture in the ornaments, wallpapers, fabrics' with 'an equally generous variety of shape, pattern, texture and vegetation in our urban exteriors. Make Highpoint lie down with the Victorian pub and the barge-boarded villa. Enjoy the railway signal and the rough stone wall and the pylon by the church'.[23] Highpoint is the neo-Corbusian slab-block that, in Rowntree's drawing, rises over the cottage-ornée; controversially, Highpoint

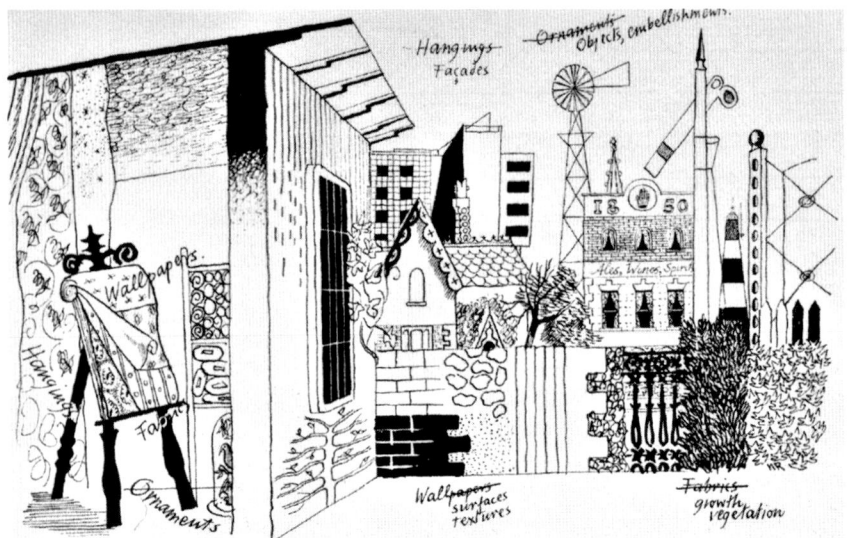

FIGURE 5.2 *Kenneth Rowntree, urban panorama of 'sharawaggi'.* The Architectural Review *(January 1944).*

had already lain down with the Victorian pub in the eyes of some hard-line modernists – Highpoint II that is. The Highpoint I flats in Highgate, London (1933–5) had been designed by Berthold Lubetkin, and the team of 'Tecton' he had assembled. Lubetkin was a Russian émigré, and the most outstanding architect working in Britain in the 1930s; another key example – along with that of Pevsner – of the major contributions émigrés made to British culture in this period. In its pure translation of Le Corbusier's 'five points of a new [white] architecture' to these eight-storey slabs, poised on pilotis, at the top of Highgate Hill – Highpoint I had unimpeachable High-Modernist credentials. Highpoint II (1936–8) took a markedly different direction; its massing aligned with Highpoint I, but it forsook its International Style purity, ingratiating itself into the English scene with texturally richer surfaces, and the notorious Surrealist-Classical introduction of Greek caryatids to support the concrete *porte-cochère*. *The Architectural Review* of October 1938 welcomed the change from the 'essentially diagrammatic' character of the first Highpoint towards 'a surface of more character and permanence': 'In the new block ... the conscious accentuation of certain forms and the variety of the materials used give a more human character to a façade that reads as a more deliberate architectural composition.'[24] An accompanying photograph of the entrance façade shows the richer palette produced in this transition from the Purist white planes of Highpoint I, to a more located richness; at Highpoint II, modulated concrete fins, framing panels of brickwork and glazed tiles, rise above the contentious caryatids. All this made Highpoint II a *cause célèbre*; for some the very deliberation in

FIGURE 5.3 *Tecton Architects, Highpoint II, North Hill, Highgate, London: the porte-cochère. Architectural Press Archive / RIBA Collections.*

composition was suspiciously historicist – even neo-Palladian; a young socialist architect, Anthony Cox, saw this as a formalist anti-societal 'turning inwards towards private formal meanings', and as a 'symptom of decline'.[25] From the standpoint of making a more rhetorical and historically contextual people's Modernism, Lubetkin may have been influenced by the turn in Soviet Russia to Socialist Realism; the façade-making of Highpoint II would also prove to be influential in the immediate post-World War II decades.[26] John Allan concludes that 'in architectural terms the situation might be crudely defined as the point in modernism's development at which the problems of surface and scale were added to the more familiar themes of mass and volume'.[27] And he points out that Lubetkin's rich autodidactic experience – encompassing Russian Orthodox iconography, Constructivist agitprop, and the work of Auguste Perret – ensured that his Modernism was never reductive; for both the Russian Orthodox iconostasis, and the mass-appeal placard, 'exploited the flat surface ... to produce cumulative installations of declamatory power'.[28]

Beyond any agendas Tecton might have had, there was the native conservatism in which the group had to operate, these anti-Modernist instincts had been given sharper bureaucratic teeth by the Town and Country Planning Act of 1932 (in law from April 1933) – Highpoint I had been approved just prior to this. The Highgate Preservation Society was formed to prevent any repeat of the 'vandalism' of Highgate I in the 'old village'. In *The Architectural Review* of 1 October 1938, a Gordon Cullen drawing showed the tweedy and pin-striped residents of Highgate on the march, waving banners proclaiming 'St George for Merrie England' and 'My Village for Ever', through streets that were already a Sharawaggi potpourri of 'stuccoed Regency houses, modern Gothic buildings in red brick and pseudo Georgian and Tudor villas' alongside the flats of Highgate I.[29] Highpoint II's heterogeneous surface syntax also emerged from extended negotiations with a Council that could now exercise a degree of aesthetic control.

Over the Highpoint-like flat-block in his Sharawaggi drawing, Rowntree strikes through 'Hangings' to write 'Façades'; within the decorator's booth he notates the 'wallpapers' on their rack, the samples of 'hangings' and 'fabrics', and the 'ornaments'; then, out in the urban scene – along with the 'Hangings' that have become 'Facades' – 'Ornaments [become] Objects, embellishments', 'Wallpapers [become] surfaces, textures' and 'Fabrics [become] growth, vegetation'. In agreement with Rowntree's panorama, Hastings finds the 'interior pattern' becoming the 'exterior pattern', as he holds out the possibility that 'the urban planner's job [might become] one of Exterior Furnishing'.[30] This trajectory in Modernism aligns with those trends we found in the work of William Morris, whereby distinctions of high and low art, architecture and ornament, public and domestic, interior and exterior, house and garden, elided into a continuum of layered pattern.

As the rediscoverer of the virtues of Sharawaggi, Christopher Tunnard led the way – both in his work, and in the ideas summated in *Gardens in the Modern Landscape* – towards an interdisciplinary vision of modern architecture and organic landscape design. *Gardens in the Modern Landscape* harnesses Gordon Cullen's representations to these new ways of seeing, wherein his 'preferences for abstraction over the illusionistic rendering of nature and his emphasis on surface' conveys a holistic vision of architecture and landscape – including houses by Raymond McGrath and Serge Chermayeff.[31]

Serge Chermayeff's Bentley Wood, as well as being one of the outstanding modern houses of the later 1930s, was notable for its Tunnard landscape design. In *Gardens in the Modern Landscape*, Tunnard captions the Cullen image as 'House and garden near Halland, Sussex', pointing out that 'except in the immediate surroundings of the house the arrangements of the beds and borders is of a non-architectural character. Irregular [Sharawaggi?] "atmospheric" plantations of flowering trees and shrubs link the house to the landscape'.[32] From a ground-level viewpoint Cullen's drawing layers the composition of house and garden as three distinct planes: a foreground sharawaggi of trees and natural meadow planting (including an alert hare), a middle plane made by the white wooden frame which marks the end of a terrace, and the modular timber rhythms of the distant house itself. Behind the frame, an abstract sculpture is indicated which would become Henry Moore's Hornton Stone figure, as described previously. In his collaboration

FIGURE 5.4 *Gordon Cullen, drawing of 'House and garden near Halland, Sussex' (Bentley Wood), garden designed by Christopher Tunnard*. The Architectural Review (April 1938). © Gordon Cullen Estate.

with Chermayeff, Tunnard wrote of their desire for 'an atmospheric planting showing an architectural character; a free yet controlled scheme, related but in contrast to the formality of the building. It was a subjective and essentially picturesque scheme which we eventually made'.[33] Tunnard had previously worked on a landscape in relation to a house by Raymond McGrath at St Ann's Hill, Chertsey, Surrey in 1935–6. In illustrating this and other projects, such as another McGrath house at Cobham in Surrey, Cullen elects for a high viewpoint rendering distant parts of the image as a flat backdrop, and folding foregrounds steeply down to the picture-plane, as in a Post-Impressionist still-life.[34]

In *The Architectural Review* of December 1949 – in 'Townscape: A Plea for an English Visual Philosophy Founded on the True Rock of Sir Uvedale Price' – Hastings (writing under his *nom-de-plume* of Ivor de Wolfe) formalized Sharawaggi as 'Townscape', as a 'radical principle' which in its individualistic and empirical 'way of looking at the world ... might be called perennially *English*'.[35] In the role of modern Sharawag, the 'radical planner has to produce his practical surrealist picture' out of the assorted givens of the urban spectacle. And, as he had done in 'Exterior Furnishing', he lists the motley urban bric-à-brac out of which this picture might be composed: 'one public-house gasolier, one bus stop, two public lavatories, one Underground station entrance, one manhole cover, . . . six plane trees, Teas with Hovis, the neon sign of the flower shop and a hundred and fifty horizontal windows . . .'.[36] Wolfe's wordy manifesto for this 'English Visual Philosophy' of a radical Picturesque has only one introductory image – a floor-scape photograph of kerb, drain-cover, and cobbles. But it leads immediately to Cullen's 'Townscape Casebook', marking his debut as a Townscape advocate. Here he makes a compelling case for a picturesque-modern visual sensibility though a lively compilation of drawings and photographs showing the eye-in-action as 'fandancer', 'netter', 'movie-camera', 'exterior decorator', etc.[37] In this pressing of the urban spectacle to the picture-plane and the retina, Mira Engler stresses Cullen's insistence on flatness as central to Townscape, for it concerned the face of things:

> [Urban] landscape is first and foremost a problem of appearance, of surface. It is a facial trait, of which a painter is continually aware. Cullen's act of flattening the city into surfaces, of extricating depth from urban space and striving for abstraction in order to see things objectively was consistent with his modern propensities. At the same time, much like his modernist predecessors, he used flatness to heighten the visual experience, to treat the city with the sensibility of atmosphere . . .[38]

Introducing his 'Casebook', Cullen accordingly makes a distinction between 'the associational and the objective' modes of seeing; in the predominant associative mode the front door signals 'home', whereas objectively it is an abstract 'rectangle of colour'. Supporting Ivor de Wolfe, Cullen urges an 'Art of the ensemble' to isolate and objectify our urban responses, while communicating them more intensely.[39] This collage-like flatness underpins all the categories of the 'Casebook'; palpably in sections such as the 'eye as painter', with images of 'floorscape', 'road surfaces', and 'wallscape', 'under [which] heading can be listed all the joys of colour, texture, creeper and weathering . . .', and 'Publicity' where Cullen enjoys how the super-graphics of 'advertising material' transform a building into 'a vivid and colourful incident'.[40] In the 'eye as matchmaker' Cullen argues for richer social imbrications than the monotony produced by the supposedly 'colourful occupation' of the two-dimensional 'zoning on paper' of functional town-planning. Instead, he shows the 'town overlaps' of real 'multiple use' where – through the legs of a giant crane – we glimpse boats and a busy river-life, a 'Bear Garden' public-house, and lorries serving workshops.[41]

'Cullen's fixation on the surfaces of the city' produced numerous essays on wallscapes and floorscapes.[42] Thus in 'The Wall', in *The Architectural Review* of November 1952, a spirited Cullen drawing frames a fragment of spot-lit wall, as seen through the window from a bar's shadowy interior. This arbitrary cropping – of segmental pediments, a statue's feet, a streetlamp, and a drainage pipe cranking downwards – awakes 'the painter's eye' to the wall's 'qualities of colour and texture, shadow and pattern and a sense of the inherent strangeness of structural and mechanical shapes'.[43] In all the images – whether stucco from France, ceramic from Brazil, or flint nodules from Norfolk – the 'walls are looked at as pictures . . . then to a large extent they become pictures, abstract to be sure, but no longer trivial or empty'.[44] In these

FIGURE 5.5 *Gordon Cullen, illustration for 'The Wall'*. The Architectural Review *(November 1952)*. © *Gordon Cullen Estate.*

respects, Townscape drew regular criticism from critics such as Joseph Rykwert (*Zodiac*, September 1959) who mistook this fascination with surfaces as a denial of the structural and social conditions of the city.[45] Surfaces *can* be superficial, and in concluding *The Picturesque*, Hussey accuses its lesser painters of a practice so 'preoccupied with surface [that it] does not feel intensely. It makes pictures but not art'.[46] These are the artists that Ruskin ranked as the Lower Picturesque. Yet even these figures opened the way to a deeper abstract vision which could 'pierce through the substance to the life', as do the works of Constable, Cézanne, and their heirs.[47] Cullen's complex picture-planes make him a perceptive heir to their discoveries.

Cullen's articles were summated in the sumptuous publication of his *Townscape* in 1961; over 300 pages of matt and gloss paper, climaxing with a portfolio of 'Proposals' strikingly imaged in full-page three-colour printing.[48] But the version that became popular was the much abbreviated *The Concise Townscape* (1971), of ten years later, which unfortunately dropped Cullen's imaginative picturesque-modern 'Proposals', such as 'Bankside Regained' – his unsought contribution to the proposed South Bank 1951 Festival of Britain, and first published in *The Architectural Review* of January 1949.[49] The centrepiece was an extended riverside pier hugging the arc of the Thames; Cullen collages the colourful accents of pennants, flags, and large-scale graphics onto an equally insistent monochrome field of – to take one view – café life, dancers, and the silhouette of the Houses of Parliament. Deanna Petherbridge explains how Picasso and Braque's Cubist experiments exploited monochromy to unify the visual field and 'to dismiss the traditional straitjacket of volumetric modelling, perspectival construction and pictorial depth . . .'.[50] Cullen's knowingly cinematic *grisaille* reprises unified surfaces of prismatic parts; in another view the sharp shadow of Waterloo Bridge arcs over the free-form flux of the muddy Thames, across a river-edge panorama of boats, terraces, graphics, and buses.

In the 1940s, when Townscape's cut-and-paste urbanism was being formulated, Britain's inhabitants were everyday confronted by the starker bricolages of blitzed cities. On *The Architectural Review*'s cover of January 1944, Sharawag artist Kenneth Rowntree découpages Alvar Aalto's gleaming Paimio Sanatorium (completed in 1932), seen through the Gothic arch of a bombed-out church, as a vision of the National Health Service which the nation had promised itself at the war's unforeseen end – the D-Day invasion of France still lay five months away. In 'The Architecture of Destruction' (*The Architectural Review*, July 1941) John Piper strove to see, beyond the immediate horror of 'a ruin manufactured in a night', how these 'instant ruins' could be as poetic as any other, as just 'like a travel-book watercolour of a Luxor temple'.[51] His pen drawings suggest the sudden shadows of many roofless naves; the 'Church of the Holy Innocents, Knowle, Bristol' has a 'nave de-roofed and arcades riven by a direct hit. Polychrome brick of the interior walls – yellow, purple, red – disclosed in all its garish majesty.

SURFACES AND SHARAWAGGI 137

FIGURE 5.6 *Gordon Cullen, illustration for 'Bankside Regained'.* The Architectural Review *(January 1949).* © *Gordon Cullen Estate.*

FIGURE 5.7 *Kenneth Rowntree, cover of* The Architectural Review *(January 1944).*

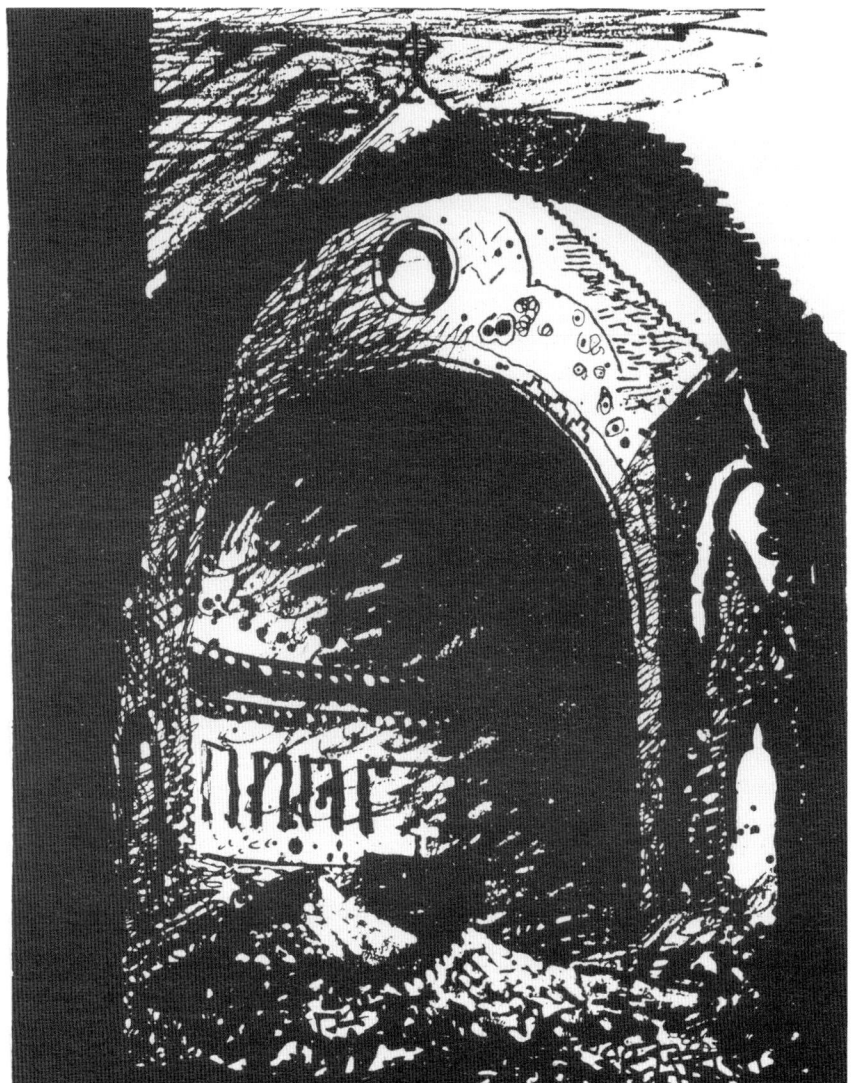

FIGURE 5.8 *John Piper, 'Church of the Holy Innocents, Knowle, Bristol'.* The Architectural Review *(July 1941).* © *The Piper Estate / DACS 2022.*

Apsidal sanctuary with coved plaster ceiling, red dado and mosaic decoration, still complete. Altar strewn with rubble and twisted iron'. At St Andrew's, Clifton, Bristol (bombed 1940) he describes:

> the walls of the church pitted, but standing, forming an enormous lidless stone box. Matrices of a collection of torn-off wall tablets framed in their black surrounds. The poor-rich ogee decoration framing the chancel arch

shredded, and disclosing itself as plaster. Panels of stained glass with transfer pattern lying on the ground among the slates . . .'[52]

In the aftermath of the war, in 'Pleasing Decay' in *The Architectural Review* of September 1947, Piper reflected further on 'the beauty as well as the horror of bomb damage', how it 'has revealed new beauties in unexpected appositions' as a stimulus to architects and town-planners 'who would retain picturesque elements from the past that can be opposed in size, colour and shape to new buildings and groups of buildings whether by way of contrast or agreement'.[53] In thus making a painter's Neo-Romanticist contribution to the visual philosophy of the post-war urban landscape, Piper appeals to Ruskin's notion of 'parasitical sublimity' whereby the Picturesque draws for its effects on characteristics more intrinsic to the sublime, such as 'angular and broken lines, vigorous oppositions of light and shadow, and grave, deep, or boldly contrasted colour'.[54] With earlier masters such as Cotman and Utrillo, Piper invoked Picasso and Matisse, Ernst and Miró, to reinforce this visuality of 'pleasing decay'.

Pevsner's Picturesque

Notwithstanding its catholic embrace of the incongruous, Sharawaggi and Townscape set a fundamentally hardcore Modernist agenda, whereas Piper's feeling for genius-loci, admixed with doses of Surrealism, contributed a Neo-Romanticist sensibility. To these harder and softer readings of the Picturesque, Nikolaus Pevsner brought the scholarly rigour of his native German training in the formal analysis of art in relation to the *zeitgeist* and to national character. Although it was Hastings's insight to recognize the potential of Hussey's *The Picturesque* to the contemporary problems that Townscape addressed, he valued the contribution of a true scholar, as Pevsner recalled:

> [H. de Cronin Hastings] had read Christopher Hussey's *The Picturesque*, the great classic of the movement. . . . I also had of course read the book – even several years before I settled down in England, but purely as a piece of English art history. It was de Cronin Hastings who dropped a remark in his studiedly casual way indicating that surely Hussey's *Picturesque* and our day-to-day work for the *Review* were really the one and same thing. This is what set me off. With de Cronin's blessing I started on a book whose subject was just this aside of the great pathfinder. In the end the book was never written, and instead only a few papers on the Georgian Picturesque came out, all but one in the *Review*.[55]

Hastings had appointed Pevsner as acting editor of *The Architectural Review* in 1942, succeeding J. M. Richards, for the duration of the war. The 'few papers' for the *Review* included 'The Genesis of the Picturesque' (1 November 1944) (beginning with Sir William Temple in 1685), and 'Sir William Temple and Sharawaggi' (with S. Lang, 1 December 1949). The untitled manuscript of the book has now been reconstructed and published as *Visual Planning and the Picturesque* (2010).[56] Pevsner's tour of Oxford, published in *The Architectural Review* of August 1949, as 'Reassessment 4: Three Oxford Colleges', drew on his research material for the book. What needs to be reassessed, argues Pevsner, is that received continental history of urbanism which measures success according to 'the degree to which plans of towns or districts approximate the perfection of all-round symmetrical ornament' where, insofar as Britain figures at all, it is the set-pieces such as Sir Christopher Wren's geometric plan for London, or the Royal Crescent at Bath, that are isolated for examination. Whereas, Pevsner argues, 'what matters is not the [Bath] Circus or the Crescent as such, but the picturesque way in which such set pieces are placed as accents in an informal composition'.[57] Pevsner structured his article as pedestrian walks through the Oxford colleges of Christ Church, Corpus Christi, and Magdalen, using the longstanding device of serial vision, and highlighting the key transitions and arrivals in the journey with commissioned photographs by Helmut Gernsheim. Pevsner knew the potential of this device from many sources, not least from how Camillo Sitte linked a rich pedestrian experience to organic urban morphologies in his *Der Städtebau* of 1889. In linking serial vision to Townscape in this way Pevsner anticipated Cullen, but although Cullen was not an architectural historian, he would make the serial vision, in his own image, with dazzling interplays of graphic imagination *and* photography.

As example, take the first of Pevsner's college tours – through Christ Church, and into Corpus Christi College – where he leads the reader on a picturesque perambulation in which passages of spatial compression and release yield the prospects staged in the photographs. Along with the excitement of these spatial transitions he alerts the reader to the surface-palette of smooth and rough textures produced, either by design, or by the natural processes of weathering and growth. In the first photograph, the gatehouse to Christ Church confronts the reader, Pevsner points to 'the old lime tree by St. Aldates's Church and the dark, rough wall of Pembroke against the much more polished wall surfaces of Christ Church [as] a setting after our picturesque tastes', making these accidents of texture equal in visual importance to Sir Christopher Wren's soaring Gothick-style gate-tower.[58] Here Pevsner consciously invokes Uvedale Price's formulation of 'roughness' as 'the most essential point of difference between the *beautiful*, and the *picturesque*'; how it arises from roughness joined to 'sudden variation' and 'irregularity'; how 'smoothness . . . conveys the idea of repose; roughness, on the contrary, conveys that of irritation, but at the same time of animation, spirit, and variety'.[59] Such picturesque alternations of smooth-rough, formal-irregular, and compression-release orchestrate the entire sequence. From the 'sunny breadth and smooth lawn' of the vast Tom Quad, confined transitions

FIGURE 5.9 *'Three Oxford Colleges by Nikolaus Pevsner'*. The Architectural Review *(1 August 1949). Tom Quad, Christ Church, Oxford. RIBA Collections.* © *Helmut Gernsheim – Curt-Engelhorn-Stiftung, Mannheim.*

lead towards Peckwater Quadrangle where 'rough walls on the left and right' and 'trailing-down wild *Vitis Coignetiae*' frame 'the smooth, trim Palladian wing of Peckwater' ahead. Turning, beyond 'the zone of vegetation' there is a 'return to pure stone-scape' where now the contrast is between smoothly genteel Palladianism and the, then, 'flaking stonework' of the giant orders of

FIGURE 5.10 *'Three Oxford Colleges by Nikolaus Pevsner'*. The Architectural Review *(1 August 1949). Passage leading from Tom Quad to Peckwater. RIBA Collections.* © *Helmut Gernsheim – Curt-Engelhorn-Stiftung, Mannheim.*

the vast Baroque Library.[60] The sequence continues 'a few steps down Merton Street', and into Corpus Christi College.

To these picturesquely inflected readings of surface and space Pevsner brought the methodologies of his intense training in Germany, extending from the beginnings of his study of the history of art, at the University of Munich in 1921, to his exile to England, following his official dismissal

FIGURE 5.11 *'Three Oxford Colleges by Nikolaus Pevsner'*. The Architectural Review *(1 August 1949). Cleft leading to Peckwater. RIBA Collections.* © *Helmut Gernsheim – Curt-Engelhorn-Stiftung, Mannheim.*

from Göttingen University in September 1933 under the Nazi race-laws. His doctorate under Wilhelm Pinder had examined the Baroque architecture of his home town of Leipzig and was published in 1928 as *Leipziger Barock. Die Baukunst der Barockzeit in Leipzig*. In contrast to the tectonic rigour of the Baroque of feudal Dresden, in that of bourgeois Leipzig there is 'the treatment of the façade as a homogeneously decorated surface'.[61] As in Leipzig's Old Stock Exchange (Alte Börse), where the pilasters of the cubic building are covered by long, thick garlands which make 'the tectonic value of the supports [to be] limited, nearly destroyed'.[62] One major influence to Pevsner's thinking was Heinrich Wölfflin, whose *Kunstgeschichtliche Grunbegriffe* (*Principles of Art History*, 1915) conceptualizes a movement, from the linearity of Classical art and architecture, towards the 'painterly' (*das Malerische*) of the Baroque and Rococo. The 'painterly' refers to the pictorial effects of the Baroque and Rococo where, writes Wölfflin, there is 'this impression of the becoming, of the unresting . . .', seen at one extreme in the 'ornamentation such as rococo art strews over its surfaces [which] produces the impression that it is in constant change'.[63]

Of equal importance to Pevsner's methodology was the other great German art historian of that era, August Schmarsow who – in *The Essence of Architectural Creation* (1893) – developed the view of architecture as essentially a spatial art. Refuting Gottfried Semper's view of architecture as an 'art of dressing' he postulated an 'aesthetics from within', based on a psychology of interior space, in difference to Wölfflin's 'aesthetics from without'. For Schmarsow, then, architecture 'is the history of the sense of space' and is in its essence a 'spatial construct'.[64] Both these 'within' and 'without' – space and surface – strands of German aesthetics exist in tension in Pevsner's introduction to *An Outline of European Architecture* (1943) where 'what distinguishes architecture from painting and sculpture is its spatial quality. . . . The history of architecture is primarily a history of man shaping space . . .'. But it is not exclusively so, for 'besides enclosing space, the architect models volume and plans surface . . .'.[65] Just prior to his exile, Pevsner clearly laid out the crux of his methodology in a German article of 1934: 'Research in art history must take on board, with passion, two highly important tasks: the sociology of art and the geography of art; that is the history of art and its connections with society and with the nation'.[66] Wölfflin had ended *Principles of Art History* with speculations on such 'National Characteristics', on how, within a certain homogeneity in European culture, 'we must reckon with the permanent differences of national types'; for example, Wölfflin contrasted an appetite for atmospheric 'unclearness' in northern architecture, to the corporeal south, where man is the 'measure of all things'.[67] Pevsner inherited the notion of a geography of art from his much admired teacher Pinder, who had taken up the task of developing these national characteristics into a whole *Kunstgeographie* (geography of art). Pinder's own flawed career demonstrates how such geographically racial ideas can elide into racism, as in his identification with Nazi xenophobia in the 1930s.

How did these German incubated notions of space, surface, and the geography of art outlast Pevsner's actual encounter with the multifarious, and often moribund, condition of British architecture as he encountered it in the 1930s? He had already developed some interest in English architecture, and had visited the country in 1930 to prepare for a course of lectures on English art and architecture at Göttingen University, where English culture was a specialism. On settling in Britain, his celebrated inter-war book, *Pioneers of the Modern Movement* (1936), had pulled together his work on the nineteenth-century origins of the Modern Movement in Britain and Germany, but had stopped at the boundary of the New Age itself. Then in 1938–9 he had planned a special issue for *The Architectural Review* of December 1939 examining the impact in Britain of the Modern Movement, an issue that came to nothing with the outbreak of war in September 1939. However, his planned essay on 'The Modern Movement in Britain' survives in manuscript and shows him – having established Modernism's origins in Victorian Britain in *Pioneers* – trying to discover to what extent Britain had taken up the Modernist baton which, in the interim, had passed to Germany and France.[68]

His essay insists that architecture 'is primarily the art of space, as sculpture is that of volume and painting that of the plane', but he concedes that 'on the whole it can safely be said that spatial movement is not what British architects wish to express in their buildings'.[69] This demonstrates longevity in the national character, for if 'the French medieval cathedral is a ravishing spatial unity, the English is a complex group of separate blocks (two transepts, not one!) screened off from each other . . .'.[70] Notwithstanding this resistance to an 'art of space' *per se*, and the predilection to the surface qualities of the picture-plane, Pevsner rejects the argument that 'the Modern Movement is essentially un-English in spirit'. For, returning to the Gothic, look at the fourteenth-century invention of the English Perpendicular which is a thoroughgoing rational 'style based entirely on hard uprights and horizontals'.[71] Significant also is the 'typically British' reversion to the traditional material of brick in its modernist architecture: 'Why has even Mr Lubetkin used brick at Highpoint II (although in almost as sophisticated a way as he used the Erecthaeum figures) . . . and Mr Goldfinger in his [terrace] house at the bottom of Downshire Hill, Hampstead . . .? Obviously, brick must have something extremely appealing and convincing for the English atmosphere, if it could attract these foreign architects working in London'.[72]

The theme of an English geography of art is powerfully revisited – much validated by his research on the Picturesque – in Pevsner's famous Reith Lectures on *The Englishness of English Art*. Pevsner was invited in the winter of 1954 to contribute to this series, inaugurated by the British Broadcasting Corporation (BBC) in 1948 in honour of is first Director-General, John Reith.[73] The lectures were broadcast in October and November 1955, published thereafter in *The Listener*, and finally in expanded form in Pevsner's book of the same title of 1956. Pevsner confessed the influence of the Viennese art historian Dagobert Frey, whose *The English Character as Reflected in English Art* (*Englisches Wesen in der bildenden Kunst*) of 1942, he thought 'written with great acumen, sensitivity and remarkably wide knowledge'. But was anxious to claim that Frey's work 'is absolutely free of any hostile remarks, let alone any Nazi bias . . .'.[74] Yet Frey is known to have willingly utilized the theories of the German anthropologist Egon Freiherr von Eickstedt, an enthusiastic Nazi member and founder of the *Zeitschrift für Rassenkunde* (*Journal of Racial Science*).[75] In conclusion to the book of his Reith Lectures, Pevsner questions that 'racial status is of use in explaining [an individual artist's] art', sceptically citing Frey on William Hogarth's origins 'in the direction of an Anglo-Mediterranean type on a Celtic-West English-Welsh sub-stratum'. But then, in the same breath, himself falls into the same racial trap: 'To this day there are two distinct racial types recognizable in England, one tall with long head and long features, little facial display and little gesticulation, the other round-faced, more agile, and more active'.[76] At the same time, *Kunstgeographie* was not exclusively German, in Britain itself ethnicity and nationhood had long formed part of the study of visual culture. It is there in John Ruskin's first publication, in John Claudius Loudon's *Architectural Magazine* (1837, 1838) on 'The Poetry of Architecture; or the Architecture of the Nations of Europe Considered in its Association with Natural Scenery and National Character'. Many other subsequent works included Geoffrey Scott's *The National Character of English Architecture* (1908), and John Gloag's *The English Tradition in Design* (1946).[77]

On the one hand, speaks Pevsner, Britain is the home of the invention of 'that most matter-of-fact, most utilitarian' industrial architecture – the spinning mill, the iron bridge and the Crystal Palace. On the other, there is a disposition to narrative in the architecture of England, to aspatially 'break the unity of interior and exterior and [to] wrap buildings in clothes not made for *them* but for buildings of other ages and purposes'. So England was a pioneer in dressing buildings in Grecian or Gothic dress 'because the costume tells a story, it is an evocative not a strictly aesthetic quality'.[78] As outlined in the 'Modern Movement' manuscript, Pevsner develops his surface-versus-space thesis most convincingly in relation to English Gothic, in the talk on 'Perpendicular England'. The great flat oak roofs of the parish churches of the later Middles Ages, and the comparative lack of interest in the stone vault, demonstrate 'a peculiarly English neglect of *moulding* space, you might even say of pulling things together. One wall, another wall, and beams across. Parts can be left as parts'.[79] In difference to a French cathedral with its three cavernous portals, an English west façade bears little organic relationship to the nave and aisles behind, indeed the cathedral is often entered from a porch placed arbitrarily against one of the aisles. Instead, there is a 'screen façade', 'with an even grid or net of blank arches or niches. . . . The English loved these long rows of blank arches, running on apparently interminably and wholly uniformly'. There is 'a great desire to stress the surface as a flat surface by such patterning'. Bringing this forward to a key 'pioneer' of Modernism, Pevsner says this is why:

William Morris was destined to become the best designer of the nineteenth century in all Europe, at least where flat surfaces are concerned, that is in chintzes, wallpapers and the like, just because he was English and had grown up with a sensitive and intelligent appreciation of the English tradition in design.[80]

Morris was also 'a great man' to John Gloag in his *The English Tradition in Design* (1946) for reopening the eyes of his compatriots – blinded in Victorian confusion – to their lineage of design.[81] This was commissioned as one of the King Penguin series, whose editorship Pevsner took over in 1942, and is among many attempts – especially intense in these years of war and reconstruction – to combine modernism, tradition, and identities of Englishness. In the King Penguins hardback keepsake format, an essay was followed by a series of full-page plates. From medieval chests to Morris's papers and fabrics, to Charles Holden's ticket machines at Piccadilly Station, Gloag's choice of images epitomizes an English tradition of 'common sense' whose threads 'run back to medieval England, back to the wisdom of men who worked with simple tools, few materials and abundant ingenuity'.[82] Gloag cites the article 'Black and White' – published by J. M. Richards in *The Architectural Review* of November 1937 – as the first outcome of a *Review* collaboration with John Piper; Piper and Richards toured Britain, seeking out what was idiomatic in national design through the everyday of harbours, signs, lighthouses, railway stations, and public houses.[83] Six pages of illustrations of striped beach-huts, lighthouse buildings, lock-gates, bollards, and whitewashed dwellings with tarred plinths gave proof of a 'national idiom of broad surface design' that achieves 'its architectural effect through the disposition of contrasted areas of black and white applied to the surface of an object'.[84] Piper developed these visual themes in 'The Nautical Style', in *The Architectural Review* of January 1938.

Pevsner's own contribution to the King Penguins was *The Leaves of Southwell* (1945), a meditation on one of the glories of the English cathedrals, the late thirteenth-century carved capitals in the Chapter House and linking corridor of Southwell Minster, followed by a fine sequence of plates by F. L. Attenborough. His essay draws out the European dimensions of Gothic culture wherein wandering English masons sketched the similarly naturalistic capitals of Rheims, in the manner of Villard de Honnecourt's sketchbooks, then returned to marry these French studies to a keen observation of their native plants: Maple, Buttercup, Hawthorn, and so on. By the first half of the next century, the masons were soon shaking off the 'foreign harness' to create 'that indigenously English version of mature Gothic, the Decorated, which, with its undulating decoration and its delightful ogee arches, remained a strictly national [English] achievement . . .'.[85] And in the first Reith Lecture on 'The Geography of Art', Pevsner again emphasizes the English impulse to surface linearity: 'Decorated is the flowing line, Perpendicular is the straight line, but both are *line* and not *body*'.[86]

In some major recent research on Decorated English Gothic, Pevsner's insights remain operative, and of more than historiographical interest. Paul Binski's *Gothic Wonder: Art, Artifice and the Decorated Style 1290–1350* (2014) applauds Pevsner as a leader in recognizing the distinct contribution of the Decorated style to European culture, citing his *Outline of European Architecture* as the epigraph to *Gothic Wonder*'s introduction: 'The architecture of England between 1250 and 1350 was, although the English do not know it, the most forward, the most important, and the most inspired in Europe'.[87] Binski develops Pevsner's suggestions further with his notion of the 'thick-wall surface'. In their Romanesque origins, the vaulted, castle-like, thick-walled, and squat Norman English cathedrals 'positively encouraged a distinctive approach to wall-surfaces and the aesthetic possibilities of the thickened wall'. English Gothic then seized on the poetic potential of these 'effects of surface', developing complex decorative patterns in its primary preoccupation 'with the aesthetics of surface, of skin and flesh'. As 'the earliest and most complete in conception of the new wave of large buildings in the Decorated Style', Exeter Cathedral epitomizes – in the multiplication of its shaft-columns (no less than sixteen to each pier), the eightfold mouldings of its nave arches, and its sumptuous tierceron vault – this language of 'multi-ribbed, highly articulated and patterned thick-wall surfaces'.[88] Pevsner saw a polarity in the mindset of Englishness between the rational-empirical, and the irrational-mystical-playful. Thus the 'Decorated is perverse, capricious, wilful, illogical, and unpredictable. It is unreasonable, where Perpendicular is reasonable'.[89] These are old stereotypes, and Binski cites the humoural theory of Pierre de Celle (Bishop of Chartres, 1181–3): 'Let English levity not be offended if Gallic maturity proves to be more solid. . . . In my experience the English are greater dreamers than the French, and the reason is that a more humid brain is much more quickly affected by the vapours of the stomach and develops all kinds of images within itself . . .'.[90] Pevsner finds both caprice *and* reason at play in the English mentality, for only such a sensibility could have produced the Picturesque.

The final chapter of *The Englishness of English Art* addresses the problems of contemporary urbanism through the idea of 'Picturesque England', confidently asserting that 'what has been said about English character shows that no country is aesthetically better provided to solve [contemporary planning issues] and thereby leave its imprint on other countries than England'.[91] Accepting that 'planning is of course largely a matter of economics, sociology, traffic engineering, and so on', Pevsner stresses the fact that urban design is 'also a visual matter', reminding the reader of 'the consistent [Townscape oriented] policy of *The Architectural Review* over the last twenty years'.[92] At the outset, in devising the sharawaggi of urban landscape, Hastings's bold insight had been to turn that picture-making aptitude – 'England's paramount contribution to the optics of rural planning' – to the optics of the contemporary city.[93] It was first necessary to make 'a picture of the kind of world the physical planner will make'. In picturing this new world, Pevsner advances an urbanism that is spatially looser than the quadrangles of his Oxford analyses yet unfolds optically as a sequence of tactile, figural precincts. This is in contrast to the totalizing object-city of the Corbusian Ville Radieuse, whose towers and slab-blocks – placed in free fields of greenery – fail to offer similar coherent visual progressions. Related to the rational-empirical typecasting seen in relation to the Gothic is that labelling of an autocratic France versus the liberty of England; Pevsner quotes Joseph Addison's (1672–1719) admiration in *The Spectator* for 'a tree in all its luxuriance and diffusion of boughs and branches' as compared to the disciplined formal parterres of the French.[94] As noted, Cullen's visual 'Townscape Casebook' reprieves the reader from the eight pages of Ivor de Wolfe's 'Townscape' manifesto which is almost entirely politico-philosophy ruminations of this kind, making the Picturesque the 'radical theory' where – in opposition to the French 'Grand Manner' – 'those who inherit the English tradition and temperament, technicians no less than poets, are potential radicals, potential Sharawags'.[95]

The Englishness of English Art gives examples of this precinctual Picturesque as applied to contemporary urban conditions but develops no analysis of them. As instances of 'picturesque principles applied to urban conditions' it illustrates Frederick Gibberd's Market Square in Harlow New Town, and the Town Square in Stevenage New Town. Pevsner also notes 'Sir William Holford's brilliant plans of 1956 for the precincts of St Paul's'.[96]

FIGURE 5.12 *Frederick Gibberd, Market Square, Harlow New Town. Architectural Press Archive / RIBA Collections.*

These were in the process of execution as his book was going to press. More detailed readings are found in the aforementioned *Visual Planning and the Picturesque* manuscript where Pevsner emphasizes the City as 'entirely a pedestrian system of contacts' which should be envisaged as 'precincts for pedestrians, with pedestrian links connecting them'. Again, the parallel is made to the morphologies of Oxbridge, and the London Inns of Court, and their imaginatively 'bold mixing up of old and new . . .'.[97] And in Cambridge itself, he praises the collegiate court principles of Hugh Casson and Neville Conder's scheme for Sidgwick Avenue, and the considered textures of its sequence of pedestrian spaces where 'the addict to floorscapes will be able to enjoy cobbles, tarmac and setts', along with lawns and sheets of water.[98]

One significant legacy of Townscape and the Picturesque was Colin Rowe and Fred Koetter's notion of the architect as *bricoleur* in 'Collage City', first advanced in a special issue of *The Architectural Review* of August 1975. The *Review* introduced Colin Rowe as developing 'views which we substantially share' in his engagement with the 'aesthetic problems of city planning', seeing the city as the product of incremental collisions wherein the architect operates as collagist. However, when *Collage City* appeared in book form in 1978, Rowe was at pains to distance his ideas from what he saw as the nostalgic and populist aspects of Townscape and, although Rowe ends up with the same kinds of precinctual spaces as Cullen and Pevsner sought, his

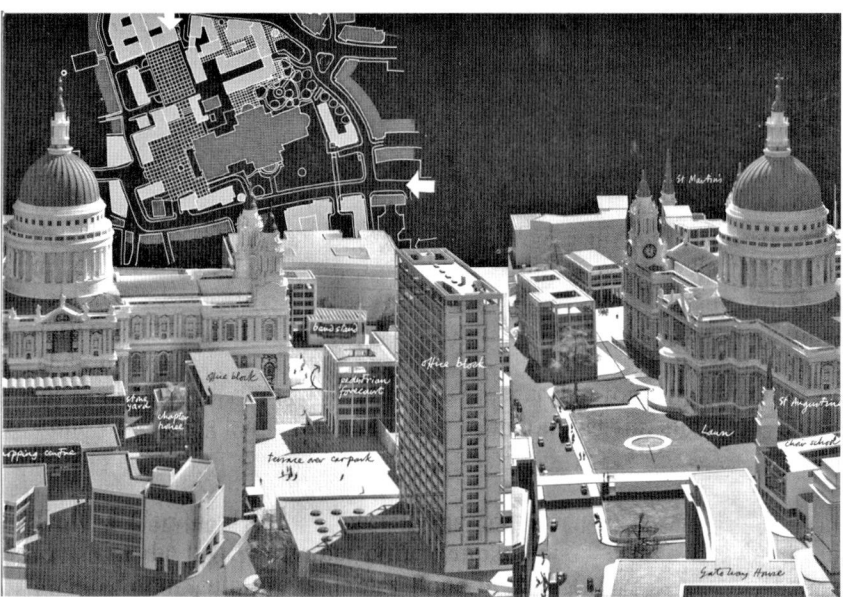

FIGURE 5.13 *William Holford, plan for the precinct of St Paul's Cathedral, London.* The Architectural Review *(June 1956).*

precedents are more broadly European than specifically English – Hadrian's Villa at Tivoli, for example.[99] Rowe's 1975 essay shows exactly the same north-west corner view of Gibberd's Market Square, in Harlow New Town, as Pevsner had illustrated in *The Englishness of English Art*, but here Rowe sees 'modern architecture and planning leaning heavily on nostalgia' in the way its self-conscious 'randomness' evokes a traditional English market-square.[100] By this point in the mid-1970s Rowe is able to contrast Gibberd's 'nostalgia' with 'the reverse', with Archigram's 'computerised dream of the expendable' – the 'plug-in city'. Yet, as the following chapters will show, it is not too difficult to unearth an English nostalgia and Picturesqueness in both Archigram *and* Gibberd.

CHAPTER SIX

As Found

Surfaces of Brutalism

Picturesque vengeance

In its enquiry into the Picturesque, the last chapter ranged into the post-World War II years, but only touched upon the debates of that period. Indeed, for the mature generation of architecture students who had fought a war for the New World of the Modern Movement, the Picturesque stood only for a compromising old-guard establishment, empowered within the pages of that leading magazine – *The Architectural Review*. Reyner Banham (1922–1988) summed up the arguments of this post-war scene in his essay 'Revenge of the Picturesque: English Architectural Polemics, 1945–1965', the last chapter of *Concerning Architecture* (1968), a collection intended to honour Nikolaus Pevsner. Pevsner had supervised Banham's doctorate for six years (for the research finally published in 1960 as *Theory and Design in the First Machine Age*) and – as evident in the attacks on him in 'Revenge of the Picturesque' – his academic connections with his former supervisor were complicated.[1] As an International Modernist, Banham was suspicious of preoccupations with Englishness, and of attempts to equate the European Masters with the Picturesque; Pevsner's *Pioneers of the Modern Movement*, for example, had already 'given modern architecture a comfortingly secure historical ancestry' and, continues Banham, 'had Pevsner deliberately set out to infuriate the young, he could hardly have done better', than in *The Architectural Review* of April 1954, to observe that: 'the Modern revolution of the early twentieth century and the Picturesque revolution of a hundred years before had all their fundamentals in common'. For this same infuriated youth looked 'to Continental modern architecture and, above all, the work of Le Corbusier ... for exemplars of a sane and rational design method (as they saw it) to set against the empiricism and compromises of the

Picturesque'.[2] At the same time, even Banham admits that *The Architectural Review*'s 'liberal policy (in spite of propaganda for "an English visual philosophy founded on the true rock of Sir Uvedale Price", otherwise known as "Townscape")' allowed it to print important articles by such Young Turks as Colin Rowe, James Stirling, and the Smithsons (Alison and Peter).[3]

Against this perceived establishment of *The Architectural Review*, there were other outlets in which the younger generation might vent their opposition to the compromises of picturesque planning; here Banham notes Colin St John Wilson's (1922–2007) dissenting pieces for *The Observer*, written by Wilson as one of the first architectural columnists in a British newspaper. In 'The Vertical City' (*The Observer*, 17 February 1952) – written four months after the Festival of Britain had closed – he excoriates Frederick Gibberd's work at Lansbury in Poplar, East London. Proposed by Gibberd for the Festival in July 1948 as a 'live' architecture display, it was a real reconstruction of a blitzed neighbourhood. It personified Picturesque planning and materiality, with its low-rise-low-density rows of two- to three-storey houses and maisonettes, traditionally constructed in stockbrick in 1950–1, and informally arranged around a shopping centre and market-place – and completed in 1952 by a jolly clock-tower with a zig-zag staircase façade.[4] Wilson's column did not pull its punches:

> There are those who maintain that the scale of London has always been 'intimate' in comparison with Rome, Paris, or New York. This extraordinary effeminacy promises to convert London into the most overblown and 'tasteful' village in the world: three- and six-storey blocks of flats with the pitched roofs, peep-hole windows and 'folky' details of the current Swedish revival, picturesquely sited around market-places, have been offered to us in the name of 'live architecture'.[5]

'On the contrary', insists Wilson, this picturesque is 'an architecture of "cold feet": fear of city-scale, fear of the machine, fear of everything that the architectural innovators of the past twenty-five years have promised us'. Unsurprisingly, the key 'innovator' is Le Corbusier, and Wilson offers as a better 'live architecture' his 'vertical garden-city' of the 1937 Paris Exhibition, tall slab-blocks, 'twenty to thirty floors high, with wide and splendid views', raised on stilts with open parkland flowing around and under.[6] In the same over-masculinized language the Corbusian rationalists liked to call themselves the 'hards' in opposition to the so-called picturesque 'softs', or the Swedish empiricists. For many looked to Sweden, inspired by its Social Democratic politics and its gentle modernist architecture; in June 1947, *The Architectural Review* had announced the 'New Empiricism' as 'Sweden's latest style' which it had developed as a regional response to the harsher aspects of the New Objectivity (*Neue Sachlichkeit*) of the inter-war period.[7]

Reflecting on the ironies of the Picturesque 'revenge', in his allotted period of 1945–65, Banham was fully conscious of the 'inner contradictions' of the

FIGURE 6.1 *Frederick Gibberd, clock tower seen from the market place at Lansbury, Poplar, London. Architectural Press Archive / RIBA Collections.*

'anti-Picturesque faction' as the polemics played themselves out. Wilson himself would make one of the most dramatic U-turns, from being a pioneer at the London County Council (LCC) in the team prototyping a British descendant of the *Unité d'Habitation* slab-block at Bentham Road, Hackney (1950–55), to his advocacy of the emollient 'other tradition' of Modernism represented by Alvar Aalto. He was electrified by the Finn's condemnation of the (Corbusian) dictatorship of Modernism in his acceptance speech of the RIBA Gold Medal in 1957.[8] At the same time Wilson, and friends such as James Stirling, were disorientated by what Banham calls the 'convulsions in the style of Le Corbusier's architecture in the mid fifties'; how could their apostle of the Machine-Age equate with the organicism of his Notre Dame du Haut at Ronchamp (1950–4), or the decided primitivism of his Jaoul houses in Paris (1956)? Stirling saw the latter dwellings as a rejection of the 'rational principles which are the basis of the modern movement'.[9] In conclusion to his essay, Banham saw Alison and Peter Smithson's 1951 shell-concrete design for the Coventry Cathedral competition as 'uncompromising and anti-picturesque', in fact as 'almost the last secure point in history on which the opponents of Picturesque compromise can rely, so total has been the triumph of the unacknowledged Picturesqueness of the Picturesque's avowed enemies'.[10] Self-evidently, 'Picturesque compromise' included Basil Spence's eclectic winning design which respectfully retained the ruins by placing his building at right-angles on a new liturgical 'west-east' axis, linking new and old with a dramatic porch. But Banham acidly points out that those of the avant-garde who had once rejected *The Architectural Review*'s 'repeated injunctions' to follow Alexander Pope's advice to 'consult the genius of the place in all', soon repeatedly did so: the Smithsons themselves in *The Economist* group in St James's Street (1959–64); James Stirling and James Gowan in the Leicester University Engineering Buildings (1959–63) – 'an asymmetrical composition of towers and low buildings that fully deserves the name of Picturesque'; and Sir Leslie Martin and Colin St John Wilson at Harvey Court, Cambridge – 'the father of Modern-Movement rationalism in England and his most able follower' – (1960–2, with Patrick Hodgkinson).[11]

The polemics of Banham's survey produced intense interrogations of surface. One clear binary that emerges is the positing of a 'hard' rational Continental Modernism against the 'soft' picturesque of Townscape and the New Empiricism. There is a 'closed' abstract aspect to rationalism – evident in the classical side of Le Corbusier and in the proportions of his *Modulor* – whose roots in the Renaissance were reinforced by Rudolf Wittkower's *Architectural Principles in the Age of Humanism* (1949, 1952). While the prefabricated 'CLASP' buildings of the Hertfordshire schools programme experimented with ideas of more 'open' indeterminate industrial systems of prefabrication. But both 'hards' and 'softs' look formalist and 'high-culture' when compared to the post-war 'low-cultures' of the 'as-found' and of USA consumerism.

The most consequential British contribution to these polemical vortices was the ethic and aesthetic of the 'New Brutalism', thought to have been coined around 1952, and demarcated in Banham's major article 'The New Brutalism' in *The Architectural Review* of December 1955; a 'Brutalist' object will exhibit three key qualities: '1, Formal legibility of plan; 2, clear exhibition of structure, and 3, valuation of materials for their inherent qualities "as found"'.[12] Banham's major point of architectural reference in coming to this definition was Alison and Peter Smithson's Hunstanton School in Norfolk (1949–54). With its steel frame and infills of yellow brick and glass, it might be taken as an undisguised homage to the language of Mies van der Rohe's Chemical Engineering and Metallurgy Building at the Illinois Institute of Technology (IIT) in Chicago (completed 1946). In fact, any apparent similarities only point up the stark differences in approach between Mies's manipulations of construction towards an ideality of form, and the Smithsons' display of building in its unadorned facticity. In their *Surface Architecture* (2002), David Leatherbarrow and Mohsen Mostafavi contrast Mies's corner column at the IIT Alumni Memorial Hall (1945) with the corner column at Hunstanton. The IIT 'columns are recessed from the planes of the exterior walls, creating a spatial void that gives the effect of an absent or missing column' – their composite closure is as much neoclassical as modern. At Hunstanton, 'the corner column is coplanar with the exterior walls.... The distinction between column and cladding is reduced; as the columns join the horizontal elements in the construction of an atectonic frame or border, they take on the appearance of surface'. Steel, brick, and glass, register as 'facts' of construction, 'understood to be expressive in their own right'.[13] Realizing that his three Brutalist criteria could as well apply to Mies's Lake Shore Drive Apartments (1951) as to the canonically Brutalist Unité d'Habitation, Marseilles (Le Corbusier,

FIGURE 6.2 *Alison and Peter Smithson, Hunstanton School, Norfolk. Architectural Press Archive / RIBA Collections.*

1947–52), Banham argues that 'in the last resort what characterizes the New Brutalism in architecture as in painting is precisely its brutality, its *je-m'en-foutisme* [I don't give-a-damn], its bloody-mindedness'. Accordingly, at the end of his essay, he revises the first of his criteria, 'Formal legibility of plan', to 'Memorability as an Image', to stress the emotive aspect of Brutalist architecture over the formalism implicit in 'formal legibility'.[14]

Banham's categories, and the comparative smoothness of Hunstanton's surfaces of steel, glass, and fair-faced brickwork are reminders that Brutalism's 'bloody-mindedness' need not entail overstated roughness of facture. In his 1966 monograph on *The New Brutalism*, Banham reasoned on that 'English architectural psychology' which, in importing a style, modified it; so, the frank materiality of Hunstanton is a correction of Miesian elegance, just as English Palladianism 'corrected' Palladio. And Banham observes how 'securely within engrained English traditions is the insistence on a pure geometrical grid of horizontals and verticals, and an air of suppressed extremism, of gentlemanly "bloody-mindedness" imprisoned within the grid'.[15] Here he remembers Pevsner's 1955 'The Englishness of English Art' with its accents on 'this barely suppressed geometrical extremism', what Pevsner calls 'Perpendicularism' – as discussed in the previous chapter – where façades, designed as 'rigid, rational grids' can be found in the English Perpendicular itself, in Anglo-Saxon churches, in Elizabethan Houses like Hardwick Hall (1590–7), and in John Wood's Circus at Bath (1754).[16] In important respects this appeal of clear façade and plan geometries was influenced by the publication of Rudolf Wittkower's *Architectural Principles in the Age of Humanism* in 1949. It might seem odd that a dense study of the geometrical principles underlying the humanism of Renaissance architecture between 1450 and 1580 – Palladio's problematics in composing his church façades, for example – could have had such far-reaching modernist influence. But in 1978, Peter Smithson again asserted that *Architectural Principles* 'confirmed, and deepened for life, a direction we had already taken; for our first real building (designed 1949–1950) – the School at Hunstanton – had been, through some inner compulsion, as regularly bayed and as strictly organized as we could make it'.[17] It chanced that Wittkower's book overlapped with the publication of Le Corbusier's *Le Modulor* (1948, English translation 1954), reinforcing the significance of proportional systems to architecture. And preceding both, in a celebrated essay in *The Architectural Review* of March 1947, Colin Rowe had compared 'The Mathematics of the Ideal Villa' in the works of Palladio and Le Corbusier.

At the same time, the New Brutalism *did* promote literal roughness of internal and external surface texture, given its other sources in Le Corbusier's *béton brut* (raw concrete) and Jean Dubuffet's *art brut*, where the architect or artist registers in the work the struggles of its creation. In 1955 the Smithsons and Theo Crosby opened the January *Architectural Design* with a manifesto on the New Brutalism. Theo Crosby had joined the journal in the previous year, swinging *AD*'s appeal towards a younger generation irritated with the old-guard picturesque empiricists associated with *The Architectural Review*. The Smithsons declared the New Brutalism as 'the only possible development for this moment from the Modern Movement', owing in part to 'the knowledge that Le Corbusier is one of its practitioners (starting with the 'béton brut' of the Unité)'. But they also drew attention to the influences of Japanese architecture on the modernisms of Frank Lloyd Wright, Le Corbusier, and Mies, and its devotion to nature and 'the materials of the built world'. 'It is this reverence for materials . . . which is at the root of the so-called New Brutalism'. New also, is the way Brutalism looks – not to the high-art of past styles – but to the primitivity of 'peasant dwelling forms. . . . We see architecture as a direct result of a way of life'.[18]

These characteristics of 'bloody-mindedness' have been seen before, in the pugnacity of Butterfield's church-building. In that context we noted the significance of Summerson's 'Christian Gothic' article (*The Architectural Review*, December 1945) in the post-war reappraisal of Butterfield, with its photographs of the gutted shells of London's St Alban, Holborn and St Matthias, Stoke Newington, and its assertion that Butterfield's churches 'are to a greater or less degree ugly. And in almost all there is power and originality transcending the ugliness'. Summerson emphasizes Butterfield's raw material integrity: 'He knows how to build – he is no studio man', his roofs are 'gawky' and 'builder-like' and he refuses the prestige of stone in his preference for 'the common, hard red brick'.[19] In her essay on 'Butterfield and Brutalism' (1994) Elain Harwood finds many parallels, 'for both [Butterfield and the Brutalists] a new, hard geometry was facilitated by new materials'.[20] James Stirling, for instance, is known to have admired Butterfield's brickwork and, at times, used both pronounced textures and smooth red engineering bricks to express his own faceted surfaces. Both made brick contemporary; Butterfield gave it an honorific status, fit for sacred architecture, whilst the Brutalists reclaimed its as-found earthiness, in contrast to the machined white-planes of inter-war modernism.

So it was that the textural brick and concrete group of flats at Ham Common, London (1955–8) – designed by James Stirling and James Gowan – were as quintessentially Brutalist as the steel-framed Hunstanton School. All three blocks, aligned on the long narrow site, have brick-bearing wall structures and expressed concrete slabs. If they pay an obvious tribute to Le Corbusier's Maisons Jaoul (1957) their surface planes are, as Banham points out in *The New Brutalism*, 'neat where Jaoul is casual and untidy. The brickwork is careful, the exposed shutter-patterned concrete is much less assertive than Le Corbusier's and brick and concrete are not allowed to run messily together (as at Jaoul) but firmly separated by a thin recessed detail'.[21] In her monumental survey of English architecture from 1945 to 1975, *Space, Hope and Brutalism*, Elain Harwood discusses the canonical Brutalist importance of Ham Common, but also includes the much less discussed Hereford Square, in London's Kensington where Colin St John

FIGURE 6.3 *Stirling and Gowan, Housing, Ham Common, Richmond, London. Colin Westwood / RIBA Collections.*

Wilson 'used the same [Ham Common] ingredients in a more formal design made in 1955–6'.[22] Wilson (working with Arthur Baker) chose an intense yellow brick for this infill development of flats and maisonettes – a strident note against the stucco of John Blore's Nash-style terraces. But, in the Wittkower-Corbusier formalism of the time, the studied proportions of the new, rhyming the old Renaissance façades, modulates a new synthesis. The aedicular frame to the deep balcony of Wilson's top-floor maisonettes – formed between sheer planes of brick – is especially striking.

The ethics of the material surface – as-found in Brutalism – demanded that what you experienced outside, was exposed within. At Hunstanton 'walls that are brick on the outside are brick (the same bricks) on the inside, fairfaced on both sides'. Within the school you see the facts of construction 'without plaster and frequently without paint', the pipes and electrical conduits are also visible.[23] In the circulation areas of Ham Common the brick and concrete runs through exposed, while within the flats the outer walls are concentrated in the central double sided chimney pier where Mark Crinson finds 'a pitch of elemental expression in the concrete mantelpieces, shelves and corbels set into their brick surrounds, a more brutish version of what Le Corbusier had created in his Maison de Weekend (1935)'.[24]

FIGURE 6.4 *Colin St John Wilson and Arthur Baker, flats at Hereford Square.* Architectural Design *(April 1959). Photograph Sam Lambert.*

Wilson's own turn-to-brick at Hereford Square is all the more remarkable, given his aforesaid fierce attack in 1952 on the 'effeminacy' of Gibberd's empirically brick Lansbury Estate, and Wilson's British architype (teamed with Peter Carter and Alan Colquhoun) of the Corbusian slab-block at Bentham Road, Hackney (1950–55). Bentham Road is unequivocally concrete in its materiality but – as Ham Common is to Jaoul – is Englishly neater than its Marseilles precedent, owing to its extensive use of pre-cast elements. Thus, the tautly elegant façade was a visibly and structurally independent pre-cast screen stretched across the face of the blocks, indexing the scale of the maisonette units, poised in ten storeys above a base of pilotis.[25] Wilson's 1957 Alvar Aalto 'conversion', as noted earlier, also confirmed his brick-turn as he discovered the vital surfaces of the master's

FIGURE 6.5 *Colin St John Wilson, Peter Carter, Alan Colquhoun, Bentham Road Estate, Hackney, London. RIBA Collections.*

Baker House Senior Students' Dormitory (MIT, Cambridge, Massachusetts, 1947–8), and Säynätsalo Town Hall (1949, 1950–2). In a later essay on 'Brick' (1994–5), he remembered how in the 1950s 'he became immersed in the writings of Adrian Stokes and very moved by [these] recent buildings of conspicuous mass'. He writes: 'And is there not also great strength in the order that the discipline of bond requires of those who practice it? (Brick is not open to the seductive freedom that is offered by the moulding of poured concrete)'.[26] Earlier, we examined Stokes's concept of 'carving', with its respect for the restraints imposed by material; here Wilson cites Stokes's condemnation, in *The Stones of Rimini* (1934), of the modelling of Le Corbusier's 'lightning concrete'.[27]

The order and discipline of brick characterizes the erudite brick box that Wilson built as extension to the Cambridge School of Architecture (1957–8, with Alex Hardy). Banham calls this 'a manifesto building' which launched the so-called 'Cambridge School' of architectural design, and represented 'the extreme intellectual wing' of the 'English Brick Brutalists'; 'Into this relatively small building were poured most of the intellectual aspirations of the Wilson, Smithson generation . . .'.[28] Leslie Martin, Colin St John Wilson, and Patrick Hodgkinson were the prominent figures in a School whose heroic period was short-lived (c. 1957–65), and whose work Kenneth Frampton regards 'as the only serious attempt, after the English [Arts and Crafts] Free Style, to create a normative, yet unequivocally modern brick architecture for the British Isles, one that, in its capacity to respond to the triad of climate, context and programme, was to prove itself capable of being generally accepted by society as a whole'.[29] Along with the School extension, key works of the Cambridge School included the above-mentioned Harvey Court, Gonville and Caius College, Cambridge (1957–62), and the Manor Road Libraries, Oxford (1959–64).

As Ham Common concentrates its exteriority in the shelves, corbels, and brick of the fireplace core, so the spaces of the School Extension – criticism-room, lecture room, staff-offices, common room, etc. – unfold in pin-wheel rotation around the off-set axle of a brickwork servant little-house, with corbelled concrete elements, including an elevated projection pulpit for the lecture room, which reminded Banham of the 'Elementarist sculpture of a Malevich or a Vanntongerloo';[30] plan and section are governed by a grid of nine-foot squares, and golden rectangles. The fact that the extension was also a live-project for the students, to reveal the processes of making, reinforced its direct expression of massive load-bearing brick, concrete floors and roof beams, and exposed finishes inside and out. In *Cambridge New Architecture* (1964, 1970), Philip Booth and Nicholas Taylor comment how this 'instructional quality is emphasized by the exposure of all structural elements. Paint and plaster which normally cover inaccuracies and birthmarks of building are excluded and even bolt-holes for shuttering are left exposed'.[31]

FIGURE 6.6 *Colin St John Wilson, with Alex Hardy, Cambridge School of Architecture extension, the lecture room. RIBA Collections.*

Brutalist wallpaper

If Brutalist architects should renounce plaster and paint and nakedly expose their surfaces, then there could surely be no place here for the ephemerality of wallpaper? And yet, in another 'revenge of the Picturesque', wallpaper would prove to be central to Brutalist formulations. Remember Rowntree's panorama to Ivor de Wolfe's January 1944 'Exterior Furnishing or sharawaggi', where wallpapers and hangings escape the domestic interior, to make urban façades and external surfaces and textures. Remember also how William Morris's projects upended the status quo of architecture, *vis-à-vis* the decorative arts, eliding barriers between inside and outside, between object, ornament, and architecture. Then, consider the following photograph of 1956 the Smithsons called 'a classic Brutalist image'; it shows a corner of the bathroom in their small terraced house in 46 Limerston Street in Chelsea, London, into which they moved in 1953. Here, as they later wrote, 'the so-called "as-found" was celebrated: the bath stood naked on its four legs; the lavatory chain hung galvanised before [Eduardo] Paolozzi wallpaper . . .'. They note this wallpaper of 1956 as in a 'style later used by Nigel Henderson at Bethnal Green and Thorpe-le-Soken'.[32] By the time this image was taken, the artist Paolozzi and photographer Henderson had set up Hammer Prints

FIGURE 6.7 *The bathroom in Limerston Street, Chelsea, with wallpaper by Eduardo Paolozzi, 1956. The Smithson Family Collection. © The Paolozzi Foundation, Licensed by DACS 2022.*

Ltd in 1954, in Thorpe-le-Soken, Essex, to produce and sell textiles, ceramics, photographs, etc. Like the lavatory wallpaper, the 'style' of these creations is one of directionless, irregular, all-over markings. In 1945, Nigel and Judith Henderson had moved into the Bethnal Green area of East London, then a war-scarred area of extreme poverty. Between 1949 and 1953, first using a Leica, then a larger-format Rolleicord, Henderson photographed the scarified surfaces of the roads and pavements, walls, and shopfronts surrounding him – as he recollects:

> I would think of the small box-like houses and shops etc. as a sort of stage set against which people were more or less unconsciously acting. Some particular marks (like the slicks and patches of tar on the roads, the cracks and slicks and erosive marks on pavement slabs, the ageing of wood and paintwork, the rich layering of billboards etc . . .) linked with the work I did more directly with the enlarger and which I later felt made some common ground with some aspects of the work of artists like Tapiés, Burri, Jean Dubuffet.[33]

Some of this reportage inspired the patterns of Hammer Prints. Banham reproduced Henderson's 'Sgraffiti on a Window' (*c.* 1949–53) in 'The New Brutalism' article (December 1955) as an 'image of human as well as formal value'. Into the paint skimmed roughly across the door-pane, swirl random

FIGURE 6.8 *Nigel Henderson, photograph of graffiti on a door window,* c. 1949–54. Tate Images © Nigel Henderson Estate.

rhythms of blackness and emphasis – circles, arcs and scratchings, not unlike the lavatory wallpaper. And collaged around the Henderson photograph, in Banham's article, are variously: a Jackson Pollock, a Burri painting on burlap, the 'sophisticated primitivism' of Paolozzi's *Head, 1953*, and a view of the 'exhibition of 100 Brutalist images', *Parallel of Life and Art*. In this show – the '*locus classicus*' of the Brutalist movement – the Smithsons collected and hung these, and other artists, at the Institute of Contemporary Arts (ICA) in London, in 1953.[34] Here they arrayed and floated a teasingly random plethora of photographs and diagrams, crossing nature, science, art, and anthropology. The year before *Parallel of Life and Art*, similar patternings of art and science had been brought together, literally over the head of Ronald Jenkins, the engineer at Ove Arup and Partners who worked with the Smithsons on their Hunstanton School. They designed the interior of his office in London's Fitzrovia, and Paolozzi contributed the ceiling wallpaper.

To examine Jenkins's ceiling, it is important to these evolving ideas of surface-depth, to introduce the art-theorist Anton Ehrenzweig (1908–1966), his influence on Paolozzi, and his contribution to the debates within the 'British School' of psychoanalytic aesthetics. Particularly regarding the role that might be accorded to oceanic states in creative experience, as opposed to outward whole-object positions – namely between the value of inarticulate form and the coherent patterns of Gestalt. This would become a key point of tension between the thinkers and artists who composed the ICA's breakaway Independent Group, and older-guard figures such as Herbert Read. Here Ehrenzweig resonated with the ideas of the psychoanalyst Melanie Klein, and debated with other key Kleinian followers such as Adrian Stokes and Marion Milner; a key forum was the Imago Group which met between 1954 and 1972, where Ehrenzweig also encountered figures such as Ernst Gombrich and Richard Wollheim.[35]

Ehrenzweig and Paolozzi had first met in 1950 when Paolozzi took up a position teaching textile design at London's Central School of Arts and Crafts where Ehrenzweig was working as a dye technician. He acted as a dye technician and screen-printer for Paolozzi, but they were also intellectually close, and Ehrenzweig's ideas encouraged Paolozzi's latent destabilizing instinct 'to look beneath the surface of things, to find fear, anxiety and fascination in works of art'.[36] Ehrenzweig's best known book is *The Hidden Order of Art* (1967) where he argues that 'conscious surface coherence has to be disrupted in order to bring unconscious form discipline into its own'.[37] But he had begun to challenge the Gestalt theory of perception much earlier, as in his 1948 paper 'Unconscious Form-creation in Art'. And his first book *The Psychoanalysis of Artistic Vision and Hearing* (1953) also examines the role of unconscious modes of perception in creativity, whether artistic or scientific; in it he argues for the 'creative accident', for the chaotic and elusive, against Gestalt theory's stress on the articulate patterns of surface perception.[38]

Ehrenzweig helped in the printing of the Jenkins ceiling paper, and from him we know the 'creative accidents' that went into its printing and pasting; the workers were allowed to arbitrarily apply the rolls creating random juxtapositions which Paolozzi accepted, only touching up a few edges. We could perhaps work this surface out as a brooding arbour of thorny thickets whose fearful depths contradict the cerebral engineer's space below, with its shiny uncluttered desk and anglepoise lamp. But a series of Henderson photographs imply readings that are both mechanistic *and* natural. One, looking up, from below the desk, through the end of Henderson's T-Square and the jointed arms of the anglepoise, brings out the hesitant grid which orders the crossings and dottings, the thickening of marks and the lacunae. Another, where a skeletal radio-mast can be seen through the window, associates the shadowy ceiling marks to industrial antennae and machine-parts.[39]

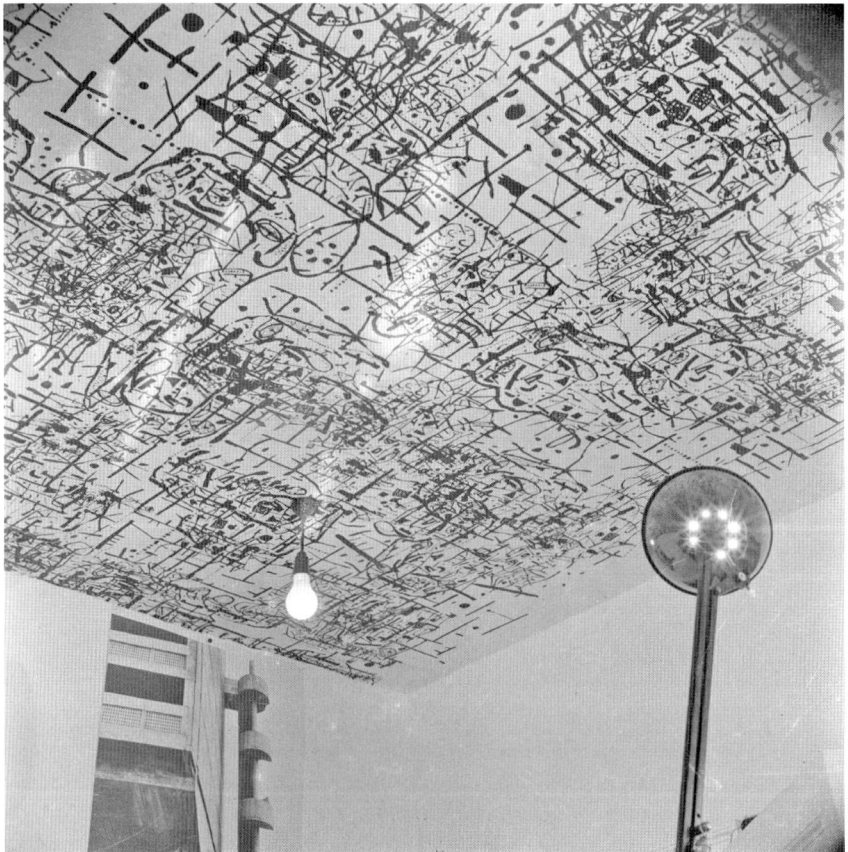

FIGURE 6.9 *Nigel Henderson, photograph of the Eduardo Paolozzi ceiling paper to Ronald Jenkins's office at Ove Arup and Partners. Tate Images © Nigel Henderson. © The Paolozzi Foundation, Licensed by DACS 2022.*

Group 10's 'This is Tomorrow'

In the first unofficial session of the Independent Group in April 1952, Paolozzi subverted pure-form Modernism with epidiascope projections of images, randomly torn from American popular magazines, and flatly juxtaposed: low art and high technology, consumer products, food, fashion, and other ephemera. Wilson, an early collector of Paolozzi's work, recalls the artist 'firing off disparate, contradictory images like a machine-gun while making grunting noises'.[40] The 'Young Independent Group' of the ICA had been meeting loosely since 1951, and were first recognized in the ICA's minutes in November 1952.[41] Banham took on the role of convenor of The Independent Group (IG) (the 'young' was dropped), while the critics Lawrence Alloway and Toni del Renzio were also prominent; key artists included Richard Hamilton, Henderson, and Paolozzi; there was also a strong architectural component involving, among others, the Smithsons, Stirling, and Wilson. As Paolozzi's projections demonstrate, in the words of Richard Hamilton, 'if there was one binding spirit amongst the people at the Independent Group, it was a distaste for Herbert Read's attitudes'.[42] Read's patrician values had been shaped in the Hampstead of the 1930s within the circle of his artist-friends Barbara Hepworth, Ben Nicholson, and Henry Moore. As Banham said, the IG was 'against direct carving, pure form, truth, beauty and all that ... what we favoured was motion studies. We also favoured rough surfaces, human images, space, machinery, ignoble materials and what we termed non-art (there was a project to bury Sir Herbert under a book entitled *Non-Art Not Now*)', a jibe at Read's *Art Now* (1933, revised 1948).[43] As has been indicated in the context of Ehrenzweig, much of this crystallized in the IG's opposition to the Gestalt theory, espoused by Read, and influential since the 1930s, which suggested human beings were patterned to seek cohesion in the visual world and to reject chaos and disorder.

The 'This is Tomorrow' exhibition, held at the Whitechapel Art Gallery in August and September 1956, also made manifest the polemics within the IG itself. Germane to the idea of the exhibition was Le Corbusier's vision of 'le synthèse des arts' by realizing collaborations of Modernist artists and architects. Wilson drew up a loose overall layout, akin to booths within a fair, which allowed autonomy to each of the twelve groups of artists and architects; the first and last booths were gateway walk-through exhibits. Representing the art and architecture extremes were the number 6, 'Patio and Pavilion' (Henderson, Paolozzi, Smithsons), and the number 2 (Richard Hamilton, John McHale, John Voelcker). At the end of the gallery, in 'Patio and Pavilion', the visitor discovered the as-found in-extremis, a bricolage shed-pavilion within an enclosure symbolizing the shelter-and-space fundamentals of the human habitat. Henderson's photocollage, *Head of a Man* (1956), glowered within in the shed, while in the sandy patio, seemingly scattered with detritus, gritty icons of human need could be detected – imprinted tiles, stones, tree and machine forms, sculptures and reliefs. The

FIGURE 6.10 *Group 6 exhibit, 'Patio and Pavilion', 'This is Tomorrow' exhibition (1956), Whitechapel Art Gallery, London. John Maltby / RIBA Collections.*

gallery-goer had to assimilate this melancholy waste-land soon after the experience of Hamilton, McHale, and Voelcker's dazzlingly vulgar images of transatlantic popular culture – a juke-box, a publicity-still of Marilyn Monroe, and a giant montage of Robbie the Robot, from the USA science-fiction film *Forbidden Planet* (1956).

With good reason many commentators focus on the distinctly opposed values of Groups 2 and 6. The Smithsons identified their earthy 'Englishness' materiality, in opposition to the Hamilton-USA glossy consumer surfaces of colour-magazines and the bodywork of Chrysler cars:

> We always considered ourselves very English. . . . We have always been oriented towards Europe and never deviated, reacting to aspirations beamed out of America that we saw as irresistible, but also, recognizing these as part of a wider threat to Europe's cultural identity.[44]

Even the Mies-IIT influenced Hunstanton School has an English ha-ha adopted from Sir John Vanbrugh's Northumberland mansion, Seaton Delaval (1718), and the very 'walking surfaces were gravel, as befitted a country school, but slightly formal, echoing the walks of nearby Sandringham [the nearby Royal Estate]'.[45] To make sense of this English-European sensibility, the Smithsons later identified their landscape language as 'Lyrical

Appropriateness' (1976) and, as noted, Banham accused the Smithsons' *The Economist* group (1959–64) of being deservedly picturesque.

In a discussion broadcast on BBC Radio's Third Programme of 17 August 1956, Wilson attacked the extremes of both Groups 2 and 6 as just sell-outs, under different guises, to the same old idea of the Picturesque – Peter Smithson and Richard Hamilton were both present: 'Neither Smithson with his ludicrously antediluvian objects, nor Hamilton with his ludicrously streamlined pop art are in fact making a constructive statement at all. They are merely lumping together formless phenomena'.[46]

From their anti-Gestalt standpoints, 'formless phenomena' were exactly what the Smithsons and Hamilton groups sought, but Wilson is acute in thus equating the formless and the Picturesque. In his study of *The Picturesque*, Macarthur puts it succinctly: 'It is a simple equation that the picturesque proposes: weaken the form of the object to foreground the forming of phenomenal experience'.[47] As for the experiential qualities of the Group 10 contribution by Wilson himself – working with architect Peter Carter, sculptor Robert Adams, and structural engineer Frank Newby – this drew praise in the discussion from the art historian David Piper for arousing sensations he had found nowhere else in the exhibition, of spectacle and heroic scale.

And in *Architectural Design* (October 1956) Theo Crosby thought Group 10 'the nearest in result to the original aim of the exhibition', as an integration of the arts, for 'here no individual work is shown: each person contributed to the total, ultimately anonymous, work'.[48] This funnelling walk-through construction of two curved planes – below a suspended concave canopy – led to a totemic eye-catcher of concave, polished aluminium sheets. As sculptor, Robert Adams's integral contribution to the ensemble was both the glinting totem, and the active modulation of the curved surfaces with cubes, cylinders, and cones. Perhaps owing to its very success in synthesis, Group 10 is much less discussed in the now extensive IG literature than the notorious Groups 2 and 6.

Group 10's construction also demonstrates the influence upon Wilson of the ideas of Adrian Stokes at this period, and the latter's contributions to the development of psychoanalytic aesthetics within the English object-relations school. Later, in an essay on 'The Natural Imagination: An Essay on the Experience of Architecture' (*The Architectural Review*, January 1989), Wilson offers a reading of Stokes that parallels the powerful experiences of compression and release generated by Group 10's installation. Between a first Melanie Klein-ian 'position' as 'an all-embracing envelopment with the mother', an 'all-enveloping environment' which is 'spatial, physical, tactile', and the sudden change to the 'contrary position of exposure and detachment', as when we are released from Group 10's impinging curved planes to the confrontation with Adams's arresting totem.[49] Then, there is the obvious homage to Le Corbusier's Ronchamp; Stirling thought that Group 10's piece was 'just right for that moment because Ronchamp had recently been built … and we were still

FIGURE 6.11 *Group 10 exhibit, 'This is Tomorrow' exhibition (1956), Whitechapel Art Gallery, London. John Maltby / RIBA Collections.*

coming to terms with the shift in Le Corbusier's work'.[50] Banham had pointedly opened his December 1955 'The New Brutalism' article with a collage of seven photographs of the exterior of Notre Dame du Haut at Ronchamp, 'one of the most personal and surprising buildings of [Le Corbusier's] career'. And, like many of his contemporaries, voiced 'consternation' at how 'a master of logical structure' could have 'set his great curving roof apparently afloat above the apexes of the massive and perforated walls', commonly associated with rude vernacular structures.[51] The one-time prophet of industrial rationalism now offered a disconcertingly enveloping form-world of rough and striated surfaces, one that was chthonic and irrational, and for many archaically monumental – hardly a manifesto for the future? But it helps to explain the organicism of Group 10's construction which also contains Wilson's proportional Wittkower side, and Frank Newby's carefully calculated intervals to the cuts of the suspended canopy element. The installation 'was mostly hardboard, though some of it had aluminium on one side, and some was matt, sprayed as roughly as possible'.[52]

Stokes and the love of wall-space

Such studied alternations of smooth and rough surfaces again indicate Wilson's immersion in the writings of Stokes in the 1950s, here a 'terribly important' book for the architect was Stokes's *Smooth and Rough* of 1951. Wilson first encountered Stokes through his *Art and Science* (1949), a study of the humanist cultures of Alberti, Piero della Francesca, and Giorgione. Here Stokes reiterates the primacy of the 'flat [architectural] surface', how in 'the early Renaissance supremely so, *the wall was the architectural focus*, its apertures, demarcations, protrusions, which were never more fruitful to the mind', and he cites Wittkower in support of Alberti's sensibility to 'the logic of the wall structure';[53] Stokes had first formulated this notion of the 'love of wall-space' in *The Quattro Cento* (1932).

Stokes underwent seven years of analysis with Melanie Klein (1882–1960), beginning in December 1929. The psychoanalytic undercurrent of the earlier texts first becomes explicitly part of his critical aesthetics in *Inside Out* (1947) and *Smooth and Rough* (1951). The latter book ends with twenty-four expressive plates mostly 'of Italian buildings of the 15th and 16th centuries, a period when change of surface carries a rich emotional directness. They are chosen for easy wall-significance, for a palpable interaction of smooth and rough surfaces....';[54] among them the two buildings which were his lifelong touchstones of wall-significance, Alberti's Tempio Malatestiano, Rimini (begun 1450), and Luciano Laurana's courtyard to the Palace of Urbino (*c*. 1465). Chapter 6, 'The Sense of Rebirth (2): Architecture', contains impassioned Kleinian readings of architectural surface:

> There is a hunger of the eyes, and doubtless there has been some permeation of the visual sense, as of touch, by the one all-embracing oral impulse. Architecturally, we experience the beloved as the provident mother. The building which provokes by its beauty a positive response, resuscitates an early hunger or greed in the disposition of morsel that are smooth with morsels that are rough, or of wall-space with the apertures ...[55]

Klein's account of infantile development posits the two 'positions' outlined in Wilson's 'The Natural Imagination', the first 'paranoid-schizoid' position followed by the second 'depressive' position. In the first position, characteristic of the earliest months of infant life, the ego lacks integration and negotiates its relations to its inner and outer worlds through part-objects such as the breast of the 'provident mother'. In the second depressive position, a level of ego integration is achieved whereby outer objects can now be grasped in their integrity, and as both 'good' and 'bad', and the mother (and father) can be comprehended as real persons, as complete outward figures. At the same time, the ego now has the capacity to experience regret, guilt, and longings. In *Smooth and Rough* Stokes remains orthodoxly Kleinian in privileging the role of the depressive position in creativity – a strong Gestalt in fact: 'Architecture draws upon the origin of all sense of wholeness'.[56] Stokes associates the first and second positions respectively with the modelling and carving distinctions – that 'direct carving' to which the IG was opposed. But a fascinating development in his subsequent books – beginning with *Michelangelo* (1955) and continuing up to *Reflections on the Nude* (1967) – is the greater value he accords to the enveloping 'oceanic' characteristics of modelling, seeing modelling and carving as reciprocal activities. A paper on 'Form in Art' (1955) problematizes the issue: 'How can it be that the homogeneity associated with idealization (the inexhaustible breast), is harnessed by the work of art to an acute sense of otherness and actuality?' He surmised that these apparently 'contrary elements' – 'a homogenous "state" into which we are drawn', and 'the mode of order and distinctiveness' – are harmoniously fused in art.[57] Stokes cautiously measures this evolution in his thinking against the ideas of Hannah Segal, whose paper on 'A Psycho-analytical Approach to Aesthetics' (1947) articulated an orthodox Kleinian aesthetic, insisting that 'the wish to create is rooted in the [second] depressive position and the capacity to create depends on a successful working through it . . .'.[58] But another important contributor to the British School, Marion Milner, found support for her own direction in Stokes's validation, in 'Form in Art', of the role of the 'oceanic feeling' in aesthetic experience. Her own work overlaps with the ideas of Ehrenzweig and urges the importance of experiences of fusion, and de-differentiation, in the creative cycle.[59]

Stokes fully embraces the idea of architecture as the 'Mother of the Arts': 'Fine building exemplifies the reparative function of art: wide feelings . . . that centre on landscape, on mother-earth, are particularized in houses'.[60] The architectonic wall-plane is the basis for painting, as in the art of fresco, and for sculpture, especially that blossoming of low-relief Stokes admired in Agostino di Duccio's carvings in the Tempio Malatestiano. Reassuring urban surfaces are fundamental to psychological health: 'Both by agriculture and architecture, and very often in the graphic arts through the example of building, a sensitiveness to surface has been employed, the lover's or the infant's precognition, evoking from stone or from canvas a unity of forms which are felt to be pre-existent . . .'.[61] Stokes venerated much fourteenth- and fifteenth-century Italian architecture, he championed Modernist artists like Ben Nicholson, Barbara Hepworth, and Henry Moore, but deplored most architecture from the mid nineteenth century onwards as lacking surface-significance.

For Stokes the surfaces of modern painting – from the Impressionists onwards – have been called upon, post-industrialization, to supply those reassuring textures once offered by the faces of architecture. Stokes explored these ideas in a lecture to the ICA on 29 February 1956 entitled: 'The Prime Influence of Building in the Graphic Arts'.[62] Here his contribution was part of a wide-ranging diet of lectures and talks showing the ICA's concentration on the interaction of different art forms; for example, also in February Reyner Banham spoke on 'Revaluation: Futurism', and the following month there was an architecture discussion on *The New Brutalism* with Toni del

Renzio and Ronald Jenkins; in June, Stokes also contributed again to a discussion on 'Freud and the Arts'.

'My talk is about what I shall call texture', Stokes begins, as he presents a series of slides stimulated by the 'everyday surfaces of smooth and rough stone', even of ordinary buildings in Italy. Texture is naturally an attribute of surface, but for him space also has a texture, and colour is also embedded in texture:

> If one sits down in front of such an [ordinary] house and thinks about the satisfying meaning of these simple proportions, an observation of the rapid changes of light and dark made by the carvings and recesses, of the pantiles on the roof, will come to mind; and soon the concept, proportion, will be abandoned, or rather proportion is there to vivify harmonious and extremely meaningful divisions of textures, surfaces and their recessions that contrast with and supplement each other.[63]

In the contemplation of such everyday 'textures, surfaces, and recessions', Stokes suggests how 'all root pleasures not only from architecture but from graphic art exist here in embryo'. Presupposing this correspondence between building and 'graphic arts in the west' it was then a matter of presenting a series of slides to show this parentage: walls and slitted shutters to a terrace; Michelangelo's allegorical *Archers shooting at a herm*; Watteau's *The Music Party* where the 'tall pillars with raised, rusticated bands are parent' to the other textures of 'wine, silks, feathery trees'. To many in the audience the lecture must have been evocative, but puzzling, having scant knowledge of the psychoanalytic aesthetics, and hinterland of Italian exploration, that underlay Stokes's ruminations. Stokes's chief complaint is that 'there is not enough good building today: consequently direct influence of building upon the graphic arts is at a minimum: in the great periods, architectural influence was ceaseless'. As he problematized this in *The Painting of our Time* (1961), painting has been forced, by this failure of architecture from the mid nineteenth century onwards, 'to fill the void, to provide the more intimate architectural pleasures ... to enwrap us with a surface ... to declaim from a wall the need for tactile passages and transitions that were once available in lovely streets'.[64] Seurat was one such filler of the void; in the ICA talk, 'the whole huge canvas' of Seurat's *The Bathers at Asnières* (1884) 'constructs a strong impression of coalescence in the manner of the flints out of which many English churches and church towers were made'. Consequently, in *The Stones of Rimini* (1934) Stokes dislikes the plasticity of modern building materials, how 'with an armature of steel, Le Corbusier can make you a room of any shape you like. He can express speed with a building'.[65] Nevertheless, he had shown *some* enthusiasm for inter-war Modernist architecture, and had even lived for a time in Wells Coates's landmark Isokon Lawn Road Flats in Hampstead, London (1934). Stokes never wrote on Le Corbusier's post-war *béton brut*, but he was 'deeply impressed' by the tactility and embracing spatial qualities of Wilson's Cambridge work. In 1966 he lectured there in the Brutalist School of Architecture extension, saw Wilson's recent load-bearing brick tower of student accommodation for Peterhouse College (William Stone Building, 1960–4), and experienced the monumental concrete-block dwelling Wilson had built for himself at Grantchester Road (1961–4).[66] And, if only in a notebook entry of 31 July 1953, there is enthusiasm for the major British public building of the post-war period, the Royal Festival Hall, opened in 1951, and realized by the design team led by Leslie Martin and Peter Moro:

> The creation of space & smooth-&-rough is the whole of the Festival Concert Hall. At last, space in London, with the surround & river. Hardly necessary to go to Italy for it. The great silent corridors with glass walls beyond which the electric trains are seen to slink on the bridge though they cannot be heard. What is this space psychologically, the essence of architecture & and all visual art. It provides both the feeling of oneness and distinctness.[67]

At the ICA Stokes alludes to this 'oneness' of the paranoid-schizoid position when he supposes 'that while depending for recognition on vision, graphic art relies for deeper effect upon the sensations that are especially developed in the blind man and soon in the infant who explores the generalized shapes and then the textures in his limited world'. This characteristic of vision to be dependent on touch, and indeed also on oral sensations, prompts Juhani Pallasmaa's exploration of vision and hapticity in *The Eyes of the Skin* (2005). After citing Stokes's *Smooth and Rough* on the 'oral and tactile notions that underlie the visual' he commends the capacity of the sensuous materials and craftsmanship of the best of modern architecture to excite oral and tactile experience: the California works of Charles and Henry Greene, Carlo Scarpa's exquisite details, the tactile colour of Luis Barragán's dwellings.[68]

* * *

Psychoanalytic aesthetics, as seen here in the work of Stokes, Ehrenzweig, and others, is surely one way of accounting for the personal and cultural traumas that fed an almost exaggerated emphasis on tactility and surface as-found within The New Brutalism and its related phenomena. The 'British School' made a major contribution in developing a Kleinian object-relations aesthetic, and Stokes was pre-eminent in placing architecture at the centre of his theory-building. Their probing of Gestalt psychology to unlock the potential of undifferentiated image-making (Ehrenzweig), and the invitation to surface-depths of unconscious phantasies (Stokes), articulated the challenge to 'good' Gestalt form-making at the heart of Brutalist and Independent Group experimentations. The Smithsons also considered themselves 'very English' in maintaining a critical distance to the allure of

USA consumer culture, in embracing an earthier materiality, while inculcating themselves in the work and ideas of Mies van der Rohe, and of Charles and Ray Eames. At the outset and throughout these years there is the working through of a persistent English Picturesque, in the case of both the Smithsons and Wilson, first unconsciously suppressed, and then unabashedly embraced. Among various other cultural legacies was an attraction to Victorian 'ugliness', to that Butterfield-ian 'bloody-mindedness' that became one of the tenets of Brutalism.

CHAPTER SEVEN

Pattern, Abstraction, Post-Modernism

Lubetkin – Pasmore – Stirling

Façadism versus Functionalism

The preceding examinations into Brutalism and the Picturesque left unexplored tendencies to formalist-abstract pattern-making – approaches that would re-emerge within Post-Modernism. Take the punchy black-and-white cover of *The Architectural Review* of November 1954, where a grouping of figures cast in Coade stone is teasingly superimposed above a graphic abstraction of part of the access elevation of one of the large blocks of Tecton's Hallfield Estate, Paddington, London (1946–54). In its note to this cover, *The Architectural Review* sees both – Coade stone and pre-cast concrete – as equally 'concerned with the application of a synthetic material as part of a system of architectural discipline', within their respective compositions. Both make a 'representational accent', and 'the intervening century of Ruskinian and Neo-Ruskinian thought would have pronounced anathema on both'.[1] Coade was an excellent artificial stone whose output, from its factory in Lambeth, provided most of the architectural ornament to the terraces of London's West End, from the mid-1770s onwards. Its embellishments livened up the potential monotony of Neo-classical developments such as Bedford Square (begun 1776), which many Modernists admired, taking the modulations of such Georgian terraces as models of functional rationalism.

The Hallfield Estate represents a climax to the issues raised by Highpoint II (1936–8) where, as considered earlier, Tecton began to exploit the declamatory potential of the architectural surface, in the face of sharp

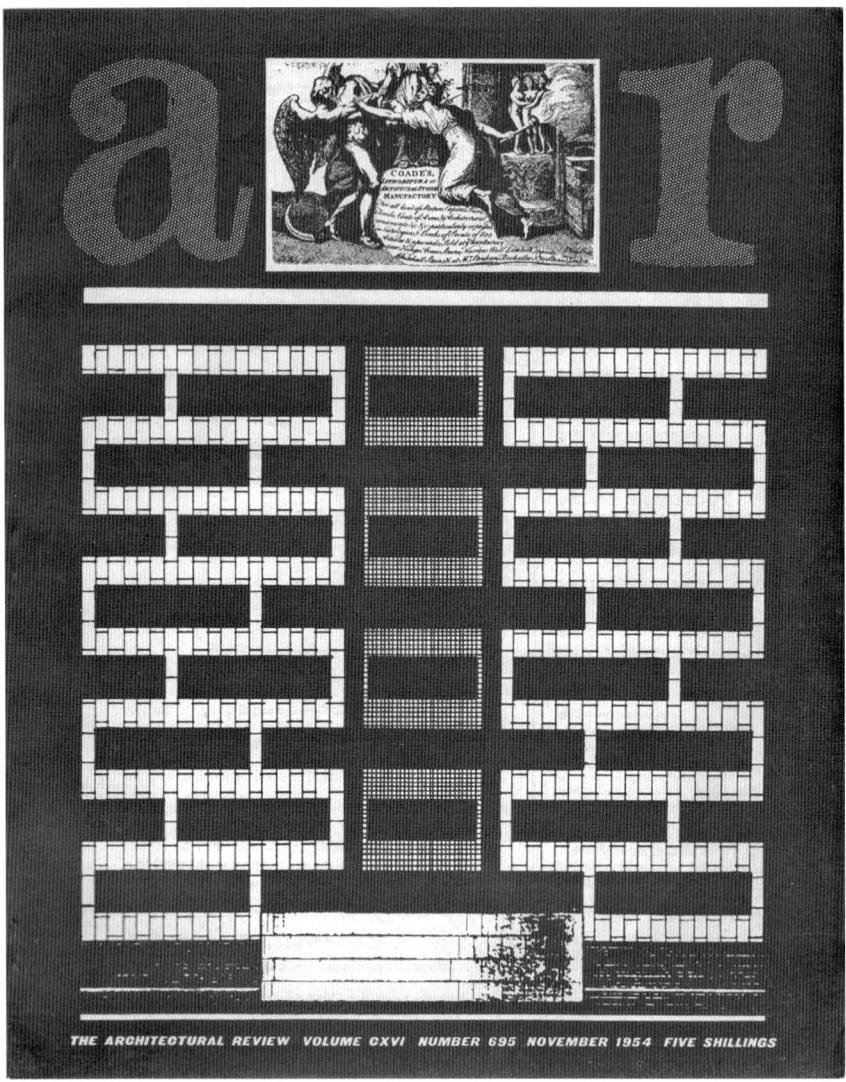

FIGURE 7.1 *Cover of* The Architectural Review *(November 1954), showing part of the access elevation of one of the large blocks of the Hallfield Estate, Paddington, London.*

criticisms of formalism. Hallfield was Tecton's swansong; it had been mostly designed before the dissolution of the firm in 1948, and was developed and executed by the practice of Lasdun and Drake from 1948–54. It is also a question of scale and repetition when the Highpoints, or a Bedford Square, are compared to an enormous estate like Hallfield – some 6,000 inhabitants occupying thirty-six acres of urban parkland; here the architects were confronted by questions of how to handle their slab-blocks, ten storeys high, of identical single-storey dwellings, when the cost-restraints did not even run to balconies.

So it was that the problems of articulating the surfaces of these giant redevelopment schemes were 'live issues at the moment' – as *The Architectural Review* stated in this November 1954 issue – and it again took Reyner Banham's perspicacity, to pull together the threads at issue, in a criticism piece on 'Façade' which preceded a closer reading, and photo-spreads of these Tecton 'Flats at Paddington'.[2] To a 'hard' modernist, the impact of Tecton's design is unsettlingly immediate when approaching the estate, from the east, on the main Bishop's Bridge Road. The flat 220-foot frontage of the access side of the first of the ten-storey slab-blocks confronts the viewer, three of which echelon along the main road, with lower six-storey blocks slotted in-between. To the road the slab-blocks present the access-deck elevation, the one shown, in part, on *The Architectural Review*'s cover; to a shocked Banham, 'the immediate impression . . . is that the architect has dealt with his facade in an original, obtrusive and alarming manner'. 'Obtrusive and alarming' because:

> Facade treatments do not form part of the common theory of the Modern Movement as our elders and betters have left it. In the pure theory the problem of the facade does not exist – form follows function, and when the problems of the interior have been correctly resolved the exterior form will be found to have crystallized into an unarguable solution. . . . So, in spite of the fact that facades must be dealt with somehow – and many of the architect's most purely aesthetic decisions are concerned with facings and fenestrations – we prefer that it should appear that these decisions were forced upon the designer by structural, technical or functional considerations which were almost beyond his control – climate, column-loadings, privacy, for instance – and feel embarrassed when we see facades like those of Paddington which have been treated as works of art in their own right.[3]

Inherently, there was not so much to express on these façades, which comprised long access balconies, with central and end staircases, together with the necessity of other intermediate widenings in the circulation where the refuse-chutes were located. Seeking to avoid the unrelieved monotony of horizontal galleries, Tecton wrapped the whole elevation in a frame of cream-coloured ceramic tiles, as if to a carpet, or – to Banham's eyes – a Baroque picture-frame with an abstract cresting. Within this frame they then hung a screen of precast concrete cladding, variegated with grey and white Cornish granite aggregate, patterned as an open-ended 'S' keymeander, stayed by discontinuous verticals. In contrast, the gallery widenings at the central staircase, and refuse chutes, are formed as distinct boxwindows framed in the cream ceramic tile (the *Review*'s cover shows these

FIGURE 7.2 *Tecton (with Drake and Lasdun), Hallfield Estate, Paddington, London. North-east elevation of large block seen from Bishop's Bridge Road. Architectural Press Archive / RIBA Collections.*

motifs of the central-stair/refuse-chute box-windows flanked by the 'S' key-meanders). Such close-readings of these 'alarming' façades gave Banham 'the clue to the shock which this building affords to routine-minded modernists', for screen-hanging like this is purely aesthetic, bearing at best only episodic connections to the fundamentals of structure, accommodation, and circulation. Banham contrasts the pattern-making of Hallfield's access elevation 'without vertical or horizontal tendency' to the strong ocean-liner like horizontals of the cantilevered access-balconies of Tecton's Priory Green Estate, Finsbury (1943–51).[4] A 'routine-minded modernist' would naturally have had no issue with these, but the other Priory Green elevations explore the same pattern-making, and chequerboard-elevation experiments, Lubetkin and Tecton had embarked upon at the Spa Green Estate, on Rosebery Avenue, in London's Finsbury area (1938–46).

Concurrent with the publication of these Rosebery Avenue flats (*The Architectural Review*, March 1951), Lubetkin wrote an apologia defending the principles underlying the philosophy of exterior design which Tecton was then evolving. 'Mechanistic tendencies', he contended, had emerged in the positivist approach to Modernism (*Sachlichkeit*) which had denied the 'individual and social aspects' of human beings, but the answer to this was *not* a romantic retreat 'into a world of *Gemütlichkeit*, suburban timidity and a conformist modesty'. In Modernism's bald solution 'formal expression [had been] left to itself as a functional resultant', considering as irrelevant 'the very material with which the architect operates', namely 'the principles of composition, the emotional impact of the visual'. Rosebery Avenue was therefore predicated on the principle of giving equal value to 'human scale, in the modelling of the whole composition, and in the treatment of details', together with the Modernist design norms of plan, volumetric articulation, and structure:

> Too often in contemporary buildings of this kind the elevational proportions, with their repetitive rhythm of openings seem to form part of a continuous band of indeterminate limits, which could be snipped off by the yard at any point. It was our endeavour to devise a design which, instead of relying solely on the interplay of the main volumes irrespective of their treatment, would take the basic rhythm proceeding from the plan, and further develop this rhythm in an overall pattern of light and shade, bringing human scale to the main abstract forms. We have already stressed the importance of the integrated relationship between planning, structure and expression in modern architecture. In the light of this it is hardly necessary to repeat that such attempts at elevational treatment have nothing in common with mere surface pattern-making.[5]

As an émigré, Lubetkin then reflects on his gradual coming-to-terms with the givens of English climate and culture, from his Russian and continental European background – issues outlined earlier. On how the Mediterranean high-modernist abstraction of Highpoint I, designed in 1934, had lacked plastic impact 'in the London climate, with its absence of light', whereas the following Highpoint II (1937–8) had experimented with 'the richness of treatment so necessary in [English] climatic conditions', by freeing the elevation from its loadbearing role and 'introducing a variety of materials and of elevational relief'. Rosebery Avenue takes this evolution a stage further. As we saw, all this marries with the conclusions of Pevsner, another great émigré, whose *Kunstgeographie* saw the linear, screen-like character, and varied materials and textures, of much English architecture – the fact that it is 'line and not body' – as appropriate to 'the mists of the north'.[6] Lubetkin settled in England in 1931 and his essay '*L'Architecture en Angleterre*' in the *L'Architecture d'Aujourd'hui* of 1932 muses on the cultural particulars of English architecture. He praises as 'powerful, impressive and persistent' the town-planning and the informal 'harmony of the landscape' of John Nash's Regent's Park in London, as compared to the formality of Haussmann's Paris: 'Urbanity, order. . . . Yes indeed, architecture is man's will in the surrounding disorder. And Paris is at least as far from London as Le Corbusier from Ruskin'. He looks sympathetically at the classical tradition of his new homeland, and its tuning of Palladio to the English context; as he in turn would nuance the abstract modernism of Highpoint I. And he applauds the variety of England's native brickwork: 'But what brick! From the softest creams, through scarlets, strong and blood-red, to violet purples – there, matured by centuries of experience, is the palette from which the English mason composes his masterpieces ... brick, this material of Pharaohs and a foundation of the English architectural tradition, shows immense vitality ... and is still flourishing in England today'.[7]

Rosebery Avenue used a Danish concrete monolithic box-frame construction, introduced to the country by the consulting engineer to the project, Ove Arup. This had the advantage of freeing the elevations from any structural role, thus allowing the desired elevational variety. In an interview between architect-planner Lionel Brett and Lubetkin (published in the same March 1951 issue of the *Review*) Brett accused Lubetkin: 'You have deliberately, and presumably with difficulty, disguised their box-frame construction'. To which Lubetkin retorted: 'I can't believe you really mean to wave [Ruskin's] Lamp of Truth in my eyes. We made the decision not to display the frame on the side elevations and we built up a consistent pattern on that decision'.[8] Ruskin was often invoked like this as a shorthand for structural positivism although – as the earlier parts of this book have demonstrated – Lubetkin's modus operandi is in truth closer to the complexities of Ruskin's wall-veil. In fact, the inner façades of the eight-storey block at Rosebery Avenue could hardly be a more direct expression of the crate of bedrooms within; 112 identical bedroom windows are stamped unremittingly into a plane of brickwork, broken only by three verticals of perforations lighting the staircase half-landings. If these relentless elevations are didactic statements, is this one saying?: 'Look, this is all you get when formal expression [is] left to itself as a functional resultant'. Yet even these austere inward-looking walls are accented, and centred, by the shadow-band of the roof-level drying-shelter and the projecting porch and entrance hall, and enclosed in a frame of light ceramic tile (as we saw also at the later Hallfield Estate) to give closure to the composition and to prevent the indeterminate 'snipped off by the yard at any point' effect.

Viewed from Rosebery Avenue, the severe brick-faced bedroom side of the eight-storey block acts as a foil to the lively living-room elevations of Sadler House; this serpentine-plan four-storey block mediates between the taller slab-blocks and the wider context of nineteenth-century terraces. In composing his façades Lubetkin drew on a rich diversity of sources; there are the rectilinear Caucasian kelims remembered from his youth, and his experiences of the collections of the Berlin Textile Academy where he was enrolled in 1922–3; the Early Renaissance, Ducal Palace of Urbino, was also an inspiration towards his chequerboard solution to surface-composition.[9] The entrance forecourt elevation to this great palace complex has three handsome portals set within a stone revetment, which make chequerboard patterns with the unaligned piano-nobile windows above, whose stone aedicules gleam in a field of pink brickwork. The chequerboards of Sadler House are particularly strong in effect, as the alternations of brick, light

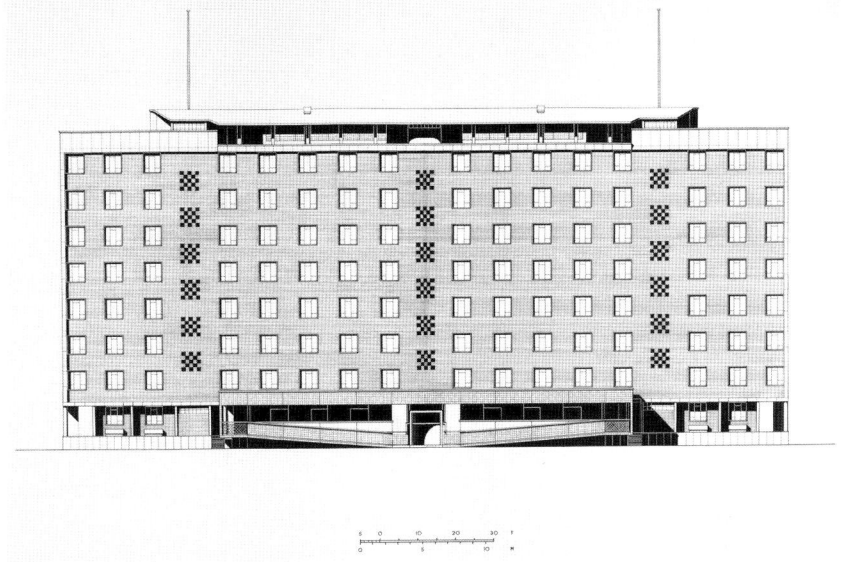

FIGURE 7.3 *Tecton, Spa Green Estate, Finsbury, London. Drawing of bedroom façade of eight-storey block. RIBA Collections.*

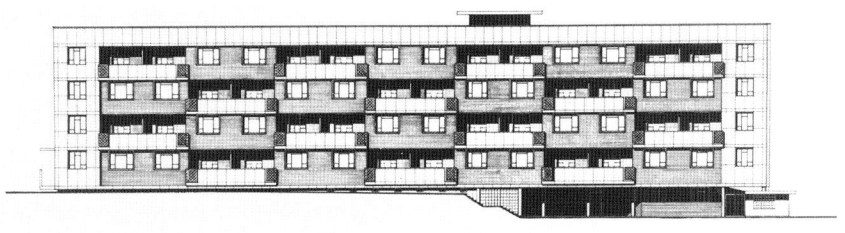

FIGURE 7.4 *Tecton, Spa Green Estate, Finsbury, London. Drawing of living-room elevation of Sadler House. RIBA Collections.*

balcony-balustrade planes, and shadowed recesses, derives organically, from an equal alternation in plan, of living rooms and bedrooms from one floor to the next. As in the other blocks, the whole façade is framed in a light tile border to allow 'the elevation to be perceived as a closed composition rather than as a series of strips cut off'.[10] In an article in *Architectural Design* (December 1951) – sharply entitled 'Knots in the

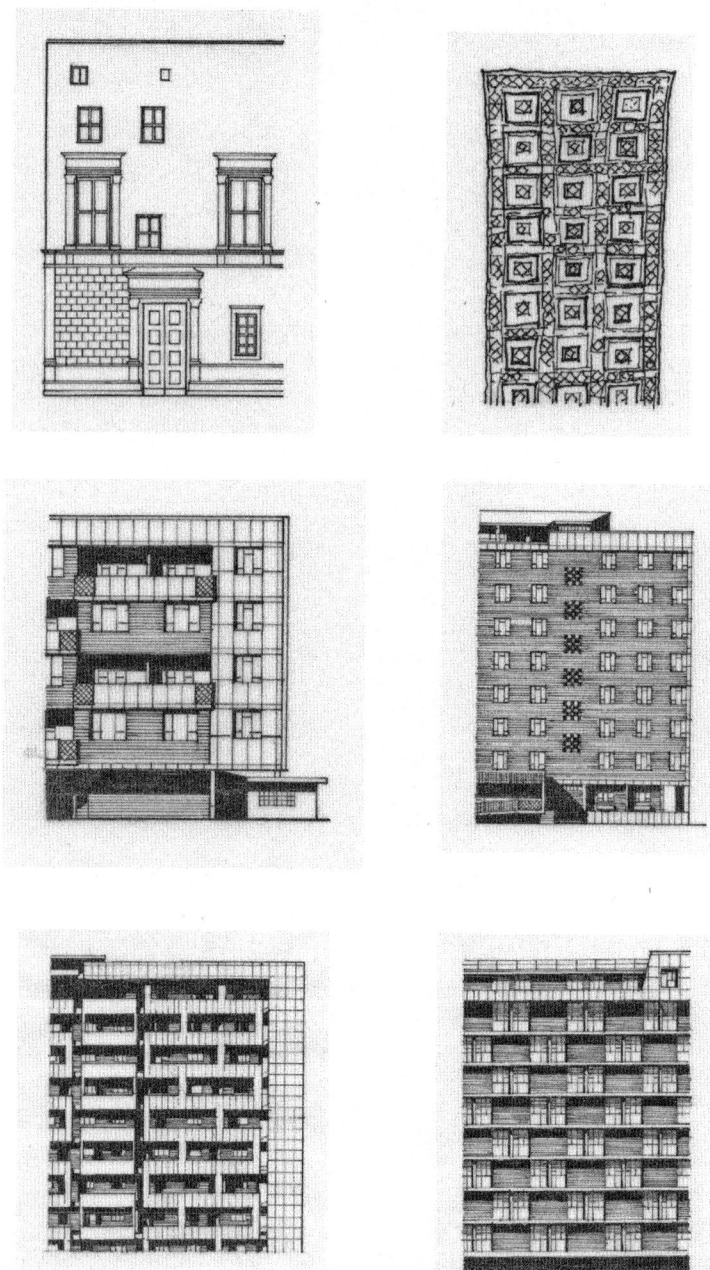

FIGURE 7.5 *Comparative patterns: top left, Palace of Urbino; top right, kelim; middle left, Sadler House, Spa Green Estate; middle right, Spa Green Estate, bedroom side of eight-storey block; bottom left, Hallfield Estate access elevation; bottom right, Hallfield Estate, living accommodation elevation. Drawings Stephen Kite.*

Master's Carpet' – the German émigré architectural-historian Julius Posener preferred *not* 'to be a knot in the master's carpet', and was critical of 'the present patternomania', 'touched off' by the 'sun-breaker' zones of pattern in certain Le Corbusier buildings, such as the Cité d'Affaires, Algiers (1938–42).[11] He favoured the self-discipline, as he saw it, of the inward-facing bedroom façades at Rosebery where the architect refrains from playing with the elemental structure, abstains 'from changing the whole thing into an ornament', as Posener regarded the carpet-like public façades. Where Lubetkin had admired Nash's Regent's Park terraces, Posener deplored their denial of the fact that they are merely repetitive rows of houses – not pedimented palaces, preferring the plain monotony of everyday Georgian-Regency terraces. No, he would rather accept the hard reality of 'being a number', in 'these enormous *unités*' of the modern world, than one of Lubetkin's 'knots'.[12]

Continuing *his* critique on 'Façade', Banham makes a comparison as provocative as the *Review*'s Coade Stone / Hallfield cover, by placing an image of Luigi Moretti's neo-Mannerist Casa del Girasole apartments in Rome (1947–50), above a view of London County Council's (LCC) Bentham Road flats in Hackney, London (1950–55). In the last chapter, the Hackney slab-block was noted as the LCC's neo-*Unité* prototype, and therefore of ostensibly impeccable Modernist credentials – designed by that team of 'hards', Colin St John Wilson, Peter Carter, and Alan Colquhoun. Yet, for Banham, both are not so different to Lubetkin at Hallfield, insofar as they 'conceal the contents and compose the façade as an independent work of art', certainly as compared to the direct expression of content found in high-modernist works such as the steel of Mies van der Rohe's Lake Shore Drive Apartments (1950–1) or the concrete of Le Corbusier's Marseilles *Unité d'Habitation* itself. In fairness to Bentham Road, Banham concedes that although it 'hangs a screen between the building's contents and the observer outside … [it] manages to look as if it were a Neutral Frame …', directly countenancing the maisonettes within, unlike the palpably composed Hallfield façades.[13] A visitor to Bentham Road today would find the block naked, as the pre-cast screen has been stripped off – the aesthetic consequences are calamitous, but the building is perfectly sound structurally without its atectonic veil. Wilson did admit to Italian influence at this time, but it was to 'a great hang-up about [Giuseppe] Terragni', to the earlier screens of his Casa del Fascio, Como (1932–6) – not Casa del Girasole.[14] Wilson and James Stirling, and other architects in Independent Group circles, knew of the Casa del Girasole; Banham himself had examined it closely in 1953 (*The Architectural Review*), there characterizing the façadism-versus-functionalism angst, as 'rationalism and eclecticism' within Italian architecture, and noting its 'disturbing quality'.[15] The Casa's paradoxically fractured façade *is* eclectic, but in the end both ingenious and rigorous – as Banham is obliged to conclude. Moretti floats a piano nobile of four storeys of apartments, behind shimmering planes of white mosaic and aluminium

FIGURE 7.6 Luigi Moretti, Casa del Girasole apartments, Rome. Architectural Press Archive / RIBA Collections.

screens, above a podium grafted with travertine *spoglia*. These bravura historical references are crowned by a sort of Mannerist-Baroque split-pediment, which continues down the façade as a cleft of shadow.

Some British architects, such as Wilson and Stirling, also drew inspiration from Moretti's journal *Spazio* – published from 1950–3 – with its dense meditations on the nature of architectural space and surface. In *Spazio 4* (January/February 1951) – from the kinds of Romanesque wall structures Ruskin had admired at Florence, Pisa, and Pistoia – Moretti theorized a 'transfiguration of wall surfaces', in 'full abstraction from any restraint or tectonic functionality'.[16] One compelling *Spazio* page-spread makes this point graphically, by comparing the square-on-the-diagonal façade revetments, of Florence's S. Miniato al Monte, to a diagonal Mondrian composition, and the rectilinear stone patterns of Pisa's Duomo, to Mondrian's equally rectilinear *Composition with Red* (1936). On Moretti's own account the problem he confronted at Il Girasole was to achieve:

Plasticity integral to the entire volume of the edifice; a break in the clarity and homogeneity of surfaces with areas of deep and violent shadows . . . full plastic freedom of expression in non-loadbearing surfaces; [as in] the importance of the travertine revetment at the base made evident through the placement of the stone panels according to purely abstract designs . . .[17]

Stirling admired Moretti, after Terragni, bracketing him between Jacob Bakema and the Smithsons as among those of Europe's 'best architects', who are 'conscious imperfectionists'; noting this in the 'Black Notebook' he kept between about 1953 and 1956. The 'conscious imperfectionists' are the art-architects who – in Stirling's accompanying sketch-diagrams – occupy one arm of a great-divide he sees occurring around 1948, between 'Antiquity' and 'Technology', between 'academic architecture / "ART"' and the 'Technological Architecture' that is non-art.[18] Therefore, the kind of splits already identified, both here and within the Independent Group debates, between closed and indeterminate form. For many Moretti was just too 'formalist', but Mark Crinson suggests that Stirling 'may have picked up more than a whiff of attractive diabolic sulphur in Moretti', in the Italian's suggestions of how Modernism could find ways forward, through re-readings of history. It is not surprising that Robert Venturi was also an admirer of Moretti; vide the split-pediment of the Vanna Venturi House (Chestnut Hill, Philadelphia, 1962) – now accepted as an icon of Post-Modernism.[19] Hereafter, I shall capitalize Post-Modernism, to distinguish the architectural style described, since the mid-1970s and 1980s, from a broader postmodernist sensibility. Stirling adds in the Black Notebook that here 'Colin Rowe's theory on Mannerism in modern architecture . . . might also apply', referring to Rowe's essay on 'Mannerism and Modern Architecture' (*The Architectural Review*, May 1950), where Rowe compares the formal ambiguities in Le Corbusier's work to certain designs of the sixteenth-century Italian Mannerists. More broadly, Moretti provides yet another instance of the importance of the reading of Italian architecture and theory, to the construction of British architectural identities – whether via Inigo Jones, Colin Campbell, Ruskin, Wittkower, Rowe or Banham. In a 1950 essay on 'Italian Eclecticism' (*The Architectural Review*, October 1952), Banham surmised that, for Moretti, 'the twentieth century is [a period] of continual eclecticism, with all the arts borrowing from one another and the past'. This, at a time when many trends in Italian architecture were challenging the purist assumptions of the Modern Movement, among them the editorial policy of Ernesto Nathan Rogers's *Casabella Continuità* magazine, and the historicism of his architectural practice BBPR.[20]

In 'Patterns in Living' (20 July 1952) – Colin St John Wilson's last contribution as an architectural columnist for *The Observer* newspaper – he complains of 'the assertively mannerist expression' of Lubetkin's Priory Green Estate in Finsbury. He was not alone in comparing Lubetkin's puzzling experiments, with the more acceptable mainstream expression of Powell and Moya's blocks at Churchill Gardens, Pimlico, which is 'fresh and sharp as a liner'. Bentham Road may have had a precast screen façade, but it nonetheless indexed the single dwelling that made up the whole, which Wilson thought 'the best way to give a true scale to large blocks of flats'. Although Tecton's breaking down 'into a checker-board of balcony, window and brick-panel' reduced the scale of their blocks, 'the unit of the checker-board pattern [did] not correspond organically with the single dwelling' – hence Wilson's accusation of assertive mannerism. Given that 'aesthetically the expression of the two schemes is very different', Wilson was driven to conclude that only the more normatively rational and coherent Churchill Gardens 'goes out wholeheartedly to meet both the machine and the modern tempo of living on their own terms . . .'.[21]

Lubetkin has been portrayed as the solitary 'outsider inside', in striving to make an *architecture parlante* more communicative of his social ideals – than the abstractness of Highpoint I – and one more mediatory towards English cultures of building.[22] So, although Lubetkin's experiments failed to impress many contemporary critics, they anticipate the best of Post-Modernism, in their aim to make an architecture more richly connected to history and place.[23] The 'overall pattern of light and shade', Lubetkin sought in Tecton's elevations, and rejected by most as formalist, attempted to figure forth the lives of individuals, by visibly knotting their activities into a wider new-order – those 'Patterns in Living' of Wilson's *Observer* column. 'Pattern' was a keyword of this period, for all kinds of urban, architectural, and societal orderings; Erwin Anton Gutkind's books – such as *Community and Environment* (1953) – had introduced terms such as 'patterns of association' and 'patterns of mobility'. Thus the Smithsons – inspired by the images circulating in the Independent Group – had argued for 'new systems of relationship'; 'It is our thesis that for every form of association there is an inherent pattern of building'.[24]

Patterns of Peterlee

An intriguing coda to Lubetkin's *architecture parlante* research – at the scale of the single dwellings – survives from the debacle of his involvement as Master-Planner for the Peterlee New-Town, designated in March 1948 for the mining communities of the north-east Durham coalfields. The site had great natural beauty, but also overlay parts of these same coalfields; the tensions between the vision of the New-Town on the one hand, and the National Coal Board's desire to extract the rich coal-seams on the other – with the related problems of subsidence undermining any new surface-developments – led to stalemate, and a frustrated Lubetkin's resignation in 1950. Nonetheless, a pilot scheme of a 'Hundred Houses' was progressed in detail, with a typology of linked dwellings, inspired by the pedimented linked semi-detached villas of Lloyd Baker Street (1819), which Lubetkin had admired from his work on the nearby Spa Green Estate, Finsbury. The houses were laid out upon an X site-plan of reflected parabolas. Owing to the subsidence problem 'the groundfloor raft and side walls were conceived as a "hollow channel" enclosing the desired accommodation, roofed by a shallow monopitch draining to a single side gutter, and cross-braced by a deep structural parapet'.[25] This internal or side-drainage is also commonly found in London's Victorian terraces, where it allows the street-façade to read as a clear frontage uncompromised by eaves or gutters. This meant that the fronts were non-loadbearing – Lubetkin called them 'gables that speak' – and, as Tecton had done with the large slab-blocks at Spa Green and the Hallfield Estate, enclosed even these small gable-ends with a frame. Seeing this use of cross-wall construction at a domestic scale, it so happens that 'Cross-Wall' versus 'Hole-in-the-Wall' had been yet another way whereby the 'hard' Corbusian Modernists marked themselves out from the disciples of Swedish Empiricism.[26] As will be seen, cross-wall construction remained integral to the post-Lubetkin phases of Peterlee. And, with his Span Developments launched in 1954, Eric Lyons would utilize cross-wall construction to make a gentle Modernism of flat-roofed terraces distinguished by lightweight façades of glass, white boarding and/or tile hanging – as at Blackheath, London, from 1956. This language cascaded to many private 1960s estates, where pitched roofs replaced flat, and site-layouts became conventionally suburban; even so, they signified an airy contemporary language as compared to the numerous sub-Poundbury twenty-first-century English estates of a 'hole-in-the-wall' retardataire Georgian-Regency – Poundbury being the Prince of Wales's neo-vernacular Dorset development conceived in 1989.

Within the 'two gables that speak', Lubetkin stated that 'any design from suburban to cubist could theoretically be inserted'. That he meant what he said, is proven by a spectrum of characterization studies in all the available languages of the time: stripped Holden-esque proto-Modernist; pure International Modernist; Festival of Britain 'soft' modernism with balconies and stone-cladding; half-timbered stockbrokers Tudorbethan; suburban semi-detached bay-window, etc. Likewise, a letter to Monica Felton – the first Chair of Peterlee Development Corporation (17 November 1947) – exhibits that same searching for a humanist language of his Rosebery Avenue apologia. He opines that the 'abstract, dematerialized expression' of the international 'modern vernacular' would not speak to the 'character of the miners'. But what would? Should it be expressive of the 'almost Piranesian environment' in which they spent their subterranean working lives, 'or would it be better to provide as the backdrop of their private lives, a setting of weightless, effortless, and optimistic aesthetic of the future atomic age?'[27] Neither in the letter, nor in the multiple characterization studies, does Lubetkin come to a conclusion, and his departure from Peterlee meant that

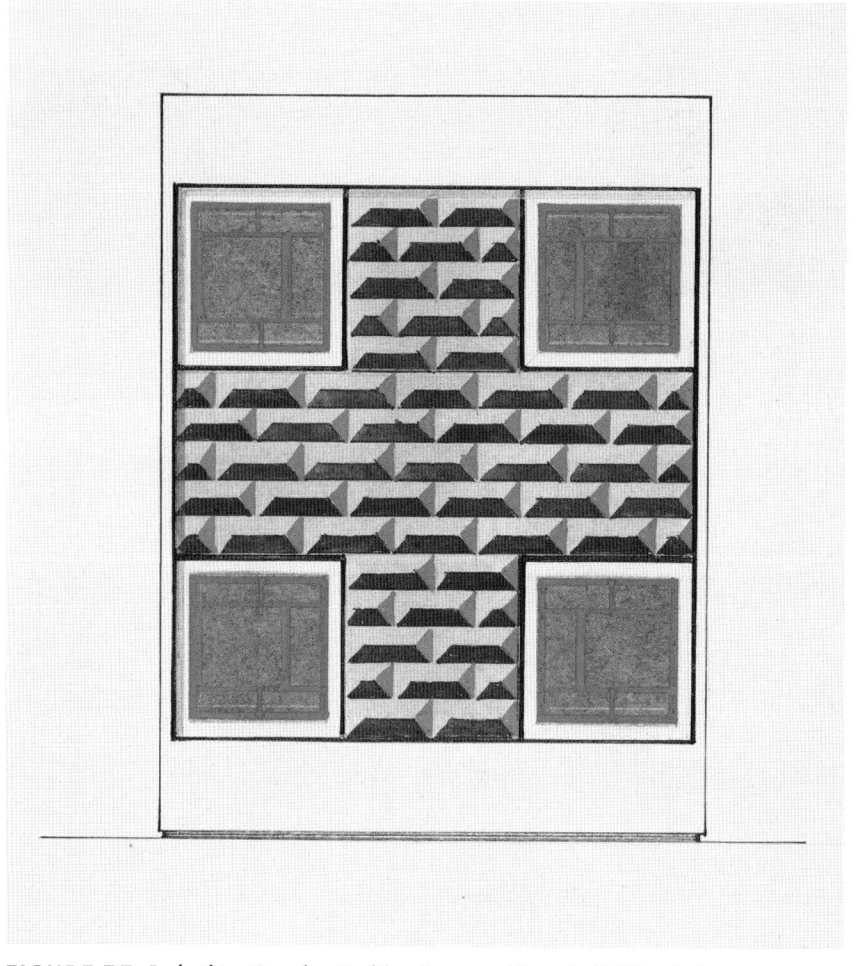

FIGURE 7.7 *Lubetkin, Peterlee, 'gables that speak' study. RIBA Collections.*

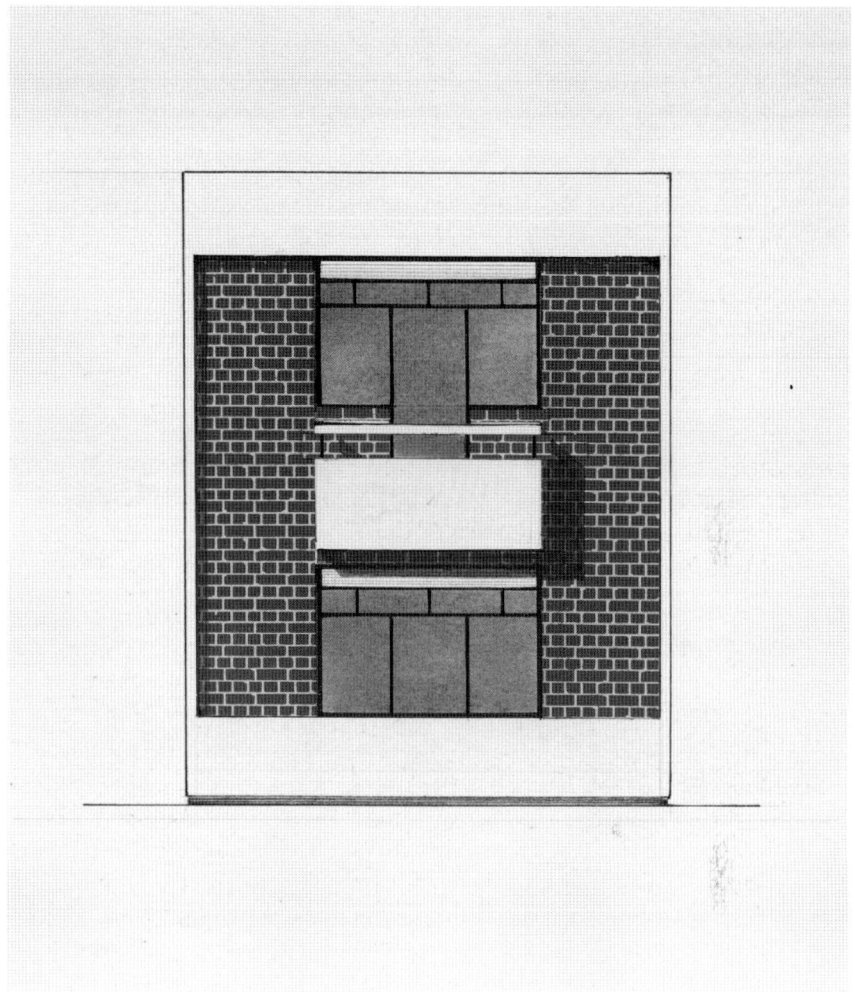

FIGURE 7.8 *Lubetkin, Peterlee, 'gables that speak' study. RIBA Collections.*

we shall never know which of the 'gables that speak' he would have chosen; it is unlikely that he would have gone for the half-timbering, or the Gothic gazebo options, which show noteworthy catholicity, yet without the self-conscious irony of later Po-Mo. Even so, these studies look remarkably proleptic of Post-Modernist semiotics; take the work of the FAT (Fashion Architecture Taste) practice – itself a highly self-conscious Po-Mo *revival* – whose housing at Islington Square, New Islington, Manchester (2006) plays with cut-out gables, patterned brickwork, and appliqué balconies, applied to repetitive plans, to speak to the characteristics of the local population. But when Lubetkin declared in his Royal Gold Medal address of 1982 that

'The sleep of Reason begets monsters' (invoking Goya's aquatint), one of the 'monsters', then in his sights, was Post-Modernist architecture.[28]

To pin down the use of this term in post-World War II British architecture, more precisely, it is necessary to again turn to Pevsner's authority, and his use of 'post-modern style' in a BBC Third Programme talk, sharply called 'The Anti-Pioneers', delivered on 3 December 1966, thirty years after the publication of his *Pioneers of Modern Design*. As he explains, although he had written on Art Nouveau, he had left 'ineffectual deviationists', such as the Expressionists (Mendelsohn, Poelzig, etc.) out of his account as, in his view, '*the* style of the century' had already been achieved in works such as Walter Gropius's Fagus Works (1910) and his Bauhaus buildings (1925) – that style Russell Hitchcock would speak of in the 1930s as the International Modern Style. And, though still *personally* committed to this High-Modernist path, he continues: 'But I am a historian and the fact that my enthusiasms can't be roused by Ronchamp or Chandigarh, by Churchill College and the Physicians does not blind me to the existence of a new style, successor to my International Modern of the 1930s, *a post-modern style, I would be tempted to call it*, but the legitimate style of the 1950s and 1960s'.[29] Here 'post-modern' encompasses the late Le Corbusier, Richard Sheppard, Robson & Partners, Brutalist brick and concrete Churchill College, Cambridge (1959–65), and the inverted ziggurat of Denys Lasdun's Royal College of Physicians at Regent's Park, London (1960–64). All exhibited what Pevsner also called 'Neo-Expressionism', by foregrounding the idioms of the artist-architect before that quiet accommodation of user-needs and programme seen in the best of International Modernism. Joseph Hudnut had been earlier in linking the term 'postmodern' to architecture in his essay of 1945, 'The Post-modern House', where he posits a house, its owner, and its architect who are all postmodern in accepting the advances of modernism and the 'collective-industrial scheme of life', while sustaining an 'ancient loyalty invulnerable against the siege of machines'.[30]

Given Ruskin's command to 'read' the surfaces of architecture, and Lubetkin's concern that his gables 'speak' to their miner inhabitants, factors immediate to our surface theme are the symbolic and semantic aspects of Post-Modernism as it becomes formulated as a style in the 1970s. Key landmarks in its definition include the aforementioned Vanna Venturi House (1962–4), Venturi's *Complexity and Contradiction in Architecture* (1966), Robert Venturi, Denise Scott Brown, and Steven Izenour's *Learning from Las Vegas* (1972), and George Baird and Charles Jencks's *Meaning in Architecture* (1969), which particularly expanded upon these semantic aspects in examining the potentials of applying F. de Saussure's structural linguistics, and concept of 'semiology' – the 'life of signs' – to architecture and urbanism. In defining the 'Decorated Shed', *Learning from Las Vegas* emphasizes 'image – image over process or form – in asserting that architecture depends in its perception and creation on past experience and emotional association and that these symbolic and representational elements may often be contradictory to the form, structure, and programme with which they convey in the same building'. In the 'decorated shed', 'space and structure are directly at the service of programme, and ornament is applied independently of them'; under this rubric the High-Renaissance Palazzo Farnese in Rome is as much a 'decorated shed' as the billboard frontages of Main Street, USA. Venturi, Scott Brown, and Izenour also 'argue for the symbolism of the ugly and ordinary in architecture and for the particular significance of the decorated shed with a rhetorical front and conventional behind: for architecture as shelter with symbols on it'.[31] Brutalism's manifestos, presented with equal urgency, told also of 'memorability as an image', and admire the 'primitive', the 'bloody-minded', the everyday and the ugly. Denise Scott Brown has acknowledged how 'our views emerged from Early Modern architecture and its postwar Brutalist admirers. These European thoughtways we linked to social protest of the 1960s, American social planning of that era, and emerging attitudes on democratic participation, popular culture, Pop Art, and new roles in architecture for history, symbolism and communication'.[32] Scott Brown studied at the Architectural Association School of Architecture in London from 1952, receiving her diploma in 1954. She describes herself as having been 'around, but not in, London's avant-garde movement' at the time, and was familiar with the work of the Independent Group members, such as the Smithsons, Paolozzi and Henderson, and Banham. Her photographs of London at this time, also evidence an 'as-found' interest in the gritty and the everyday.[33] In these European-USA 'thoughtways', Paolozzi and Hamilton's consumption of images of American mass-culture, and the Smithsons' absorption in journal photographs of Mies's IIT campus, work to inform Scott Brown and Venturi's theory and *modus operandi*, as mediated through Brutalist rhetoric.

Peterlee, Pasmore, and constructed abstract art

To take the Peterlee story forward, after Lubetkin's departure, is to pick up yet another significant strand from the 1950s, one Alastair Grieve has called 'a neglected avant-garde', that of 'constructed abstract art in England',[34] and the noteworthy story of artist-sculptor Victor Pasmore's experimental involvement in the next stages of the New-Town over a twenty-three-year period, from 1955 to 1978. It turns out to have been an isolated experiment, yet it represents a major and sustained attempt to carry through the abstract potentials inherent – at the larger scale – in the inter-relations of infrastructure, dwelling, and landscape, and – at the scale of the dwelling-cluster – within the wall-planes of cross-wall and flat-roof construction. Just as Group 10's Ronchamp-esque contribution to the 'This is Tomorrow' exhibition (1956) has dropped from view – as compared to the critical flux around the Hamilton and Smithsons installations (Groups 2 and 6) – so have those of the abstract artists gathered around Victor Pasmore with their roots in

Russian Constructivism and Suprematism, De Stijl and the Bauhaus.[35] As a leading 'constructivist', Pasmore collaborated with the architect Ernö Goldfinger and sculptor Helen Phillips, as 'Group 7'. *Architectural Design* (October 1956) showed a photograph of a 'relief by Pasmore and sculpture by Helen Phillips [as] related within the 16 foot square pavilion' – 'perhaps the most sophisticated space in the show', according to Theo Crosby.[36] Crosby saw the basic divide in the exhibition as between 'sections which ultimately derive from the constructivists and those who take their cue from the other movements of the twenties, Dadaism and surrealism'. Although at least four Groups can be said to have made settings representing the constructivist wing, it is the latter – Independent Group centred movements – that subsequent criticism of 'This is Tomorrow' has chosen to foreground. Crosby maintains that 'the constructivists have already had a great influence on architecture, but no actual constructivist building has ever been built; it remains a comprehensive and stimulating theory . . .'.[37] Pasmore's Peterlee remains a rare English attempt to work out these theories at large-scale in urbanism, landscape, and architecture.

Pin-wheeling planes steered visitors through the square modular plan of Group 7, in an architectural grammar whose well-known roots can be traced in Van Doesburg, Rietveld, De Stijl, and ultimately to Frank Lloyd Wright's 'destruction of the [architectural] box' into independent screens – a discovery made known to Europe by his Wasmuth portfolios published there in 1910 and 1911. To confront the viewer on entry, Pasmore mounted a large orthogonal relief on the central screen, of a type of his wherein horizontal rib-elements are disposed about a central spine – in contrast to Phillips's organic crab-like sculpture as discovered round the corner. From being an admired realist painter of the Euston Road School, Pasmore had made a dramatic conversion to abstraction in 1948, exhibiting his first reliefs in March 1952, and much of his art-practice continued to be devoted to relief-making from 1952 up to around 1960.[38] In 1954 he became Master of Painting at King's College, University of Durham, at Newcastle-upon-Tyne and it was at this time that his work was spotted by Arthur Vivian Williams, the combative and perceptive General Manager of Peterlee (1948–74), who was looking to revitalize the aesthetic direction of the town. Although much housing had been constructed since Lubetkin's departure in 1950, they were conventional two-storey semi-detached dwellings to dull layouts. Williams thought Peterlee could be improved by 'the employment of an artist capable of organizing small units of building in terms of mass and colour' and, liking the architectonic quality of the constructions of Pasmore's he had seen, he realized he had found that artist, whom he consequently appointed in 1955 as a consultant to Peterlee – a post he held up till 1978.[39] Pasmore established Five Points to govern the application of his modern spatial concepts to the urban design of his given area – the 300-acre southwest part of the New-Town, bordered to south and east by the topography of the deep wooded ravine of Blunts Dene:

He sought a more modern architectural style, with a cross-wall construction whose use of timber cladding was honestly expressed and which was flat roofed. He substituted black brick for red and developed with his two young architectural assistants, Peter Daniel and Frank Dixon, a system where the principal windows were placed in the non load-bearing walls, the windows stained brown and the main panels painted white. *Secondly, thirdly and fourthly*, the layouts were to articulate the topography, to break down the multiplicity of repeated units and to reduce them to a pedestrian scale. Public space, private gardens and garaging were to be integrated into the overall scheme as 'positive' features. His net-like treatment of private spaces is important in understanding how Pasmore's abstract grids of broken lines – in his planning work and paintings alike – translated themselves into housing layouts. *The fifth principle* was one found in other new towns, yet it produced radical results in Pasmore's hands. That was to free the housing from the road system.[40]

Pasmore's first sketch of the organization of the four housing groups of the south-west area, as free squares and spines, represents the distinct communities (with no through-traffic) inter-related by structures of circulation, hardscape, and softscape, and aligns with his reliefs of the time where, within a strict rectilinear discipline, 'quite large, flat rectangles are matched by rhythms of thin, linear slats'.[41] The first stage was the zone to the east, nearest the Dene, comprising 388 houses each with access to a private screened patio-space. Again, akin to the relief-making process, the first housing layouts were not conceived on paper, but by laying out wooden blocks upon a workshop floor. In a shared procedure, the architects and the artist then developed these into scale-models, testing the ideas which produced an intricate tapestry of dwellings, patios, parking zones, and courtyards structured on the open-grid pattern.[42] The cubic volumes, and their multitudinous connections to these immediate spaces, and the contours of the landscape flowing around, produced ostensibly picturesque results, but Pasmore's planning aims – conceived to attack 'the existing practices common in the New Town layouts' – refused 'the mistaken concept of the picturesque'.[43] His open grid pattern abjures winding roads and romantic landscape and his language, in actuality, derives from a belief in the 'complete autonomy of form' achieved by the revolution that, following Cubism, produced abstract art. In a statement on 'What is Abstract Art' – summarizing the ideas that had driven his 1948 conversion – Pasmore declared his belief in a development 'which is altogether independent of imitative techniques, literary associations and decorative functions. In abstract form, painting and sculpture have attained an objective status analogous to that of music. . . . The abstract artist must move from the two-dimensional medium of painting to the actual three-dimensional world of sculpture, "construction" or pure architecture'.[44] In thus liberating form from narrative and figuration,

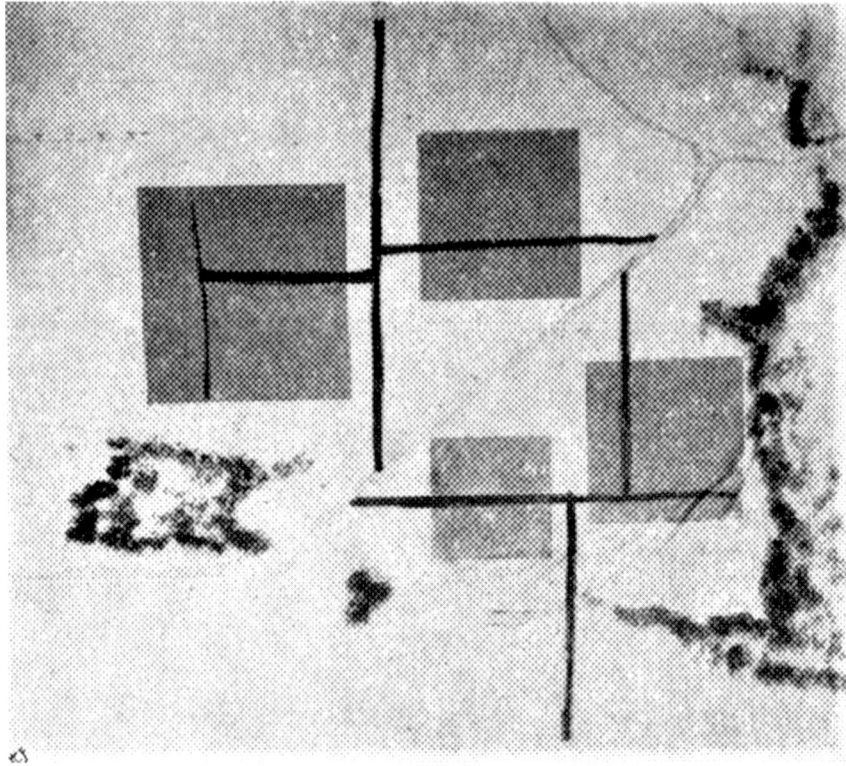

FIGURE 7.9 *Victor Pasmore, Peterlee, first sketch for disposition of housing groups of the South West Area.* The Architectural Review *(February 1961).* © *Estate of Victor Pasmore. All Rights Reserved, DACS 2022.*

the artists and architects of Constructivism or De Stijl sought to discover the objective significance of line, form, colour, and their relationships. Any such lingering beliefs in total abstraction that had survived into the 1970s – namely, that the constituents of art might possess such inherent properties – would be overturned by the semiotics and language-based theories that drove Post-Modernism. In his many writings Rudolf Arnheim also examined the psychodynamics of form in detached scientific language, in works such as *Art and Visual Perception* (1954, 1974) and *The Dynamics of Architectural Form* (1977). The latter book unabashedly examines the formal principles of the discipline through chapters, for example, as 'Elements of Space', 'Vertical and Horizontal', 'Solids and Hollows', and expresses puzzlement as to why architects 'neglect the active study of design', and read so much on linguistics, information theory, structuralism, sociology, and so forth, while evading 'the discission of architecture itself', whose 'design, of course, is nothing more or less than the creation of a building's tangible and visible shapes'.[45]

PATTERN, ABSTRACTION, POST-MODERNISM

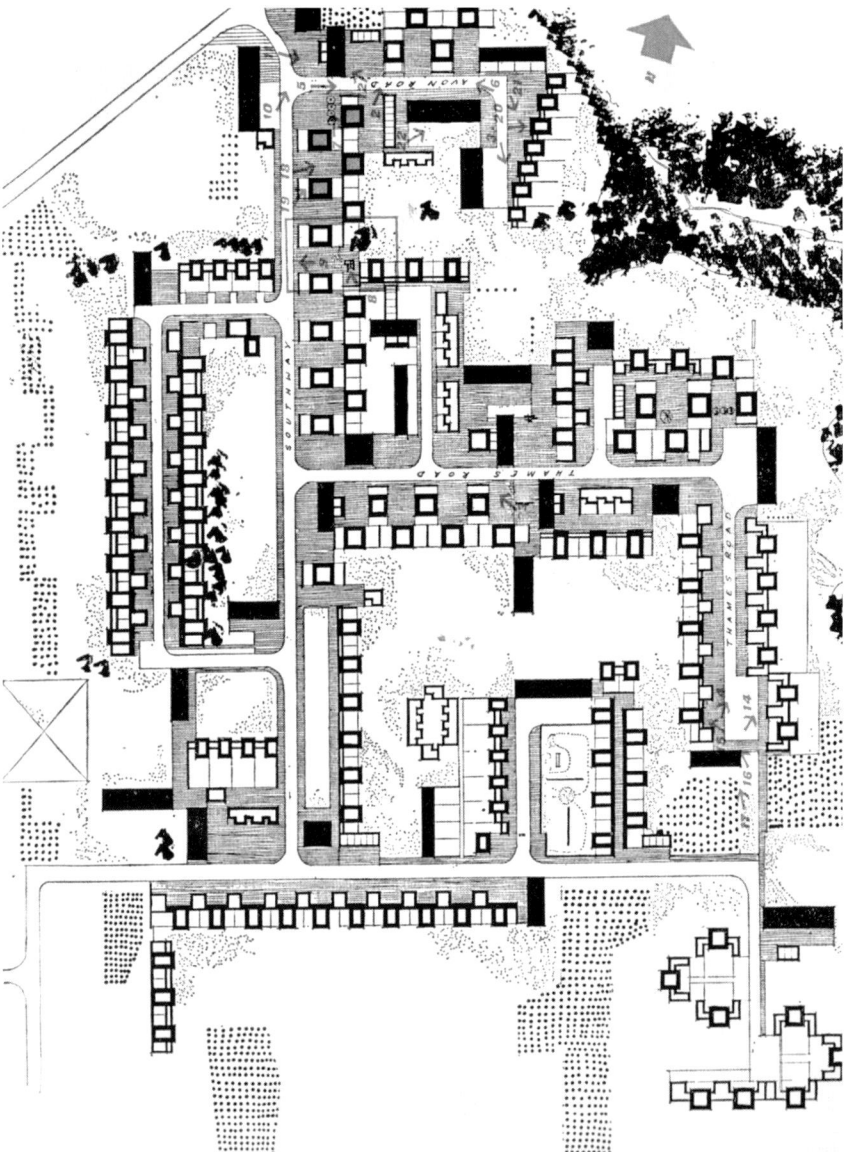

FIGURE 7.10 *Peterlee, South West Area, layout plan of the first major housing group.* The Architectural Review *(February 1961).*

It is to be expected that Pasmore and the architects would exploit the abstract potential of the planar language of flat-roofed – or very shallow-pitch – cross-wall construction, patterning a neutral palette of white or black brickwork, white-painted glazed screens, and vertical and horizontal timber boarding, stained grey or black. Slatted screen elements extend out

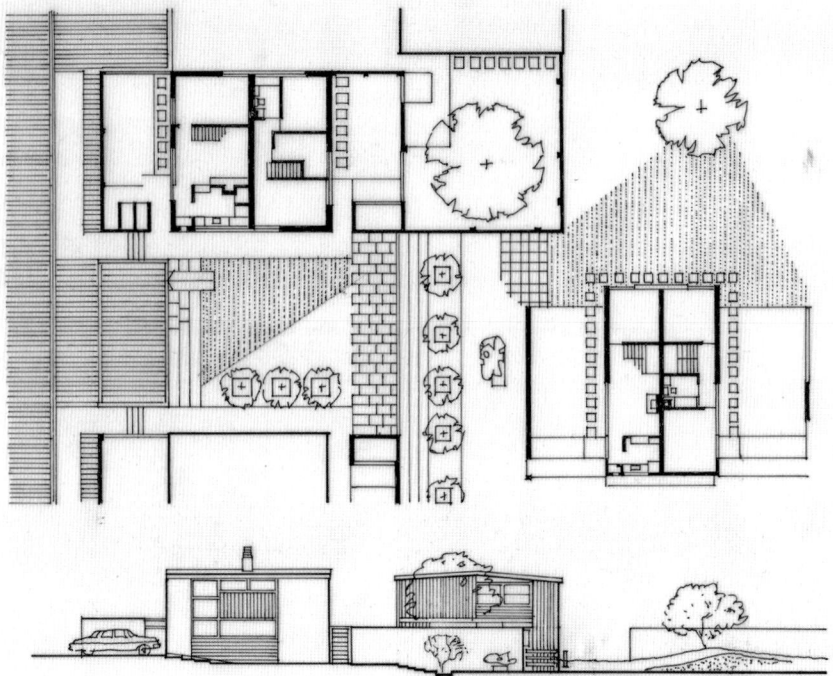

FIGURE 7.11 *Peterlee, group of houses, South West Area. Drawing Stephen Kite, based on* The Architectural Review *(February 1961).*

from the dwellings, which at one point Pasmore made into a complete extended timber relief construction – an artwork in its own right. But – avoiding the two-dimensional – the vertical also inter-relates with groundscapes, constituted of three structured planes: the inclined planes of roads and forecourts; the horizontal planes of the houses and their related outdoor spaces; and the free contour form of major open space. These three planes are linked together by stepped terraces of paving, and by bollards, and short pram-ramps, and are restricted to three materials: concrete paving, dolomite gravel, and tarmac – a five-foot construction module orders everything.[46] The most common house in this area – a two-storey, three-bedroom semi-detached – does not seem a type likely to produce the rich tessellation of space, and experiential variety found here. But there are no front and backs to the streets in the normal sense; instead, the house-clusters are accessed from intermediate courts, via off-street parking, at one point leading to a further space with a play-sculpture – designed by architect Peter Daniel – and thence onto the parkland. Private screened patio gardens hug the *long* side of the dwelling, accessed from the spatially conventional kitchen, living, and sitting areas.

FIGURE 7.12 *Peterlee, group of houses, South West Area. Inside the courtyard of the group of houses shown in Figure 7.11, with a play sculpture designed by Peter Daniel. Architectural Press Archive / RIBA Collections.*

The open-grid, of this first phase, respects Mondrian's focusing of the rules of art on the right angle: 'We find that in nature all relations are dominated by a single primordial relation, which is defined by the opposition of two extremes. Abstract plasticism represents this primordial relation in a precise manner by means of the two positions which form the right angle'.[47] However, Pasmore was also beginning to make less strictly geometrical works reciprocally inspired, as he admitted, by his work on Peterlee; with some likeness to Mondrian's *Pier and Ocean* series, in his oil and charcoal on board, *Abstract in Black and White* (1957), small arcs dance among straight lines – the vestiges of a grid, circumscribed within an oval upon a rectangular ground.[48] In others, such as *Line and Space No 23* (1964), the straight and curved oil and gravure markings, on the as-found material surface of warped board, duplicate the linear and biomorphic responses to the undulations of the Peterlee landscape.[49] These fluid qualities come out in Sunny Blunts – the last part of the south-west area to be completed – where Pasmore played spines and clusters of cubic housing against an interdependent curvilinear road-system, and the topographies of the Dene and Burn, to achieve a fuller unity of dwelling and landscape.

FIGURE 7.13 *Peterlee, view looking outwards from the courtyard shown in Figures 7.11 and 7.12. Architectural Press Archive / RIBA Collections.*

The focus here has been on the abstract surface interplays of the housing and wider landscape, rather than the once-neglected, but now celebrated and restored, monumental Apollo Pavilion – constructed in 1968, and named after the NASA space-programme – Pasmore designed as an 'eye-catcher' for Sunny Blunts, and a crossing-point to the small artificial lake created within the Dene. The pavilion's cantilevers, planes, and blocks, rhyme with the Cubistic language of the houses, but it was far more robustly constructed of reinforced concrete; Pasmore described it as 'an architecture and sculpture of purely abstract form through which to walk, in which to linger and on which to play; a free and anonymous monument which, because of its independence, can lift the activity and psychology of an urban housing community onto a universal plane'.[50] While the Apollo Pavilion has now been well restored, it takes a sympathetic eye – and a reading between what little survives of the original concept, and the photographs in journals, contemporary to its construction – to grasp the qualities of those wider ambitions for the settlement-patterns of south-west Peterlee. The difficulty of the enterprise was exacerbated by the innovation of the housing, the exposed site, and a team of inexperienced architects and builders. The houses leaked, and by the 1980s most had been drastically remodelled, with pitched roofs added. In an unpublished article, 'Where the Artist Comes In', Pasmore said that 'the professional architect has to make two kinds of environment. He has to make a utilitarian one – the house to keep out the wind and the rain. But he has also to create a social and spiritual environment'. Pasmore wanted the flat roofs 'to emphasize the cubic concept of the total architectural form', but given the poor technology and Peterlee's long windy winters, they contributed to failures from the 'utilitarian' aspect, while enhancing the unity of the 'spiritual environment'.[51]

If Peterlee is yet another narrative of New-Town disappointments, it is also 'the largest collaboration between artist and architect in the history of British architecture', as Alan Powers has described it.[52] In striving for a unity of art and architecture it can be seen as a continuity of the inter-war British Constructive tradition represented by Leslie Martin's 1937 book *Circle: International Survey of Constructive Art*, where Pasmore stands as heir to Ben Nicholson. However, the breaks with these inter-war ambitions are just as strong; as the other aforesaid groupings, represented in 'This is Tomorrow', had revolted against the 'soft' Modernism represented by the Festival of Britain (opened May 1951), so the Constructionist idea was to recover the pioneering principles of Modernism, as their offering to post-war reconstruction.[53] But both the pre- and post-war abstractionists drew inspiration from Mondrian, as in Pasmore's ambition to synthesize 'fundamental principles, both spiritual and material'.[54]

James Stirling – homo ludens

James Stirling has already figured as an important actor in these surface-narratives of the post-World War II years, as member of the Independent Group, as commentator and critic, and as Brutalist architect. His work continues to be of great interest to us; as the author of the Engineering Faculty, Leicester University (1959, with James Gowan), with both High-Modern and 'Expressionist' credentials – depending on your point of view – in its collaging of features of canonic Modernism, Victorian industrialism, Butterfield-ian bloody-mindedness, and Brutalist bombast. Then, in his transition from this complicated Late-Modernist stance, to an equally involved Post-Modernist embrace of history and context, examined here briefly in the Staatsgalerie, Stuttgart (1977–83) and, more closely, in his Clore Gallery extension to Tate Britain, London (1978–86). Even though, Stirling himself, always ferociously tore off any Po-Mo labels attached to his work.

Stirling's sense of surface, of smooth and rough, can be seen in his Competition Design for Sheffield University (1953, with Alan Cordingley) where a square smooth-surfaced library – like a 'centralized church plan of the Renaissance' – completes the vista of an extended piazza, opposite to the more plastically Baroque Arts and Administration block.[55] Here this curiosity in surface effects is directed upon English Baroque architecture, as evidenced by jottings in his 'Black Notebook' of circa 1953–4. Stirling complains: 'Frequently I awake in the morning and wonder how it is that I can be an architect and an Englishman at the same time, particularly a modern architect'. For, post-Gothic, he can only find six great British architects: Charles Rennie Mackintosh, Thomas Archer, Nicholas Hawksmoor, Sir John Vanbrugh, Inigo Jones, and 'perhaps Soane'; of these half – Archer, Hawksmoor, Vanbrugh – are English Baroque:

> Four of these (the first) are all sculpture or plastic school, which would suggest that it is in this aspect which our future architects will excel and this against the conventional (wrongly) attitude to climate, the attitude which says the Unité is alright on the Mediterranean. While Renaissance architecture is useless here . . . through a lack of sun or snow, Baroque or heavily sculptured architecture is not, as it does not rely on sun but on the juxtaposition of solid and void and the resulting pattern, also because the amount of wet and dirt, our buildings must be of such powerful domination that dirt and staining do not matter (they will be inevitably), thus although Seaton Delaval and Archer's Westminster church [St John's, Smith Square, Westminster] have burnt out innards and damaged exteriors, they are such dominating and powerful designs that they are still today still two of the most magnificent buildings. This appreciation has nothing whatever to do with the 'cult of ruins'.[56]

The last sentence rejects any Picturesque, Piper-esque appetite for the 'pleasing decay' of these war-ruins. Stirling observes that cills and cornices *invite* staining, admiring instead the clear-cut cill-less apertures of Joseph Emberton's modern Empire Hall, Olympia (1929). His friend, Colin St John (Sandy) Wilson, also remembers Stirling's admiration for Hawksmoor's churches in London's East End, of 'sitting in the churchyard of [Hawksmoor's] St Georges in the East [where Stirling] argued that in a climate with little sunlight one might be able to model a building better by facets of glass – and that was many years before Leicester Engineering Laboratories'.[57] In his notes, and these conversations with Sandy Wilson, Stirling is pondering the possibilities of the British architectural surface, as it adjusts languages imported from sunnier regions, to the wet and misty native climate – whether Gothic, Palladian, Baroque, or International Modernism. The solution Stirling advances at Sheffield – one of bold elemental volumes, marshalled in distinct patterns of solid and void, and those volumes of direct surface expression – will characterize his work to come. So, in the Sheffield Competition, Stirling saw 'the façade of the Arts-Admin block [as] essentially a wall (perforated)', its Baroque movement contrasting with the stasis of the

Library, and with 'only two materials on [the] façade – solid and void. Dirt staining would be of no consequence like "rust on a battleship"'.[58] Talking at London's Architectural Association (21 February 1954) on his Sheffield competition project, Stirling disapproved of the current trend of 'disguising the interior' with a 'curtain wall' – as had the winners Gollins, Melvin, Ward; while this might have some legitimacy when all the accommodation is similar – as in Skidmore, Owings & Merrill's internationally recognized Lever House office building, New York (1952) – 'it could not possibly apply in [Sheffield's] instance when the accommodation is of such highly diverse function'.[59]

The concept of the megastructure would not be defined until 1964, when Fumihiko Maki conceived it as a large frame containing the diverse functions of a city or part-city – an idea that would be seized upon by Japan's Metabolists, and England's Archigram. Stirling's giant wall foreshadows the megastructure, as a vast container into which he packs the different institutional functions, separated by vertical circulation-shafts negatively expressed as shadow-voids. At the centre, in a compositional coup de grâce, he joggles the lecture-theatre wedges (eight to each long façade) into a neo-Constructivist assemblage.

Maintaining the surface tension of his extended wall, Stirling brings the elevational play of these lecture-theatre elements to a single plane, while secreting plan-libre curves of glazing within the voids. Mark Crinson draws

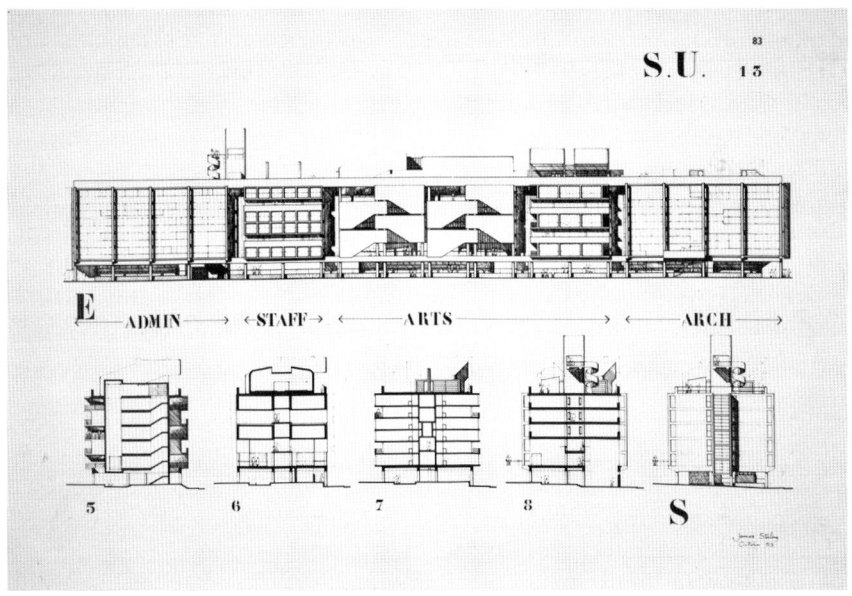

FIGURE 7.14 *James Frazer Stirling and Alan Cordingley. Photograph of elevations and sections for University of Sheffield, Sheffield, England, 1953. Gelatin silver print, 23 × 34 cm, AP140.S2.SS1.D7.P4.2. James Stirling/Michael Wilford fonds, Canadian Centre for Architecture © CCA.*

out the Mannerist aspects of Stirling's composition – this concentration of blank surfaces as a negative centre – with reference to Colin Rowe's aforementioned essay on 'Mannerism and Modern Architecture' (May 1950); Rowe was Stirling's tutor for his final-year thesis at Liverpool School of Architecture (1950) and quickly became a friend and mentor.[60] In illustrating Le Corbusier's early villa, at La Chaux-de-Fonds (1916), Rowe is 'both ravished and immensely irritated' by the ambiguities of a façade where 'the flat vertical surface of the two upper floors is divided into three panels. The outer ones, narrow and vertical, are pierced by elliptical lunettes, while the central one, elaborately framed, comprises an unrelieved blank, white surface'.[61] For Rowe, this centripetal attraction to an absence is 'both a disturbance and a delight', equal in sophistry to Italian Mannerist façades like the Casa di Palladio, Vicenza (1572), or Zuccheri's casino at Florence (1578). Rowe discovers intentions 'in the choice of texture, surface and detail', typical of the Mannerist architect – whether Renaissance or Modern: 'The surface of the Mannerist wall is either primitive or over-refined, and a brutally direct rustication frequently occurs in combination with an excess of attenuated and rigid delicacy'.[62] Rowe stimulated Stirling to explore architecture's potential to modulate the 'flat vertical surface'. In the context of the complexities of Sheffield, there is Rowe's isolation of 'a further Mannerist device, the discord between elements of different scale placed in immediate juxtaposition', as occurs in Michelangelo's apses at St Peter's, Rome – praised by Le Corbusier for the sublime drama in their 'gigantic geometry of harmonious relationships'[63] – or the dissonant assemblages of Le Corbusier's own Salvation Army Refuge in Paris (1929).

Rowe's 'Mannerism and Modern Architecture' was introduced earlier in the context of Luigi Moretti's work and writings, including those pages in *Spazio* that showed the automorphism between Mondrian's paintings and Romanesque walls. Equally original was Moretti's article in the last issue of *Spazio*, '*Strutture e sequenze di spazi*' ('Structures and Sequences of Spaces', *Spazio* 7, December 1952-April 1953) where he makes a stereometry of spatial analysis by casting plaster models of Renaissance interior sequences, such as St Peter's, Rome, and Palladio's Villa Rotonda. This has the threefold result of: abstracting and making contemporary the spatial essence of these historic interiors; dramatizing the 'modalities of their succession and . . . the structure of their composition'; and allowing these voids to seem solid and carveable. Moretti believes that 'internal volumes . . . have a concrete presence of their own, independent of the figure and corposity of the material that enclose them . . .'.[64] In his report on his Sheffield entry, Stirling refers to Moretti's plaster castings as illustrated in *Spazio*:

> By treating the external surface of the inner constructions of a building as a three-dimensional negative or mould, [Moretti] was able to obtain solidified space. If space can be imagined as a solid mass determined in shape and size by the proportion of a room or the function of a corridor,

then an architectural solution could be perceived by the consideration of alternative ways in which the various elements of the programme could be plastically assembled.[65]

This plastic assembly of discrete spatial prisms – like machined parts, or the 'crystalline organisms' of which Moretti speaks – can be seen in Stirling's axonometric sketch studying the conjoining of corridor, glazed curvilinear foyers, vertical circulation shafts, and lecture theatres.[66]

Stirling again had Italy in mind when he wrote: 'the layout of the [Sheffield] site could be thought of as having a Renaissance quality about it (superficial resemblance to St Mark's Venice) – this sort of thing is not unlikely to arise, as I consider there is nothing fundamentally new about modern architecture'.[67] He then quotes from Le Corbusier's *Towards a New Architecture* (1927), from 'Mass' – the first of his 'Three Reminders to Architects' (Mass, Surface, Plan): 'Architecture is the masterly, correct and magnificent play of masses brought together in light'.[68]

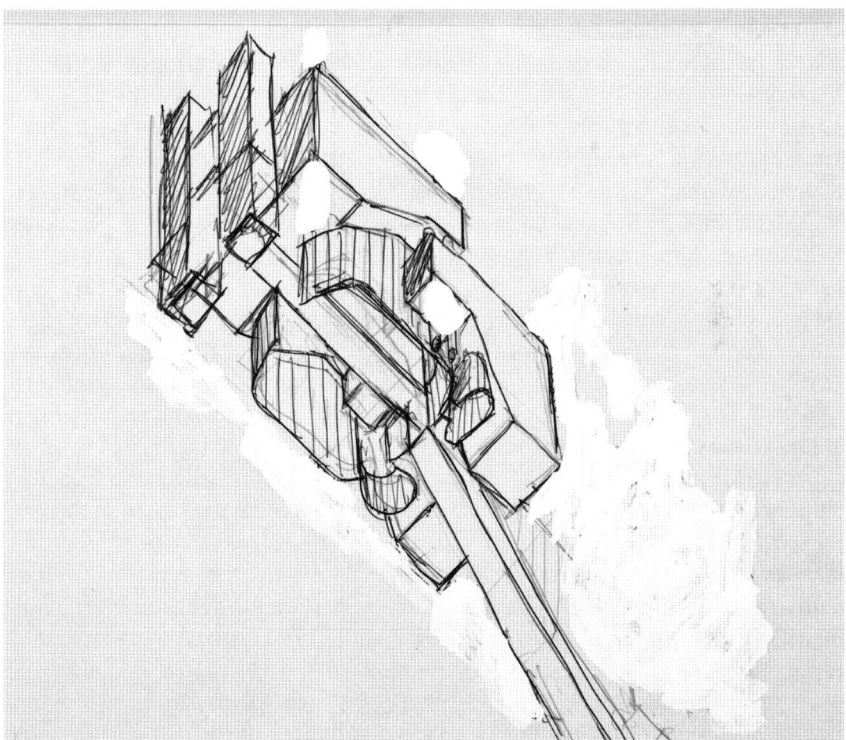

FIGURE 7.15 *James Frazer Stirling and Alan Cordingley. Axonometric sketch for University of Sheffield, Sheffield. England, 1953. Ink, graphite and gouache on paper, 21 × 29.7 cm, AP140.S2.SS1.D7.P2.4. James Stirling/Michael Wilford fonds, Canadian Centre for Architecture © CCA.*

Equal in Le Corbusier's triad is the 'Second Reminder: Surface', where 'the task of the architect is to vitalize the surfaces' of the 'masses brought together in light' without 'eating up the mass'. The simple grids of an American factory, or the serene classicism of the Rue de Rivoli, Paris, '*modulate* and still remain within the mass', as compared to Paris's fussy Boulevard Raspail or – as Le Corbusier's English translator Frederick Etchells notes – London's Edwardian Baroque, Regent Street.[69] Sheffield's ensemble of cubic library and Arts-Administration block on its tapered square resembles the modulated urban-walls of Scamozzi's Procuratie Nuove (1582), and Sansovino's Library (begun 1537), as they define the perspectives of the piazza and adjacent piazzetta of St Mark's, in the presence of the campanile and San Marco itself.

As for contemporary Renaissance studies, it was not so much the aforementioned Wittkower's *Architectural Principles in the Age of Humanism* (1949, 1952) that influenced Stirling, but Wittkower and Fritz Saxl's folio-size volume *British Art and the Mediterranean* (1948). Stirling recollects: 'This large book was the one that none of us students could ever fit on our bookshelves, it just lay on the floor and got looked at'.[70] While *Architectural Principles* is a cerebral probing into humanist geometry, *British Art and the Mediterranean* is superlatively visual, for it was published in 1948 as the catalogue of the 1941 photographic exhibition on the connections between British and Mediterranean cultures, organized by London's Warburg Institute. Wittkower curated the second part of the exhibition, from the sixteenth to the nineteenth century, translating the sober exhibition panels to the vivid spreads of the large printed pages. In the catalogue's preface Wittkower wrote of how 'every section bears witness to the extent to which English art is indebted to Greece and Italy, and should show the fascinating transformation which the foreign elements have undergone as soon as they were introduced'. How 'in the kaleidoscopic survey ... which is unrolled before the eyes of the reader ... the second [post 1500] half is like those which show a horse jumping a fence, in a number of shots recording every single position of the leaping animal'.[71]

Hence, packed into the two-page spread on 'The Italianized Architecture of Inigo Jones and his School' are antecedents, in elevation and plan, including the Villa Medici at Poggio a Caiano, and Scamozzi's Villa Polini, compared to Jones's own Queen's House, Greenwich (begun 1616), and its legacies like Roger Pratt's Coleshill House (1650–62). The distinction which Wittkower makes is that, even though Jones closely followed his Italian models, 'there is still an English element in the flat appearance of the elevations and in the excessive length of the building compared with its height'.[72] We have seen how Pevsner made similar points on such English mutations. Then, in Lord Burlington's Chiswick House (begun 1725), the organic unity of Palladio's Villa Rotonda model translates to 'the creation of isolated balanced surface patterns', and each façade, component, and motif is unrelated.[73] Wittkower called this Burlington-ian, over-articulated separateness of components, a *staccato* manner.⁷⁴ As an example of how 'Italian architectural motives ... were given a completely new meaning in the new context in which they were used', consider that of the Venetian window (or Serliana), the motif of three lights where the central one is arched and wider than the others: 'In Italy it had always had a plastic quality and functional importance, while in the new English setting it emerged as a decorative pattern'; thus at Houghton Hall (1722) and Holkham Hall (1734), both in Norfolk, it is found as a decorative element in the blank walls of the corner-pavilions.⁷⁵ As has been reported, Pevsner also made similar points in *The Englishness of English Art* on this English tendency to leave parts as parts, and to *compartment* space, rather than to *mould* it. This *staccato* character is consistent also with the Baroque of Vanbrugh whose 'architecture is conceived in blocks', adjusted together to 'the effect of overwhelming masses'.⁷⁶ One suggestive page on 'Classical Features in the Gothic Revival' frames a portrait of Horace Walpole (his Gothic Strawberry Hill in the background) with the tower of Hawksmoor's St Anne's Church, Limehouse, London (1712–24), and Vanbrugh's blocky Belvedere at Claremont House, Esher (*c*. 1715), to stress a persistent archaic medievalism in the work of these architects, where memories of Gothic steeples and castle-walls stimulate their massing.⁷⁷ In ways like these, as Claire Zimmerman explains it, the book 'curated a set of objects and endowed them with an aggregate identity as reflections of a British approach to art and internationalism', in that 'transposition from tangible object to memorable image' that Brutalism sought.⁷⁸

Saxl and Wittkower unquestionably fuelled Stirling's omnivorous visual imagination, reinforcing the presentness of the past. Although an early design, Sheffield deserves detailed analysis for it is embryonic of Stirling's mature manner: the bold joinings of solid and void to sharp visions of programme and poetry; the sustained surface-tension in the play of material and tectonics; and the T. S. Eliot-like insights into the reciprocity of historical order and contemporaneity.

Surfaces as skins – Leicester University Engineering Building

The last chapter pointed to the influence of Le Corbusier's Jaoul houses on Stirling and Gowan's Ham Common, London (1955–8), at the same time recording Stirling's perplexity – in his 'Garches to Jaoul' article (September 1955) – that they make so 'little reference to the rational principles which are the basis of the modern movement'; how can it be that the Jaoul dwellings under construction in 1953 are so primitive, when the Villa Garches of 1927 'is an excellent example of Le Corbusier's particular interpretation of the machine aesthetic'?⁷⁹ In *The New Brutalism* (1966), Banham's section on

'Les Maison Jaoul, Neuilly' contains much commentary on Stirling's 1955 article. In Jaoul, Banham sees the 'vacuum of architectural meaning', posited by Brutalism, 'dramatically filled'. Where even Hunstanton's as-found steel and glass 'seemed too thin, too elegant' to match the consequences of the word, archaic Jaoul with its raw concrete and exposed brickwork,'*"became"* Brutalism', became 'the common standard by which the Brutalism of other buildings could be classified'. In Banham's reading, 'Brutalism, as a going style, proved to be largely a matter of surfaces derived from Jaoul', and he draws out the sustained attention to surface in Stirling's critique of the dwellings.[80] Stirling illustrates 'Garches to Jaoul' with his own photographs of the houses under construction, making yet stronger the contrast between the rough load-bearing, nine-inch brick cross walls and the dark apertures. In *Smooth and Rough* (1951), Adrian Stokes relishes 'the qualities of that smooth-rough disposal which we observe plainly in the simple Mediterranean house; best known, perhaps, in process of being built, before glass has tamed yawning apertures of velvet-smooth blackness which confer an ordered sense of voluminous depth . . .'.[81] Another oddity of Jaoul is that it *is* more Mediterranean than Parisian, 'recalling the Provençal farmhouse', and this 'within half a mile of the Champs-Élysées', Stirling complains. Colin St John Wilson would certainly have shared his *Smooth and Rough* enthusiasms with his friend, but Stirling himself does not seem to have been a reader of Stokes. And the windows that close these apertures, says Stirling, 'are either "holes in the wall" or "fourth wall" units in the larger floor-to-beam openings'; this '"fourth wall" – the incorporation of shelving and opaque materials into the window opening – is symptomatic of Le Corbusier's recent attitude to surface depth. Windows are no longer to be looked through but looked at. The eye finding interest in every part of the surface impasto', as compared to the black *fenêtre en longueur* banding, the 'hard textureless finish' of the wall-planes of Villa Garches.[82] Banham finds Stirling's use of the painterly term 'impasto' here 'telling', for 'elsewhere Stirling observes that "the wall is considered as a surface and not as a pattern", and it was at this time that the Brutalist sculpture of Paolozzi was an "art of surface, not of mass"'.[83] Jaoul's impasto translated to the neater concrete and brick surfaces of Stirling and Gowan's Ham Common, where the chunky windows are also designed to be 'looked at'.

Leicester University Engineering Building (1959–63) is the avowed climax to this phase of Stirling's journey, and also his partnership with James Gowan, and presents surface impasto of an evidently different kind. In *Surface Architecture*, Leatherbarrow and Mostafavi refer to Leicester as the building of its era 'that most productively explored the erosion of the singular and coherent volume, both conceptually and literally . . . In this building, as in the collages of Paolozzi and the readymades of Duchamp, there is an acceptance of "found" objects and their transformation. But not only materials and surfaces are juxtaposed; entire volumes are as well'.[84] Leicester could never have been a liner, like Garches, or the muscular vessel of the Sheffield Arts and Administration block with its nautical roofscape; the programme requirements and the tight left-over site dictated that it instead came out – not as a Corbusian Cunarder – but as 'an aircraft carrier with its island structure to one side of an offset deck, says Stirling';[85] a parti akin to Wright's Johnson Wax at Racine, Wisconsin (1936–9, laboratory tower 1944–50), with its laboratory tower and stratum of workspaces and, like Leicester, a strikingly red building – but Gowan says 'our models were English, not Wright'.[86] Banham had also published the Futurist visions of Sant' Elia; another more mechanistic-looking project of the time – also with a folded-roof warehouse and an articulated corner tower – was an Architectural Association (AA) student project by Edward Reynolds of 1957–8, for a Bristol warehouse, which Gowan knew of, as an AA tutor. The programme was short and to the point: northlight-lit flexible workshop spaces; a water-tank one hundred feet above the ground-level workshops where hydraulic experiments would be carried out; a requirement for the architects not to use exposed concrete finishes on the exterior. Once the workshops were disposed on the constricted plot, it soon proved logical to pile up the remaining accommodation – the lecture theatres, offices, and research laboratories – into a tower-cluster supporting the water-tank.

The 'negative matrix' (Moretti's term) of these elements are grafted onto the vertical circulation spines, as distinct prisms, into a Moretti-like stereotomy of space: the glazed faceted mini-skyscraper of the office tower supporting the water-tank; the laboratory-tower with its hooded hopper-vents; and the cantilevered lecture theatres (the smaller for 100 students, the larger for 200) reminiscent of Constantin Melnikov's Moscow Worker's Club (1926) – although unknown to Stirling and Gowan at the time. With concrete disallowed, Leicester became rich in colour and surface, but still faced in just three materials: hard red Accrington engineering bricks, red Dutch clay tiles, and industrial patent glazing. John McKean thinks this complex assemblage 'so impenetrable it could be solid; hewn, facetted on a grinding stone. The surfaces are skins; the podium, solid above its splayed base, is a brick curtain'. Reinforcing the skinness are the double doors under the ramp 'covered by brick almost as if wallpaper',[87] a telling detail which foreshadows an equally significant moment in the podium of Stuttgart's Staatsgalerie (1977–83), where stones that look as if they have fallen out of the wall, allow ventilation into the parking zone; they also imply the building's eventual ruin, and joke that the building's apparent mass is, in tectonic reality, just a veneer of cladding. Even the standard glazing at Leicester is made to seem solid; it is faceted in the taller tower, as in that vision Stirling had shared with Wilson in the blitzed shell of Hawksmoor's St George-in-the-East, 'that in a climate with little sunlight one might be able to model a building better by facets of glass', it sparkles like a frozen waterfall down the circulation shaft, is visored in the hopper windows of the squat research laboratory tower, and is alternately translucent and opaque in the workshops, where the north-lights are interlayered with semi-opaque

FIGURE 7.16 Stirling and Gowan, Leicester University Engineering Building. Photograph Richard Einzig / Arcaid.

glass fibre, and the remainder with aluminium foil. Peter Eisenman's article, 'Real and English: The Destruction of the Box I' (1974), also interrogates Leicester's interrelation of surface and volume, claiming that it 'takes the compositional attitude of Constructivism, rather than its vocabulary and brings it into some sort of dialectic with the concept of the vertical plane in Le Corbusier';[88] but it is no longer the 'paper-thin surfaces' of Garches, here 'all potential planes are cut, chamfered or splayed to imply depth in volume'.[89]

So much did the glass and red-skinned Leicester defy as-found material expectations that the percipient Pevsner – who could normally spot a fifteenth-century moulding from one end of a parish-church nave – claimed, after 'a good look at [the building]', that the jutting lecture theatres were 'of exposed concrete [and] the rest is faced with blue engineering bricks'. He made this error in the above-mentioned 'The Anti-Pioneers' BBC talk of December 1966, where he makes Leicester a 'test case' of that Neo-Expressionism in new English building which he found deplorable. Everywhere he looked at Leicester he saw the repetition of 'aggressive angularity' akin to the Expressionism of Bruno Taut's fantastic *Stadtkrone*, whether in the jutting lecture-theatres, the angular thrust of the podium and ramp, or the cutting angles of the towers and workshops.[90] But the same spikiness reminds Colin Rowe of 'magnificently quirky' High Victorianism, and he places Leicester circa 1860 as 'aboriginally English *and* nineteenth century' – rejecting any foreign influences like De Stijl and Constructivism: 'At Leicester most intimately this architect wished to be someone like a Butterfield (perhaps at Keble), or something like a Woodward (perhaps at the Oxford Museum), and all this with more than a touch of the long vanished Paxton conservatory at Chatsworth'.[91]

Stirling certainly shared Le Corbusier's admiration of the functional tradition, represented by Joseph Paxton and industrial architecture generally; his personal photograph collection contains many images of colliery structures, gantries, kilns, and so on.[92] If you do not look too hard at Leicester, one of the formal games it plays is to denote the *appearance* of direct industrial building, but its ostensible legibility belies a Mannerist work of art-architecture, whose structure is both disclosed and dissembled, whose parts are as much rhetorical as functional, and whose surface-skins are as ambiguously alluring as that telling brick-wallpaper door in the podium. Rowe's parallels to Woodward and the Oxford Museum are persuasive, equally the many Butterfield connections have been noted. Through his friend, Henry Wentworth Acland – the client of the University Museum, Oxford – John Ruskin played an influential consultant role in the design of Thomas Deane and Benjamin Woodward's building, which opened in June 1860. Evidencing Ruskin's belief in the rational Changefulness of Gothic, the Museum cascades – in wall-veils of polychromatic Veronese Gothic – as a cadence of boldly distinct volumes, from the sturdy pyramidal central tower of the main front block, through the polygonal spired turret of the end-staircase, to the pyramidal Large Laboratory, inspired by the Abbot's Kitchen at Glastonbury.

Confessedly 'addicted to walls', Rowe would become increasingly exercised by a lack of 'face' in Stirling's architecture, an aspect notably absent in his Neue Staatsgalerie, Stuttgart (1977–83), where receding Praeneste-like strata of ramps and terraces make the Gallery's principal frontage to Konrad-Adenauer-Strasse. Even Stirling was concerned to 'counteract the possible appearance of a monumental stone quarry', hence his introduction of fiercely coloured, pink and blue steel handrails, and bright metallic porches clinging like butterflies to the wall-faces.[93] But Stirling also wanted planting to complement the stone surfaces, and these haphazard mantles of creeper only intensify the atmosphere of a quarry, or a lost ruin. So Rowe finds Stuttgart simply 'a building with *no* face'; in plan, ethos, and material, it develops all kinds of assonances with the Neo-Classicism of its neighbouring earlier gallery, but 'the primary [classical] concept, the vertical surface, as a presentation to the eye', as the 'primary percept', is lacking.[94]

FIGURE 7.17 *James Stirling, Michael Wilford, and Associates. Photograph Peter Walser. View of the public footpaths, Staatsgalerie, Stuttgart, Germany, 1983–4. Image from colour transparency, AP140.S2.SS1.D52.P.79.6. James Stirling/Michael Wilford fonds, Canadian Centre for Architecture © CCA.*

Nor can Leicester be expected to have a representational frontage in the way of Wallis Gilbert's neo-Modernist Hoover Building (1932–5), on London's Great West Road, yet its skins *do* partake of a broader corporeal presence. The stance of the towers, before the workshops, has the swagger of that legendary photograph of Isambard Kingdom Brunel, posed in front of the launching chains of his *The Great Eastern* (1857). The diagonal corners of the office tower (cf. the Smithsons' Economist Building, London) activate this 'physically invigorating quality', as Rowe described it, especially where 'knees' of canted concrete effect the transition from the four muscular columns, which carry the large lecture theatre and offices, to the paired triangular corner-columns, which continue support upwards, now *within* the patent-glazing. The undeniable anthropomorphism of the tower-cluster triggers different responses, where some might see the persona of a vigorous engineer, others imagine a 'mechanical hobgoblin', poised to clank off across the campus.[95] For architect M. J. Long (who worked closely with her husband Colin St John Wilson on the Aalto-inspired British Library, 1974–97), and a number of her peers, 'the Leicester building embodied for me the idea that a building was a creature – a practical organism with its own rules, its own almost visible bones and connective tissue'.[96]

The Clore Gallery – arcadian walls

As described, Banham included Leicester, with its 'asymmetrical composition of towers and low buildings', as an outstanding example of the 'Revenge of the Picturesque'.[97] Peter Davey also said of the Stuttgart Staatsgalerie – the acknowledged masterpiece of Stirling's conspicuously post-modern phase – that it was Picturesque, both in its compositional collaging of form and vista, and in the opportunities it offered for individual exploration and experience.[98] At Stuttgart, Stirling's picturesque is conjured from the ruination of Schinkel's Altes Museum in Berlin (1825–30). In his essay 'Losing Face', Anthony Vidler argues that the erosion of 'face', which troubled Rowe as a persistent failing in modern architecture, had already begun in the Altes Museum, whose 'façade' is an endless democratic stoa, veiling the wall-plane behind, and beyond that the intricate turns of the staircase. Stirling continues the deconstruction by '[stripping] away not one but two faces, in order to reveal the [now roofless] drum of the central space not now as interior but as exterior surface'.[99] The Schinkel of the Altes Museum is of the 'Tragic' scenography, the first of the 'three kinds of scenes' Vitruvius describes in Book Five of *The Ten Books of Architecture*, a noble, public, and formal architecture of columns and statues. Counter to this is the Schinkel of The Gardener's House at Charlottenhof, near Potsdam (1829–40) where he admixes the 'Comic' and 'Satyric' modes; 'comic scenes' are 'after the manner of ordinary dwellings', says Vitruvius, and 'satyric scenes are decorated with trees, caverns, mountains, and other rustic objects delineated in landscape style'. At Potsdam, Schinkel's buildings harmonize with the 'free' landscaping, on the English model, of Peter Joseph Lenné; Schinkel had toured England in 1826, and his friend Hermann Fürst von Pückler-Muskau's *Hints on Landscape Gardening* (*Andeutungen über Landschaftsgärtnerei*, 1834) is based on John Nash and Humphrey Repton. In Schinkel, this English Picturesque is imbued with German Romantic Neo-Classicism, and inflected by his direct experience of Italy and its villa architecture. On these themes Schinkel writes that in the house of the gardener, 'the intention was to create a picturesque environment ... and to produce a great variety of architectural objects, which would fit pleasantly with the surrounding landscape'.[100] A tower is the pivot of a complex composition, which orchestrates the main court-gardener's house, the gardener's assistant's house, the linking vine-clad 'great arbour', and other pergolas and elements, into patterns of figure and ground, open and closed. Schinkel's fusion of Romantic Neo-Classicism, and the poetics of the picturesque, would appeal strongly to Stirling as his work took a more contextual and historically referential turn in the 1970s; at the same time he began to collect the Neo-Classical furniture of Thomas Hope. He contemplated Schinkel in the pages of a facsimile edition of his *Collection of Architectural Designs* (*Sammlung Architektonischer Entwürfe*, 1866) whose exquisite engravings capture the aura of his buildings in their lucidity and lyricism.

Given its Altes Museum precedent, the Staatsgalerie can be claimed for the tragic scena; its gravitas emolliated by the comic and satyric aspects of its butterfly canopies, its *ruinenlust,* and its cloaks of creeper. In some other ensuing works of Stirling (and his partner, from 1971, Michael Wilford), the comic and satyric moods predominate, together with those related Charlottenhof-like elements of arcadian garden, tower, and loggia; these include the Center for the Performing Arts, Cornell University (1982–9), and the work next to be examined, the Clore Gallery, Tate Britain, London (1978–86). Owing to the notoriety of the 'red trilogy' of his University buildings at Leicester, Cambridge, and Oxford, Stirling became persona non grata in Britain for a decade; as a consequence his major subsequent work has been achieved abroad. The opening of the Clore Gallery in April 1987 signalled a return from exile; it is still quite a small work and one less critically examined, but highly representative, and of interest to this study as meeting Rowe's desire for intercourse with evocative vertical surfaces.

Designed to house the collection of the work of the artist J. M. W. Turner, the practice was faced with the problem of extending the closed composition of Sidney Smith's laborious classical composition of 1896, comprising a central Corinthian portico, and flanking wings terminated by pedimented pavilions with blind Venetian windows, all superimposed upon a rusticated stone plinth. Stirling refers to his new wing as 'a garden wall containing the gardens of the Tate', and as a non-monumental accretion to Smith's building 'like the orangery extension to a country house';[101] a problem analogous to that which confronted Gunnar Asplund when extending the Neo-Classical Göteborg Law Courts (1934–7). Stirling arrived at a similar solution by applying a panelled grid of stone and stucco to his 'garden wall', with the important distinction that Stirling's grid is just a decorative veneer, whereas the grid of Asplund's extension expresses the structural steel frame within, in accordance with the tenets of rational Modernism.[102] Moreover, Stirling had *two* contexts to contend with at each end of his wall; Sidney Smith's Portland stone monument, and the red-brick Neo-Georgian of the Commandant's Lodge of the former Military Hospital. The Portland stone grid allows a chequer-play of materials within the panels, ochre render to tone with Smith, and red facing brickwork – laid in English bond – stepping up to marry with the Lodge. Ochre was also Asplund's choice for his Göteborg panels, but where the Swede takes his cue from the ochre render within the stone pilasters of the original building, Stirling's might be taken as a gesture to the buff colour of London's everyday brickwork, like the one he uses for the side and service-road elevations where the language switches suddenly to factory-like Modernist.

In two important critiques John Summerson is, surprisingly, affirmative of Stirling's playfulness: the first, a survey in *The Architectural Review* of March 1983, characterizes him as 'Vitruvius Ludens'; in the second – his review of the Clore Gallery specifically (*The Architectural Review*, June 1987) – 'ludens' has become 'Vitruvius Ridens or Laughter at the Clore'.

FIGURE 7.18 *Stirling and Wilford, Clore Gallery, Tate Britain. Photograph Stephen Kite.*

Summerson admits to being initially wrongheaded about Leicester, seeing as 'exhibitionism' what 'was really the acting-out of a deeply felt thesis', what 'was brilliant, arrogant play'. And, notwithstanding the harsh elements of The Florey Building, Oxford (1966–71) it remains 'a powerful piece of "deep" functionalism'. Continuing his survey, Summerson reports Stirling's increasing absorption in explicitly Neo-Classical ideas of imagery and urbanism, while stressing how 'the Neo-Classical has been the "natural" alternative to the Modern ever since Gropius stated the converse in his Werkbund building of 1914. The Modern Movement sprang from Neo-Classical soil and to that soil it is always liable to return, and return it does in Stirling's work …'. The Clore – known by 1983, in near-final project models and drawings – represents 'a new gamble of Stirling the player. The play here is as much with styles as with forms …'. He concludes: Stirling 'has, as Norman Shaw had, a marvellous streak of comic inventiveness which has to be rigorously (and inventively) corrected'.[103]

At the Clore, the entrance is the focus of this comic invention; as compared to the ascent to Smith's portico, here the visitor descends by Lutyensesque semi-circular steps to a stone-flagged pond-court, delineated by the loggia, and the confrontation of the entrance with Smith's southern pavilion. Stirling tells how he made his entrance by 'reversing what happens on the corner of the Tate, where a pediment sits above a lunette window', placing instead a lunette over the triangle of a cut-out pediment, whose gaping void then makes his gateway.[104] So, says Summerson, he 'out-faces Tate with a yawn and a wink'[105] – or is it a guffaw and a wink from 'Vitruvius Ridens'? Descent to such a gateway also invokes the graver associations of cyclopean tombs, while the lunette, with its stepped mouldings, is a direct quotation from the forbidding steeple of Hawksmoor's St George-in-the-East. Stirling clearly had such literal facial metaphors in mind, as when 'pressed as to what that façade represents', of the entrance to his contemporary Fogg Museum (1979–84), Harvard University – an equally primitivist square-slot-triangle motif, flanked by watchful pylons – replied: 'I would say that there is a big cleft or opening, an entrance which can also be seen as a head with a face, a visage overlooking the campus. Maybe it has a slightly Eastern and antique gaze, ambiguous as to its origin. It is not exactly a Western face; perhaps I was trying to make a face which was, shall I say, not British'.[106] Stirling is as confessedly clear on the atectonic nature of his surfaces:

> The Clore is not made of solid stone or structural brickwork like the Tate and the Lodge. Its materials are all veneers (as is the case with most modern buildings). We have tried to indicate that these veneered surfaces are not structural, hence the scissoring of walls in strategic places. When using traditional materials in an untraditional way it should be explicit that they are applied; here there's a kind of abstract slashing and cutting which can only mean these materials (and symbols) are not as substantial as they appear.[107]

In Britain, Charles Jencks was early in codifying Post-Modernism, in *The Language of Post-Modern Architecture* (1977), and he interviewed Stirling at the time of the Clore's launch. Questioned by Jencks on 'Mannerist notions of tension and contrast' in his building, Stirling admits that 'some of the architects in history I most admire must have been Mannerist architects. Certainly it is intended that there are balances of symmetries and asymmetries as well as continuities and discontinuities'. Hence the 'scissoring' produces a host of minor jests, reminding Summerson of 'Giulio Romano's slipping voussoirs at [the Palazzo del Te, 1525] Mantua'.[108] For example, over the corner to the bay-window of the reading room, the horizontal member of the grid is simply cut off, leaving the brick-panels above, outwardly unsupported, and making the veneered materiality unambiguous. Or there are the 'missing' stones at one end of the loggia – reminiscent of the fallen stones in the podium of the Staatsgalerie – that allow daylight into the supervisors' rest room. Many saw these games as aimed at a coterie, and as an irresponsible disavowal of architecture's public role. In conclusion to his review of the Clore, Peter Blundell Jones complained how 'the elevated conversations between Stirling and Jencks or Summerson start to look distinctly like fiddling while Rome burns.[109]

Enthusiast Summerson also enjoyed the many Soanian aspects of the Clore; Sir John Soane (1753–1837) was another architect-hero of Stirling's, and Summerson had been curator of the Soane Museum for almost forty years up to 1984. In his own house in Lincoln's Inn Fields, Soane had enlarged the domestic to a near-public scale by layering surfaces, by shaping labyrinthine routes, and by his *lumière mystérieuse* conducted magically into the volumes via fissures and hidden skylights. The Clore's entrance is also not large, in scale it is like the hall of a medium country-house, so to extend the experience of progression Stirling made a chicane of his staircase and gallery, pulling visitors away from, then drawing them back towards the galleries by the strong 'Regency' colours of an arch outlined in turquoise and ultramarine; circumventing this, gallery-goers finally arrive in a calm sequence of picture-rooms where the light-scoops, says Stirling, 'may contribute to the feeling of a slightly mysterious light source, like Soane's interiors, where he reflects daylight down walls and you're not quite sure where it's coming from'.[110] A tall Soanian light-slot also illuminates the entrance staircase and its surfaces, where the external grid of stone and ochre is rediscovered on the back walls, as if internally projected, and arbitrarily cut at the levels of balustrade and soffit.

Of those arcadian, comic and satyric elements – tower, wall, loggia, and garden – which reference Schinkel at Charlottenhof, the tower is an equally pronounced component in earlier Clore studies of November 1980, where it is almost a prospect-tower which looks down upon the water-garden through openings variously imagined as pointed, segmental, or rectangular. It is rendered, and grows from an eroded field of stone-cladding which returns as a backcloth to the loggia, with a simple projecting coping. As the

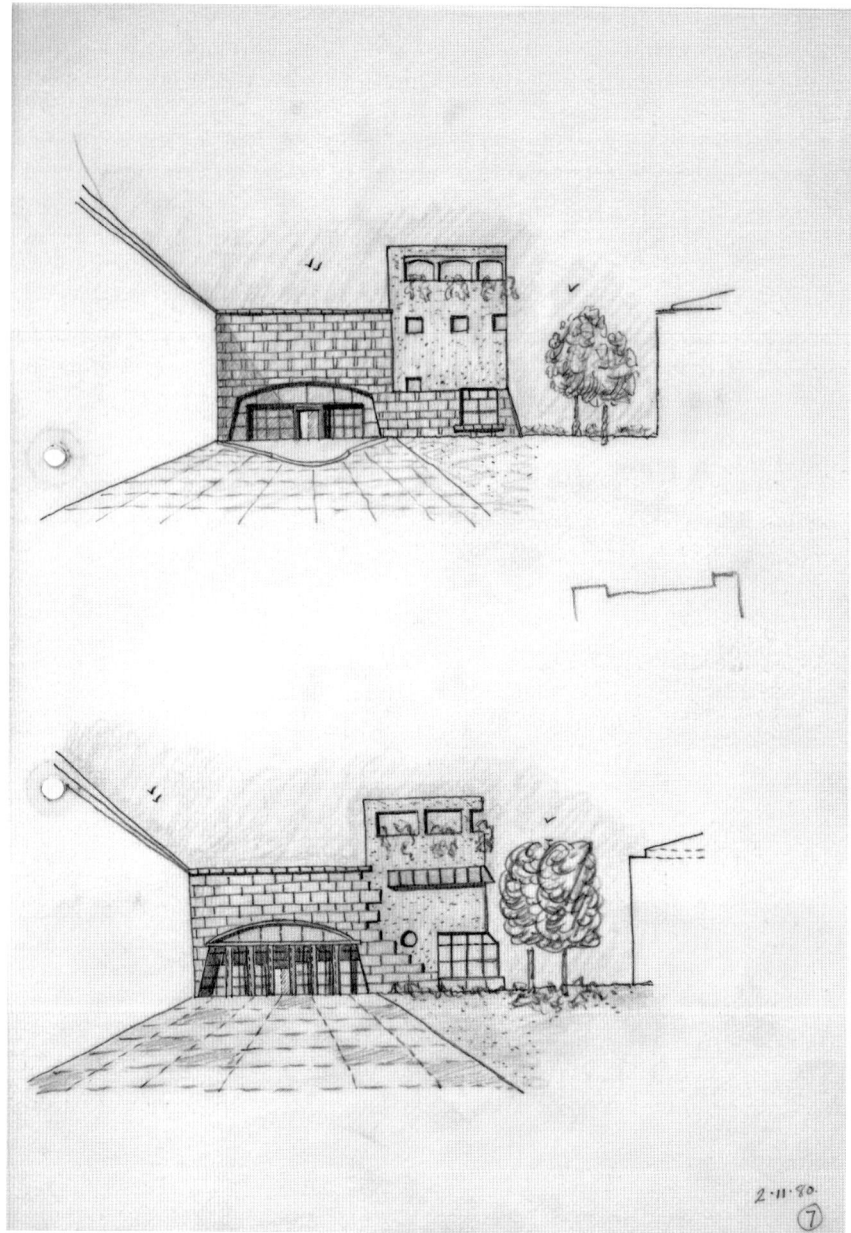

FIGURE 7.19 *James Stirling, Michael Wilford, and Associates. Perspectives for Clore Gallery, London, England, 2 November 1980. Graphite and coloured pencil on paper, 29.9 × 21 cm, AP140.S2.SS1.D60.SD1.P4.8. James Stirling/Michael Wilford fonds, Canadian Centre for Architecture © CCA.*

idea of the binding Asplund-esque grid developed, so did the thought of continuing Smith's classical cornice; with that development the tower disappeared as an independent vertical element, surviving only as an attic storey, carried up above the mouldings, as in Smith's pavilion. Stirling's loving attention to surface is evident in the suite of up-view axonometric presentation drawings he produced. Such drawings are perplexing to the layperson, but Stirling nonetheless strove to explain them to a bemused Queen Mother when she opened the Gallery; they are from Stirling's own hand, and few offices could have allowed so much of a principal's time to this meticulous hatching of skies and walls, in coloured pencil.

Stirling and Wilford described their museums, such as the Staatsgalerie and the Clore, and other related urban projects, 'as a fresh reading and

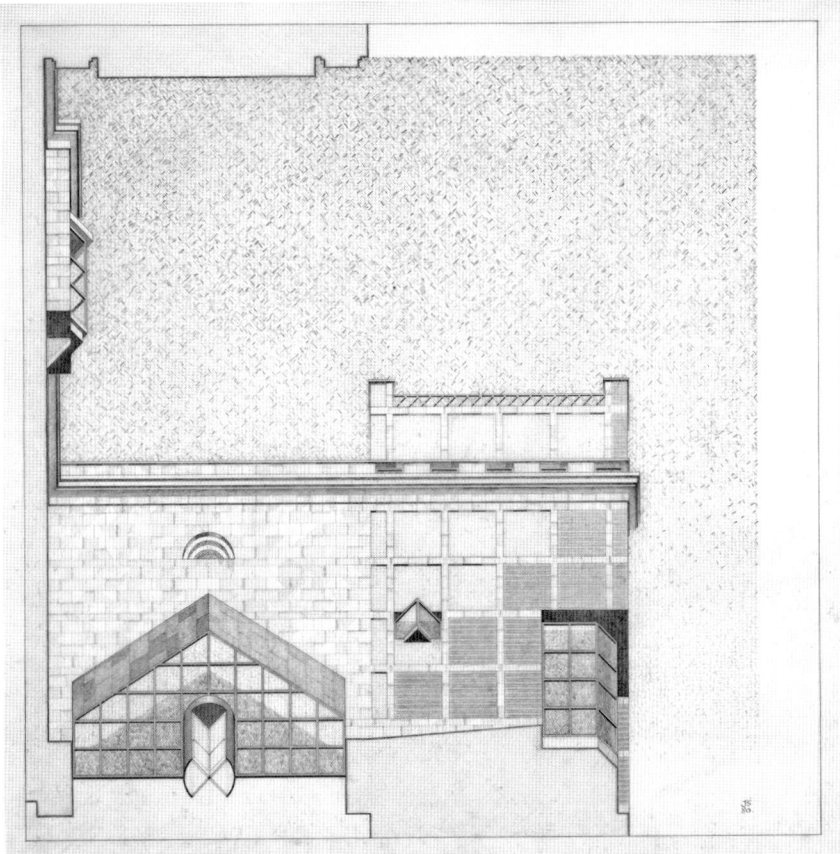

FIGURE 7.20 *James Stirling, Michael Wilford, and Associates. Axonometric of façade for Clore Gallery, London, England, 1980. Graphite and coloured pencil on translucent paper, 75.5 × 75.7 cm, AP140.S2.SS1.D60.SD1.P14.3. James Stirling/ Michael Wilford fonds, Canadian Centre for Architecture © CCA.*

commentary on the complex patterns and textures of the city', and as initiating 'richer dialogues between past and present without the use of ingratiating historic pastiche . . .'.[111] At the same time, they fiercely rebutted the standpoint of many commentators, that these projects heralded 'a dramatic change in design', or that the 'occasional incorporation of neo-classical details, proclaimed that direction as "post modern" – a categorization always dismissed by us as glib and self-serving'.[112] Instead, they underlined the continuities in the work, in the compositional strategies employed, in the use of collage, and the occasional 'use of façade or "veneer" buildings'. The projects examined here also show continuities in the handling of surface and materiality: the surface 'impasto' of Ham Common; the skin-surfaces of Leicester's stereotomy of space; the expressive tragic or arcadian faces of the Staatsgalerie or the Clore, where the 'incorporation of neo-classical details' becomes explicit. Turn the pages of that foundational text of Post-Modernism – Venturi's *Complexity and Contradiction in Architecture* (1966) – and images of the work of many of Stirling's architect-heroes appear in succession: Vanbrugh, Moretti, Hawksmoor, Le Corbusier, various Italian Mannerists, Soane, Butterfield, etc., demonstrating the sorts of serious play at which Stirling excelled: contradictory complexity, ambiguity, expressive surface and texture, difficult wholes, and so on. In their late-Modernist context, these stratagems undoubtedly do come within the (lower-case) post-modernism of Pevsner's definition, and in its Neo-Classical turn, of (upper-case) Po-Mo. But, unlike the crude 'this-means-that' of much Po-Mo, Stirling's work stands comfortably with his heroes, across time and the international stage, in its dense multi-valency.

CHAPTER EIGHT

High-Tech, Neo-Vernacular, New Materiality

Richard Rogers – Ralph Erskine – Caruso St John

High-Tech and the Exo-skeleton – Archigram to Lloyds

So chameleonic is Leicester University's 'mechanical hobgoblin', that it has even been branded as 'High-Tech'; in one book on *Pioneering British 'High-Tech'* (McKean, Bramante, Powell, 1999), for example, it figures as one of three case-studies, together with Norman Foster's smooth-skinned Willis Faber and Dumas Building, Ipswich (1975), and the skeletal bravura of Richard Rogers's Lloyd's Building (1978–86), in the City of London. Lloyds turned architecture inside-out, exposing its structure and services as urban spectacle. Fire regulations disallowed the structural steel desired by the Richard Rogers Partnership, so instead they detailed structural concrete with the smoothness, precision, and diagonal bracing associated with steel, as engineer Peter Rice explains: 'Our aim was to exploit the natural qualities of concrete while trying to achieve the visual articulation and legibility normally associated with steel'.[1] The High-Tech developed by English architects in the 1970s, such as Rogers and Foster, demanded the lightness and flexibility of steel, for its space-age imagery of lightness, flexibility, and expendability – the heaviness of concrete Brutalism was no longer regarded as Modern. Anyhow, according to Adrian Forty, 'the designation of concrete as "modern" was always fragile, always open to question and constantly in need of refreshment. Concrete's inherent backwardness, its earthbound origins in the peasant process of *pisé*, is never far away . . .'.² As we saw, Brutalism had revelled in this atavistic character of concrete, in its very fusion of the primitive and modern. At Lloyds, any heaviness in the steel-looking concrete structure, 'is successfully balanced by the airy and elegant lightness of the atrium roof, a startling re-enactment of the Victorian drama of The Crystal Palace and the great nineteenth-century railway termini – though wrought iron is, of course, replaced by tubular steel'.³ The absence, from British architecture, of such Crystal Palace spectacle – until this 1960s/1970s High-Tech explosion – rests in large part with Ruskin, yet it is equally British. In Rogers's work, the Archigram pioneer, Peter Cook, finds an 'enthusiasm for production and invention. It comes from that part of the English psychology that has not forgotten the audacities and imagination of the young boy constructing a model airplane, or a few years later, lying under the engine of a small car, or later still, watching the technicians strip out the world's longest neoprene gasket'.⁴

In a lecture to the Architectural Association (AA) in January 1857, on the 'Influence of Imagination in Architecture', Ruskin had scorned the desire to create a 'new style' based on the mechanistic language of Paxton's Crystal Palace:

> The furnace and the forge shall be at your service: you shall draw out your plates of glass and beat out your bars of iron till you have encompassed us all, – if your style is of the practical kind, – with endless perspective of black skeleton and blinding square . . .⁵

Although – even in rejecting the quest for a new iron-architecture – Ruskin anticipated Paul Scheerbart (or the *Stadtkrone* of Lloyds), by tantalizing his AA audience with a vision of an iron style of the 'ideal kind', where 'you shall wreathe your streets with ductile leafage, and roof them with variegated crystal – you shall put, if you will, all London under one blazing dome of many colours that shall light the clouds round it with its flashing, as far as to the sea'.⁶ The path to the skeletal Lloyds takes it course via the Centre Pompidou in Paris (Richard Rogers and Renzo Piano, 1977), back to the English avant-garde group of the 1960s known as 'Archigram'.

Momentous ambitions were contained in the first *Archigram 1* printed on just two sheets in London in May 1961: 'WE HAVE CHOSEN TO BY-PASS THE DECAYING BAUHAUS IMAGE WHICH IS AN INSULT TO FUNCTIONALISM'. The publication's collaborators – Peter Cook, David Greene, and Mike Webb – declared: 'The poetry in bricks is lost. We want to drag into building some of the poetry of countdown, orbital helmets, discord of mechanical body transportation and leg walking . . .'.⁷ In May 1961, Alan Shepard had become the first American in space, and President Kennedy had announced to Congress the ambition to land men on the Moon, and return them to Earth, within the decade. In 1967, Peter Cook explained 'the first *Archigram* [as] an outburst against the crap going up in

HIGH-TECH, NEO-VERNACULAR, NEW MATERIALITY 225

London, against the attitude of a continuing European tradition of well-mannered but gutless architecture that had absorbed the label "Modern", but had betrayed most of the philosophies of the earliest "Modern"'.[8] The 'crap' included the expanses of glass curtain-walling that 'had begun to seal city streets. Lustrous office block surfaces', emulating the corporate architecture of New York.[9] Refuting these well-mannered boxes, all the works in the project-spread of *Archigram 1* exaggerate contour, 'skin' is a recurrent term, as membranes are pushed, penetrated, and folded, in organic responses to movement, change, and light. Tilted centre-page is an elevation of Michael Webb's Furniture Manufacturers Association Building in High Wycombe (1957–8), a fourth-year student project he made at London's Regent Street Polytechnic; regarded as one of the most striking student projects of the late 1950s, it was chosen for exhibition in 1961, by New York's Museum of Modern Art, as an example of 'visionary' architecture.[10] It was also published in detail in *The Architects' Journal* of 14 March 1959, in pages given over to work of the British Architectural Students Association (BASA), and attributed to one Mike de Webb.[11] The labels applied to this elevation in *Archigram 1*: 'movement', 'move', 'skin' and – most tellingly – 'tubism', characterize the pulsation of biomorphic elements and tubes inserted into, or attendant upon, a slender concrete skeleton; 'space enclosure is effected by means of pre-cast and in-situ Ferro-Cimento (a technique pioneered by Luigi Nervi, whereby various types of concrete are applied to layers of steel mesh)'.[12] Wordsmith and critic Reyner Banham captured the

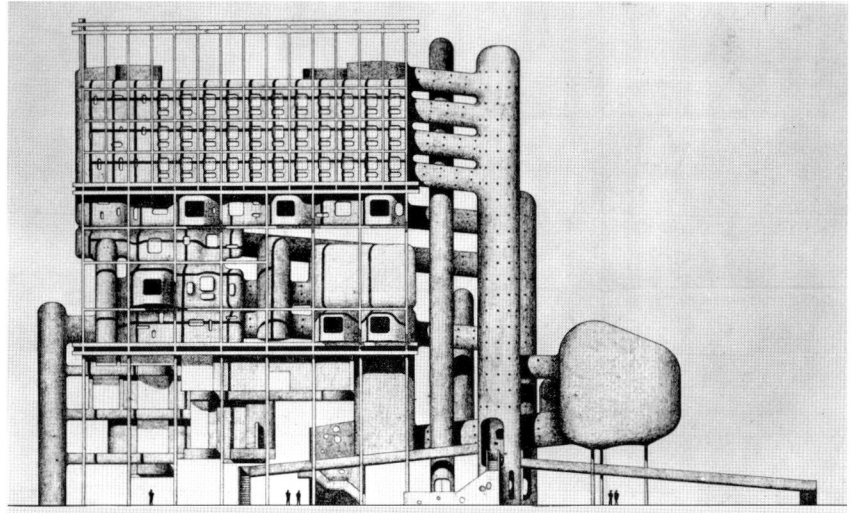

FIGURE 8.1 *North elevation, Furniture Manufacturers Association Headquarters, High Wycombe, England (Furniture Factory), Michael Webb. © Archigram 1957–8.*

disgust inherent in this 'Tubism' of exposed innards by christening it as 'Bowellism'; movement is made visible, and in the accommodation of the Furniture Manufacturers Association we can observe the peristalsis of the intestines. Banham also coined the term 'topological' to describe 'the facts of circulation' in earlier Brutalist projects like the Smithsons' Sheffield University extension of 1953. Sheffield was extreme for the time, as an anti-building of blocks, decks, and ducts, where for Banham, the 'flourishing display of the circulation system, the unifying principle of the design – in the absence of any comprehensible visual aesthetic, – becomes the connectivity of the circulation'.[13]

A key built work, connecting this Brutalist vein of anti-building to the space-age topologies and exo-skeletons of Archigram, was the South Bank Arts Centre (1960–7), designed by Warren Chalk, Ron Herron, Dennis Crompton, and John Attenborough for Group Leader Norman Engleback, within the Special Works Division of the London County Council. Cook, Greene, and Webb, 'who were still only a couple of years out of [architecture] school were still a bit in awe of Ron [Herron], Warren [Chalk], and Dennis [Crompton] who had built stuff', and invited them to contribute their competition drawings for the Lillington Street Housing, Westminster, to *Archigram 2* in 1962, thereby completing the Archigram group of six.[14] The Arts Centre juggles two concert halls – the Queen Elizabeth Hall and the Purcell Room – and the Hayward Gallery, between the Waterloo Bridge and the light-hearted Modernism of the Royal Festival Hall; as Warren Chalk wrote on the project's publication in *Architectural Design* in 1967, 'a special trap the architects were determined to avoid was the nautical whimsy of the 1951 Festival of Britain'. Instead, they aspired to 'the message of the city as a single building', a key inspiration being the Smithsons' entry for the Berlin Haupstadt Competition of 1958, where the movement patterns of people and cars were celebrated with the superimposition of a shifting angular network of pedestrian decks above the vehicular grid below, connected by escalators.[15] The South Bank Centre remains rebarbative, in its purposely inchoate collisions of raised promenades and sparring volumes. Where Brutalism had used concrete to 'bloody-mindedly' underscore physical presence and surface facture, here the meticulously detailed shuttered ducts and beams, and Cornish granite aggregate panels, tend to dissolution; as Forty explains it: 'The continuous concrete surface was a way to lose sight altogether of the buildings as individual objects, and instead to allow them to merge into a generic urban infrastructure'.[16]

The South Bank Arts Centre looks as if it could withstand a major attack, nonetheless expendability is encoded in these infrastructural notions of the 'city as a single building'. 'Expendability' is already there as a keyword in *Archigram 1*, written against Peter Cook and Gordon Sainsbury's project for a Piccadilly Circus competition (*The Star* newspaper, 1961); but by *Archigram 3*, 'EXPENDABILITY towards throwaway architecture' is emblazoned on the cover as a core manifesto. The projects illustrated in

HIGH-TECH, NEO-VERNACULAR, NEW MATERIALITY   227

FIGURE 8.2 *Warren Chalk, Ron Herron, Dennis Crompton, and John Attenborough for Group Leader Norman Engleback within the Special Works Division of the London County Council, South Bank Arts Centre (1960–7), detail view. Photograph Stephen Kite.*

the seven pages of yellow paper embrace the ideas advanced in Peter Cook's editorial, of longer-term infrastructure, and shorter-term expendable units:

> Perhaps it will not be until such things as housing, amenity place and work place become recognized as consumer products that can be 'bought off the peg' – with all that this implies in terms of expendability (foremost), industrialization, up-to-date-ness, consumer choice, and basic product-design – that we can begin to make an environment that is really part of a developing human culture.[17]

All this would reach its climax in the city-sized megastructure of the celebrated Plug-in City of 1964, but the plug-in proposition of 'planned obsolescence' is even now embryonic in *Archigram 3*, in the Nottingham Shopping Centre Project (1962) of Peter Cook and David Greene, where the 'service road generates permanent crane railway which serves, builds, maintains and replaces district.... Expendable shop units can multiply'; as written on one concept section: 'The cranes can handle anything from grand pianos, crates, general goods to [expendable] shops ...'.[18] Cranes have become the leitmotif pinnacles of the bony Gothic-esque aesthetic of expendability and High-Tech, climaxing in the blue cranes that crown Richard Rogers's Lloyds Building. Like the images of Antonio Sant'Elia's *La Città Nuovo* (1914), that partly inspired Archigram, all these visualizations would mostly remain as paper-architecture, until the completion of Renzo Piano and Richard Rogers's Pompidou Centre in Paris in 1977. For Peter

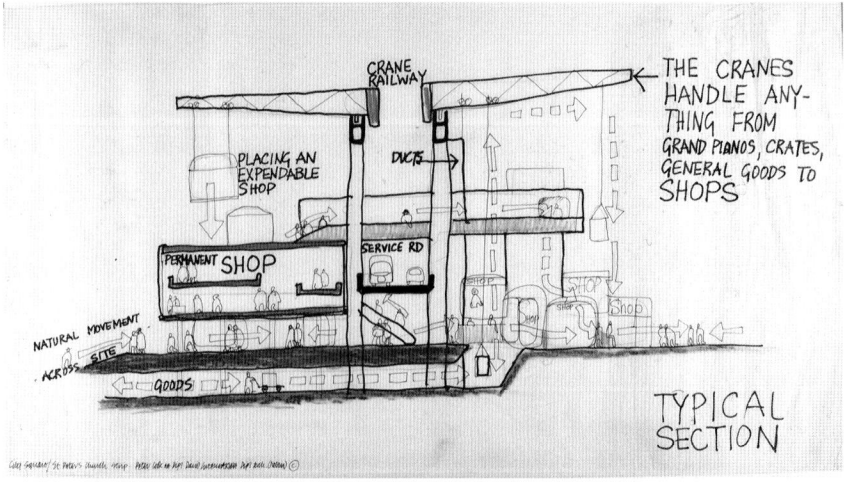

FIGURE 8.3 *Nottingham Shopping Viaduct sketch. Peter Cook and David Greene.* © Archigram 1962.

Cook himself, the Pompidou Centre was predictably 'too consistent'[19] in the rationality of its form, as an expression of Archigram's rhetorics of indeterminancy. But for many critics at the time, they were unlikely to get anything closer; Banham writing in 1977 certainly saw Pompidou as 'a kind of terminal monument to [the megastructure] movement. Even that colour scheme [of the services side] seems to say "Archigram" (if not [The Beatles] "Yellow Submarine"!) . . .'.[20] Piano had his own longstanding fascinations with building processes and detail, while Rogers had direct experience of the USA from his studies at Yale University (begun 1961), and admired the work and ideas of Buckminster Fuller, and Charles and Ray Eames. From the graphics of Archigram, and early experiments such as Team 4's Reliance Controls Factory (Rogers, Foster, Brumwell, Cheesman, 1967), Pompidou became a test-bed for the working out of 'the whole British-based "high-tech" alliance between architecture and engineering [as an] updating of an older passion for craft and detail';[21] and a demonstration of the performance of the exo-skeleton in making urban surfaces, in the most challenging of historical contexts.

Unquestionably, the Beaubourg official competition programme was visionary in wanting 'the Centre's internal flexibility [to] be as large as possible', responding 'in a living and complex organism such as the Centre [to] the evolution of needs . . .'.[22] But the Piano and Rogers team's competition design, partnered with engineers Ove Arup and Partners, took this pursuit of indeterminancy to an evangelical extreme, even including moveable floors – the latter over-ambitious idea was soon dropped, once the competition had been won. The concept evolved early of 'a clearly defined and rational framework', where everything was pushed outside of a totally clear deep-plan envelope; on the west side the user circulation and other movements, facing a new public square, and on the east side, hard against the Rue du Renard, all the mechanical equipment. So the architects envisioned Beaubourg as 'a giant Meccano set rather than a traditional static transparent or solid doll's house';[23] as Simon Sadler points out, 'a typical British boy of Archigram's generation, growing up in the 1940s, was apt to play with Meccano sets . . .'.[24] This toy, based on mechanical engineering and sold as kits of plates and girders, nuts and bolts, was invented by Frank Hornby, in Liverpool, England in 1901; its influence might be paralleled to that of the Froebel blocks of Frank Lloyd Wright's childhood. Having pushed all the innards out then, as Piano describes, 'we took a decision: are we going to show all this, or cover it with a false façade? That was it. Our design. It was absolutely super-simple'.[25] A far greater loss to the Beaubourg as realized, than the moveable floors, has been the omission of the media surfaces that were so crucial to the competition concept of a 'Live Centre of Information' for Paris, and beyond. Piano and Rogers visualized their 'screen façade as a site for the convergence of multiple, formerly distinct entities into a single surface of appearance, relaying "constantly changing information, news, what's on in Paris, artworks, robots, television, temporary structures, electronic two-way games, and

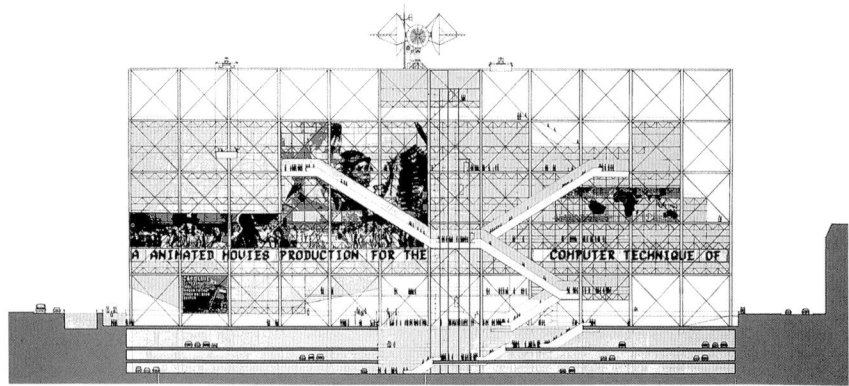

FIGURE 8.4 *Elevation of competition design, Centre Georges Pompidou, Paris, France. Piano + Rogers. © Fondazione Renzo Piano; Rogers Stirk Harbour + Partners (RSHP).*

information, etc."'; the competition elevation to the public square conveyed these media-systems as photo-montages and message-streams.[26]

As it turned out, realizing any of this proved to be more challenging than the structure itself, though the ligatures are there, if needed, for fixing media tools that are now readily available. Pompidou can therefore be seen as a point of origin for subsequent developments of the media façade; at the same time it represents the culmination of the media-envelope experimentation that had intensified with the spread of electrification at the turn of the twentieth century. The Piano and Rogers team were certainly aware, for example, of Oscar Nitzchke's *Maison de la Publicité* project for Paris of 1934–6; this media-machine would have emblazoned the nocturnal Champs-Élysées with illuminated, interchangeable graphics, arrayed on a diagonally braced steel-grid – all strikingly similar to Piano and Rogers's montages. Kenneth Frampton would later complain about Pompidou's 'under-provision of wall surface', and its 'over-provision of flexibility';[27] the stripping of its communicative media-surfaces would only place further onus upon the naked exo-skeletal structure to signify the status of a great public institution. This High-Tech tendency to elaborate structure-as-ornament can be seen at its outset in Team 4's Reliance Controls (1965–6), where the diagonal bracing, to every structural steel bay, goes far beyond engineering requirements. Rogers's biographer, Bryan Appleyard, tells of his 'desire to produce a layered building in which the surface is replete with interest and incident', one equal to 'the more elaborate surfaces of the Gothic and Classical styles'; the double skeleton was a way to achieving this.[28] In the competition entry this layering was achieved with an excess twinning of structure, a double line of columns, embracing the pushed-out circulation

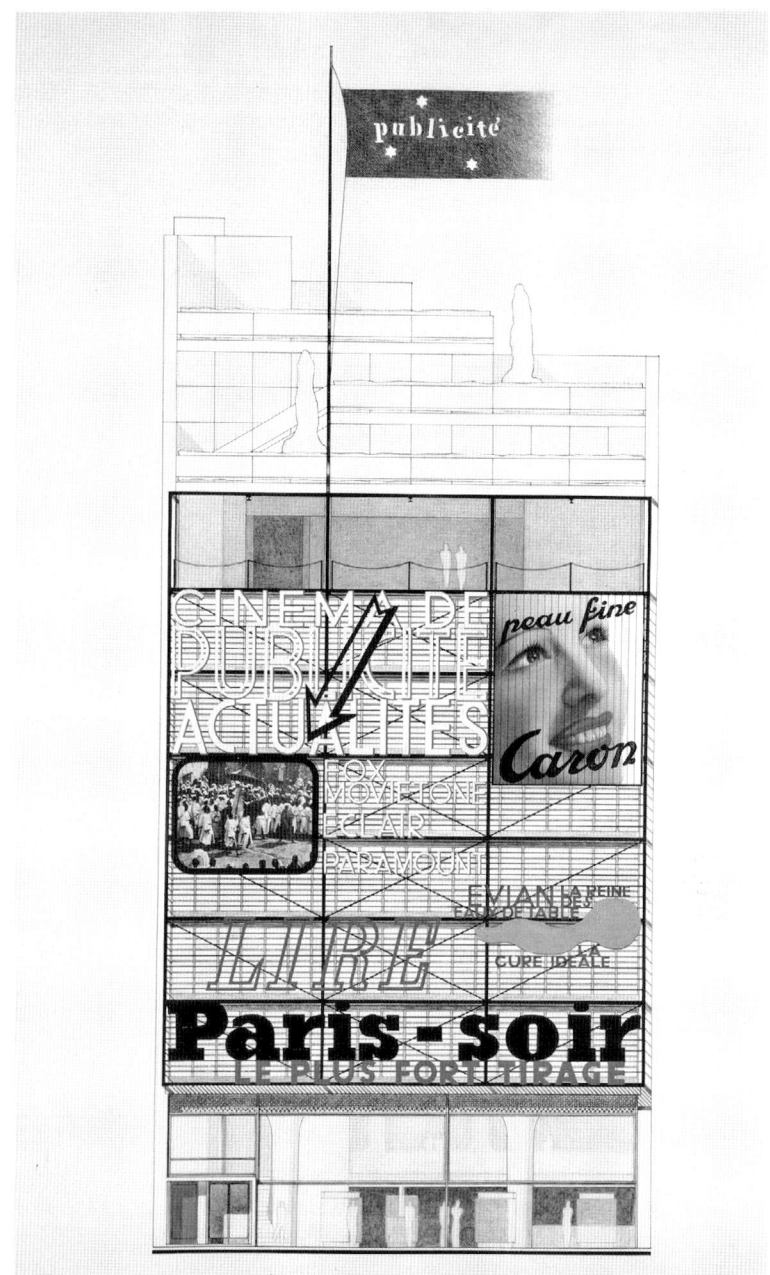

FIGURE 8.5 *Oscar Nitzchke,* Maison de la Publicité *project, Paris, 1934–6, elevation (drawing date 1936). Ink, colour, pencil, gouache, and graphite on lithograph on board, 71.1 × 52.1 cm. Gift of Lily Auchinloss, Barbara Jakobson, and Walter Randel. Acc. No. 424.1976.2. Digital image, The Museum of Modern Art, New York/Scala, Florence.*

and servicing zones, at the ends of the great girders. To the Arup engineers this was both illogical and expensive, and in April 1972, Peter Rice conceived the idea of placing all the compressive load on the inner columns, making the outer layer as verticals in tension, and linking the two by a cantilevered beam; these became the feted 'gerberettes', named after the German engineer Heinrich Gerber (1832–1912) who had patented such a cantilever structural element in 1866. Rice empathized with the architect's emotive approach to form and making, also seeking 'a feeling of contact and warmth between the person looking and the maker'.[29] On this theme, Andrew Saint amplifies upon a key relation:

> Here is an echo of Ruskin and the Arts and Crafts Movement. Not just Rice's work at the Pompidou Centre and after, but the whole British-based 'high-tech' alliance between architecture and engineering, can be read as the updating of an older passion for craft and detail. Structural particulars are picked out, honed and polished, pointed to and hallowed as significant; components and connectors are fetishized and lovingly pictured, from the first sketch through manufacturing, assembly and installation to the unveiling. The image of the identifiable, photogenic particular stands in for the baffling complexity of the whole.[30]

Rice, himself, recognized these historical perspectives, in the belief 'which comes from the past, that the building process is a craft process, a process by which you design and define something by understanding how it works'.[31] As they developed, the gerberettes – so animate at the ends of the 48-metre-span main trusses – became the totemic element which epitomized the intricacy of Pompidou as a whole. The craft aspect only intensified when the decision was made to cast them; looking back to the individuality of Victorian cast-iron, they evolved as magnificently bone-like products of the foundry, each ground to an individual finish – the main columns were also centrifugally cast. All these components were fabricated off-site, and assembled together as a giant Meccano set; while the horizontal connecting galleries are supported within the gerberette zone, the escalators are suspended outside in a final celebratory layering of movement systems. The animation of this populated long diagonal, tracking across the public façade, compensates for the absent media screens.

'We have here an exact parallel with the human body . . . that is, they have put all the guts outside . . . .', protested René Barjavel in *Le Journal du Dimanche* of January 1977, unwittingly spotting Pompidou's genealogy going back to 'Bowellism', and typical of many critics who were shocked to find a major art institution, in the heart of historic Paris, that looked 'like a construction which will never be finished . . .'.[32] But more specialist critics also questioned the absence of symbolism of these urban surfaces; Alan Colquhoun (*Architectural Design*, 1977) was troubled by a building whose exo-skeleton 'presents an image of total mechanization but makes no

HIGH-TECH, NEO-VERNACULAR, NEW MATERIALITY 233

FIGURE 8.6 *Centre Georges Pompidou, Paris, France. Piano + Rogers. Construction of the gerber beam of 'gerberette'. Photograph Bernard Vincent. © Fondazione Renzo Piano; Rogers Stirk Harbour + Partners (RSHP).*

connection between this image and the other possible images of our own culture'. Colquhoun doubts:

> This attitude [that] assumes that architecture has no further task other than to perfect its own technology. It turns the problem of architecture as a representation of social values into a purely aesthetic one, since it assumes that the purpose of architecture is merely to accommodate any form of activity which may be required and has no positive attitude towards these activities. It creates institutions, while pretending that no institutionalization is necessary.[33]

Richard Rogers's Lloyds Building in Leadenhall Street (1978–86) realized a more monochromatic version of High-Tech, within the dense urban grain of the City of London; again a strategy of pushing out circulation and services allowed prisms of unencumbered floor space, supported by six independent service towers, in glittering realization of Louis Kahn's concept of 'served and servant' spaces. Like the Portland stone steeples of Wren and Hawksmoor, these towers are glimpsed as perspectival fragments from within the labyrinths of the City, as they guard the core volume of the soaring barrel-vaulted Underwriting Room. Here Rogers, and his team, produced a masterpiece out of the language assembled at Pompidou, but the iconographical questions remained unresolved, as to how much stacks of expendable lavatory units can equate to the gravitas of a great City institution. And, as a consequence, Lloyds attracted similar vitriol, in one case from the now aged pioneer Berthold Lubetkin, as 'an assembly of nuts and bolts, scrap iron, celebrating a confusion of fancy props, the glorification of ironmongery and triumph of mega-technology for its own sake'.[34] Lubetkin's jaundiced remarks undermine High-Tech's claim to be the continuity line of Modernism, against the cross-currents of Post-Modernism, Neo-Vernacular, and so forth. In theory-averse Britain, High-Tech assembled

FIGURE 8.7 *Richard Rogers Partnership, Lloyds Building, City of London. Photograph Stephen Kite.*

its principles empirically – in a kind of theoretical Meccano of part-to-whole – adapting ideas from 'urbanism, the social uses of space, energy saving and mass production that seemed relevant ...'.[35] As the following section demonstrates, very different outcomes could result from not dissimilar lines of reasoning.

Ralph Erskine, Byker Wall, and Romantic Functionalism

When Banham came to critique the completed Centre Pompidou (*The Architectural Review*, May 1977), he saw the decision to locate it, hard against the Rue de Renard, with its public and ceremonial aspects to the piazza on the west, in the context of Townscape English site-planning practice, as 'directly comparable to the Smithson's decision to put the housing blocks at Robin Hood Gardens on the noisy perimeter of the site, in order to create a quite zone within. [And as] even more directly comparable to the [Ralph] Erskine's team decision to back up their Byker brick "wall" in Newcastle against the threat of traffic noise'.[36] The muscularity of the Smithsons' concretely Brutalist project in Poplar, London (1966–72), can be considered to rhyme with aspects of Pompidou; but the comparison to the 'Byker Wall' (1973–80), in this 'High-Tech' context is, on the face of it, surprising. *The Architectural Review* had published the 'Byker Wall' much earlier in December 1974, and Banham himself had written on 'The great wall of Tyne' in the *New Society* of February 1975, characterizing Erskine as an 'eccentric Anglo-Swedish designer, [as] outstandingly the most *messy* architect practising in Europe today', and the aesthetics of the Wall, and the lower-rise housing it embraces, as 'Higher Shambolism', and as 'a tidal wave of sheddery and pergolation'; the on-site architects' studio proudly seized upon the latter expression as an office catchphrase.[37] But too much can be made of the ostensible disjunction between the languages of High-Tech and the Neo-Vernacular of Byker's 'sheddery'; in both approaches, architecture *per se* almost disappears, to become an enabling infrastructure that empowers consumer-culture's desires or, in Erskine's case, fosters popular participation; and both enjoy ad hoc *bricolage*, whether in steel tubing or timber 'pergolation'.

Erskine presents yet another instance of émigré injections to British architectural culture, in this case a revenant English-Swedish-English one. For Erskine was English, born in 1914 in Northumberland, and studied architecture and planning at Regent Street Polytechnic; he moved to Sweden in 1938, initially attracted by the optimistic Functionalism represented by the 1930 Stockholm Exhibition. But he took with him certain English influences, including a thorough knowledge of Ebenezer Howard's Garden City ideas; as a newly qualified architect he had worked for Louis de Soissons on Welwyn Garden City in 1920; he had also befriended the inspirational Gordon Cullen as a fellow student – his *Townscape* would become one of Erskine's most-thumbed books.[38] Characterized in Britain as 'The New Empiricism' – from a text the Swedish architect Sven Backström contributed to *The Architectural Review* in June 1947 – the country's gentle Modernism contributed to that Festival of Britain ethos, against which the Brutalists had revolted. But by 1965 Sweden itself, under the 'Million Dwellings Programme' launched by its social democratic government, had swung to a mechanically Fordist model of planning and construction, antipathetic to Erskine as backwardly seizing upon the 'early Functionalisms simplistic planning and interest for the techniques and materials of the industrial age . . .'.[39] As a result, in the 1960s, Erskine was attracted by opportunities to build in the region of his birth, where his emollient version of Swedish Modernism had a following, and whose Nordic affinities were demonstrated in the, decidedly Scandinavian, Newcastle Civic Centre (George Kenyon, 1958–68), whose carillon tower pays homage to Ragnar Östberg's Stockholm City Hall (1911–23) – appropriately, the Civic Centre was opened by King Olav V of Norway in November 1968. Erskine's local esteem obtained him work at Killingworth New Town to the north-east of Newcastle, where his concept of a village community on the lakeside site, intended to evoke 'simple fishermen's huts on Skye', was only partially realized.[40] His scheme for 800 dwellings in Eaglestone, for developer Bovis (begun 1973), in the New Town of Milton Keynes (designated 1967), was also only half-completed to Erskine's designs, and followed similar Townscape and Camillo Sitte principles, to optimize the topography and the variety in the patterns of spaces. The developer's standard houses are clad in brickwork, and a mixture of brightly stained tongue and groove or feather edge boarding, which sometimes comes low to nearly clad the whole house, or stays high as an eaves band. In his 1980 survey of *The State of British Architecture*, Sutherland Lyall saw such 1970s Neo-Vernacular housing (as he described it) as 'the most prevalent consequence of the agonies of post tower block *triste*', he mocked the sentiment of its 'supposed grass roots connections with the everyday building of a (long dead) rural village England', and the way it was 'entirely concerned with what houses look like on the outside'. Eaglestone's surface appearances received this withering critique:

> Eaglestone appear[s] to have attempted to design out the appearance of design. . . . A collection of otherwise modest and conventional developer dwellings on a slightly hilly site, the appearance of their having been developed piece-meal is created by arbitrary changes in the colour of roof tiles and brickwork from one set of dwellings to another. The appearance of non-architect-designed downmarket ordinariness is suggested by details such as projecting bow windows, rough wooden balconies, and whimsical folksy suburban timberwork. The appearance of having been comfortably lived in by a race of ardent build-it-yourselfers is broadly hinted at by the proliferation of large quantities of unplaned timber posts and frames, porches and balconies.

FIGURE 8.8 *Ralph Erskine, Eaglestone housing, Milton Keynes, Buckinghamshire. Architectural Press Archive / RIBA Collections.*

Lyall had more time for 'Erskine's Byker housing megastructure at Newcastle', where similar techniques 'are developed with remarkable bravura and with some meaning', and where there had been stronger attempts to involve the occupants in the outcomes.[41] Bernard Rudofsky's exhibition at The Museum of Modern Art, New York of 1964–5, and subsequent publication as *Architecture without Architects* (1964), summates this enthusiasm to design out the appearance of design; his inspirational illustrations gathered together works of the 'vernacular, anonymous, spontaneous, indigenous', across space and time, to introduce the 'unfamiliar world of nonpedigreed architecture'.[42] Eaglestone's Neo-Vernacular is one of a number of experiments at Milton Keynes, whose loose grid-squares shaped by the road network, became test-beds of housing form and layout. In opposing approach to the jumbly Eaglestone, is the High-Tech looking housing of Netherfield, just one grid-square to the south, where regimented, parallel rows of terraces are clad in industrial-looking silver profiled metal sheeting, and fibreglass fins applied to the ends of the party-walls act as pilasters (design team: Chris Cross, Jeremy Dixon, Mike Gold, Ed Jones, Jim Muldrew, Don Ritson, Derek Walker, Philip Ware). Yet both design teams could validly claim to reference English traditions; Eaglestone, the informality of the village-green; Netherfield, the rational repetition of Georgian-Regency terraces. A criticism of the two schemes by Robert Maxwell (*The Architects' Journal*, 10 December 1975), begins with pointedly contrasting photographs of the façades of industrial metal-sheeted

FIGURE 8.9 *Design team: Chris Cross, Jeremy Dixon, Mike Gold, Ed Jones, Jim Muldrew, Don Ritson, Derek Walker, Philip Ware: Netherfield housing, Milton Keynes, Buckinghamshire. Architectural Press Archive / RIBA Collections.*

Netherfield, and timber-boarded Eaglestone; the imagery of each can be seen as an artifice, for Netherfield 'revives and recasts an eighteenth century aesthetic', whereas Eaglestone 'recasts a medieval aesthetic', in deploying 'an expressionist language of nooks and crannies'.[43] Erskine's Nordic-ness has both this broader identity that encompasses Northumberland and Britain, and specific Scandinavian-Swedish dimensions. In his study of Nordic building, *Nightlands* (1996), Christian Norberg-Schulz isolates Erskine as then alone in attacking the problem of Nordic urbanism, with projects for subarctic settlements that 'are both new and representative of a Nordic interpretation of place'.[44] As for the vernacular of Erskine's Swedish roots, Norberg-Schulz distinguishes the half-timbered frame traditions of Denmark from Swedish log construction, whose basic element is 'an embracive rectangle of stacked timbers'. In such construction openings must be cut out; adzing is also common to Swedish log-construction with 'the squared timbers forming a unified surface'. And in the Swedish *längor* (long house), 'in all cases, the outer wall is treated as a continuous surface, in accordance with the original interpretation of log construction; this is evidenced by the proportions of the wall surface and the sporadic openings'. Ever since the seventeenth century this unity of timber wall-surface has been intensified by applications of 'barn red'.[45] The home Erskine built for his family in Drottningholm (1963), assimilates this log folk construction of *knut-timring*

HIGH-TECH, NEO-VERNACULAR, NEW MATERIALITY

(a 'knot-ring' around space) into a contemporary making of the long house volumes of house and studio, around a sheltered court, where the planks are of prefabricated lightweight concrete, grained with a rake with irregular teeth; rounded corner and roof elements emphasize the unity of broad surface. Openings are irregular and carefully tuned to internal use and external aspect, some horizontal in proportion, some more square. Erskine notably did not repeat the experiment of his earlier single-room war-time house at Lissma (1941–2), where the family had learnt the environmental drawbacks of wholly glazed walls. As Erskine has said: 'Certainly opening the house to the view is just one way of working; another way is to appreciate the landscape through a small opening'.[46]

Norberg-Schulz's praise for Erskine's innovative Nordic urbanism originates in his research, in the mid-1950s, into the challenge of realizing an ideal city north of the Arctic Circle. One of Erskine's powerful drawings looks down upon the settlement of 'An Ecological Arctic Town', spectacularly located in the snows halfway up the south-east facing slopes of a mountain. A great wall cranks angularly around the whole town, pierced by small windows and patterned in bold, warm-hued patterns, of red and gold on its sunny side, and cooler blue and green hues to the shaded perimeter – all very prescient of the Byker Wall. Erskine presented his Arctic city thinking to his Team 10 peers at the CIAM (Congrès Internationaux d'Architecture Moderne) at Otterlo, Holland in 1959. In the ensuing discussion both Aldo

FIGURE 8.10 *Ralph Erskine, 'Project for an Arctic Town' (1958). From ArkDes Collections ARKM 1986 17 0349.*

Van Eyck and Peter Smithson were perturbed by what they saw as a tendency to 'exaggerate' in Erskine's work. Van Eyck praised the Nordic projects as 'beautifully done', but found wanting a sublimity in the architectural response equal to 'the majestic power of the event up there'; he was troubled by the humour in Erskine's projects, how they were 'so fanatically involved with looking after cosiness'. Smithson brutally dismissed 'the tendency in this work to what we call "Mickey Mouse styling". You have deliberately exaggerated certain features in order to more clearly communicate the intention of the functions'. And he spoke of reports from visitors to the houses and shopping centres of the Nordic regions, being 'very disturbed with the number of materials used, the number of apparently arbitrary colours, or the number of arbitrary changes in colour and the mixture of symbols used'; he warned Erskine against this and 'to be a little less like Walt Disney ... and a bit more like Charles Eames'.[47] Words like 'exaggeration', 'arbitrariness', 'cosiness', are the familiar coded put-downs the guardians of the 'true paths' of Modernism fire against Expressionist-Organicist tendencies. Even though the leading organic-architecture historian, Peter Blundell Jones, was keen to include Erskine within the marginalized organic canon of Modernism – along with the likes of Scharoun and Häring – he has acknowledged Erskine's 'protest about "organic" and inclusion in any such grouping'.[48] Also, accepting Erskine's refusal of the 'organic' label, Peter Collymore suggests 'Romantic Functionalist' to capture the pragmatic, adaptable humanism of the English-Swede's architecture.[49]

Erskine's Arctic Town gave a Nordic inflection to the idea of inhabited walls as urban identifiers that had stimulated modernist thinking ever since Le Corbusier's city-planning ideas for Algiers of 1930–4, ideas that are evident in much of the thinking of Team 10 and the Smithsons, as in the topologies of their entry for the aforementioned Haupstadt Berlin Competition of 1958. Cutting as the east wind can be in Newcastle-upon-Tyne, in its location at the north-eastern edge of England, it is not an arctic climate; however, by applying the same perimeter wall principles as in his Nordic town, Erskine greatly enhanced the environmental conditions of the exposed south-western slopes of the Byker area, situated a mile to the east of the centre of Newcastle, on the north side of the River Tyne. As well as protecting against north and east winds, the wall was designed to be an acoustic barrier to a proposed urban motorway that was never constructed. Byker had grown up in the 1880s as housing for skilled workers in the shipbuilding and heavy engineering works on the banks of the Tyne. Very dense two-storey terraces of 'Tyneside flats' (one flat over the other, each with its own front door to the street) ran straight up the hill, offering little environmental or spatial quality, except for thrilling views back to the centre of Newcastle, of the course of the Tyne and its many bridges. Following his commission in 1968, in 1970 Erskine produced a 'Plan of Intent' for Byker, in outline his objectives were: to create an 'integrated environment for living in its widest sense'; to maintain the traditions of characterful and close-knit neighbourhood; to phase rehousing so as not to break family and community ties; to maximize the potential of the site in terms of view and insolation; to create a characterful settlement with a network of pedestrian routes; 'to provide a recognizable physical form' and a '"local" individuality to each group of houses'.[50]

The Wall is far from being the whole story of Byker – it provides only 20% of the accommodation, 80% is in the low-rise housing within its protective embrace – but it is the most 'recognizable physical form' in giving identity to the whole, as it curves down the hillside, incorporating historical elements along its course, such as the church of St Lawrence near the top of the hill, and the Public Baths and Shipley Hall halfway down. Its heroic presence is greater than its actual height, at the centre at Raby Gate it only reaches eight storeys, and the perimeter block of the later phase of Dunn Terrace climaxes in the twelve storeys 'recognition point' of the sheltered-housing wedge of Tom Collins House.[51] In places mini-walls dock into it the main Wall, to mitigate its presence and to reinforce settlement boundaries. The fins of the blue metal-clad lift machine-rooms are important townscape elements, punctuating the skyline of the Wall as it descends. The vivid ad-hocism of the Wall's sunny side reflects its social organization; at its base two-storey planes of buff brickwork express ground-level family maisonettes; smaller one-bed maisonettes populate the upper levels, the result of the original demography where there was a housing need for a high proportion of elderly residents. These upper stages are clad in off-white fibre-cement panels, making a neutral field for the lively 'sheddery' of projecting access galleries and balconies – later stages, like Tom Collins House, use the better weathering properties of white-finished aluminium sheeting. For these galleries and balconies, green and blue-stained horizontal timber slatting was applied to red timber sub-frames. The course of the Roman Hadrian's Wall passes nearby, and the north-face of Erskine's wall is equally defensive looking, with small windows, and a peppering of red and yellow ventilators, being 'lavishly patterned in coloured bricks. It represents one of the longest exercises in conscious decoration that has been built'.[52] Brick-cladding was intrinsic to the Neo-Vernacular turn in the 1960s and 1970s; appropriate to housing, less appropriate to a major Civic Centre like the one Robert Matthew Johnson-Marshall designed in 1978, for Middlesex, as an overblown evocation of a Norman Shaw mansion. The abstract patterns of Erskine's giant mural use a metric format brick (290 × 90 × 65mm) in five different colours – deep reds, greys, and ochre. In the earlier phase they rhyme with the geometry of the Wall as bands, or vertical panels, or zip-bands, that interact with the facets of its curves. Intensifications of pattern mark out entrances through the Wall, at one gateway they make a sort of pediment, whilst at the important axis to Raby Street, a Mondrian-esque, Boogie-Woogie, brick design runs the full eight-storey height of the Wall. A change of idiom in the lower, later phase of Dunn Terrace produces diagonals and chevrons, reminiscent of warship camouflage, which break up the Wall's

FIGURE 8.11 *Ralph Erskine, Byker Wall, Newcastle upon Tyne, south side. From ArkDes Collections ARKM 1986 122 1938.*

HIGH-TECH, NEO-VERNACULAR, NEW MATERIALITY

FIGURE 8.12 *Ralph Erskine, Byker Wall, Newcastle upon Tyne, north side. From ArkDes Collections ARKM 1986 122 1904.*

form as a foreground to the Newcastle skyline. The low-rise, predominantly two-storey housing that makes up 80% of Byker, utilizes a similar palette of brick, colour-stained timber, and bright metal sheeting, to shape a network of connected pedestrian spaces of intimate villagey character. Rich Cullenesque floorscapes typify these outdoor rooms; the small square where Raby Street meets the Wall is paved with salvaged flagstones, and is ornamented with spoils of column-fragments from demolished Newcastle buildings; an alley might have stone flags set in a sea of cobbles; and even asphalt streets are edged with cobble-channels and broken by lines of granite slabs.[53]

The community of Byker had no say in the look and form of the Wall, and participation in the low-rise housing was also marginal; the on-site presence of the architects' office in the middle of Byker – opened in September 1969 – ensured some lines of communication, but on the level of keeping the community informed on progress, and the design-team receiving limited input on needs and preferences.[54] So Lyall's criticism of developer-led Eaglestone rings true, even at Byker; in its fragmentation and bricolage we have an *aesthetic* of self-build and participation, which is highly designed, to design out the look of design. There can be no doubt that the 'revenge of the Picturesque' is hard-wired into British Modernism, whether it manifests itself as the bricolages of metallic High-Tech, or timbery Romantic Functionalism.

In September 1983, *The Architectural Review* included Erskine's place-making at Newcastle, and his brand of Romantic Functionalism, under the rubric of a special issue on what it called 'Romantic Pragmatism'. The *Review* sought to capture an ethos in British architecture of the 1970s and early 1980s that was described neither by Structural-Rationalism, nor by the worst indulgences of Neo-Vernacular. In the leading article, Editor Peter Davey (together with Gillian Darley) stressed the rigour of thinking and geometry in the 'sense and sensibility' of this manner, drawing on 'a legacy of that turn of the century marriage between freedom and discipline. Arts and Crafts architects, Frank Lloyd Wright and Ralph Erskine – all have pursued this line'; other key contemporary representatives included the work of Edward Cullinan, and MacCormac, Jamieson, Prichard.[55] Then, in the following year (May 1984), the *Review* asked 'five distinguished foreign observers', and a range of native British architects to respond to the question, 'Is there a British tradition?' In the context of the conservative British atmosphere of the 1980s, of the architects discussed here, Stirling was robust in his rebuttal: 'No. Except in the worst sense of the word: English Noddyland and I am not part of it'. But, in *his* response, Richard Rogers viewed 'Stirling's maverick, witty eccentricity [as] rooted in the [British] architecture of the eighteenth and nineteenth centuries . . .'. From his own standpoint, not surprisingly, Rogers saw 'the steel technology [as] rooted in British railway architecture. Paxton and Brunel, and the birth of the industrial revolution . . .'. Just as expectedly, Richard MacCormac empathized with the Romantic Pragmatist concern 'for individuals rather than abstractions', and 'a concern for quality in making things'. Disowning his own thoughts on the English Meccano-esque aspects of Archigram, Peter Cook protested: 'Screw the English tradition. It's a great big trap. . . . We force ourselves into utter provinciality. I feel Romantic Pragmatism is the enemy. It's only the second- or third-rate who use it as a prop'. Of the 'foreign observers', the US architect and theorist Peter Eisenman warmed most to the idea: 'There is no question that England has such a tradition: this can easily be seen when it is compared to a place like the United States, which in these terms, does not. . . . Equally, there is no question that after the Second World War . . . England was the post-war leader of Western architecture, not only in architectural journalism and education, but also in theory and practice . . .'.[56]

Caruso St John and the New Materiality

Eisenman was generous, given the eclectic state British architecture had arrived at by the 1980s – a spent field scattered with remnants of the battles of Brutalism, Post-Modernism, High-Tech, Neo-Vernacular, and the rest. In the pragmatism of Romantic Functionalism, or the functionality of Romantic

Pragmatism, some had sought a neo-Ruskinian middle-way forward, by harnessing making to social purpose, as demonstrated in the rough-sawn joints of Erskine's Byker, or the devotedly elaborate details of Cullinan's work – for example, his Fountains Abbey Visitor Centre, Yorkshire (1988–92). Lyall had concluded his survey of the state of the nation's architecture (1980) pessimistically, troubled by 'British architecture's . . . growing interest in the apparently unserious – an interest in impermanence, flexibility, in the joke, irony and the frivolity of knowing eclecticism and stylism . . .'.[57] For a conservative observer and admirer of the Classical tradition, like the architectural historian David Watkin, this very eclecticism and stylism was a source of 'hope for the future. The restricting ideologies of the modern movement have finally been overcome . . .'. Watkin concluded his *History of Western Architecture* (1986), entirely with images of emphatically Post-Modernist or Classical-Revival projects; in this company (Charles Moore, Quinlan Terry, Ricardo Bofill, Léon Krier), Stirling's Staatsgalerie, Stuttgart stands out for its Modernist credentials – even within its Post-Modernity.[58] But for significant numbers of that generation of architects, emergent from the mid-1980s and into the 1990s, making and meaning would again provide the *rappel à l'ordre*. Their work is tauter and more Minimalist than that of the Romantic Pragmatists, though like them it also draws strength from the ethics and aesthetics of the Arts and Crafts movement. Once again, there is a modus operandi of looking both outward, and inward, for renewal – at this juncture, to Switzerland and Austria, to the boxy architecture of the Swiss School, and the writings and works of Adolf Loos. Models and ideas which are then transmogrified to the British condition; for his part, we know how much Loos was devoted 'to the standard products of British equipment of 1900, men's suits and chairs'.[59]

As an advocate of this sensibility to the qualities of 'plainness and a sense of naturalness', Tony Fretton, and his Lisson Gallery in Marylebone, London (1985–93), stands out as significant. Fretton had worked as a fine artist, and there are concordances between the practice of these architects, and the fine-grained interrogative ways of working of fine artists. Note how Fretton's Minimalism replicates in architecture, 'the formal discipline, intellectual reach and the "power to be affecting and communicative" that he found in Donald Judd, Barnett Newman and Louis Kahn'.[60] The Lisson's poetic façade to Bell Street is a testament to the international art boom of the 1980s, conspicuously hidden in what was then an everyday backwater to the Edgeware Road. On the question of its significance, Kenneth Frampton writes of its 'laconic Bell Street façade, painted white, which speaks of an architecture this country has never known . . .'. This street-face has four bands which approximate the levels of the adjoining classically stuccoed shop; the first two levels are fully-glazed, above is a plain band punctuated by a square oculus which reminds Frampton of 'the oculus on the façade of the Villa Garches';[61] the planes are as shrewdly 'carved' and proportioned, as a low-relief by Ben Nicholson. In thus setting a new paradigm for

FIGURE 8.13 *Tony Fretton Architects, Lisson Gallery, London. Photograph Lorenzo Elbaz.*

Modernism in Britain, architecture like the Lisson Gallery plainly rejects the scenography of Post-Modernism. Architecture like this overlaps with theories of 'New Materialism', and its emphasis on material expression, within an 'approach to design that seeks to challenge the hegemony of top-down processes of form making and replace it with bottom-up logic of form-finding', underscoring 'formation rather than form', in grappling with the givens of locale and matter.⁶² However, it is problematic that New Materialism has become a broad discourse encompassing, in some cases, the instrumental extremes of parametric digital computation – so once again displacing architecture's agency as a liberal art. I shall therefore adopt the term 'New Materiality', to differentiate the buildings examined in this section of the chapter. The 'New Materiality' reclaims the authenticity of material and making, in resistance to the commodification of architecture and the flows of capital; as Kenneth Frampton opines: 'To stress tectonic rather than scenographic values in the constitution of architectural form is evidently a strategy by which to stiffen the resistance of the field to its further dissolution through the instrumental maximization of international capital'.⁶³

In the second stage of the competition for the New Art Gallery Walsall (announced in March 1995), it finally came down to a choice between Tony Fretton's proposal for 'an exquisite glass box that offered flexibility', and Caruso St John's design which 'was more fixed, with a stronger civic presence' – Caruso St John were chosen.⁶⁴ Their practice (founded 1990) represents a younger cohort than Fretton's (born 1945); Adam Caruso was born in 1962 in Canada, and studied at McGill University, Montreal. Peter St John is English, born 1959, and studied at the Bartlett and the Architectural Association. In their concerns for authenticity Caruso St John admire the rebarbative material instincts of Lewerentz, of the Smithsons and – back to where we began – the awkward Picturesque of Philip Webb and Red House, 'painstakingly built from raw, garish locally sourced brick and tile . . .'.⁶⁵ For instance, Adam Caruso has spoken of the Picturesque as 'a very powerful way of working and is what in Britain great nineteenth-century architects like Webb and Shaw were masters of: making a picture which isn't classical, but puts different elements together to achieve a kind of coherence of balance'.⁶⁶ They had also become greatly interested in the Swiss scene in the 1980s – especially the work of Herzog and de Meuron – and the ways in which this work reprised certain Team 10 concerns, again including the British contributions of the Smithsons.⁶⁷

Therefore Caruso St John's Walsall Gallery embraces many references: the gaunt factories of Walsall itself and the tower of St Matthew's Church; Florence's Palazzo del Popolo, whose tower extrudes from the body of the building to loom above the urban space of the Piazza della Signoria; Adolf Loos's Müller House in Prague; Hardwick Hall, Derbyshire. Bess of Hardwick's great Elizabethan prodigy house (1590–7) merits attention as a near at hand inspiration – its six proud towers crown its Derbyshire hilltop just sixty miles north-east of Walsall. Nor is it necessary to look to Florence, or Loos, or Switzerland, for a boxy architectonic, for it is easy to imagine Walsall as a chunk of building cleft from Hardwick's cubic masses. In the passages from Pevsner on Perpendicular England examined earlier, he underlined an Englishness of compartmented parts; so Hardwick Hall's 'plan is like that of a thirteenth-century cathedral – the outcome of rectangle

FIGURE 8.14 *Hardwick Hall, Derbyshire, the west front. Edwin Smith / RIBA Collections.*

or square added to rectangle or square. The elevation is of blocks pushed against blocks, and the roofs are unrelievedly flat'.[68] Loos is important to Walsall, but the Gallery's organization is not a Raumplan in the manner of the Müller House. Hardwick was inventively early in having a cross-hall which its probable architect, Robert Smythson, would have known from du Cerceau, Serlio, and possibly Palladio. Mark Girouard points to the 'most unique and daring feature' of its interior as the staircases; the most ceremonial one starts just off the south-east side of the cross-hall to reach its end 'only after many windings, doublings back, long runs and spacious landings', finally curling up to arrive at the tall vestibule to Bess's High Great Chamber, which Sacheverell Sitwell considered 'the most beautiful room, not in England alone, but in the whole of Europe, with a great frieze of parget work, ten or twelve feet deep, of coloured plaster, representing a stag hunt, and a boar hunt, the court of Diana, and the story of Orpheus'; he also agreed with Pevsner in finding in it 'the lesson and precursor of much modern architecture'.[69]

Walsall's New Art Gallery opened at the turn of the new century on 15 February 2000; like its English Midlands precursor, the sombre and lofty place of arrival is a space whose close-set precast concrete beams the architects explain as 'joist members [which] are spatially analogous to the timber ceiling of a medieval hall'.[70] The staircase starts off grandly broad to a mezzanine level, then in declension to a more domestic scale, turns into a dog-leg which arrives at the Long Gallery – as the architects knowingly call it – forming the vestibule to the galleries housing the Garman Ryan Collection at the heart of the building. This collection was formed by Kathleen Garman (1901–79), wife of the sculptor Jacob Epstein (whose carving was earlier examined in relation to the surfaces of Charles Holden), and her friend Sally Ryan (1916–18), and was gifted by Kathleen Garman in 1974 to her native Walsall and Black Country. This intimate, adventurous, and wide-ranging collection, comprises paintings, drawings, and sculptures by artists of the stature of Dürer, Rembrandt, Constable, Van Gogh, Monet, and Epstein himself. Appropriate to the intimacy of this core-collection, the architects thought of the Gallery as a whole, 'as being like a big house to be explored and discovered by visitors as they moved between floors'.[71] So the Garman Ryan galleries – grouped in thirteen modestly scaled rooms around a double-height hall-space – can be considered multifariously as a house-within-a-house, as an Upper Hall, or as a Cabinet of Curiosities; the material lining of Douglas fir strips reinforces the warmth of these rooms as spaces apart. The Garman Ryan core has its own internal circulation, and a stair within the hall-space. Outside this Cabinet, other staircases lure visitors upwards to further temporary exhibition galleries, the progress reaching its climax at the fourth floor in the lofty tower-room of the restaurant (a space since re-designated in use), an imposing prospect-turret equating to Hardwick Hall's highpoint of the High Great Chamber.

Caruso St John's approaches to surface, imbricate experiential and tectonic complexity, striving for an authenticity that is true to structure and material *and* to the legitimate realization of atmosphere, eliding positivist structural expression for its own sake *or* the superficial make-up of Post-Modernism.[72] So, whereas Walsall's structural beams frankly express the

FIGURE 8.15 *Caruso St John, New Art Gallery Walsall, exterior. Photograph Hélène Binet.*

pre-cast structure in ways a Brutalist might admire, their excess multiplication and depth – well beyond structural calculation – reinforces the atmosphere of a joisted medieval hall. Caruso St John turn Loos's observations on 'The Principle of Cladding' (1898) into a critique of the obsession with wall construction – as in British High-Tech architecture – at the expense of the character of the room; as long-term teachers of architecture they point to

HIGH-TECH, NEO-VERNACULAR, NEW MATERIALITY

FIGURE 8.16 *Caruso St John, New Art Gallery Walsall, entrance hall. Photograph Hélène Binet.*

this Loos text as 'one that we have discussed with students for many years'.[73] Loos argues that the correct way to build is to follow our ancestors: 'In the beginning we sought to clad ourselves, to protect ourselves from the elements.... Originally consisting of animal furs or textiles, this covering [as in Semper] is the first architectural feature'. Walls *followed* from this cladding instinct, but many architects work illogically: 'Their imagination creates not rooms but walls. . . . Then they clad the internal walls with the material that seems most appropriate.' Whereas 'the true artist, the great architect . . . first of all gets a feeling for the effect he wants to produce and then sees in his mind's eye the rooms he wants to create'.[74] Caruso St John 'definitely subscribe to Loos's position, but [they] are interested in the matter of walls, in how [they] can make their construction somehow responsive to a spatial imperative'.[75] Caruso St John wanted all the visible structural walls of Walsall to be cast, not for the sake of technological rhetoric, but from an interest in 'a seamless web that can engage material and shape in the function of spatial character'.[76] So where the shell of the building is visible, the visitor sees the internal surfaces of the cast *in situ* concrete walls as-made with vertical boarded shuttering of 75mm-wide planed Douglas fir. Then, in some locations, a 75mm-wide lining of Douglas fir boards is placed *onto* the concrete as characterful cladding, but the scale and grain of this lining is identical to the concrete surfaces. A teasing assonance results between the fictitious formwork of this timber-lining – reminiscent also of the warm embrace of Elizabethan timber-panelling – and the grain of the concrete structure. Preoccupations with a seamless web of surface-effect also characterize the external cladding at Walsall, where Caruso St John liken their use of terracotta tiles to a coat worn over a stainless-steel shirt. In a well-known local saying, Hardwick Hall was 'more glass than wall', but in this aspect Walsall departs markedly from its illustrious precedent, as just a scattering of flush windows mark its intriguing skin. The stainless-steel rain screen is the inner layer of the external cladding, as face to the 300mm-thick external concrete walls, appearing in its own right as a skin at ground and roof levels. The outer layer is the textured cloak of large-scale terracotta tiles, whose scale reduces towards the top of the building; the choice of clay being in part a tribute to Walsall's heritage of pottery-making. Peter St John also recalls Adam Caruso's attraction to 'a pretty Victorian building on Walsall High Street in carved stone', and how they sought to make an urban contribution with an equally characterful civic building. 'The idea of the tiles was about the surface of the building having a texture to it, and a shadow, and a sense of detail, that was equivalent to the Victorian carving', by these means marrying an interpretation of old surfaces to a contemporary countenance.[77] Stainless steel is also used for the external window frames which are positioned just forward from the plane of the surrounding tiles, in homage to the flush glazing applied to the raw brickwork of Lewerentz's Church of St Peter, at Klippan, Sweden. The random placing of these modest windows is tuned both to the desired overall house-like character, and keyed to moments within the gallery journey; at one happy point a view through one of these openings – along the canal on which the Gallery is sited – might be taken as a picture-in-itself, 'hung' within the Garman Ryan collection.[78]

    Caruso St John's relish for the potentialities of surface can be seen in their use of this quotation from Richard Serra: 'To roll, to crease, to hold, to store, to bend, to shorten, to twist, to dapple, to shave, to crumple, to tear, to chip, to split, to cut, to sever, to drop'.[79] Meditating upon their approach to surface, Philip Ursprung imagines that Caruso St John 'treat the material in such a way that it looks more like a drawing on a surface which is bent and folded elastically than like a rigid structure. It is more about pictorial inscription than about tectonic solidity. It is about surface, not about essence'. This is not, in any way, to deny the import of materiality: 'The spatiality of Caruso St John is the product of cultural and economic pressure, an appearance in which ideas and matter intertwine, somewhere between a thing and an idea'.[80] Into the twenty-first century they have continued to research deeply – if more eclectically – into the performative and material potentials of surface, as in the polychromatic façade of their entrance addition for the Museum of Childhood, Bethnal Green, London (2002–6), which draws direct inspiration from Owen Jones's *The Grammar of Ornament*, and the Ruskinian 'incrustation' of the façades of patterned marble Peter St John had admired in Venice and Florence.[81]

* * *

With the opening of the New Art Gallery Walsall, in February 2000, we end this investigation of the surfaces and materiality of British architecture; this turn-of-century endpoint is undoubtedly arbitrary, but it has allowed some detailed perspectives into the values that have shaped British architectural surfaces over a span of some 150 years. More recent studies, projects, and built works, demonstrate the persistence of many of the strands of surface expression that have been identified under the themes of: Reading the Wall-Surface; Surfaces of Romance; Smooth and Rough; Carving the Surface; Surfaces and Sharawaggi (the Picturesque); Surfaces of Brutalism; Pattern, Abstraction, Post-Modernism; High-Tech, Neo-Vernacular, New Materiality. In the twenty-first century, the powerful tools of digital computation and parametrics have continued to demonstrate their own untrammelled capacities, often more successfully when mediated by user and environmental constraints.

We witnessed Colin Rowe's dismay at the lack of '*face*, as the metaphorical plane of intersection between the eyes of the observer and what one may dare to call the *soul* of the building', in James Stirling's Staatsgalerie in Stuttgart, where Rowe deplored its absence of façade, and its failure, in his view, to 'premiate a specific vertical surface'.[82] From the foregoing, what might be nonetheless surprising has been the persistence of the surface as a shaping factor in British architecture, through all the powerful forces of Modernity that might have tended to its dissolution. Readers will draw their own inferences from the preceding chapters, but here we must seek to draw out some concluding strands.

Ruskin's instruction to '*Read* the sculpture' and the faces of architecture, like the pages of a book, carried force within British cultures, that are as much literary as visual. These architectural texts were to be construed through iconography, the age-mark of their weathering, their truth-to-material, and the ethical lessons conveyed by all of this. Bored by the incommunicative surfaces of High Modernism, through a linguistic turn, Post-Modernism revisited the potential for iconography, and material interest, to provide meaning in architecture; often the results were over-literal, but the projects of the later Stirling promulgated these Po-Mo themes with sophistication – although he always rejected the Post-Modernist label. The Picturesque was also born out of literary cultures steeped in the Gothic novel, the pages of Sir Walter Scott, and Romantic poetry; it has been a pervasive theme of these pages, even appearing as a 'revenge' to Modernism, in places where it might be least expected – in aspects of Brutalism or High-Tech, for example. The Picturesque nurtures naturalism, a love of surface-texture and weathering, and its affection for ruins and fragments encourages the bricolage of a part-to-whole aesthetic.

Ruskin loved the broad patterned wall-surfaces of Venetian Gothic architecture as they developed from the busy arcades of the Byzantine *palazzo* and *fondaco*, and his geo-aesthetics contrasts the wall-veils of Italian Gothic with the linearity of the North. Thereby he exerted a powerful influence on the predilection to surface in High Victorian architecture with its potential for the display of the aforesaid iconography, weathering, and material richness. At the same time British Gothic architecture had never aspired to the thorny, or lace-like, excesses of French Flamboyant; the national mania for beauty of surface, that Nikolaus Pevsner discovered as a German émigré in England, married a love for over-all linear patterning with integrity of the wall-plane. Even in the great gridded cages of Perpendicular chapels, or Elizabethan prodigy houses such as Hardwick Hall, the wall-face invariably coheres within an overall massing that is blocky, rather than plastic. So, although King's College Chapel or Hardwick Hall can be glibly understood as precursors of Modernist frame-architecture, outbreaks of the purely skeletal in Britain have customarily been circumscribed. Again, Ruskin's influence was strong, his hatred of iron-architecture ensuring that the railway engine-sheds met the city, mediated by piles of polychromatic Gothic. Despite the propaganda for the Modernist frame it is rare to find it nakedly expressed; the proto-Modernism of Charles Holden's 55 Broadway – where Portland stone veils a steel-frame – typifies the bulk of actual production. The exo-skeletal expressions of the structure and the innards of buildings – as literally burst out in the neo-Bowellist drawings of Archigram, and the built works of High-Tech – were but a transitory moment of cultural intensity. These can also be recovered for a British functional tradition, for a William Heath Robinson pleasure in elaborate contrivance, not unrelated to the Arts and Crafts, matching Peter Cook's description of that inventively eccentric aspect of English psychology represented by the young child's fascination in construction – be it a model aeroplane or a Meccano assembly.

Ruskin's geo-aesthetics also engendered a cult of the Savage surface as, in his 'Nature of Gothic', he opposed the jasper-like earth-veils of the South to the wild heathy moors of the North. Ethic becomes Aesthetic, as ostensibly negative qualities – like ignorance, ugliness, or formlessness – testify to the unbridled liberty of the workman who strikes the surface. William Butterfield's archetypal churches demonstrate this search for truth-in-ugliness, and authenticity-in-awkwardness, an inclination made manifest in surfaces as examined, from Webb and Butterfield, through to Brutalism, to Stirling, and the New Materiality. As a reduced form of the Sublime, the Picturesque shares this appetite for wildness.

William Morris admired Gothic architecture for its unashamed wall-surfaces which, as viewed through the lens of Medieval romance, could be left plainly whitewashed or ornamented with flat layered planes of painting, tapestry, and wallpaper. In the democracy of the Arts and Crafts, all such productions are now imagined as the domain of the anonymous artisan-maker. From its moorings to the architectonic surface, ornament slips away to migrate across the surfaces of objects, furnishings, and other artefacts, blurring or upending boundaries between the 'higher' Fine Arts and the 'lower' decorative ones. Not for the first time, the apparently ephemeral art of wallpaper pattern-designing becomes a site of intense surface investigation; other important cases include Eduardo Paolozzi's Brutalist wallpaper pasted to the Smithsons' bathroom in Limerston Street, Chelsea, and the exterior furnishing of Picturesque 'Sharawaggi', where wallpaper escapes the domestic interior to generate urban façades. But within the scope of this study, it has not been possible for interior surfaces to hold our attention unduly, at the expense of examining the external surfaces of architecture.

And, just as the 'minor' decorative arts can 'propel' the 'major' ones in the Arts and Crafts, so the part can generate the whole. This tunes with a bottom-up, theory-averse empiricist English sensibility, with Picturesque *ruinenlust* and its composition-by-fragment, and with the investigative methods of natural science. Again – in what has been called his synecdochic method – Ruskin exemplifies this potent microcosm-to-macrocosm approach, fusing his romantic-symbolical imagination, with the scientific analysis of the geologist or archaeologist, to inspect the material and textural palimpsests of architecture. Although Ruskin had scorned the desire to make a new style based on iron and glass, the forge was at the service of Piano, Rogers, and Rice, when casting Pompidou's gerberette cantilever elements – reflecting this Arts and Crafts fetishization of craft and detail.

In *Smooth and Rough* (1951), Adrian Stokes underscores the haptic and oral precognitions of the infant, or the lover, that drive our experience of the details of surface-texture; these pages have unpacked rich interchanges of smooth and rough in exploring that 'national mania' for surface. It is too simplistic to say that the savage surface is rough and shaggy, and the smooth gentle and refined; savage sensibilities can be found as much in the smooth surfaces of Butterfield's strident polychromatic brickwork, or Stirling's shining red tilework, as in the rawness of *béton-brut*. I can think of no better illustration of smooth-and-rough surface complexities than the comparisons that have been made here between the Arts and Crafts works of George

Frederick Bodley, and those of Edward Schröder Prior; between Bodley's search for a refined Englishness in breadth of surface – in reaction to the muscularity of Ruskinian 'rogue architects' – and the stern Anglo-Saxon look of Prior's work, vehemently handmade in its Fair-Isle sweater-like textures. Both architects, however, reprised later English Gothic models for their effects, including the Perpendicular – so-hated by Ruskin for its gridiron patterns.

Insofar as white-rendered surfaces have been considered the uniform of International Modernism, their hold has proved uncertain in British architecture, despite successful precedents in Regency stucco villas and terraces. As the last of the Edwardians, and first of the English Moderns – as John Summerson described him – Charles Holden's architecture found a proto-Modern middle-way, in its virility of elemental massing, sheer stonework surfaces, and integration of the truth-to-material code of 'carving direct' in the work of sculptors such as Jacob Epstein (whose work is housed in the New Art Gallery Walsall – the last of our surface-exemplars). Holden's naked Modernism is 'white' in its catholic way, with its cliffs of bleached Portland stone alluding to the abstraction of Nicholas Hawksmoor's Baroque, and to similarly elemental skyscrapers in the USA. But the conservatism of Holden's 55 Broadway (1926–9) is shown up, a few years later, by the starkly white Le Corbusian modernism of Berthold Lubetkin's Highpoint I flats in Highgate, London (1933–5). This assessment of the British surface has insisted upon the importance of the constant importation of ideas, models, and émigré architects and critics themselves – such as Lubetkin and Pevsner. Undeniably, only the Picturesque can be claimed as a wholly indigenous British body of theory and work. As imported models and ideas were customarily recalibrated to native needs and conditions, so the émigrés themselves underwent processes of adaptation, the *cause-célèbre* being the transformation, from the clean white walls of Highpoint I, to the complicated surface syntax of Highpoint II (1936–8). That this was far more than a simple deferring to the contexts of English conservatism and planning constraints, is proven by how strongly Lubetkin and Tecton maintained the pattern-making direction in their façades post-World War II as, for example, at the Hallfield Estate, Paddington, London (1946–54). From his Russian and continental European background Lubetkin had felt compelled to adapt the High-Modernist abstraction he had brought in his suitcases, to the fundamentals of the damp, misty London climate, and its variety of materials and textures – alarming as his Baroque tendencies proved to positivist Modernist critics. The notion that patterns of living might make patterns on the façade looks back to traditions of *architecture parlante*, and anticipates the semiology of Post-Modernism; Lubetkin explored these possibilities further in his short-term involvement with the north-east New-Town of Peterlee. The Peterlee story was taken forward by the artist-sculptor Victor Pasmore's experiments with his Mondrian-esque constructed abstract art, in a sustained involvement lasting from 1955 to

1978. Pasmore at Peterlee, is just one step further in the halting Arts and Crafts aspiration to make architecture a total-work-of-art, as seen in: Ruskin's call that an architect should be also a painter or sculptor; the partnerships of Webb, Burne-Jones, and Morris; in Epstein's carvings for Holden; in Leslie Martin's *Circle* (1937); in the architect-artist-engineer collaborations of the 'This is Tomorrow' (1956) exhibition; in Paolozzi and Henderson's dialogues with the Smithsons, and so on.

Here, the supreme example of an émigré critic and scholar, and interpreter of Englishness in architecture, has of course been Nikolaus Pevsner; even though others, such as Rudolf Wittkower, have also proved significant. As has been seen in Ruskin's geo-aesthetics, Pevsner is far from being the first to deploy *Kunstgeographie* in architectural interpretation, and as clearly problematic as such racial-geographic approaches can be, his *The Englishness of English Art* provides fascinating readings into the English predilection for pattern and surface, that are of more than historiographical interest. As we saw in the recent scholarship of Paul Binski's *Gothic Wonder: Art, Artifice and the Decorated Style* (2014), Pevsner's insights remain operative, as Binski expands upon the origins of the 'thick-wall surface' in the squat Norman English cathedrals, and its development, in English Gothic, into an 'aesthetics of surface, of skin and flesh'. And finally – as in the last chapter of *The Englishness of English Art* – it is once again 'Picturesque England' that is the key to understanding the flat, picture-making propensities, of architecture and urbanism in Britain, in its medley of caprice and reason, and in its giving form to national ideas of personal liberty – as compared to the autocratically over-determined city.

NOTES

Introduction

1. Luciano Fabro quoted in Robert Hoozee (ed.), *British Vision: Observation and Imagination in British Art 1750–1950* (Brussels: Mercatorfonds/Ghent: Museum voor Schone Kunsten, 2008). See also Mark A. Cheetham, *Artwriting, Nation, and Cosmopolitanism in Britain: The 'Englishness' of English Art Theory since the Eighteenth Century* (Farnham: Ashgate, 2012).

Chapter One

1. E. T. Cook and Alexander Wedderburn (eds.), *John Ruskin Collected Works*, The Library Edition, 39 vols. (London: George Allen, 1903–12), vol. 24, *St Mark's Rest*, pp. 203–4; subsequent references in the form: Ruskin, *Works*, 24: 203–4, *St Mark's Rest*.
2. Ruskin, *Works*, 24: 241, *St Mark's Rest*.
3. Ruskin, *Works*, 24: 263, *St Mark's Rest*.
4. Shakespeare, *Henry VI*, Part 3, Act 3, Scene 2.
5. Charles Eastlake, *A History of the Gothic Revival*, ed. J. Mordaunt Crook (Leicester: Leicester University Press, 1978 [1872], 2nd edition), p. 278.
6. Ruskin, *Works*, 10: 269, *Stones of Venice*, vol. 2.
7. See Stephen Kite, *Building Ruskin's Italy: Watching Architecture* (Farnham: Ashgate, 2012).
8. Elizabeth K. Helsinger, *Ruskin and the Art of the Beholder* (Cambridge, MA: Harvard University Press, 1982), p. 212.
9. Ruskin, *Works*, 11: 182–3, *Stones of Venice*, vol. 3.
10. Ruskin, *Works*, 8: 234, *Seven Lamps*.
11. Ruskin, *Works*, 11: 38, 41, *Stones of Venice*, vol. 3.
12. Ruskin, *Works*, 11: 41, *Stones of Venice*, vol. 3; George Landow, *The Aesthetic and Critical Theories of John Ruskin* (Princeton, NJ: Princeton University Press, 1971), chapters 4, 5.
13. Quoted in Adrian Forty, *Words and Buildings: A Vocabulary of Modern Architecture* (London: Thames & Hudson, 2000), p. 72.
14. Ruskin, *Works*, 36: 212, letter to F. J. Furnivall, 22 May 1855.

15 G. R. Lewis, *Illustrations of Kilpeck Church, Herefordshire: In a Series of Drawings Made on the Spot. With an Essay on Ecclesiastical Design, and a Descriptive Interpretation* (London: G. R. Lewis and William Pickering, 1842), p. xiii; see also Edward N. Kaufmann, 'Architectural Representation in Victorian England', *Journal of the Society of Architectural Historians*, vol. 46, no. 1 (March 1987), pp. 30–8, p. 30.

16 Lewis, *Illustrations of Kilpeck Church*, p. 16.

17 Lewis, *Illustrations of Kilpeck Church*, p. 33.

18 William Whyte, *Unlocking the Church: The lost secrets of Victorian sacred space* (Oxford: Oxford University Press, 2017), chapter 1, 'Seeing'.

19 Quoted in Whyte, *Unlocking the Church*, p. 33.

20 Ruskin, *Works*, 7: 14, *Modern Painters*, vol. 5.

21 William Morris, *News from Nowhere* (London: Thames & Hudson, 2017 [1892]), pp. 189–90.

22 Michael W. Brooks, *John Ruskin and Victorian Architecture* (London: Thames & Hudson, 1989), p. 88.

23 Eastlake, *History of the Gothic Revival*, p. 278.

24 Ruskin, *Works*, 9: 75, *Stones of Venice*, vol. 1.

25 Anuradha Chatterjee, *John Ruskin and the Fabric of Architecture* (Abingdon: Routledge, 2018), expands on the fabric/dress theme.

26 Semper quoted in David Leatherbarrow and Mohsen Mostafavi, *Surface Architecture* (Cambridge, MA: MIT Press, 2002), p. 91.

27 Ruskin, *Works*, 9: 351, *Stones of Venice*, vol. 1, Kite's emphasis.

28 Deborah Howard, *The Architectural History of Venice* (New Haven and London: Yale University Press, 2002), p. 34.

29 Ruskin, *Works*, 10: 276, *Stones of Venice*, vol. 2.

30 Michael W. Brooks, 'Describing Buildings: John Ruskin and Nineteenth-Century Architectural Prose', *Prose Studies*, vol. 3 (1980), pp. 241–53.

31 Ruskin, *Works*, 10: 212, *Stones of Venice*, vol. 2.

32 Juergen Schulz, *The New Palaces of Medieval Venice* (University Park, PA: Pennsylvania State University Press, 2004), chapter 1, figs. 20, 21. See also Paolo Maretto, *La Casa Veneziana: nella storia della città dale origini all'ottocento* (Venezia: Marsilio Editori, 1986), pp. 66–70, fig. 33; Edoardo Arslan, *Gothic Architecture in Venice*, trans. A. Engel (London: Phaidon, 1971), pp. 30–1.

33 Ruskin, *Works*, 10: 295, *Stones of Venice*, vol. 2.

34 Brooks, 'Describing Buildings', p. 245.

35 Ruskin, *Works*, 10: 275–6, *Stones of Venice*, vol. 2, Kite's emphasis to last sentence. There are also field notes and details in Ruskin's *Venice-Notebook* 'House Book 1': 'House No 43. very interesting in a courtyard in the Calle del Rimedio'. He notes the 'old wooden bracketed beam' (p. 52) and draws its capitals on the opposite page, and the '4 at[tached arches] of 2nd. [order] on a long plinth'. On the following page he records: 'I got up to its second story and marked the section and angle leaf of this capital which are important thus – The shafts stand on this plinth. and I think always have stood without

any base'. (The Ruskin, Lancaster University / Venetian Notebooks Electronic Edition; accessed February 2018.)

36 Ruskin, *Works*, 11: 22–3, *Stones of Venice*, vol. 3.
37 Ruskin, *Works*, 11: 27, *Stones of Venice*, vol. 3.
38 Ruskin, *Works*, 24: 163, *Guide to the . . . Academy of Fine Arts at Venice*.
39 Ruskin, *Works*, 24: 163, *Guide to the . . . Academy of Fine Arts at Venice*.
40 Manfred Schuller, 'Le facciate dei palazzo medioevale di Venezia. Ricerche su singoli esempi architettonici', in Francesco Valcanover and Wolfgang Wolters (eds.), *L'Architettura Gotica Veneziana* (Venice: Instituto Veneto di Scienze, Lettere ed Arti, 2000), pp. 280–349, p. 338.
41 Jacob Burckhardt, *The Architecture of the Italian Renaissance* (Harmondsworth: Penguin Books, 1987 [1867]), p. 46.
42 Ruskin, *Works*, 9: 323, *Stones of Venice*, vol. 1.
43 See Paul Hills, *Venetian Colour: Marble, Mosaic and Glass 1250–1550* (New Haven and London: Yale University Press, 1999), p. 12.
44 Ruskin, *Works*, 11: 23, *Stones of Venice*, vol. 3.
45 Ruskin, *Works*, 11: 28, *Stones of Venice*, vol. 3.
46 Hills, *Venetian Colour*, pp. 66–7.
47 Ruskin, *Works*, 10: 264, *Stones of Venice*, vol. 2.
48 Ruskin, *Works*, 8: 108, *Seven Lamps*.
49 Ruskin, *Works*, 8: 109, *Seven Lamps*.
50 Nikolaus Pevsner, *The Englishness of English Art* (Harmondsworth: Penguin Books, 1964, [1956]), chapter 4, 'Perpendicular England'.
51 Ruskin, *Works*, 10: 17, *Stones of Venice*, vol. 2.
52 Ruskin, *Works*, 10: 38, *Stones of Venice*, vol. 2.
53 Ruskin, *Works*, 9: 85, *Stones of Venice*, vol. 1.
54 Ruskin, *Works*, 9: 88, *Stones of Venice*, vol. 1.
55 Ruskin, *Works*, 9: 87, *Stones of Venice*, vol. 1.
56 Ruskin, *Works*, 9: 87, *Stones of Venice*, vol. 1.
57 Ruskin, *Works*, 9: 88, *Stones of Venice*, vol. 1.
58 Ruskin, *Works*, 9: 88, *Stones of Venice*, vol. 1.
59 Ruskin, *Works*, 4: 292, *Modern Painters*, vol. 2.
60 Ruskin, *Works*, 35: 116, *Praeterita*. Robert Hewison, *Ruskin on Venice* (New Haven and London: Yale University Press, 2009), p. 50.
61 Ruskin letter to his father from Venice dated 26 April 1852, quoted in E. T. Cook, *The Life of John Ruskin*, 2 vols. (London: George Allen, 1911), vol. 1, p. 300. Anthony Ozturk, 'Geo-Aesthetics: Venice and the Architecture of the Alps', in K. Hanley and E. Sdegno (eds.), *Ruskin, Venice and Nineteenth-Century Cultural Travel* (Venice: Università Ca' Foscari Venezia, 2010), pp. 187–211, expands on these 'inter-textual narratives' as 'Geo-aesthetics'.
62 Joan Evans and John Howard Whitehouse (eds.), *The Diaries of John Ruskin* (Oxford: Clarendon Press, 1956), vol. 1, p. 445.

63 Evans and Whitehouse, *Diaries*, vol. 1, p. 446.
64 Ruskin, *Works*, 9: 196–7, *Stones of Venice*, vol. 1.
65 *Architectural Notebook ('N' Book)*, 1849, p. 40, Ruskin Foundation (The Ruskin, Lancaster University).
66 Ruskin, *Works*, 9: 88, *Stones of Venice*, vol. 1.
67 Ruskin, *Works*, 9: 347, *Stones of Venice*, vol. 1.
68 Ruskin letter to his father dated 7 October 1845, in Harold I. Shapiro (ed.), *Ruskin in Italy: Letters to His Parents 1845* (Oxford: Clarendon Press, 1972), p. 220.
69 Ken Jacobson and Jenny Jacobson, *Carrying Off the Palaces: John Ruskin's Lost Daguerreotypes* (London: Quaritch, 2015), p. 41
70 Ruskin, *Works*, 10: xxv (letter to his father from Verona dated 2 June 1852). See also Karen Burns, 'Topographies of Tourism: "Documentary" Photography and *The Stones of Venice*', *Assemblage*, 32 (April 1997), pp. 22–4, among many studies of Ruskin and photography, including the comprehensive Jacobsons' *Carrying Off the Palaces*.
71 Eastlake, *History of the Gothic Revival*, p. 278.
72 Ruskin, *Works*, 9: 347, *Stones of Venice*, vol. 1.
73 Ruskin, *Works*, 9: 349–50, *Stones of Venice*, vol. 1.
74 Neil Jackson, 'Christ Church, Streatham, and the Rise of Constructional Polychromy', *Architectural History*, vol. 43 (2000), pp. 219–52, p. 232. See also J. B. Bullen, *Byzantium Rediscovered* (London: Phaidon, 2003), pp. 108–9.
75 Jackson, 'Christ Church, Streatham', pp. 237–8.
76 Ruskin, *Works*, 9: 39, *Stones of Venice*, vol. 1.
77 Ruskin, *Works*, 10: 110, *Stones of Venice*, vol. 2.
78 Deborah Howard, *Venice and the East: The Impact of the Islamic World on Venetian Architecture 1100–1500* (New Haven and London: Yale University Press, 2000), pp. 2–3; Ruskin, *Works*, 9: 38, *Stones of Venice*, vol. 1.
79 Owen Jones, *The Grammar of Ornament* (Lewes: Ivy Press, 2016 [1856]), p. 173.
80 Quoted in Jackson, 'Christ Church, Streatham', p. 242; *The Ecclesiologist* (April 1850), pp. 432–3.
81 Paul Thompson, 'All Saints' Church, Margaret Street, Reconsidered', *Architectural History*, vol. 8 (1965), pp. 73–94, p. 76.
82 Quoted in Thompson, 'All Saints' Church, Margaret Street', p. 76.
83 Ruskin, *Works*, 8: 176, *Seven Lamps*.
84 Ruskin, *Works*, 8: 177, *Seven Lamps*.
85 Thompson, 'All Saints' Church, Margaret Street', p. 76.
86 Paul Thompson, *William Butterfield* (Cambridge, MA: MIT Press, 1971), p. 163.
87 Thompson, *William Butterfield*, p. 377.

88 Henry-Russell Hitchcock, *Early Victorian Architecture in Britain*, 2 vols. (London: Trewin Copplestone, 1954), vol. 1, p. 573.
89 Ruskin, *Works*, 8: 219, *Seven Lamps*.
90 Ruskin, *Works*, 8: 167, *Seven Lamps*.
91 Ruskin, *Works*, 9: 351, *Stones of Venice*, vol. 1.
92 Ruskin, *Works*, 9: 460, *Stones of Venice*, vol. 1.
93 James Stevens Curl, 'All Saints' Margaret Street', *The Architects' Journal*, vol. 191, no. 25 (20 June 1990), pp. 36–55, p. 52; Bullen, *Byzantium Rediscovered*, p. 142.
94 Hitchcock, *Early Victorian Architecture*, vol. 1, p. 585.
95 Thompson, *William Butterfield*, p. 164.
96 Thompson, *William Butterfield*, p. 250.
97 Ruskin, *Works*, 10: 186–7, *Stones of Venice*, vol. 2.
98 Ruskin, *Works*, 10: 193–4, *Stones of Venice*, vol. 2.
99 Ruskin, *Works*, 11: 144–5, *Stones of Venice*, vol. 3.
100 Ruskin, *Works*, 5: 132, *Modern Painters*, vol. 3.
101 Ruskin, *Works*, 11: 133, *Stones of Venice*, vol. 3.
102 Ruskin, *Works*, 11: 134, *Stones of Venice*, vol. 3.
103 John Summerson, 'Act 3: Christian Gothic. Scene 1: William Butterfield', *The Architectural Review*, vol. 98, no. 588 (1 December 1945), pp. 166–75; see also Elain Harwood, 'Butterfield and Brutalism', *AA Files*, no. 27 (Summer 1994), pp. 39–46.
104 Summerson, 'William Butterfield', p. 170.
105 Summerson, 'William Butterfield', p. 170.
106 Summerson, 'William Butterfield', p. 170.
107 Quoted in Summerson, 'William Butterfield', p. 170; *Ecclesiologist*, no. 20 (1859).
108 Quoted in Christopher Wood, *The Pre-Raphaelites* (London: Weidenfeld & Nicolson, 1981), p. 17.
109 H. S. Goodhart-Rendel, *English Architecture Since the Regency: An Interpretation* (London: Constable, 1953), p. 129.
110 Ian Nairn, *Nairn's London* (London: Penguin Books, 2014 [1966]), p. 95.
111 Quoted in Harwood, 'Butterfield and Brutalism', p. 45.
112 Henry-Russell Hitchcock, 'G. E. Street in the 1850s', *Journal of the Society of Architectural Historians*, vol. 19, no. 4 (December 1960), pp. 145–71, p. 148.
113 George Edmund Street, 'The True Principles of Architecture, and the Possibility of Development', *Ecclesiologist*, vol. 13 (1852), pp. 247–62, p. 248.
114 Street, 'True Principles', p. 248.
115 Street, 'True Principles', p. 249.
116 Alec Clifton-Taylor and A. S. Ireson, *English Stone Building* (London: Victor Gollancz, 1983), p. 28.

117 Hitchcock, *Early Victorian Architecture*, vol. 1, p. 149, p. 604.
118 George Edmund Street, 'On the Proper Characteristics of a Town Church', *Ecclesiologist*, vol. 11 (1850), pp. 227–33, p. 229.
119 Eastlake, *History of the Gothic Revival*, p. 278.
120 Street, 'True Principles', p. 261.
121 Street, 'True Principles', pp. 254–5.
122 Street, 'True Principles', p. 255.
123 Julian Flannery, *Fifty English Steeples: The Finest Medieval Parish Church Towers and Spires in England* (London: Thames & Hudson, 2016), p. 352.
124 Street, 'True Principles', p. 255.
125 Michael Hall, 'What Do Victorian Churches Mean? Symbolism and Sacramentalism in Anglican Church Architecture, 1850–1870', *Journal of the Society of Architectural Historians*, vol. 59, no. 1 (March 2000), pp. 78–95, p. 83.
126 Ruskin, *Works*, 36: 115, letter to Henry Acland, 24 May 1851.
127 Quoted in Hall, 'What do Victorian Churches Mean?', p. 82.
128 *Ecclesiologist*, vol. 15 (1854), p. 429.
129 *Ecclesiologist*, vol. 19 (1858), p. 316.
130 *Ecclesiologist*, vol. 19 (1858), p. 316.
131 Paul Joyce, 'Boyne Hill (Maidenhead), Berkshire *All Saints*', in P. Howell and I. Sutton (eds.), *The Faber Guide to Victorian Churches* (London: Faber & Faber, 1989), p. 16.
132 George Edmund Street, *Brick and Marble in the Middle Ages: Notes of Tours in the North of Italy* (London: John Murray, 1874 [1855], 2nd edition), Palazzo Pubblico, Udine, p. 249 and plates 36 and 37; Palazzo Scaligeri, p. 95. See also Antony Branfoot and Suzanna Branfoot, 'The Old and the New: influences and style in the work of G. E. Street in Berkshire', in J. Elliott and J. Pritchard (eds.), *George Edmund Street: A Victorian Architect in Berkshire* (Reading: Centre for Continuing Education, The University of Reading, 1998), pp. 29–45, p. 44.
133 Arthur Edmund Street, *Memoir of George Edmund Street, RA* (London: John Murray, 1888), p. 204.
134 Ruskin, *Works*, 8: 104, *Seven Lamps*.
135 'Specification of the works to be done in the erection of a New Steeple at the North West angle of the Church of All Saints Boyne Hill, G. E. Street, September 1864', PRJ/4/1/10, Paul Joyce Archive, The Paul Mellon Centre for Studies in British Art, London.
136 All Saints, Boyne Hill, 'Church No. 5 – Buttresses and lower part of Tower', Colour ink on paper original drawing, G. E. Street, September 1864. PRJ/4/1/2, Paul Joyce Archive, The Paul Mellon Centre for Studies in British Art, London.
137 Street, 'True Principles', p. 261; see also Hitchcock, 'Street in the 1850s', p. 149.

138 Street, *Brick and Marble in the Middle Ages*, plate 'Italian Brickwork', f. p. 122.

139 'Specification of the works to be done in the erection of a New Steeple at the North West angle of the Church of All Saints Boyne Hill, G. E. Street, September 1864', p. 2. PRJ/4/1/10, Paul Joyce Archive, The Paul Mellon Centre for Studies in British Art, London.

140 'Interior of All Saints Church, Both Hill, Maidenhead [After an Original Sketch by our own Artist]', *The Illustrated News of the World* (2 October 1858), p. 217.

141 *Ecclesiologist*, vol. 19 (1858), p. 316.

142 Street, *Brick and Marble in the Middle Ages*, p. 115 (Kite's emphasis).

143 Street, *Brick and Marble in the Middle Ages*, p. 117.

144 Street, *Brick and Marble in the Middle Ages*, p. 400.

145 Street, *Brick and Marble in the Middle Ages*, p. 405.

146 Street, *Brick and Marble in the Middle Ages*, p. 405.

147 George Edmund Street, 'On Colour as Applied to Architecture', *Associated Architectural Societies, Reports and Papers*, vol. 3, part 2 (1855), p. 365.

148 Edward N. Kaufman, '"The weight and vigour of their masses": Mid-Victorian county churches and the "Lamp of Power"', in John Dixon Hunt and Faith M. Holland (eds.), *The Ruskin Polygon: Essays on the Imagination of John Ruskin* (Manchester: Manchester University Press, 1982), pp. 94–121, p. 97.

149 Kaufman, 'The weight and vigour of their masses', p. 96.

150 Kaufman, 'The weight and vigour of their masses', p. 96.

151 George Truefitt, *Designs for Country Churches* (London: Joseph Masters, 1850); see, for example, No. IV.

152 Truefitt, *Designs for Country Churches*, p. 6, p. 7.

153 Evelyn Eames and Joyce Gregory, 'Influence and Heritage', in J. Elliott and J. Pritchard (eds.), *George Edmund Street: A Victorian Architect in Berkshire* (Reading: Centre for Continuing Education, The University of Reading, 1998), pp. 71–80, pp. 73–7.

Chapter Two

1 William Morris, *News from Nowhere* (London: Thames & Hudson, 2017 [1892]), pp. 189–90.

2 William Morris, 'Address on the collection of paintings of the English Pre-Raphaelite school in the City of Birmingham Museum and Art Gallery on Friday, October 24, 1891', in May Morris, *William Morris, Artist, Writer, Socialist. Vol. 1: The Art of William Morris; Morris as a Writer* (Cambridge: Cambridge University Press, 2012 [1936]), pp. 296–310, pp. 302–3.

3 Percy Lubbock, *Shades of Eton* (London: Jonathan Cape, 1932 [1929]), pp. 93–4. See also May Morris, *William Morris, Artist, Writer, Socialist. Vol. 1*, pp. 38–9.

4   Lubbock, *Shades of Eton*, pp. 93–4.
5   Nikolaus Pevsner, *Pioneers of Modern Design: From William Morris to Walter Gropius* (London: Pelican Books, 1960 [1936]), pp. 58–9. First published in 1936 under the title *Pioneers of the Modern Movement* by Faber & Faber.
6   See, for example, Peter Davey, *Arts and Crafts Architecture* (London: Phaidon, 1995), pp. 39-40.
7   J. W. Mackail, *The Life of William Morris*, Vol. 1 (London: Longmans, Green, 1901), p. 142.
8   See Rob Aben and Saskia de Wit, *The Enclosed Garden: History and Development of the Hortus Conclusus and its Reintroduction into the Present-day Urban Landscape* (Rotterdam: 010 Publishers, 2001), pp. 37-40.
9   Aben and de Wit, *The Enclosed Garden*, p. 247; see also Tessa Wild, *William Morris and His Palace of Art* (London: Philip Wilson, 2018), p. 201.
10 British Library, Harley MS 4425. Acquired by the nation in 1753 under the Act of Parliament that established the British Museum, and one of the foundation collections of the British Library. See also Fiona MacCarthy, *The Last Pre-Raphaelite: Edward Burne-Jones and the Victorian Imagination* (London: Faber & Faber, 2012), p. 151.
11 William Morris, *Earthly Paradise*, 'The Man Born to Be King: The Medieval Tale for March', lines 1660–88, 1890–3.
12 William Morris, 'Making the Best of It' (a paper read before the Trades' Guild of Learning and the Birmingham Society of Artists, 1879), in William Morris, *Hopes and Fears for Art. Five lectures delivered in Birmingham, London, and Nottingham, 1878–1881* (London: Ellis & White, 1882), p. 128.
13 See 'The garden path' chapter in Davey, *Arts and Crafts Architecture*, p. 125ff.
14 Quoted in MacCarthy, *Burne-Jones*, p. 169.
15 Peter Blundell Jones, 'Red House', *The Architects' Journal*, vol. 183, no. 3 (15 January 1986), pp. 37–56, p. 47. See also Wild, *William Morris and his Palace of Art*, pp. 233–42.
16 See Marjorie Quennell and C. H. B. Quennell, *A History of Everyday Things in England: The Age of Production 1851–1934* (London: Batsford, 1934), fig. 77 illustrating Devey's cottages in the context of Red House, and Sheila Kirk, *Philip Webb: Pioneer of Arts and Crafts Architecture* (Chichester: Wiley-Academy, 2005), p. 85.
17 Ray Watkinson, *William Morris as Designer* (London: Studio Vista, 1967), p. 42.
18 Ruskin, *Works*, 9: 285, *Stones of Venice*, vol. 1. See also Michaela Braesel, 'The Influence of Medieval Illuminated Manuscripts on the Pre-Raphaelites and the Early Poetry of William Morris', *Journal of William Morris Studies*, vol. 15, no. 4 (2004), pp. 41–54, p. 41.
19 Aben and de Wit, *Enclosed Garden*, p. 44.
20 See similar diagram in Aben and de Wit, *Enclosed Garden*, p. 43.
21 See Linda Parry (ed.), *William Morris*, V & A exhibition catalogue (London: Philip Wilson, V & A Museum, 1996), pp. 172–3.

NOTES

22 Braesel, 'Medieval Illuminated Manuscripts', p. 41.
23 Illustrated in Kim Sloan (ed.), *Places of the Mind: British watercolour landscapes 1850–1950* (London: British Museum and Thames & Hudson, 2017), fig. 15, p. 31; Wood, *Pre-Raphaelites*, p. 26.
24 Hermann Muthesius, *The English House*, 3 vols., ed. Dennis Sharp, trans. Janet Seligman and Stewart Spencer (London: Frances Lincoln, 2007, first complete English edition, first published as *Das Englische Haus*, Berlin: Wasmuth, 1904, 1905), vol. 3, p. 95.
25 William Morris, *Gothic Architecture: A Lecture for the Arts and Crafts Exhibition by William Morris* (London: Kelmscott Press, 1893, first spoken as a lecture at the New Gallery, for the Arts and Crafts Exhibition Society, 1889), p. 61.
26 Watkinson, *Morris as Designer*, p. 68.
27 William Morris, 'The Lesser Arts of Life' (1878), in William Morris, *Architecture, Industry and Wealth* (London: Longmans, Green, 1902), p. 45.
28 May Morris, 'Morris as a Designer', in May Morris, *William Morris, Artist, Writer, Socialist. Vol. 1: The Art of William Morris; Morris as a Writer* (Cambridge: Cambridge University Press, 2012 [1936]), pp. 34–62, p. 43.
29 William Morris, *Some Hints on Pattern-Designing* (London: Longmans, 1899, lecture given at The Working Men's College, London, 10 December 1881), p. 2.
30 Morris, *Hints on Pattern-Designing*, p. 2.
31 Morris, *Hints on Pattern-Designing*, p. 4.
32 Morris, *Hints on Pattern-Designing*, p. 22.
33 Morris, *Hints on Pattern-Designing*, p. 27.
34 Morris, *Earthly Paradise*, 'The Watching of the Falcon: The Medieval Tale for July', lines 223–6.
35 Morris, 'The Lesser Arts of Life', p. 69.
36 Henry James, *The Wings of the Dove* (Harmondsworth: Penguin Books, 1965), pp. 54–5.
37 Alina Payne, *From Ornament to Object: Genealogies of Architectural Modernism* (New Haven and London: Yale University Press, 2012), p. 89.
38 Payne, *Ornament to Object*, p. 90.
39 Morris, *Hints on Pattern-Designing*, p. 29.
40 Morris, *Hints on Pattern-Designing*, p. 30.
41 Morris, 'The Lesser Arts of Life', p. 70.
42 Morris, 'The Lesser Arts of Life', p. 70.
43 Morris, 'The Lesser Arts of Life', p. 71.
44 See J. Mordaunt Crook, *William Burges and the High Victorian Dream* (London: Frances Lincoln, 2013), p. 289.
45 Muthesius, *English House*, vol. 3, p. 89.
46 Mackail, *Life of William Morris*, vol. 1, pp. 158–9.

47 Mackail, *Life of William Morris*, vol. 1, p. 159.
48 See Wild, *Morris and His Palace of Art*, pp. 119–25.
49 Wild, *Morris and His Palace of Art*, pp. 119–28.
50 Mackail, *Life of William Morris*, vol. 1, pp. 372–3.
51 See also Linda Parry, *William Morris Textiles* (London: V & A Publishing, 2013), p. 185, and Imogen Hart, 'An "Enchanted" Interior: William Morris at Kelmscott House', in Jason Edwards and Imogen Hart (eds.), *Rethinking the Interior, c. 1867–1896: Aestheticism and Arts and Crafts* (Farnham: Ashgate, 2010), pp. 67–84.
52 See Charlotte Gere, *Artistic Circles: Design and Decoration in the Aesthetic Movement* (London: V & A Publishing, 2010), pp. 161–2.
53 Morris, *Earthly Paradise*, 'The Watching of the Falcon: The Medieval Tale for July', lines 193–4.
54 Morris, *Hints on Pattern-Designing*, p. 6.
55 George Wardle, 'Morris Exhibit at The Foreign Fair Boston, 1883–84', www.burrows.com [accessed February 2017].
56 May Morris, *Morris*, vol. 1, p. 37.
57 Morris, 'The Lesser Arts of Life', p. 68.
58 Watkinson, *Morris as Designer*, p. 52.
59 Joanna Banham, 'The English Response: Mechanization and Design Reform', in Lesley Hoskins (ed.), *The Papered Wall: The History, Patterns and Techniques of Wallpaper* (London: Thames & Hudson, 2005), pp. 132–49, pp. 138–9.
60 Mackail, *Life of William Morris*, vol. 1, p. 176.
61 See Clare Latimer, 'The Division of the Wall: The Use of Wallpapers in Decorative Schemes, 1870–1910', *Journal of the Decorative Arts Society 1850 – the Present*, no. 12 (1988), pp. 18–25,mm p. 18, and Gere, *Artistic Circles*, pp. 61–2.
62 William Lethaby, *Philip Webb and His Work* (London: Raven Oak Press, 1979), p. 44.
63 Lethaby, *Webb*, p. 135.
64 Lethaby, *Webb*, p. 137.
65 See detailed symbolic readings in Sally-Anne Huxtable, 'Re-reading the Green Dining Room', in Jason Edwards and Imogen Hart (eds.), *Rethinking the Interior, c. 1867–1896: Aestheticism and Arts and Crafts* (Farnham: Ashgate, 2010), pp. 25–40.
66 J. Mordaunt Crook, 'Eastlake's Career', in Charles L. Eastlake, *A History of the Gothic Revival* (Leicester: Leicester University Press, 1978 [1872]), pp. 18–26, p. 19.
67 Charles Eastlake, *Hints on Household Taste* (London: Longmans Green, 1869, 2nd edition), p. 111.
68 Morris, 'Making the Best of It', p. 136.
69 Morris, 'Making the Best of It', p. 136.

70 Fiona MacCarthy, *William Morris: A Life for our Time* (London: Faber & Faber, 1995), p. 107 (Kite's emphasis).
71 Quoted in Hart, 'An "Enchanted" Interior', p. 79.
72 Quoted in Gere, *Artistic Circles*, p. 165.
73 See Caroline Dakers, *The Holland Park Circle: Artists and Victorian Society* (New Haven and London: Yale University Press, 1999), and Charles Harvey and Jon Press, *Art Enterprise and Ethics: Essays on the Life and Work of William Morris* (London: Frank Cass, 1996), 'Ionides Family'.
74 Gleeson White, 'An Epoch Making House', *The Studio*, vol. 14 (1898), pp. 102–12, p. 102
75 Quoted in Harvey and Press, 'The Ionides Family and 1 Holland Park' (January 1994), p. 2.
76 Lewis F. Day, 'A Kensington Interior', *The Art Journal* (1893), pp. 139–44, p. 140.
77 Day, 'Kensington Interior', p. 140.
78 George Llewellyn Morris, 'On Mr. Philip Webb's Town Work; illustrated with drawings by E. A. Rickards', *The Architectural Review*, vol. 2 (1 June 1897), pp. 199–208, p. 206.
79 Day, 'Kensington Interior', p. 141.
80 Day, 'Kensington Interior', p. 141.
81 White, 'An Epoch-Making House', p. 107.
82 Parry, *Morris Textiles*, p. 115.
83 G. L. Morris, 'Webb's Town Work', p. 206.
84 White, 'An Epoch-Making House', p. 104.
85 Mackail, *Life of Morris*, vol. 1, p. 197.
86 Mackail, *Life of Morris*, vol. 1, pp. 197–8.
87 Morris, *Earthly Paradise*, lines 1–4.
88 Quoted in Peter Ackroyd, *London: The Biography* (London: Vintage, 2001), p. 110.
89 Quoted in Dakers, *Holland Park Circle*, p. 238.
90 See Elizabeth Wilhide, *William Morris: Decor and Design* (London: Pavilion, 2014), p. 40.
91 Norman Kelvin (ed.), *The Collected Letters of William Morris, Vol. 2, 1881–1884* (Princeton, NJ: Princeton University Press, 1987), letter to Alfred James Hipkins, dated 17 March 1883, p. 177.
92 Kelvin, *Letters of Morris, Vol. 2, 1881–84*, letter to Thomas Coglan Horsfall, 11–28 February 1881, p. 17.
93 Robert Edis, *The Furniture and Decoration of Town Houses* (New York: Scribner & Welford, 1881), p. vi. See also Gere, *Artistic Circles*, pp. 88–91.
94 Ruskin, *Works*, 16: 320, *The Two Paths*.
95 Edis, *Decoration of Town Houses*, p. 70.
96 Payne, *Ornament to Object*, p. 253.

97 Lesley Hoskins, 'Wallpaper', in Linda Parry (ed.), *William Morris*, V & A exhibition catalogue (London: Philip Wilson, V & A Museum, 1996), pp. 198–205, p. 202.

98 May Morris, 'Morris as a Designer', pp. 39–40.

99 See Parry, *Textiles*, pp. 136–8.

100 Day, 'Kensington Interior', p. 144.

101 Kelvin, *Letters of Morris, Vol. 2, 1881–84*, letter to Andreas Scheu, 15 September 1883, pp. 227–8.

Chapter Three

1 Bodley quoted in Michael Hall, 'The Rise of Refinement: G. F. Bodley's All Saint's, Cambridge, and the Return to English Models in Gothic Architecture of the 1860s', *Architectural History*, vol. 36 (1993), pp. 103–26, p. 121.

2 John Betjeman (ed.), *Collins Pocket Guide to English Parish Churches: The South* (London: Collins, 1968), p. 94.

3 'Holy Trinity Church, Prince Consort Rd.', *Survey of London: Vol. 78 South Kensington Museum Area*, http://www.british-history.ac.uk/survey-london/vol38/pp349-356 [accessed 23 July 2018]

4 Michael Hall, *George Frederick Bodley and the Later Gothic Revival in Britain and America* (New Haven and London: Yale University Press, 2014), p. 240.

5 Hall, *Bodley*, p. 240.

6 Bodley, quoted in Hall, *Bodley*, p. 245.

7 Pevsner, quoted in David Verey, 'George Frederick Bodley: Climax of the Gothic Revival', in J. Fawcett (ed.), *Seven Victorian Architects* (London: Thames & Hudson, 1976), pp. 75–101, p. 91.

8 James Cubitt, *Church Design for Congregations: Its Development and Possibilities* (London: Smith, Elder, 1870), p. 46.

9 Edward Warren, 'The Life and Work of George Frederick Bodley', *Journal of the Royal Institute of British Architects*, vol. 17 (1910), pp. 305–40, p. 334.

10 Quoted in Verey, 'Bodley', p. 95.

11 See Alan Crawford, 'Englishness in Arts and Crafts Architecture', in D. Crellin and I. Dugavell (eds.), *Architecture and Englishness 1880–1914* (London: Society of Architectural Historians of Great Britain, 2006), pp. 25–36, p. 29.

12 George Frederick Bodley, 'Some Principles that may be Guides for the Applied Arts', *Journal of the Society of Arts*, vol. 51, no. 2619 (30 January 1903), pp. 181–9, p. 182.

13 Bodley, 'Guides for the Applied Arts', p. 183.

14 Bodley, 'Guides for the Applied Arts', p. 183.

15 Bodley, 'Guides for the Applied Arts', p. 184.

16 Goodhart-Rendel, *English Architecture Since the Regency*, pp. 214–16.

17 H. S. Goodhart-Rendel, 'Rogue Architects of the Victorian Era', *RIBA Journal*, vol. 56 (1949), pp. 251–9, p. 255.
18 George Frederick Bodley, 'On Some Principles and Characteristics of Ancient Architecture and their Application to the Modern Practice of the Art', *The Builder*, vol. 108 (1885), pp. 294–7, p. 295.
19 Goodhart-Rendel, *English Architecture Since the Regency*, p. 221.
20 Scott, quoted in Hall, 'Rise of Refinement', p. 116.
21 Quoted in Hall, *Bodley*, p. 239.
22 Warren, 'The Life and Work of George Frederick Bodley', p. 331.
23 Goodhart-Rendel, quoted in John Newman, *Glamorgan: The Buildings of Wales* (New Haven and London: Yale University Press, 1995), p. 300.
24 Bodley, 'Characteristics of Ancient Architecture', p. 295.
25 Warren, 'The Life and Work of George Frederick Bodley', p. 333.
26 Quoted in Verey, 'Bodley', p. 87.
27 Warren, 'The Life and Work of George Frederick Bodley', p. 310.
28 George Frederick Bodley, *Poems* (London: George Bell, 1899), p. 41.
29 Eastlake, *History of the Gothic Revival*, p. 369.
30 Eastlake, *History of the Gothic Revival*, p. 369.
31 C. M. Smart, *Muscular Churches: Ecclesiastical Architecture of the High Victorian Period* (Fayetteville, AK: University of Arkansas Press, 1989), p. 219.
32 Eastlake, *History of the Gothic Revival*, p. 371.
33 Eastlake, *History of the Gothic Revival*, p. 371.
34 Trevor Garnham, 'St Andrew's Church, Roker, Sunderland 1905', in *Arts and Crafts Masterpieces* (London: Phaidon, 1999) (unpaginated).
35 Garnham, 'St Andrew's Church, Roker', fig. 28.
36 Edward S. Prior, 'Texture as a Quality of Art and a Condition of Architecture' (1889, pub. 1890), in D. Valinsky (ed.), *An Architect Speaks: The Writings and Buildings of Edward Schröder Prior* (Exeter: Short Run Press, David Valinsky, 2014), pp. 44–56, p. 44.
37 Prior, 'Texture as a Quality of Art', p. 54.
38 Prior, 'Texture as a Quality of Art', p. 44.
39 Prior, 'Texture as a Quality of Art', p. 45.
40 Prior, 'Texture as a Quality of Art', p. 46.
41 Prior, 'Texture as a Quality of Art', p. 46.
42 Prior, 'Texture as a Quality of Art', p. 46.
43 Prior, 'Texture as a Quality of Art', p. 51.
44 Christophe Grillet, 'Edward Prior', *The Architectural Review*, vol. 112, no. 671 (November 1952), pp. 302–8, p. 304.
45 Prior, 'Texture as a Quality of Art', p. 47.
46 Prior, 'Texture as a Quality of Art', p. 47.
47 Prior, 'Texture as a Quality of Art', p. 48.

48 Ruskin, *Works*, 9: 301, *Stones of Venice*, vol. 1.
49 Rudolf Arnheim, *The Dynamics of Architectural Form* (Berkeley, CA: University of California Press, 1977), p. 131.
50 Edward S. Prior, *The Cathedral Builders in England* (London: Seeley, 1905), p. 16
51 Prior, *Cathedral Builders*, p. 17.
52 Lawrence Weaver (attrib. signed 'W'), 'Country Homes Gardens Old and New: Home Place, Holt, The Residence of the Rev. F. M. Meyrick-Jones', *Country Life*, vol. 26, no. 670 (6 November 1909), pp. 634–42. The article is signed 'W' and is generally attributed to *Country Life*'s editor.
53 Jill Franklin, 'Edwardian Butterfly Houses', *The Architectural Review*, vol. 157, no. 938 (April 1975), pp. 220–5, p. 220; Jill Franklin, *The Gentleman's Country House and its Plan 1835–1914* (London: Routledge & Kegan Paul, 1981), pp. 232–7; Andrew Saint, *Richard Norman Shaw* (New Haven and London: Yale University Press, 2010, revised edition), pp. 359–62. Prior also must have known of Viollet-le-Duc's butterfly design for a French town mansion of 1864; see Martin Godfrey Cook, *Edward Prior: Arts and Crafts Architect* (Ramsbury: Crowood Press, 2015), pp. 70–3.
54 Quoted in David Valinsky (ed.), *An Architect Speaks: The Writings and Buildings of Edward Schröder Prior* (Exeter: Short Run Press, David Valinsky, 2014), p. 75.
55 Edward S. Prior, 'Architectural Modelling' (June 1895), in D. Valinsky (ed.), *An Architect Speaks: The Writings and Buildings of Edward Schröder Prior* (Exeter: Short Run Press, David Valinsky, 2014), pp. 80–3, p. 81.
56 Juhani Pallasmaa, *The Thinking Hand: Existential and Embodied Wisdom in Architecture* (Chichester: John Wiley, 2009), p. 57.
57 Prior,' Architectural Modelling', p. 83.
58 Prior,' Architectural Modelling', p. 83.
59 Muthesius, *The English House*, vol. 2, figs. 101–3, pp. 128, 131.
60 The thatch was replaced with tiles after a fire in 1905.
61 Grillet, 'Edward Prior', p. 304.
62 Weaver, 'Home Place, Holt', p. 638.
63 Prior, 'Texture as a Quality of Art', p. 48.
64 Weaver, 'Home Place, Holt', p. 641.
65 Weaver, 'Home Place, Holt', p. 641.
66 See also the photograph essay in: Jeremy Musson, *Romantics and Classics: Style in the English Country House*, photography by Hugo Rittson Thomas (New York: Rizzoli, 2021), 'Voewood: Made by its materials', pp. 214–27.
67 Prior, 'Texture as a Quality of Art', p. 48.
68 Bullen, *Byzantium Rediscovered*, pp. 168–9.
69 M. Hill, J. Newman, and N. Pevsner, *The Buildings of England: Dorset* (New Haven and London: Yale University Press, 2018), p. 475.
70 Cook, *Prior*, p. 151.

71 Hill, Newman, Pevsner, *Dorset*, p. 475.
72 As suggested in Hill, Newman, Pevsner, *Dorset*, p. 475. The balustrade has been dismantled (September 2018).
73 William Lethaby, *Architecture, Mysticism and Myth* (London: The Architectural Press, 1974 [1891]), p. 180.
74 Quoted in Davey, *Arts and Crafts Architecture*, p. 87.
75 Davey, *Arts and Crafts Architecture*, p. 87.
76 A. S. G. Butler, *The Architecture of Sir Edwin Lutyens*, 3 vols. (Woodbridge: Antique Collectors' Club, 1984 [1950]), vol. 2, p. 13. See also Roderick Gradidge, *Edwin Lutyens: Architect Laureate* (London: George Allen & Unwin, 1981), pp. 55–6.

Chapter Four

1 Reyner Banham, *Age of the Masters: A Personal View of Modern Architecture* (London: The Architectural Press, 1975 [1962]), p. 35.
2 Banham, *Age of the Masters*, p. 39.
3 Mark Wigley, *White Walls, Designer Dresses* (Cambridge, MA: MIT Press, 1995), pp. xiv–xiv.
4 Banham, *Age of the Masters*, p. 39.
5 Le Corbusier (Charles-Edouard Jeanneret), *Journey to the East*, ed. and trans. Ivan Žaknić (Cambridge, MA: MIT Press, 2007 [1966]), p. 60.
6 J. M. Richards, *An Introduction to Modern Architecture* (Aylesbury: Penguin Books, 1953 [1940]), p. 57; see also Wigley, *White Walls*, p. xix.
7 F. R. S. Yorke, *The Modern House* (London: The Architectural Press, 1957 [1934]), p. 47, p. 49.
8 Wigley, *White Walls*, p. xxi.
9 Yorke, *The Modern House*, p. 25.
10 Yorke, *The Modern House*, p. 46.
11 See Gavin Stamp, 'Introduction', in G. Stamp (ed.), 'Britain in the Thirties', *Architectural Design*, vol. 49, nos. 10/11 (1979), pp. 2–43, p. 6.
12 John Summerson, 'Foreword', in Eitan Karol and Finch Allibone, *Charles Holden Architect 1875–1960*, exhibition catalogue (London: RIBA Heinz Gallery, 1988), p. 5.
13 Summerson, 'Foreword', in Karol and Allibone, *Charles Holden*, p. 5.
14 Charles Holden, 'Letter on Art and Industry', *The Architects' Journal* (9 September 1931), p. 343.
15 Penelope Curtis, 'How Direct Carving Stole the Idea of Modern British Sculpture', in David J. Getsy (ed.), *Sculpture and the Pursuit of a Modern Ideal in Britain, c. 1880–1930* (Aldershot: Ashgate, 2004), pp. 291–318, p. 299.
16 Anon., 'Awards at the Royal Institute of British Architects: The Soane and the Pugin', *The Architectural Review* (1 March 1897), pp. 200–11, p. 210.

17 Nikolaus Pevsner, 'Obituary, C. H. Holden 1874–1960', *The Architectural Review*, vol. 128, no. 766 (1 December 1960), pp. 446–8, p. 446.

18 Eitan Karol, *Charles Holden 1875–1960* (Donington: Shaun Tyas, 2007), p. 65

19 Susan Beattie, *The New Sculpture* (New Haven and London: Yale University Press, 1983), p. 46.

20 Penelope Curtis, Denise Raine, Matthew Withey, Jon Wood, and Victoria Worsley (eds.), *Sculpture in 20th-century Britain*, 2 vols. (Leeds: Henry Moore Institute, 2003), vol. 2, pp. 336–7.

21 Beattie, *The New Sculpture*, p. 68.

22 Beattie, *The New Sculpture*, p. 69.

23 Beattie, *The New Sculpture*, p. 69.

24 Adrian Stokes, *The Critical Writings of Adrian Stokes*, 3 vols., ed. Lawrence Gowing (London: Thames & Hudson, 1978), *The Stones of Rimini*, vol. 1, p. 230.; subsequent references in the form: Stokes, *Critical Writings*, *Stones of Rimini*, vol. 1, p. 230.

25 Beattie, *The New Sculpture*, p. 131.

26 The competition for the new library was won in the name of H. Percy Adams, but the designer was Holden, then the the firm's chief draughtsman.

27 Anthony Beeson, *Bristol Central Library and Charles Holden: A History and Guide* (Bristol: Redcliffe Press, 2006), p. 13.

28 For example, Andrew Foyle, *Bristol. Pevsner Architectural Guides* (New Haven and London: Yale University Press, 2004), p. 76.

29 Quoted in Karol, *Holden*, p. 32.

30 Charles Holden, 'If Whitman had been an Architect', *The Architectural Review*, vol. 17, no. 103 (1 June 1905), p. 258.

31 Holden, 'If Whitman Had Been an Architect', p. 258.

32 Charles Holden, 'Thoughts for the Strong', *The Architectural Review*, vol. 18, no. 104 (1 July 1905), p. 27.

33 Brian Hanson, 'Singing the Body Electric with Charles Holden', *The Architectural Review*, vol. 158, no. 946 (1 December 1975), pp. 349–56, p. 350.

34 Nikolaus Pevsner, *The Buildings of England, London, 1 The Cities of London and Westminster* (Harmondsworth: Penguin Books, 1973, 3rd edition), p. 378.

35 Holden quoted in Richard Cork, *Art Beyond the Gallery in Early 20th Century England* (New Haven and London: Yale University Press, 1985), p. 14.

36 Jacob Epstein, *An Autobiography* (London: Hulton Press, 1955, revised edition of *Let There be Sculpture*, 1940), p. 21.

37 Epstein, *Autobiography*, p. 5.

38 Epstein, *Autobiography*, p. 5.

39 Holden quoted in Karol, *Holden*, p. 122.

40 Cork, *Art Beyond the Gallery*, p. 22.

41 Epstein, *Autobiography*, p. 22.
42 Epstein, *Autobiography*, p. 22.
43 See Richard Cork, *Wild Thing: Epstein, Gaudier-Brzeska, Gill* (London: Royal Academy of Arts, 2010), chapter 1, 'Scandal on the Strand'.
44 Quoted in Epstein, *Autobiography*, p. 243, p. 244.
45 Jacob Epstein, 'The Artist's Description of his Work', *The British Medical Journal* (4 July 1908), p. 40.
46 Epstein, 'The Artist's Description of his Work', p. 40.
47 Holden quoted in Hanson, 'Singing the Body Electric', p. 352.
48 Hanson, 'Singing the Body Electric', p. 352.
49 Walter Bayes, 'Sense and Sensibility. The New Head Offices of the Underground Railway, Westminster, London', *The Architectural Review*, vol. 66, no. 396 (1 November 1929), pp. 225–39, p. 225.
50 See also Gavin Stamp, *The Great Perspectivists* (London: Trefoil Books, 1982), p. 134.
51 Stamp, *Great Perspectivists*, p. 118.
52 Quoted in Cork, *Art Beyond the Gallery*, p. 252.
53 Pevsner, *The Buildings of England, London, 1 The Cities of London and Westminster*, p. 562.
54 Stamp, *Great Perspectivists*, p. 133.
55 See Cork, *Art Beyond the Gallery*, p. 260.
56 A.T.E. (Anon) '"No. 55 Broadway, Westminster", New Headquarters for the London Electric Railways at St James's Park', *The Architects' Journal* (16 October 1929), pp. 558–63, p. 561.
57 Alan Wilkinson (ed.), *Henry Moore: Writings and Conversations* (Aldershot: Lund Humphries, 2002), p. 253.
58 Wilkinson, *Moore: Writings and Conversations*, p. 252.
59 Wilkinson, *Moore: Writings and Conversations*, p. 253.
60 Moore quoted in Herbert Read (ed.), *Unit 1: The Modern Movement in English Architecture, Painting and Sculpture* (London: Cassell, 1934), p. 29.
61 Moore quoted in Read, *Unit 1*, p. 29.
62 Cork, *Art Beyond the Gallery*, p. 267.
63 See Cork, *Art Beyond the Gallery*, pp. 274–5.
64 Wilkinson, *Moore: Writings and Conversations*, p. 98.
65 Moore quoted in Cork, *Art Beyond the Gallery*, p. 277.
66 Curtis, 'How Direct Carving Stole the Idea of Modern British Sculpture', p. 11.
67 Curtis, 'How Direct Carving Stole the Idea of Modern British Sculpture', p. 298.
68 See Hanson, 'Singing the Body Electric', p. 353, from *The Graphic* of 14 April 1929.
69 See Cork, *Art Beyond the Gallery*, pp. 260–1.

70 Quoted in Cork, *Art Beyond the Gallery*, p. 259.
71 Curtis, 'How Direct Carving Stole the Idea of Modern British Sculpture', p. 299.
72 Underwood quoted in Curtis, 'How Direct Carving Stole the Idea of Modern British Sculpture', p. 301.
73 Blomfield quoted in Epstein, *Autobiography*, p. 271.
74 Bayes, 'Sense and Sensibility', p. 230.
75 Bayes, 'Sense and Sensibility', p. 230.
76 Epstein quoted in Cork, *Art Beyond the Gallery*, p. 290.
77 Epstein, *Autobiography*, p. 136.
78 Epstein, *Autobiography*, p. 136.
79 Bone quoted in Epstein, *Autobiography*, pp. 272–3.
80 See Dennis Wardleworth, 'Passing By: Architectural Sculpture in Inter-War London', Henry Moore Institute Essays on Sculpture, no. 47 (Leeds: Henry Moore Institute, 2005), p. 3.
81 This Moore and Stokes section draws on hitherto unpublished material from Stephen Kite, 'Adrian Stokes: The Critical Writings – An Architectonic Perspective', Newcastle upon Tyne University, PhD Thesis, 2002. See also Stephen Kite, *Adrian Stokes: An Architectonic Eye* (London: Legenda, Modern Humanities Research Association and Maney Publishing, 2009), chapter 7, 'Architectonics of the Relief'. Richard Read, 'Circling Each Other: Henry Moore and Adrian Stokes', http://www.tate.org.uk/art/research-publications/henry-moore/richard-read-circling-each-other-henry-moore-and-adrian-stokes-r1151308 [accessed 6 March 2018], probes thoroughly into the ambivalent Stokes-Moore relationship.
82 Stokes, *Critical Writings*, *Three Essays on the Painting of our Time*, vol. 3, p. 146.
83 Henry Moore quoted from interview transcript, '*Henry Moore interviewed by John and Vera Russell*' (1961), Tate Archive (TAV 23B). Reproduced by permission of the Henry Moore Foundation.
84 '*Henry Moore interviewed*', Tate Archive (TAV 23B)
85 Moore quoted in Sophie Bowness, 'An Anthology of Sculptor's Writings on Stone Carving', in *Carving Mountains: Modern Stone Sculpture in England 1907–37* (Cambridge: Kettle's Yard, 1998), pp. 8–21, p. 17.
86 Stokes, *Critical Writings*, *Reviews of Modern Art*, vol. 1, p. 311.
87 Stokes, *Critical Writings*, *Reviews of Modern Art*, vol. 1, p. 312.
88 Moore quoted in Bowness, 'Anthology of Sculptor's Writings', p. 17.
89 '*Henry Moore interviewed*', Tate Archive (TAV 23B).
90 '*Henry Moore interviewed*', Tate Archive (TAV 23B).
91 Stokes, *Critical Writings*, *Stones of Rimini*, vol. 1, p. 252.
92 Wilkinson, *Moore: Writings and Conversations*, p. 258. See also Alan Powers, *Serge Chermayeff: Designer, Architect, Teacher* (London: RIBA Publications, 2001), Chapter 5, 'Beloved Bentley'.

93 Wilkinson, *Moore: Writings and Conversations*, pp. 258–9.
94 Wardleworth, 'Passing By', p. 3.
95 Wardleworth, 'Passing By', p. 7.
96 Stamp, 'Introduction: Britain in the Thirties', p. 24.

Chapter Five

1   See Kitty Hauser, *Shadow Sites: Photography, Archaeology, and the British Landscape 1927–1955* (Oxford: Oxford University Press, 2007), p. 127.
2   H. J. Randall, 'History in the Open Air', *Antiquity*, vol. 8, no. 29 (March 1934), pp. 5–23, p. 5.
3   Hauser, *Shadow Sites*, p. 142.
4   O. G. S. Crawford, 'Historical Cycles', *Antiquity*, vol. 5, no. 17 (March 1931), pp. 5–20, p. 5.
5   Piper quoted in Hauser, *Shadow Sites*, p. 151.
6   Frances Spalding, *John Piper, Myfanwy Piper: Lives in Art* (Oxford: Oxford University Press, 2009), p. 123.
7   See John Macarthur, 'Townscape, Anti-scrape and Surrealism: Paul Nash and John Piper in *The Architectural Review*', *The Journal of Architecture*, vol. 14, no. 3 (2009), pp. 387–406, p. 396.
8   John Piper, 'England's Early Sculptors', *The Architectural Review*, vol. 80, no. 479 (1 October 1936), pp. 157–62, p. 158.
9   Piper, 'England's Early Sculptors', p. 158, p. 160.
10 Blake quoted in Piper, 'England's Early Sculptors', p. 160.
11 Hubert de Cronin Hastings (the Editor), 'Exterior Furnishing or Sharawaggi: The Art of Making Urban Landscape', *The Architectural Review*, vol. 95, no. 565 (1 January 1944), pp. 3–8.
12 Hastings (the Editor), 'Exterior Furnishing', p. 3.
13 Hastings (the Editor), 'Exterior Furnishing', p. 5; Christopher Hussey, *The Picturesque: Studies in a Point of View* (London: Frank Cass, 1983 [1927]).
14 Hussey, *The Picturesque*, p. 205.
15 Sir Thomas Dick Lauder, *Sir Uvedale Price on the Picturesque: With an Essay on the Origin of Taste* (Edinburgh: Caldwell, Lloyd, 1842), pp. 347–8. Kite's emphasis.
16 Price quoted in Hussey, *The Picturesque*, p. 204; Lauder, *Price on the Picturesque*, p. 348.
17 Christopher Tunnard, 'Colour and the Cottage Garden', *The Architectural Review*, vol. 83, no. 494 (1 January 1938), pp. 37–9, p. 39; Christopher Tunnard, *Gardens in the Modern Landscape* (Philadelphia, PA: University of Pennsylvania Press, 2014 [1948, 2nd edition, originally published 1938]), p. 61.

18 Tunnard, *Gardens in the Modern Landscape*, p. 61.
19 Sir William Temple, *The Works of Sir William Temple in Two Volumes* (London: J. Round et al., 1731), vol. 1, p. 186.
20 Temple, *Works of Sir William Temple*, vol. 1, p. 186.
21 Takau Shimada, 'Is Sharawadgi Derived from the Japanese Word Sorowaji?', *The Review of English Studies*, vol. 48, no. 191 (August 1997), pp. 350–2, p. 352.
22 Walpole quoted in Tunnard, *Gardens in the Modern Landscape*, fn. p. 61.
23 Hastings (the Editor), 'Exterior Furnishing', p. 6.
24 Anon., 'Highpoint Number Two. Tecton, Architects', *The Architectural Review*, vol. 84, no. 503 (1 October 1938), pp. 165–76, p. 166.
25 Cox quoted in William J. R. Curtis, *Modern Architecture since 1900* (London: Phaidon, 1992), p. 228.
26 See Kenneth Frampton, *Modern Architecture: A Critical History* (London: Thames & Hudson, 1993, 3rd edition), pp. 252–3.
27 John Allan, 'Rediscovering Lubetkin', in S. Charlton (ed.), *British Modern: Architecture and Design in the 1930s* (London: The Twentieth Century Society, 2007), pp. 89–104, p. 100.
28 Allan, 'Rediscovering Lubetkin', p. 94.
29 Anon., 'Modern Flats in Highgate', *The Architectural Review*, vol. 84, no. 503 (1 October 1938), pp. 161–4, p. 161.
30 Hastings (the Editor), 'Exterior Furnishing', p. 6.
31 Mira Engler, *Cut and Paste Urban Landscape: The Work of Gordon Cullen* (Abingdon: Routledge, 2016), p. 74.
32 Tunnard, *Gardens in the Modern Landscape*, p. 76.
33 Tunnard quoted in Powers, *Chermayeff*, p. 134.
34 Tunnard, *Gardens in the Modern Landscape*, pp. 72–4.
35 Ivor de Wolfe, 'Townscape: A Plea for an English Visual Philosophy founded on the True Rock of Sir Uvedale Price', *The Architectural Review*, vol. 106, no. 636 (1 December 1949), pp. 354–62, p. 355.
36 Wolfe, 'Townscape', p. 361.
37 Gordon Cullen, 'Townscape Casebook', *The Architectural Review*, vol. 106, no. 636 (1 December 1949), pp. 363–74.
38 Engler, *Cut and Paste Urban Landscape*, p. 124.
39 Cullen, 'Townscape Casebook', p. 363.
40 Cullen, 'Townscape Casebook', p. 372.
41 See Gordon Cullen, 'Bankside Regained', *The Architectural Review*, vol. 105, no. 625 (1 January 1949), pp. 15–24.
42 Engler, *Cut and Paste Urban Landscape*, p. 124.
43 Gordon Cullen, 'The Wall', *The Architectural Review*, vol. 112, no. 671 (1 November 1952), pp. 294–301, pp. 296–7.
44 Cullen, 'The Wall', p. 298.

45 See Engler, *Cut and Paste Urban Landscape*, p. 124.
46 Hussey, *The Picturesque*, pp. 247–8.
47 Hussey, *The Picturesque*, p. 247.
48 See John Macarthur, *The Picturesque: Architecture, Disgust and Other Irregularities* (Abingdon: Routledge, 2007), p. 204; David Gosling, *Gordon Cullen: Visions of Urban Design* (London: Academy Editions, 1996), p. 92.
49 Cullen, 'Bankside Regained'.
50 Deanna Petherbridge, *The Primacy of Drawing: Histories and Theories of Practice* (New Haven and London: Yale University Press, 2010), p. 83.
51 John Piper, 'The Architecture of Destruction', *The Architectural Review*, vol. 535, no. 90 (1 July 1941), pp. 25–30, p. 26.
52 Piper, 'Architecture of Destruction', pp. 25–6.
53 John Piper, 'Pleasing Decay', *The Architectural Review*, vol. 102, no. 609 (1 September 1947), pp. 85–94, p. 93.
54 Ruskin quoted in Piper, 'Pleasing Decay', p. 93, from the 'Lamp of Memory' of *The Seven Lamps of Architecture*.
55 Pevsner, Nikolaus, *Visual Planning and the Picturesque*, ed. Mathew Aitchison (Los Angeles, CA: Getty Publications, 2010), p. 9.
56 Pevsner, *Visual Planning and the Picturesque*.
57 Nikolaus Pevsner, 'Reassessment 4: Three Oxford Colleges', *The Architectural Review*, vol. 106, no. 632 (1 August 1949), pp. 120–4, p. 120.
58 Pevsner, 'Three Oxford Colleges', p. 121.
59 Price quoted in Pevsner, *Visual Planning and the Picturesque*, pp. 132–3.
60 Pevsner, 'Three Oxford Colleges', pp. 122–3.
61 Ute Engel, 'The Formation of Pevsner's Art History: Nikolaus Pevsner in Germany 1902–1935', in Peter Draper (ed.), *Reassessing Nikolaus Pevsner* (Aldershot: Ashgate, 2004), pp. 29–55, p. 31.
62 Pevsner quoted in Engel, 'The Formation of Pevsner's Art History', p. 31.
63 Heinrich Wölfflin, *Principles of Art History: The Problem of the Development of Style in Later Art*, trans. M. D. Hottinger of the 7th edition of 1929 of *Kunstgeschichtliche Grunbegriffe*, originally published 1915 (Mineola, NY: Dover Publications, 1950), p. 63.
64 August Schmarzow, 'The Essence of Architectural Creation', in H. F. Mallgrave and Eleftherios Ikonomou (eds.), *Empathy, Form and Space: Problems in German Aesthetics 1873–1893* (Santa Monica, CA: Getty Center for the History of Art and the Humanities, 1994), pp. 281–97, p. 296, p. 286.
65 Nikolaus Pevsner, *An Outline of European Architecture* (Harmondsworth: Penguin Books, 1963 [1943], 7th edition), pp. 15–16.
66 Pevsner quoted in Stefan Muthesius, 'Germanness, Englishness, Jewishness, Scientificness, Popularization', in Peter Draper (ed.), *Reassessing Nikolaus Pevsner* (Aldershot: Ashgate, 2004), pp. 57–69, p. 59.
67 Wölfflin, *Principles of Art History*, pp. 235–6. See also Pevsner, *Visual Planning and the Picturesque*, pp. 4–5.

68 Nikolaus Pevsner, 'The Modern Movement in Britain (Introduction by Bridget Cherry)', in S. Charlton (ed.), *British Modern: Architecture and Design in the 1930s* (London: The Twentieth Century Society, 2007), pp. 13–38.
69 Pevsner, 'The Modern Movement in Britain', p. 22, p. 30.
70 Pevsner, 'The Modern Movement in Britain', p. 33.
71 Pevsner, 'The Modern Movement in Britain', pp. 32–3.
72 Pevsner, 'The Modern Movement in Britain', p. 37.
73 See Susan Harries, *Nikolaus Pevsner: The Life* (London: Pimlico, 2013), chapter 31.
74 Nikolaus Pevsner, *Pevsner: The Complete Broadcast Talks: Architecture and Art on Radio and Television, 1945–1977*, ed. Stephen Games (Farnham: Ashgate, 2014), p. 261.
75 Iain Boyd Whyte, 'Nikolaus Pevsner: Art History, Nation, and Exile', *RIHA Journal*, 0075 (23 October 2013), http://www.riha-journal.org/articles/2013/2013-oct-dec/whyte-pevsner [accessed 26 November 2019].
76 Pevsner, *Englishness of English Art*, p. 197.
77 On Pevsner's *Kunstgeographie*, see Andrew Leach and John Macarthur, *The Baroque in Architectural Culture 1880–1980* (London: Routledge, 2016), chapter 9.
78 Pevsner, *Complete Broadcast Talks*, p. 266, p. 267.
79 Pevsner, *Complete Broadcast Talks*, p. 276.
80 Pevsner, *Complete Broadcast Talks*, p. 278.
81 John Gloag, *The English Tradition in Design* (Harmondsworth: Penguin Books, 1946), p. 24. Gloag later wrote a much larger study of *The English Tradition in Architecture* (1963). On King Penguins, see also Harries, *Pevsner: The Life*, pp. 322–3.
82 Gloag, *The English Tradition in Design*, p. 35.
83 Spalding, *Lives in Art*, p. 135.
84 Gloag, *The English Tradition in Design*, p. 35; J. M. Richards, 'Black and White: An Introductory Study of a National Design Idiom', *The Architectural Review*, vol. 82, no. 492 (1 November 1937), pp. 165–76, p. 165.
85 Nikolaus Pevsner, *The Leaves of Southwell* (Harmondsworth: Penguin Books, 1945), p. 50.
86 Pevsner, *Complete Broadcast Talks*, p. 259.
87 Paul Binski, *Gothic Wonder: Art, Artifice and the Decorated Style 1290–1350* (New Haven and London: Yale University Press, 2014), p. 1; Pevsner, *Outline of European Architecture*, p. 128.
88 Binski, *Gothic Wonder*, pp. 23–4.
89 Pevsner quoted in Binski, *Gothic Wonder*, p. 49.
90 Binski, *Gothic Wonder*, p. 49.
91 Pevsner, *Englishness of English Art*, p. 188.
92 Pevsner, *Englishness of English Art*, p. 188.

93 Hastings (the Editor), 'Exterior Furnishing', p. 4.
94 Addison quoted in Pevsner, *Englishness of English Art*, p. 177.
95 Wolfe, 'Townscape', p. 361.
96 Pevsner, *Englishness of English Art*, pp. 188–9, p. 192.
97 Pevsner, *Visual Planning and the Picturesque*, p. 189.
98 Pevsner, *Visual Planning and the Picturesque*, p. 193.
99 See Pevsner, *Visual Planning and the Picturesque* (Macarthur and Aitchison, introduction 'Pevsner's Townscape'), p. 30.
100 Colin Rowe and Fred Koetter, 'Collage City', *The Architectural Review*, vol. 158, no. 942 (1 August 1975), pp. 66–92, p. 74.

Chapter Six

1 See Nigel Whiteley, *Reyner Banham: Historian of the Immediate Future* (Cambridge, MA: MIT Press, 2002), pp. 11–16; Reyner Banham, 'Revenge of the Picturesque: English Architectural Polemics, 1945–1965', in John Summerson (ed.), *Concerning Architecture: Essays on Architectural Writers and Writing Presented to Nikolaus Pevsner* (London: Allen Lane The Penguin Press, 1968), pp. 265–73.
2 Banham, 'Revenge of the Picturesque', p. 265, p. 267.
3 Banham, 'Revenge of the Picturesque', p. 267.
4 See Elain Harwood, *Space Hope and Brutalism: English Architecture 1945–1975* (New Haven and London: Yale University Press, 2015), pp. 18–19.
5 Colin St John Wilson, 'The Vertical City', *The Observer* (17 February 1952); see also Stephen Kite, 'Softs and Hards: Colin St John Wilson and the Contested Visions of 1950s London', in Mark Crinson and Claire Zimmerman (eds.), *Neo-avant-garde and Postmodern: Postwar Architecture in Britain and Beyond* (New Haven, CT: The Yale Center for British Art, 2010), p. 58.
6 Wilson, 'The Vertical City'.
7 Anon., 'The New Empiricism: Sweden's Latest Style', *The Architectural Review*, vol. 101, no. 606 (June 1947), pp. 199–204.
8 See Sarah Menin and Stephen Kite, *An Architecture of Invitation: Colin St John Wilson* (Aldershot: Ashgate, 2005).
9 James Stirling, 'Garches to Jaoul', *The Architectural Review*, vol. 118, no. 705 (September 1955), pp. 145–51, p. 151.
10 Banham, 'Revenge of the Picturesque', p. 273.
11 Banham, 'Revenge of the Picturesque', p. 272–3.
12 Reyner Banham, 'The New Brutalism', *The Architectural Review* (December 1955), pp. 355–61, p. 357.
13 Leatherbarrow and Mostafavi, *Surface Architecture*, p. 166.
14 Banham, 'The New Brutalism', p. 357, p. 361.

15 Reyner Banham, *The New Brutalism: Ethic or Aesthetic?* (London: The Architectural Press, 1966), p. 19.
16 Banham, *The New Brutalism: Ethic or Aesthetic?*, pp. 19–20; Games (ed.), *Pevsner: The Complete Broadcast Talks*, pp. 279–80.
17 Peter Smithson quoted in M. Christine Boyer, *Not Quite Architecture: Writing around Alison and Peter Smithson* (Cambridge, MA: MIT Press, 2017), p. 44.
18 Alison Amithson, Peter Smithson, and Theo Crosby, manifesto of "The New Brutalism', *Architectural Design*, vol. 25, no. 1 (January 1955), p. 1. Reprinted in Banham, Reyner, *The New Brutalism: Ethic or Aesthetic?* (London: The Architectural Press, 1966), pp. 45–6.
19 Summerson, 'Act 3: Christian Gothic. Scene 1: William Butterfield', *The Architectural Review*, vol. 98, no. 588 (1 December 1945), pp. 166–75, pp. 170–2.
20 Harwood, 'Butterfield and Brutalism', p. 45.
21 Banham, *The New Brutalism: Ethic or Aesthetic?*, p. 88.
22 Harwood, *Space Hope and Brutalism*, p. xxvi. Hereford Square was contentiously delisted in November 2008, and subsequently demolished and replaced by stuccoed pastiches of the existing terrace.
23 Banham, *The New Brutalism: Ethic or Aesthetic?*, p. 19.
24 Mark Crinson, *Stirling and Gowan: Architecture from Austerity to Affluence* (New Haven and London: Yale University Press, 2012), p. 144.
25 See Menin and Kite, *An Architecture of Invitation*, pp. 50–5. The independence of the façade screen has been unfortunately attested to by its subsequent removal, with disastrous consequences to the scale and expression of the building.
26 Colin St John Wilson, 'Brick', *Scroope: The Cambridge Architecture Journal*, no. 6 (1994–5).
27 Stokes, *Critical Writings, Stones of Rimini*, vol. 1, p. 244, p. 258.
28 Banham, *The New Brutalism: Ethic or Aesthetic?*, p. 126.
29 Kenneth Frampton, 'On Leslie Martin', *Architectural Research Quarterly*, vol. 5, no. 1 (2001), pp. 11–12.
30 Banham, *The New Brutalism: Ethic or Aesthetic?*, p. 126.
31 Philip Booth and Nicholas Taylor, *Cambridge New Architecture* (London: Leonard Hill Books, 1970 [1964], 3rd edition), p. 59.
32 Smithsons quoted in Ben Highmore, 'Brutalist Wallpaper and the Independent Group', *Journal of Visual Culture*', vol. 12, no. 2 (2013), pp. 205–21, pp. 206–7.
33 Henderson quoted in Claude Lichtenstein and Thomas Schregenberger (eds.), *As Found: The Discovery of the Ordinary* (Baden: Lars Müller, 2001), p. 94. See also Victoria Walsh, *Nigel Henderson: Parallel of Life and Art* (London: Thames & Hudson, 2001), pp. 49ff.
34 Banham, 'The New Brutalism', p. 354, p. 359.
35 See Beth Williamson, *Between Art Practice and Psychoanalysis Mid-Twentieth Century: Anton Ehrenzweig in Context* (Farnham: Ashgate, 2015), p. 38, n. 4.

36 Williamson, *Ehrenzweig in Context*, p. 60.
37 Ehrenzweig quoted in Nicky Glover, *Psychoanalytic Aesthetics: An Introduction to the British School* (London: Karnac Books, 2009), p. 143.
38 See Glover, *Psychoanalytic Aesthetics*, pp. 137–58; see also Mark Crinson, 'Eye Wandering the Ceiling: Ornament and New Brutalism', *Art History*, vol. 41, no. 2 (April 2018), pp. 318–43.
39 Images in Williamson, *Ehrenzweig in Context*, pp. 84–8
40 Wilson quoted in Menin and Kite, *An Architecture of Invitation*, p. 40.
41 Among the extensive sources on The Independent Group, see Anne Massey, *The Independent Group: Modernism and Mass Culture, 1945–59* (Manchester: Manchester University Press, 1995), and David Robbins (ed.), *The Independent Group: Postwar Britain and the Aesthetics of Plenty* (Cambridge, MA: MIT Press, 1990).
42 Hamilton quoted in Martin Harrison, *Transition: The London Art Scene in the Fifties* (London: Merrell, 2002), p. 95.
43 Banham quoted in Whiteley, *Banham*, p. 84.
44 Smithsons quoted in Boyer, *Not Quite Architecture*, p. 293.
45 Smithsons quoted in Boyer, *Not Quite Architecture*, p. 294.
46 'This is Tomorrow', BBC Radio 3, 17 August 1956, Peter Smithson, Colin St John Wilson, William Turnbull, Richard Hamilton in discussion with Theo Crosby and David Piper; Wilson quoted in Menin and Kite, *An Architecture of Invitation*, p. 57.
47 John Macarthur, *The Picturesque: Architecture, Disgust and Other Irregularities* (Abingdon: Routledge, 2007), p. 156.
48 Theo Crosby, 'This Is Tomorrow', *Architectural Design* (October 1956), pp. 334–6, p. 336.
49 Colin St John Wilson, *Architectural Reflections: Studies in the Philosophy and Practice of Architecture* (Manchester: Manchester University Press, 2000), p. 6.
50 Stirling quoted in Stephen Kite, 'Colin St John Wilson and the Independent Group', *Journal of Visual Culture*, vol. 12, no. 2 (August 2013), pp. 245–61, p. 257.
51 Banham, 'The New Brutalism', p. 356.
52 Wilson quoted in Kite, 'Wilson and the Independent Group', p. 257.
53 Stokes, *Critical Writings, Art and Science*, vol. 2, p. 193, Stokes's emphasis.
54 Stokes, *Critical Writings, Smooth and Rough*, vol. 2, facing p. 256.
55 Stokes, *Critical Writings, Smooth and Rough*, vol. 2, p. 243.
56 Stokes, *Critical Writings, Smooth and Rough*, vol. 2, p. 244.
57 Adrian Stokes, 'Form in Art', in M. Klein, P. Heimann, and R. E. Money-Kyrle (eds.), *New Directions in Psychoanalysis: The Significance of Infant Conflict in the Pattern of Adult Behaviour* (London: Tavistock, 1955), pp. 406–20, pp. 414–15.
58 Hannah Segal, 'A Psycho-Analytical Approach to Aesthetics', in M. Klein, P. Heimann, and R. E. Money-Kyrle (eds.), *New Directions in Psychoanalysis*,

pp. 384–405, p. 390. Segal later also moved closer to Stokes's position in giving more emphasis in creativity to the idealization arising from the paranoid-schizoid position.

59 See Glover, 'Psychoanalytic Aesthetics'.
60 Stokes, *Critical Writings*, *Smooth and Rough*, vol. 2, p. 241.
61 Stokes, *Critical Writings*, *Smooth and Rough*, vol. 2, p. 241.
62 Adrian Stokes, 'An Influence of Buildings on the Graphic Arts in the West', typescript with handwritten amendments and additions by Stokes, Tate Archive (TGA 8816/181), quotations by permission of Telfer Stokes. Given as a talk to the Institute of Contemporary Arts, February 1956: 'The Prime Influence of Buildings on the Graphic Arts of the West'. See http://www.helpmego.to/ica/OldWEBSITE/history/50years.pdf [accessed 31 October 2013]
63 Stokes, Adrian, 'An Influence of Buildings on the Graphic Arts in the West'.
64 Stokes, *Critical Writings*, *The Painting of Our Time*, vol. 3, p. 146.
65 Stokes, *Critical Writings*, *Stones of Rimini*, vol. 1, p. 258.
66 See Stephen Kite, 'Building and the Graphic Arts: Adrian Stokes at the ICA', https://www.tate.org.uk/research/publications/tate-papers/20 [accessed 20 February 2020].
67 Stokes quoted in Menin and Kite, *An Architecture of Invitation*, p. 203.
68 Juhani Pallasmaa, *The Eyes of the Skin: Architecture and the Senses* (Chichester: Wiley-Academy, 2005), pp. 59–61.

Chapter Seven

1 *The Architectural Review*, vol. 116, no. 695 (November 1954), The cover, and notes to the cover, p. 283.
2 Reyner Banham, 'Façade: Elevational treatment of the Hallfield Estate Paddington', *The Architectural Review*, vol. 116, no. 695 (November 1954), pp. 302–18.
3 Banham, 'Façade', p. 303.
4 Banham, 'Façade', p. 307.
5 Berthold Lubetkin, 'Flats in Rosebery Avenue, Finsbury', *The Architectural Review*, vol. 409, no. 651 (1 March 1951), pp. 138–49.
6 Pevsner, *The Englishness of English Art*, p. 24, p. 18.
7 Lubetkin quoted in John Allan, *Berthold Lubetkin: Architecture and the Tradition of Progress* (London: Artifice, 2012), pp. 102–3.
8 Lionel Brett and Berthold Lubetkin, 'Canons of Criticism: 2', *The Architectural Review*, vol. 109, no. 651 (March 1951), pp. 135–7, p. 136.
9 See Allan, *Lubetkin*, p. 47, p. 387.
10 Lubetkin, 'Flats in Rosebery Avenue', p. 140.
11 Julius Posener, 'Knots in the Master's Carpet', *Architectural Design* (December 1951), pp. 353–7.

12 Posener, 'Knots in the Master's Carpet'; see also Allan, *Lubetkin*, pp. 390–1.
13 Banham, 'Façade', p. 306.
14 Wilson quoted in Menin and Kite, *An Architecture of Invitation*, pp. 52–3.
15 Reyner Banham, 'Casa del Girasole', *The Architectural Review*, vol. 113, no. 674 (1 February 1953), pp. 73–7.
16 Moretti quoted in Marco Mulazzani and Federico Bucci, *Luigi Moretti: Works and Writings* (New York: Princeton Architectural Press, 2000), p. 169.
17 Moretti quoted in Mulazzani and Bucci, *Luigi Moretti*, p. 30, n. 62.
18 Stirling quoted in Mark Crinson (ed.), *James Stirling: Early Unpublished Writings on Architecture* (Abingdon: Routledge, 2010), pp. 37–9.
19 Crinson, *Stirling: Early Unpublished Writings*, pp. 9–10.
20 Banham quoted in Andrew Leach, 'Continuity in Rupture: Postmodern Architecture before Architectural Postmodernism', in Mark Crinson and Claire Zimmerman (eds.), *Neo-avant-garde and Postmodern: Postwar Architecture in Britain and Beyond* (New Haven, CT: The Yale Center for British Art, 2010), pp. 127–49, p. 136, which expands on British readings of Italian architectural culture, and vice-versa, at this time.
21 Colin St John Wilson, 'Patterns in Living', *The Observer* (20 July 1952).
22 Allan, *Lubetkin*, p. 391.
23 Lubetkin himself rejected Post-Modernism tout court, see Allan, *Lubetkin*, p. 573.
24 See Boyer, *Not Quite Architecture*, p. 76, p. 107.
25 Allan, *Lubetkin*, p. 490.
26 See Menin and Kite, *An Architecture of Invitation*, p. 34.
27 Lubetkin quoted in Allan, *Lubetkin*, pp. 490–3.
28 Lubetkin quoted in Allan, *Lubetkin*, p. 572.
29 Pevsner, *The Complete Broadcast Talks*, p. 478 (my emphasis). See also Leach, 'Continuity in Rupture', pp. 130–4.
30 Hudnut quoted in Leach, 'Continuity in Rupture', p. 127.
31 Robert Venturi, Denise Scott Brown, and Steven Izenour, *Learning from Las Vegas* (Cambridge, MA: MIT Press, 2017, facsimile of 1972 edition), p. 64.
32 Scott Brown, preface to *Learning from Las Vegas* (facsimile of first edition).
33 See Martino Stierli, 'Taking on Mies: Mimicry and Parody of Modernism in the Architecture of Alison and Peter Smithson and Venturi / Scott Brown', in Crinson and Zimmerman (eds.), *Neo-avant-garde and Postmodern: Postwar Architecture in Britain and Beyond*, pp. 151–74.
34 Alastair Grieve, *Constructed Abstract Art in England: A Neglected Avant-Garde* (New Haven and London: Yale University Press, 2005).
35 See Alastair Grieve, '"This is Tomorrow": A Remarkable Exhibition Born from Contention', *The Burlington Magazine*, vol. 136, no. 1093 (April 1994), pp. 225–32.
36 Theo Crosby, 'This Is Tomorrow', *Architectural Design* (October 1956), pp. 334–6, p. 335.

37 Crosby, 'This is Tomorrow', p. 334.
38 See Grieve, *Constructed Abstract Art in England*, chapter 4.
39 Williams quoted in Elain Harwood, 'Neurath, Riley and Bilston, Pasmore and Peterlee', in E. Harwood and A. Powers (eds.), *Housing the Twentieth Century Nation, Twentieth Century Architecture 9* (London: Twentieth Century Society, 2008), pp. 84–96, p. 92.
40 Harwood, 'Pasmore and Peterlee', p. 93 (my emphasis)
41 Grieve, *Constructed Abstract Art in England*, p. 120. Diagram illustrated in 'Housing in Peterlee New Town' (Anon.), *The Architects' Journal*, vol. 133 (23 February 1961), pp. 291–302, p. 292; 'Housing at Peterlee. Peter Daniel, Frank Dixon, Victor Pasmore' (Anon.), *The Architectural Review*, vol. 129, no. 768 (1 February 1961), pp. 88–97, p. 91.
42 'Housing at Peterlee', *The Architectural Review*, 1 February 1961, p. 88.
43 'Housing in Peterlee New Town', *The Architects' Journal*, 23 February 1961, p. 298.
44 Pasmore quoted in Grieve, *Constructed Abstract Art in England*, p. 123, p. 124.
45 Arnheim, *The Dynamics of Architectural Form*, p. 2.
46 'Housing at Peterlee', *The Architectural Review*, 1 February 1961, p. 92.
47 Petherbridge, *The Primacy of Drawing*, p. 205.
48 Grieve, *Constructed Abstract Art in England*, p. 121.
49 See Sam Gathercole, 'Art and Construction in Britain in the 1950s', *Art History*, vol. 29, no. 5 (November 2006), pp. 887–925, pp. 900–1.
50 Pasmore quoted in Graham Farmer and John Pendlebury, 'Conserving Dirty Concrete: The Decline and Rise of Pasmore's Apollo Pavilion, Peterlee', *Journal of Urban Design*, vol. 18, no. 2 (2013), pp. 263–80, p. 270.
51 Pasmore quoted in Garry Philipson, *Aycliffe and Peterlee New Towns 1946–1988: Swords into Ploughshares and Farewell Squalor* (Cambridge: Publications for Companies, 1988), p. 115.
52 Alan Powers, 'New Town Artistry', *The Architects' Journal*, vol. 24, no. 13 (11 October 2001), pp. 44–8, p. 44.
53 See Gathercole, 'Art and Construction in Britain', pp. 904–7.
54 Pasmore quoted in Gathercole, 'Art and Construction in Britain', p. 905.
55 Stirling quoted in Crinson, *Stirling and Gowan*, p. 77.
56 Stirling, *Early Unpublished Writings*, p. 35.
57 Colin St John Wilson, 'Sandy Wilson: Living Dangerously' [James Frazer Stirling 1926–1992: in memoriam], *The Architectural Review*, vol. 191, no. 1150 (December 1992), p. 13.
58 Stirling, *Early Unpublished Writings*, p. 25.
59 Stirling, *Early Unpublished Writings*, pp. 25–6.
60 See Crinson, *Stirling and Gowan*, pp. 79–80.
61 Colin Rowe, 'Mannerism and Modern Architecture', *The Architectural Review*, vol. 107, no. 641 (1 May 1950), pp. 289–99, p. 290.

62 Rowe, 'Mannerism and Modern Architecture', pp. 298–9.
63 Le Corbusier, *Towards a New Architecture*, trans. F. Etchells (London: The Architectural Press, 1970 [1927]), p. 157.
64 Moretti quoted in Mulazzani and Bucci, *Luigi Moretti*, p. 178.
65 Stirling quoted in Crinson, *Stirling and Gowan*, p. 81.
66 See Crinson, *Stirling and Gowan*, p. 83; Geoffrey H. Baker, *The Architecture of James Stirling and His Partners James Gowan and Michael Wilford* (Abingdon: Routledge, 2016), p. 31. The composition was made yet more crystalline in Leon Krier's up-view axonometric rendition of *c*. 1974.
67 Stirling, *Early Unpublished Writings*, p. 24.
68 Le Corbusier, *Towards a New Architecture*, p. 11.
69 Le Corbusier, *Towards a New Architecture*, p. 37, p. 41.
70 Stirling quoted in John McKean, 'James Stirling and James Gowan: Leicester University Engineering Building 1959–63', in *Pioneering British 'High-Tech'* (London: Phaidon, 1999) (unpaginated).
71 F. Saxl and R. Wittkower, *British Art and the Mediterranean* (London: Oxford University Press, 1969 [reprint of 1948]), 'Preface'; see also Katia Mazzucco, '1941 *English Art and the Mediterranean*. A photographic exhibition by the Warburg Institute in London', *Journal of Art Historiography*, no. 5 (December 2011).
72 Saxl and Wittkower, *English Art and the Mediterranean*, no. 44.
73 Saxl and Wittkower, *English Art and the Mediterranean*, no. 54.
74 See John Summerson, *Architecture in Britain 1530 to 1830* (Harmondsworth: Penguin Books, 1970), p. 333.
75 Saxl and Wittkower, *English Art and the Mediterranean*, no. 55.
76 Saxl and Wittkower, *English Art and the Mediterranean*, no. 49.
77 Saxl and Wittkower, *English Art and the Mediterranean*, no. 81.
78 Claire Zimmerman, 'Photography into Building in Post-war Architecture: The Smithsons and James Stirling', *Art History*, vol. 35, no. 2 (April 2012), pp. 270–87, p. 284.
79 Stirling, 'Garches to Jaoul', p. 151.
80 Banham, *The New Brutalism*, p. 85 (my emphasis).
81 Stokes, *Critical Writings*, Smooth *and* Rough, vol. 2, pp. 242–3.
82 Stirling, 'Garches to Jaoul', p. 146, p. 150, p. 148.
83 Banham, *The New Brutalism*, p. 85.
84 Leatherbarrow and Mostafavi, *Surface Architecture*, p. 190.
85 John Jacobus, 'Engineering Building, Leicester University', *The Architectural Review*, vol. 135, no. 806 (April 1964), pp. 252–60, p. 260.
86 Gowan quoted in McKean, 'Stirling and Gowan'.
87 McKean, 'Stirling and Gowan'.
88 Peter Eisenman, 'Real and English: The Destruction of the Box. 1', *Oppositions*, no. 4 (October 1974), pp. 5–34, p. 20.

89 Eisenmann quoted in Anthony Vidler, *James Frazer Stirling: Notes from the Archive* (Montreal: Canadian Center for Architecture, and Yale University, 2010), p. 140.
90 Pevsner, *The Complete Broadcast Talks*, pp. 478–9.
91 Colin Rowe, 'James Stirling: A Highly Personal and Very Disjointed Memoir', in P. Arnell and T. Bickford (eds.), *James Stirling: Buildings and Projects, James Stirling, Michael Wilford and Associates* (London: The Architectural Press, 1984), p. 15.
92 See Baker, *The Architecture of James Stirling*, pp. 8–9.
93 Stirling quoted in Davey, 'Stuttgart', p. 42.
94 Rowe, 'Very Disjointed Memoir', pp. 22–3.
95 See Crinson, *Stirling and Gowan*, p. 253
96 Long quoted in Alan Berman (ed.), *Jim Stirling and the Red Trilogy: Three Radical Buildings* (London: Frances Lincoln, 2010), p. 111.
97 Banham, 'Revenge of the Picturesque', pp. 272–3.
98 Peter Davey, 'Stuttgart', *The Architectural Review*, vol. 191, no. 1150 (December 1992), pp. 38–46, p. 46.
99 Anthony Vidler, *The Architectural Uncanny: Essays in the Modern Unhomely* (Cambridge, MA: MIT Press, 1992), p. 91.
100 Karl Friedrich Schinkel, *Collection of Architectural Designs* (Guildford: Butterworth Architecture, 1989, facsimile of 1866 edition of *Sammlung Architektonischer Entwürfe*), p. 53.
101 James Stirling, 'Design Philosophy and Recent Work', *James Stirling Michael Wilford and Associates* (London: Academy Editions, 1990), pp. 7–13.
102 See David Jenkins, *Clore Gallery, Tate Gallery, Liverpool, James Stirling, Michael Wilford and Associates* (London: Phaidon, 1992) (unpaginated).
103 John Summerson, 'Vitruvius Ludens', *The Architectural Review*, vol. 173, no. 1033 (March 1983), pp. 18–21.
104 Stirling, 'Design Philosophy and Recent Work', p. 9.
105 John Summerson, 'Vitruvius Ridens or Laughter at the Clore', *The Architectural Review*, vol. 181, no. 1034 (June 1987), pp. 45–6, p. 45.
106 Stirling, 'Design Philosophy and Recent Work', p. 9.
107 Stirling, 'Design Philosophy and Recent Work', p. 9.
108 Summerson, 'Vitruvius Ludens', p. 45.
109 Peter Blundell Jones, 'Stirling's Last Laugh', *The Architects' Journal*, vol. 186, no. 29 (22 July 1987), pp. 32–44, p. 44.
110 Charles Jencks, 'Clore Contextualisms' (Charles Jencks in interview with James Stirling), *The Architectural Review*, vol. 181, no. 1084 (June 1987), pp. 47–50, p. 47.
111 Michael Wilford, 'An Evolving Design Philosophy', in *James Stirling and Michael Wilford: Architectural Monographs*, no. 32 (London: Academy Editions, 1993), p. 7.
112 Wilford, 'An Evolving Design Philosophy', p. 7.

Chapter Eight

1. Peter Rice quoted in Adrian Forty, *Concrete and Culture: A Material History* (London: Reaktion Books, 2012), pp. 45–6.
2. Forty, *Concrete and Culture*, p. 28.
3. Kenneth Powell, 'Richard Rogers Partnership: Lloyd's Building, London, 1978–86', in *Pioneering British 'High-Tech'* (London: Phaidon, 1999), unpaginated.
4. Cook, quoted in Richard Burdett, *Richard Rogers Partnership: Works and Projects* (New York: The Monacelli Press, 1996), p. 23.
5. Ruskin, *Works*, 16: 349, 'Influence of Imagination in Architecture'.
6. Ruskin, *Works*, 16: 349, 'Influence of Imagination in Architecture'.
7. *Archigram 1* (1961), Archigram archive: archigram.westminster.ac.uk [accessed October 2020].
8. Cook quoted in Simon Sadler, *Archigram: Architecture without Architecture* (Cambridge, MA: MIT Press, 2005), p. 11.
9. Sadler, *Archigram*, p. 11.
10. See Sadler, *Archigram*, pp. 22–4.
11. Webb, M. de [*sic*], 'Furniture Manufacturers Association Showrooms, High Wycombe', *The Architects' Journal*, vol. 129, no. 3342 (14 March 1959), pp. 451–4.
12. Webb, 'Furniture Manufacturers Association Showrooms', p. 454.
13. Banham, *The New Brutalism*, p. 43.
14. Dennis Crompton (ed.), *A Guide to Archigram 1961–74* (New York: Princeton Architectural Press, 2012, 3rd revised edition), p. 9.
15. Warren Chalk, 'South Bank Arts Centre, London', *Architectural Design* (March 1967), pp. 120–3, pp. 120–2.
16. Forty, *Concrete and Culture*, p. 282.
17. Crompton (ed.), *Guide to Archigram*, p. 68; *Archigram 3* (1963), Archigram archive: archigram.westminster.ac.uk [accessed November 2020].
18. *Archigram 3*, p. 4 (1963); Nottingham Shopping Centre Project (1962), Project No. 34; Archigram archive: archigram.westminster.ac.uk [accessed November 2020].
19. Cook quoted in Bryan Appleyard, *Richard Rogers: A Biography* (London: Faber & Faber, 1986), p. 185.
20. Reyner Banham, 'Enigma of the Rue du Renard', *The Architectural Review*, vol. 161, no. 693 (May 1977), pp. 277–8, p. 277.
21. Andrew Saint, *Architect and Engineer: A Study in Sibling Rivalry* (New Haven and London: Yale University Press, 2007), p. 382.
22. Nathan Silver, *The Making of Beaubourg: A Building Biography of the Centre Pompidou, Paris* (Cambridge, MA: MIT Press, 1994), p. 24.
23. Anon., 'The Pompidolium', *The Architectural Review*, vol. 161, no. 693 (1 May 1977), pp. 271–94, p. 282.

24 Sadler, *Archigram*, p. 18.
25 Piano quoted in Silver, *The Making of Beaubourg*, p. 25.
26 See Craig Buckley, 'Face and Screen: Towards a Genealogy of the Media Façade', in Francesco Casetti, Rüdiger Campe, and Craig Buckley (eds.), *Screen Genealogies: From Optical Device to Environmental Medium* (Amsterdam: Amsterdam University Press, 2019), pp. 73–114, also for a genealogy of the media façade.
27 Frampton, *Modern Architecture*, p. 285.
28 Appleyard, *Richard Rogers*, p. 212.
29 Rice quoted in Saint, *Architect and Engineer*, p. 382.
30 Saint, *Architect and Engineer*, p. 382.
31 Rice quoted in Saint, *Architect and Engineer*, p. 382.
32 Barjavel quoted in 'The Pompidolium', *Architectural Review* (May 1977), p. 287.
33 Colquhoun quoted in Appleyard, *Richard Rogers*, p. 223.
34 Lubetkin quoted in Alan Powers, *Britain: Modern Architectures in History* (London: Reaktion Books, 2007), p. 213.
35 Powers, *Britain*, p. 195.
36 Banham, 'Enigma of the Rue du Renard', p. 277.
37 Reyner Banham, 'The Great Wall of Tyne', *New Society*, vol. 31, no. 644 (6 February 1975), pp. 330–1, p. 330; Michael Drage, 'Byker: Surprising the Colleagues for 35 Years – A Social History of Ralph Erskine's Arkitektkontor AB in Newcastle', in E. Harwood and A. Powers (eds.), *Housing the Twentieth Century Nation*, Twentieth Century Architecture 9 (London: Twentieth Century Society, 2008), pp. 148–62, p. 149.
38 Mats Egelius, *Ralph Erskine, Architect* (Stockholm: Byggförlaget, 1990), p. 7, p. 21; see also Natasha Vall, 'Social Engineering and Participation in Anglo-Swedish Housing 1945–1976: Ralph Erskine's Vernacular Plan', *Planning Perspectives*, vol. 28, no. 2 (2013), pp. 23–45.
39 Erskine quoted in Vall, 'Social Engineering and Participation in Anglo-Swedish Housing 1945–1976', p. 228.
40 Erskine quoted in Egelius, *Ralph Erskine, Architect*, p. 136.
41 Sutherland Lyall, *The State of British Architecture* (London: The Architectural Press, 1980), p. 70, pp. 75–6.
42 Bernard Rudofsky, *Architecture without Architects: A Short Introduction to Non-pedigreed Architecture* (London: Academy Editions, 1964).
43 Robert Maxwell, 'Two Housing Schemes at Milton Keynes', *The Architect's Journal*, vol. 162, no. 50 (10 December 1975), pp. 1247–60, p. 1260.
44 Christian Norberg-Schulz, *Nightlands: Nordic Building* (Cambridge, MA: MIT Press, 1996), p. 193.
45 Norberg-Schulz, *Nightlands*, pp. 60–1.
46 Egelius, *Ralph Erskine, Architect*, pp. 9–11, pp. 60–6; Erskine quoted in Oscar Newman, *CIAM '59 in Otterlo* (London: Alec Tiranti, 1961), p. 50.

47 Van Eyck and Smithson quoted in Newman, *CIAM '59 in Otterlo*, p. 169.
48 Peter Blundell Jones, 'Ralph Erskine: An Organic Architect', *Architectural Research Quarterly*, vol. 18, no. 3 (2014), pp. 210–17, p. 210.
49 Peter Collymore, *The Architecture of Ralph Erskine* (London: Academy Editions, 1994, revised edition), p. 34.
50 Mats Egelius, *Ralph Erskine Byker Redevelopment, Byker Area of Newcastle upon Tyne* (Tokyo: A. D. A. Edita, GA 55, 1980), p. 3.
51 Peter Malpass, 'A Reappraisal of Byker. Part 2: Magic, Myth and the Architect', *The Architects' Journal*, vol. 169, no. 20 (16 May 1979), pp. 1011–21.
52 Colin Amery, 'Housing, Byker, Newcastle Upon Tyne', *The Architectural Review*, vol. 156, no. 934 (1 December 1974), pp. 350–62, p. 359.
53 See Peter Buchanan, 'Landscaping at Byker, Newcastle Upon Tyne', *The Architectural Review*, vol. 170, no. 1018 (December 1981), pp. 334–43.
54 Malpass, 'A Reappraisal of Byker. Part 2', pp. 1011–21.
55 Gillian Darley and Peter Davey, 'Sense and Sensibility', *The Architectural Review*, vol. 174, no. 1039 (September 1983), pp. 22–5.
56 Anon., 'Is there a British Tradition', *The Architectural Review*, vol. 175, no. 1047 (May 1984), pp. 40–7.
57 Lyall, *The State of British Architecture*, p. 146.
58 David Watkin, *A History of Western Architecture* (London: Laurence King, 1992 [1986]), pp. 571–6.
59 Powers, *Britain*, p. 231.
60 Powers, *Britain*, pp. 228–31.
61 Tony Fretton and Kenneth Frampton, 'Lisson Gallery, London', *AA Files*, no. 23 (Summer 1992), pp. 19–23.
62 Neil Leach, 'Design and New Materialism', in E. Grierson, H. Edquist, and Hélène Frichot (eds.), *De-signing Design: Cartographies of Theory and Practice* (Lanham, MD: Lexington Books, 2015), p. 206; the 'New Materialism' is a term coined by Manuel DeLanda in the 1990s.
63 Frampton quoted in Peter Davey, 'Materiality and Resistance', *The Architectural Review*, vol. 194, no. 1167 (May 1994), pp. 4–5, p. 5.
64 Deborah Smith (ed.), *The New Art Gallery Walsall* (London: Batsford, 2002), p. 64.
65 Christopher Woodward quoted in Aurora Fernández Per (ed.), *As Built: Caruso St John Architects* (Vitoria-Gasteiz: a+t ediciones, 2005), p. 13.
66 Adam Caruso quoted in Luca Deon and Toni Häfliger (eds.), *Caruso St John: Knitting, Weaving, Wrapping, Pressing* (Basel: Birkhäuser, 2002), p. 80.
67 See Adam Caruso and Peter St John, 'Caruso St John 2013–19: The Physical Quality of Space', *El Croquis*, issue 201 (Madrid, 2019), p. 287.
68 Pevsner, *The Englishness of English Art*, p. 120.
69 Mark Girouard, *Robert Smythson and The Elizabethan Country House* (New Haven and London: Yale University Press, 1983), p. 157; Sacheverell Sitwell,

British Architects and Craftsmen (London: Batsford, 1946–7, 3rd edition), pp. 26–7; see also Brian Carter, 'Solid Citizen: Art Gallery, Walsall. Caruso St John Architects', *The Architectural Review*, vol. 207, no. 1239 (May 2000), pp. 62–6.

70 Caruso St John quoted in Peter Allison, 'The Presence of Construction: Walsall Art Gallery by Caruso St John: AA Exhibition Gallery, 12 January–14 February 1998', *AA Files*, no. 35 (Spring 1998), pp. 70–9, p. 70.

71 Smith (ed.), *The New Art Gallery Walsall*, p. 36.

72 See Fernández Per, *As Built: Caruso St John Architects*, p. 163.

73 Adam Caruso quoted in Deon and Häfliger (eds.) *Caruso St John: Knitting, Weaving, Wrapping, Pressing*, p. 76.

74 Adolf Loos, *On Architecture. Adolf Loos; Selected and Introduced by Adolf and Daniel Opel*, trans. M. Mitchell (Riverside, CA: Ariadne Press, 2002), p. 42.

75 Adam Caruso quoted in Deon and Häfliger (eds.) *Caruso St John: Knitting, Weaving, Wrapping, Pressing*, p. 76.

76 Allison, 'The Presence of Construction', p. 74.

77 See Caruso and St John, *El Croquis*, issue 201, p. 291.

78 Allison, 'The Presence of Construction', pp. 71–2.

79 Serra quoted in Allison, 'The Presence of Construction', p. 72.

80 Philip Ursprung, *Caruso St John: Almost Everything* (Barcelona: Ediciones Polígrafa, 2008), p. 79.

81 See Mhairi McVicar, *Precision in Architecture: Certainty, Ambiguity and Deviation* (Abingdon: Routledge, 2019), chapter 7.

82 Rowe, 'Very Disjointed Memoir', p. 11.

BIBLIOGRAPHY

Aben, Rob, and Saskia de Wit, *The Enclosed Garden: History and Development of the Hortus Conclusus and its Reintroduction into the Present-day Urban Landscape* (Rotterdam: 010 Publishers, 2001).
Ackroyd, Peter, *London: The Biography* (London: Vintage, 2001).
Alexander, Michael, *Medievalism: The Middle Ages in Modern England* (New Haven and London: Yale University Press, 2017).
Allan, John, 'Rediscovering Lubetkin', in S. Charlton (ed.), *British Modern: Architecture and Design in the 1930s* (London: The Twentieth Century Society, 2007), pp. 89–104.
Allan, John, *Berthold Lubetkin: Architecture and the Tradition of Progress* (London: Artifice, 2012).
Allison, Peter, 'The Presence of Construction: Walsall Art Gallery by Caruso St John: AA Exhibition Gallery, 12 January–14 February 1998', *AA Files*, no. 35 (Spring 1998), pp. 70–9.
Amato, Joseph A., *Surfaces: A History* (Berkeley, CA: University of California Press, 2013).
Amery, Colin, 'Housing, Byker, Newcastle Upon Tyne', *The Architectural Review*, vol. 156, no. 934 (1 December 1974), pp. 350–62.
Anon., 'Awards at the Royal Institute of British Architects: The Soane and the Pugin', *The Architectural Review* (1 March 1897), pp. 200–11.
Anon., 'Highpoint Number Two. Tecton, Architects', *The Architectural Review*, vol. 84, no. 503 (1 October 1938), pp. 165–76.
Anon., 'Modern Flats in Highgate', *The Architectural Review*, vol. 84, no. 503 (1 October 1938), pp. 161–4.
Anon., 'The New Empiricism: Sweden's Latest Style', *The Architectural Review*, vol. 101, no. 606 (June 1947), pp. 199–204.
Anon., 'Housing at Peterlee. Peter Daniel, Frank Dixon, Victor Pasmore', *The Architectural Review*, vol. 129, no. 768 (1 February 1961), pp. 88–97.
Anon., 'Housing in Peterlee New Town', *The Architects' Journal*, vol. 133 (23 February 1961), pp. 291–302.
Anon., 'The Pompidolium', *The Architectural Review*, vol. 161, no. 693 (1 May 1977), pp. 271–94.
Anon., 'Is there a British Tradition', *The Architectural Review*, vol. 175, no. 1047 (May 1984), pp. 40–7.
Appleyard, Bryan, *Richard Rogers: A Biography* (London: Faber & Faber, 1986).
Arnheim, Rudolf, *The Dynamics of Architectural Form* (Berkeley, CA: University of California Press, 1977).
Arslan, Edoardo, *Gothic Architecture in Venice*, trans. A. Engel (London: Phaidon, 1971).

A.T.E. (Anon.), '"No. 55 Broadway, Westminster", New Headquarters for the London Electric Railways at St James's Park', *The Architects' Journal* (16 October 1929), pp. 558–63.

Baker, Geoffrey H., *The Architecture of James Stirling and His Partners James Gowan and Michael Wilford* (Abingdon: Routledge, 2016).

Banham, Joanna, 'The English Response: Mechanization and Design Reform', in Lesley Hoskins (ed.), *The Papered Wall: The History, Patterns and Techniques of Wallpaper* (London: Thames & Hudson, 2005), pp. 132–49.

Banham, Reyner, 'Casa del Girasole', *The Architectural Review*, vol. 113, no. 674 (1 February 1953), pp. 73–7.

Banham, Reyner, 'Façade: Elevational Treatment of the Hallfield Estate Paddington', *The Architectural Review*, vol. 116, no. 695 (November 1954), pp. 302–18.

Banham, Reyner, 'The New Brutalism', *The Architectural Review* (December 1955), pp. 355–61.

Banham, Reyner, *The New Brutalism: Ethic or Aesthetic?* (London: The Architectural Press, 1966).

Banham, Reyner, 'Revenge of the Picturesque: English Architectural Polemics, 1945–1965', in John Summerson (ed.), *Concerning Architecture: Essays on Architectural Writers and Writing Presented to Nikolaus Pevsner* (London: Allen Lane The Penguin Press, 1968), pp. 265–73.

Banham, Reyner, *Age of the Masters: A Personal View of Modern Architecture* (London: The Architectural Press, 1975 [1962]).

Banham, Reyner, 'The Great Wall of Tyne', *New Society*, vol. 31, no. 644 (6 February 1975), pp. 330–1.

Banham, Reyner, 'Enigma of the Rue du Renard', *The Architectural Review*, vol. 161, no. 693 (May 1977), pp. 277–8.

Bayes, Walter, 'Sense and Sensibility. The New Head Offices of the Underground Railway, Westminster, London', *The Architectural Review*, vol. 66, no. 396 (1 November 1929), pp. 225–39.

BBC Radio 3, '"This is Tomorrow", 17 August 1956, Peter Smithson, Colin St John Wilson, William Turnbull, Richard Hamilton in discussion with Theo Crosby and David Piper'.

Beattie, Susan, *The New Sculpture* (New Haven and London: Yale University Press, 1983).

Beeson, Anthony, *Bristol Central Library and Charles Holden: A History and Guide* (Bristol: Redcliffe Press, 2006).

Berman, Alan (ed.), *Jim Stirling and the Red Trilogy: Three Radical Buildings* (London: Frances Lincoln, 2010).

Betjeman, John (ed.), *Collins Pocket Guide to English Parish Churches: The South* (London: Collins, 1968).

Binski, Paul, *Gothic Wonder: Art, Artifice and the Decorated Style 1290–1350* (New Haven and London: Yale University Press, 2014).

Blundell Jones, Peter, 'Red House', *The Architects' Journal*, vol. 183, no. 3 (15 January 1986), pp. 37–56.

Blundell Jones, Peter, 'Stirling's Last Laugh', *The Architects' Journal*, vol. 186, no. 29 (22 July 1987), pp. 32–44.

Blundell Jones, Peter, 'Ralph Erskine: An Organic Architect', *Architectural Research Quarterly*, vol. 18, no. 3 (2014), pp. 210–17.

Bodley, George Frederick, 'On Some Principles and Characteristics of Ancient Architecture and their Application to the Modern Practice of the Art', *The Builder*, vol. 108 (1885), pp. 294–7.

Bodley, George Frederick, *Poems* (London: George Bell, 1899).

Bodley, George Frederick, 'Some Principles that may be Guides for the Applied Arts', *Journal of the Society of Arts*, vol. 51, no. 2619 (30 January 1903), pp. 181–9.

Booth, Philip, and Nicholas Taylor, *Cambridge New Architecture* (London: Leonard Hill Books, 1970 [1964], 3rd edition).

Bowness, Sophie, 'An Anthology of Sculptor's Writings on Stone Carving', in *Carving Mountains: Modern Stone Sculpture in England 1907–37* (Cambridge: Kettle's Yard, 1998), pp. 8–21.

Boyd Whyte, Iain, 'Nikolaus Pevsner: Art History, Nation, and Exile', *RIHA Journal*, 0075 (23 October 2013), http://www.riha-journal.org/articles/2013/2013-oct-dec/whyte-pevsner [accessed 26 November 2019].

Boyer, M. Christine, *Not Quite Architecture: Writing Around Alison and Peter Smithson* (Cambridge, MA: MIT Press, 2017).

Braesel, Michaela, 'The Influence of Medieval Illuminated Manuscripts on the Pre-Raphaelites and the Early Poetry of William Morris', *Journal of William Morris Studies*, vol. 15, no. 4 (2004), pp. 41–54.

Branfoot, Antony and Suzanna Branfoot, 'The Old and the New: Influences and Style in the Work of G. E. Street in Berkshire', in J. Elliott and J. Pritchard (eds.), *George Edmund Street: A Victorian Architect in Berkshire* (Reading: Centre for Continuing Education, The University of Reading, 1998), pp. 29–45.

Brett, Lionel, and Berthold Lubetkin, 'Canons of Criticism: 2', *The Architectural Review*, vol. 109, no. 651 (March 1951), pp. 135–7.

Brooks, Michael W., 'Describing Buildings: John Ruskin and Nineteenth-Century Architectural Prose', *Prose Studies*, vol. 3 (1980), pp. 241–53.

Brooks, Michael W., *John Ruskin and Victorian Architecture* (London: Thames & Hudson, 1989).

Buchanan, Peter, 'Landscaping at Byker, Newcastle Upon Tyne', *The Architectural Review*, vol. 170, no. 1018 (December 1981), pp. 334–43.

Buckley, Craig, 'Face and Screen: Towards a Genealogy of the Media Façade', in Francesco Casetti, Rüdiger Campe, and Craig Buckley (eds.), *Screen Genealogies: From Optical Device to Environmental Medium* (Amsterdam: Amsterdam University Press, 2019), pp. 73–114.

Bullen, J. B., *Byzantium Rediscovered* (London: Phaidon, 2003).

Burckhardt, Jacob, *The Architecture of the Italian Renaissance* (Harmondsworth: Penguin Books, 1987 [1867]).

Burdett, Richard, *Richard Rogers Partnership: Works and Projects* (New York: The Monacelli Press, 1996).

Burns, Karen, 'Topographies of Tourism: "Documentary" Photography and *The Stones of Venice*', *Assemblage*, 32 (April 1997), pp. 22–44.

Butler, A. S. G., *The Architecture of Sir Edwin Lutyens*, 3 vols. (Woodbridge: Antique Collectors' Club, 1984 [1950]).

Carter, Brian, 'Solid Citizen: Art Gallery, Walsall. Caruso St John Architects', *The Architectural Review*, vol. 207, no. 1239 (May 2000), pp. 62–6.

Caruso, Adam, and Peter St John, 'Caruso St John 2013–2019: The Physical Quality of Space', *El Croquis*, issue 201 (Madrid, 2019).

Chalk, Warren, 'South Bank Arts Centre, London', *Architectural Design* (March 1967), pp. 120–3.
Chatterjee, Anuradha, *John Ruskin and the Fabric of Architecture* (Abingdon: Routledge, 2018).
Cheetham, Mark A., *Artwriting, Nation, and Cosmopolitanism in Britain: The 'Englishness' of English Art Theory since the Eighteenth Century* (Farnham: Ashgate, 2012).
Clifton-Taylor, Alec, *The Pattern of English Building* (London: Batsford, 1962).
Clifton-Taylor, Alec, and A. S. Ireson, *English Stone Building* (London: Victor Gollancz, 1983).
Collymore, Peter, *The Architecture of Ralph Erskine* (London: Academy Editions, 1994, revised edition).
Cook, E. T., *The Life of John Ruskin*, 2 vols. (London: George Allen, 1911).
Cook, E. T., and Alexander Wedderburn (eds.), *John Ruskin Collected Works*, The Library Edition, 39 vols. (London: George Allen, 1903–12).
Cook, Martin Godfrey, *Edward Prior: Arts and Crafts Architect* (Ramsbury: Crowood Press, 2015).
Cork, Richard, *Art Beyond the Gallery in Early 20th Century England* (New Haven and London: Yale University Press, 1985).
Cork, Richard, *Wild Thing: Epstein, Gaudier-Brzeska, Gill* (London: Royal Academy of Arts, 2010).
Crawford, Alan, 'Englishness in Arts and Crafts Architecture', in D. Crellin and I. Dugavell (eds.), *Architecture and Englishness 1880–1914* (London: Society of Architectural Historians of Great Britain, 2006), pp. 25–36.
Crawford, O. G. S., 'Historical Cycles', *Antiquity*, vol. 5, no. 17 (March 1931), pp. 5–20.
Crinson, Mark (ed.), *James Stirling: Early Unpublished Writings on Architecture* (Abingdon: Routledge, 2010).
Crinson, Mark, *Stirling and Gowan: Architecture from Austerity to Affluence* (New Haven and London: Yale University Press, 2012).
Crinson, Mark, 'Eye Wandering the Ceiling: Ornament and New Brutalism', *Art History*, vol. 41, no. 2 (April 2018), pp. 318–43.
Crompton, Dennis (ed.), *A Guide to Archigram 1961–74* (New York: Princeton Architectural Press, 2012, 3rd revised edition).
Crosby, Theo, 'This Is Tomorrow', *Architectural Design* (October 1956), pp. 334–6.
Cubitt, James, *Church Design for Congregations: Its Development and Possibilities* (London: Smith, Elder, 1870).
Cullen, Gordon, 'Bankside Regained', *The Architectural Review*, vol. 105, no. 625 (1 January 1949), pp. 15–24.
Cullen, Gordon, 'Townscape Casebook', *The Architectural Review*, vol. 106, no. 636 (1 December 1949), pp. 363–74.
Cullen, Gordon, 'The Wall', *The Architectural Review*, vol. 112, no. 671 (1 November 1952), pp. 294–301.
Cullen, Gordon, *Townscape* (London: The Architectural Press, 1961).
Curl, James Stevens, 'All Saints' Margaret Street', *The Architects' Journal*, vol. 191, no. 25 (20 June 1990), pp. 36–55.
Curtis, Penelope, 'How Direct Carving Stole the Idea of Modern British Sculpture', in David J. Getsy (ed.), *Sculpture and the Pursuit of a Modern Ideal in Britain, c. 1880–1930* (Aldershot: Ashgate, 2004), pp. 291–318.

Curtis, Penelope, Denise Raine, Matthew Withey, Jon Wood, and Victoria Worsley (eds.), *Sculpture in 20th-Century Britain*, 2 vols. (Leeds: Henry Moore Institute, 2003).
Curtis, William J. R., *Modern Architecture since 1900* (London: Phaidon, 1992).
Dakers, Caroline, *The Holland Park Circle: Artists and Victorian Society* (New Haven and London: Yale University Press, 1999).
Darley, Gillian, and Peter Davey, 'Sense and Sensibility', *The Architectural Review*, vol. 174, no. 1039 (September 1983), pp. 22–5.
Davey, Peter, 'Stuttgart', *The Architectural Review*, vol. 191, no. 1150 (December 1992), pp. 38–46.
Davey, Peter, 'Materiality and Resistance', *The Architectural Review*, vol. 194, no. 1167 (May 1994), pp. 4–5.
Davey, Peter, *Arts and Crafts Architecture* (London: Phaidon, 1995).
Day, Lewis F., 'A Kensington Interior', *The Art Journal* (1893), pp. 139–44.
Deon, Luca, and Toni Häfliger (eds.), *Caruso St John: Knitting, Weaving, Wrapping, Pressing* (Basel: Birkhäuser, 2002).
Drage, Michael, 'Byker: Surprising the Colleagues for 35 Years – A Social History of Ralph Erskine's Arkitektkontor AB in Newcastle', in E. Harwood and A. Powers (eds.), *Housing the Twentieth Century Nation*, Twentieth Century Architecture 9 (London: Twentieth Century Society, 2008), pp. 148–62.
Eames, Evelyn, and Joyce Gregory, 'Influence and Heritage', in J. Elliott and J. Pritchard (eds.), *George Edmund Street: A Victorian Architect in Berkshire* (Reading: Centre for Continuing Education, The University of Reading, 1998), pp. 71–80.
Eastlake, Charles, *Hints on Household Taste* (London: Longmans Green, 1869, 2nd edition).
Eastlake, Charles, *A History of the Gothic Revival*, ed. J. Mordaunt Crook (Leicester: Leicester University Press, 1978 [1872], 2nd edition).
Edis, Robert, *The Furniture and Decoration of Town Houses* (New York: Scribner & Welford, 1881).
Egelius, Mats, *Ralph Erskine Byker Redevelopment, Byker Area of Newcastle upon Tyne* (Tokyo: A. D. A. Edita, GA 55, 1980).
Egelius, Mats, *Ralph Erskine, Architect* (Stockholm: Byggförlaget, 1990).
Eisenman, Peter, 'Real and English: The Destruction of the Box. 1', *Oppositions*, no. 4 (October 1974), pp. 5–34.
Engel, Ute, 'The Formation of Pevsner's Art History: Nikolaus Pevsner in Germany 1902–1935', in Peter Draper (ed.), *Reassessing Nikolaus Pevsner* (Aldershot: Ashgate, 2004), pp. 29–55.
Engler, Mira, *Cut and Paste Urban Landscape: The Work of Gordon Cullen* (Abingdon: Routledge, 2016).
Epstein, Jacob, 'The Artist's Description of his Work', *The British Medical Journal* (4 July 1908), p. 40.
Epstein, Jacob, *An Autobiography* (London: Hulton Press, 1955, revised edition of *Let There be Sculpture*, 1940).
Evans, Joan, and John Howard Whitehouse (eds.), *The Diaries of John Ruskin* (Oxford: Clarendon Press, 1956).
Farmer, Graham, and John Pendlebury, 'Conserving Dirty Concrete: The Decline and Rise of Pasmore's Apollo Pavilion, Peterlee', *Journal of Urban Design*, vol. 18, no. 2 (2013), pp. 263–80.

Fernández Per, Aurora (ed.), *As Built: Caruso St John Architects* (Vitoria-Gasteiz: a+t ediciones, 2005).
Flannery, Julian, *Fifty English Steeples: The Finest Medieval Parish Church Towers and Spires in England* (London: Thames & Hudson, 2016).
Forty, Adrian, *Words and Buildings: A Vocabulary of Modern Architecture* (London: Thames & Hudson, 2000).
Forty, Adrian, *Concrete and Culture: A Material History* (London: Reaktion Books, 2012).
Fox, Bridgeen, 'The Church of All Saints, Boyne Hill, Maidenhead', in J. Elliott and J. Pritchard (eds.), *George Edmund Street: A Victorian Architect in Berkshire* (Reading: Centre for Continuing Education, The University of Reading, 1998), pp. 46–59.
Foyle, Andrew, *Bristol. Pevsner Architectural Guides* (New Haven and London: Yale University Press, 2004).
Frampton, Kenneth, *Modern Architecture: A Critical History* (London: Thames & Hudson, 1993, 3rd edition).
Frampton, Kenneth, 'On Leslie Martin', *Architectural Research Quarterly*, vol. 5, no. 1 (2001), pp. 11–12.
Franklin, Jill, 'Edwardian Butterfly Houses', *The Architectural Review*, vol. 157, no. 938 (April 1975), pp. 220–5.
Franklin, Jill, *The Gentleman's Country House and its Plan 1835–1914* (London: Routledge & Kegan Paul, 1981).
Fretton, Tony, and Kenneth Frampton, 'Lisson Gallery, London', *AA Files*, no. 23 (Summer 1992), pp. 19–23.
Garnham, Trevor, 'St Andrew's Church, Roker, Sunderland 1905', in *Arts and Crafts Masterpieces* (London: Phaidon, 1999).
Gathercole, Sam, 'Art and Construction in Britain in the 1950s', *Art History*, vol. 29, no. 5 (November 2006), pp. 887–925.
Gere, Charlotte, *Artistic Circles: Design and Decoration in the Aesthetic Movement* (London: V & A Publishing, 2010).
Girouard, Mark, *Robert Smythson and the Elizabethan Country House* (New Haven and London: Yale University Press, 1983).
Gloag, John, *The English Tradition in Design* (Harmondsworth: Penguin Books, 1946).
Glover, Nicky, *Psychoanalytic Aesthetics: An Introduction to the British School* (London: Karnac Books, 2009).
Goodhart-Rendel, H. S., 'Rogue Architects of the Victorian Era', *RIBA Journal*, vol. 56 (1949), pp. 251–9.
Goodhart-Rendel, H. S., *English Architecture Since the Regency: An Interpretation* (London: Constable, 1953).
Gosling, David, *Gordon Cullen: Visions of Urban Design* (London: Academy Editions, 1996).
Gradidge, Roderick, *Edwin Lutyens: Architect Laureate* (London: George Allen & Unwin, 1981).
Grieve, Alastair, '"This is Tomorrow": A Remarkable Exhibition Born from Contention', *The Burlington Magazine*, vol. 136, no. 1093 (April 1994), pp. 225–32.
Grieve, Alastair, *Constructed Abstract Art in England: A Neglected Avant-Garde* (New Haven and London: Yale University Press, 2005).

Grillet, Christophe, 'Edward Prior', *The Architectural Review*, vol. 112, no. 671 (November 1952), pp. 302–8.

Hall, Michael, 'The Rise of Refinement: G. F. Bodley's All Saint's, Cambridge, and the Return to English Models in Gothic Architecture of the 1860s', *Architectural History*, vol. 36 (1993), pp. 103–26.

Hall, Michael, 'What Do Victorian Churches Mean? Symbolism and Sacramentalism in Anglican Church Architecture, 1850–1870', *Journal of the Society of Architectural Historians*, vol. 59, no. 1 (March 2000), pp. 78–95.

Hall, Michael, *Gothic Architecture and Its Meanings: 1550–1830* (Reading: Spire Books, 2002).

Hall, Michael, '"A Patriotism in our Art": Ideas of Englishness in the Architecture of G. F. Bodley', in D. Crellin and I. Dugavell (eds.) *Architecture and Englishness 1880–1914* (London: Society of Architectural Historians of Great Britain, 2006), pp. 7–24.

Hall, Michael, *George Frederick Bodley and the Later Gothic Revival in Britain and America* (New Haven and London: Yale University Press, 2014).

Hanson, Brian, 'Singing the Body Electric with Charles Holden', *The Architectural Review*, vol. 158, no. 946 (1 December 1975), pp. 349–56.

Harries, Susan, *Nikolaus Pevsner: The Life* (London: Pimlico, 2013).

Harris, Alexandra, *Weatherland: Writers and Artists Under English Skies* (London: Thames & Hudson, 2015).

Harrison, Martin, *Transition: The London Art Scene in the Fifties* (London: Merrell, 2002).

Hart, Imogen, 'An "Enchanted" Interior: William Morris at Kelmscott House', in Jason Edwards and Imogen Hart (eds.), *Rethinking the Interior, c. 1867–1896: Aestheticism and Arts and Crafts* (Farnham: Ashgate, 2010), pp. 67–84.

Harvey, Charles Edward, and Jon Press, 'The Ionides Family and 1 Holland Park' (January 1994): https://www.researchgate.net/publication/259810860_The_Ionides_Family_and_1_Holland_Park [accessed October 2017].

Harvey, Charles, and Jon Press, *Art Enterprise and Ethics: Essays on the Life and Work of William Morris* (London: Frank Cass, 1996).

Harwood, Elain, 'Butterfield and Brutalism', *AA Files*, no. 27 (Summer 1994), pp. 39–46.

Harwood, Elain, 'Neurath, Riley and Bilston, Pasmore and Peterlee', in E. Harwood and A. Powers (eds.), *Housing the Twentieth Century Nation*, Twentieth Century Architecture 9 (London: Twentieth Century Society, 2008), pp. 84–96.

Harwood, Elain, *Space, Hope and Brutalism: English Architecture 1945–1975* (New Haven and London: Yale University Press, 2015).

Hastings, Hubert de Cronin (the Editor), 'Exterior Furnishing or Sharawaggi: The Art of Making Urban Landscape', *The Architectural Review*, vol. 95, no. 565 (1 January 1944), pp. 3–8.

Hauser, Kitty, *Shadow Sites: Photography, Archaeology, and the British Landscape 1927–1955* (Oxford: Oxford University Press, 2007).

Helsinger, Elizabeth K., *Ruskin and the Art of the Beholder* (Cambridge, MA: Harvard University Press, 1982).

Hewison, Robert, *Ruskin on Venice* (New Haven and London: Yale University Press, 2009).

Highmore, Ben, 'Brutalist Wallpaper and the Independent Group', *Journal of Visual Culture*, vol. 12, no. 2 (2013), pp. 205–21.

Hill, M., J. Newman, and N. Pevsner, *The Buildings of England: Dorset* (New Haven and London: Yale University Press, 2018).
Hills, Paul, *Venetian Colour: Marble, Mosaic and Glass 1250–1550* (New Haven and London: Yale University Press, 1999).
Hitchcock, Henry-Russell, *Early Victorian Architecture in Britain*, 2 vols. (London: Trewin Copplestone, 1954).
Hitchcock, Henry-Russell, 'G. E. Street in the 1850s', *Journal of the Society of Architectural Historians*, vol. 19, no. 4 (December 1960), pp. 145–71.
Holden, Charles, 'If Whitman had been an Architect', *The Architectural Review*, vol. 17, no. 103 (1 June 1905), p. 258.
Holden, Charles, 'Thoughts for the Strong', *The Architectural Review*, vol. 18, no. 104 (1 July 1905), p. 27.
Holden, Charles, 'Letter on Art and Industry', *The Architects' Journal* (9 September 1931), p. 343.
Hoozee, Robert (ed.), *British Vision: Observation and Imagination in British Art 1750–1950* (Brussels: Mercatorfonds/Ghent: Museum voor Schone Kunsten, 2008).
Hoskins, Lesley, 'Wallpaper', in Linda Parry (ed.), *William Morris*, V & A exhibition catalogue (London: Philip Wilson, V & A Museum, 1996), pp. 198–205.
Hoskins, Lesley (ed.), *The Papered Wall: The History, Patterns and Techniques of Wallpaper* (London: Thames & Hudson, 2005).
Howard, Deborah, *Venice and the East: The Impact of the Islamic World on Venetian Architecture 1100–1500* (New Haven and London: Yale University Press, 2000).
Howard, Deborah, *The Architectural History of Venice* (New Haven and London: Yale University Press, 2002).
Hussey, Christopher, *The Picturesque: Studies in a Point of View* (London: Frank Cass, 1983 [1927]).
Huxtable, Sally-Anne, 'Re-reading the Green Dining Room', in Jason Edwards and Imogen Hart (eds.), *Rethinking the Interior, c. 1867–1896: Aestheticism and Arts and Crafts* (Farnham: Ashgate, 2010), pp. 25–40.
Jackson, Neil, 'Christ Church, Streatham, and the Rise of Constructional Polychromy', *Architectural History*, vol. 43 (2000), pp. 219–52.
Jacobson, Ken, and Jenny Jacobson, *Carrying Off the Palaces: John Ruskin's Lost Daguerreotypes* (London: Quaritch, 2015).
Jacobus, John, 'Engineering Building, Leicester University', *The Architectural Review*, vol. 135, no. 806 (April 1964), pp. 252–60.
James, Henry, *The Wings of the Dove* (Harmondsworth: Penguin Books, 1965).
Jencks, Charles, 'Clore Contextualisms' (Charles Jencks in interview with James Stirling), *The Architectural Review*, vol. 181, no. 1084 (June 1987), pp. 47–50.
Jencks, Charles, and George Baird, *Meaning in Architecture* (New York: George Braziller, 1970).
Jenkins, David, *Clore Gallery, Tate Gallery, Liverpool, James Stirling, Michael Wilford and Associates* (London: Phaidon, 1992).
Jones, Owen, *The Grammar of Ornament* (Lewes: Ivy Press, 2016 [1856]).
Joyce, Paul, 'Boyne Hill (Maidenhead), Berkshire *All Saints*', in P. Howell and I. Sutton (eds.), *The Faber Guide to Victorian Churches* (London: Faber & Faber, 1989), p. 16.
Karol, Eitan, *Charles Holden 1875–1960* (Donington: Shaun Tyas, 2007).

Karol, Eitan, and Finch Allibone, *Charles Holden Architect 1875–1960*, exhibition catalogue (London: RIBA Heinz Gallery, 1988).
Kaufman, Edward N., '"The Weight and Vigour of Their Masses": Mid-Victorian County Churches and the "Lamp of Power"', in John Dixon Hunt and Faith M. Holland (eds.), *The Ruskin Polygon: Essays on the Imagination of John Ruskin* (Manchester: Manchester University Press, 1982), pp. 94–121.
Kaufmann, Edward, N., 'Architectural Representation in Victorian England', *Journal of the Society of Architectural Historians*, vol. 46, no. 1 (March 1987), pp. 30–8.
Kelvin, Norman (ed.), *The Collected Letters of William Morris, Vol. 2, 1881–1884* (Princeton, NJ: Princeton University Press, 1987).
Kirk, Sheila, *Philip Webb: Pioneer of Arts and Crafts Architecture* (Chichester: Wiley-Academy, 2005).
Kite, Stephen, 'Adrian Stokes: The Critical Writings – An Architectonic Perspective', Newcastle upon Tyne University, PhD Thesis, 2002.
Kite, Stephen, *Adrian Stokes: An Architectonic Eye* (London: Legenda, Modern Humanities Research Association and Maney Publishing, 2009).
Kite, Stephen, 'Softs and Hards: Colin St John Wilson and the Contested Visions of 1950s London', in Mark Crinson and Claire Zimmerman (eds.), *Neo-avant-garde and Postmodern: Postwar Architecture in Britain and Beyond* (New Haven, CT: The Yale Center for British Art, 2010).
Kite, Stephen, *Building Ruskin's Italy: Watching Architecture* (Farnham: Ashgate, 2012).
Kite, Stephen, 'Colin St John Wilson and the Independent Group', *Journal of Visual Culture*, vol. 12, no. 2 (August 2013), pp. 245–61.
Kite, Stephen, 'Building and the Graphic Arts: Adrian Stokes at the ICA', https://www.tate.org.uk/research/publications/tate-papers/20 [accessed 20 February 2020].
Landow, George, *The Aesthetic and Critical Theories of John Ruskin* (Princeton, NJ: Princeton University Press, 1971).
Latimer, Clare, 'The Division of the Wall: The Use of Wallpapers in Decorative Schemes, 1870–1910', *Journal of the Decorative Arts Society 1850 – the Present*, no. 12 (1988), pp. 18–25.
Lauder, Sir Thomas Dick, *Sir Uvedale Price on the Picturesque: With an Essay on the Origin of Taste* (Edinburgh: Caldwell, Lloyd, 1842).
Le Corbusier, *Towards a New Architecture*, trans. F. Etchells (London: The Architectural Press, 1970 [1927]).
Le Corbusier (Charles-Edouard Jeanneret), *Journey to the East*, ed. and trans. Ivan Žaknić (Cambridge, MA: MIT Press, 2007 [1966]).
Leach, Andrew and John Macarthur, *The Baroque in Architectural Culture 1880–1980* (London: Routledge, 2016).
Leach, Andrew, 'Continuity in Rupture: Postmodern Architecture before Architectural Postmodernism', in Mark Crinson and Claire Zimmerman (eds.), *Neo-avant-garde and Postmodern: Postwar Architecture in Britain and Beyond* (New Haven, CT: The Yale Center for British Art, 2010), pp. 127–49.
Leach, Neil, 'Design and New Materialism', in E. Grierson, H. Edquist, and Hélène Frichot (eds.), *De-signing Design: Cartographies of Theory and Practice* (Lanham, MD: Lexington Books, 2015).
Leatherbarrow, David, and Mohsen Mostafavi, *Surface Architecture* (Cambridge, MA: MIT Press, 2002).

Lethaby, William, *Architecture, Mysticism and Myth* (London: The Architectural Press, 1974 [1891]).
Lethaby, William, *Philip Webb and his Work* (London: Raven Oak Press, 1979).
Lewis, G. R., *Illustrations of Kilpeck Church, Herefordshire: In a Series of Drawings Made on the Spot. With an Essay on Ecclesiastical Design, and a Descriptive Interpretation* (London: G. R. Lewis and William Pickering, 1842).
Lichtenstein, Claude, and Thomas Schregenberger (eds.), *As Found: The Discovery of the Ordinary* (Baden: Lars Müller, 2001).
Loos, Adolf, *On Architecture. Adolf Loos; Selected and Introduced by Adolf and Daniel Opel*, trans. M. Mitchell (Riverside, CA: Ariadne Press, 2002).
Lubbock, Percy, *Shades of Eton* (London: Jonathan Cape, 1932 [1929]).
Lubetkin, Berthold, 'Flats in Rosebery Avenue, Finsbury', *The Architectural Review*, vol. 409, no. 651 (1 March 1951), pp. 138–49.
Lyall, Sutherland, *The State of British Architecture* (London: The Architectural Press, 1980).
Macarthur, John, *The Picturesque: Architecture, Disgust and Other Irregularities* (Abingdon: Routledge, 2007).
Macarthur, John, 'Townscape, Anti-scrape and Surrealism: Paul Nash and John Piper in The Architectural Review', *The Journal of Architecture*, vol. 14, no. 3 (2009), pp. 387–406.
MacCarthy, Fiona, *William Morris: A Life for Our Time* (London: Faber & Faber, 1995).
MacCarthy, Fiona, *The Last Pre-Raphaelite: Edward Burne-Jones and the Victorian Imagination* (London: Faber & Faber, 2012).
Mackail, J. W., *The Life of William Morris*, Vol. 1 (London: Longmans, Green, 1901).
Malpass, Peter, 'A Reappraisal of Byker. Part 2: Magic, Myth and the Architect', *The Architects' Journal*, vol. 169, no. 20 (16 May 1979), pp. 1011–21.
Maretto, Paolo, *La Casa Veneziana: nella storia della città dale origini all'ottocento* (Venezia: Marsilio Editori, 1986).
Massey, Anne, *The Independent Group: Modernism and Mass Culture, 1945–59* (Manchester: Manchester University Press, 1995).
Matless, David, *Landscape and Englishness* (London: Reaktion Books, 1998).
Maxwell, Robert, 'Two housing schemes at Milton Keynes', *The Architect's Journal*, vol. 162, no. 50 (10 December 1975), pp. 1247–60.
Mazzucco, Katia, '1941 *English Art and the Mediterranean*. A photographic exhibition by the Warburg Institute in London', *Journal of Art Historiography*, no. 5 (December 2011).
McKean, John, 'James Stirling and James Gowan: Leicester University Engineering Building 1959–63', in *Pioneering British 'High-Tech'* (London: Phaidon, 1999).
McVicar, Mhairi, *Precision in Architecture: Certainty, Ambiguity and Deviation* (Abingdon: Routledge, 2019).
Menin, Sarah, and Stephen Kite, *An Architecture of Invitation: Colin St John Wilson* (Aldershot: Ashgate, 2005).
Mordaunt Crook, J., 'Eastlake's Career', in Charles L. Eastlake, *A History of the Gothic Revival* (Leicester: Leicester University Press, 1978 [1872]), pp. 18–26.
Mordaunt Crook, J., *William Burges and the High Victorian Dream* (London: Frances Lincoln, 2013).

Morris, George Llewellyn, 'On Mr. Philip Webb's Town Work; Illustrated with Drawings by E. A. Rickards', *The Architectural Review*, vol. 2 (1 June 1897), pp. 199–208.

Morris, May, 'Morris as a Designer', in May Morris, *William Morris, Artist, Writer, Socialist. Vol. 1: The Art of William Morris; Morris as a Writer* (Cambridge: Cambridge University Press, 2012 [1936]), pp. 34–62.

Morris, William, 'Address on the collection of paintings of the English Pre-Raphaelite school in the City of Birmingham Museum and Art Gallery on Friday, October 24, 1891', in May Morris, *William Morris, Artist, Writer, Socialist. Vol. 1: The Art of William Morris; Morris as a Writer* (Cambridge: Cambridge University Press, 2012 [1936]), pp. 296–310.

Morris, William, 'Making the Best of It' (a paper read before the Trades' Guild of Learning and the Birmingham Society of Artists, 1879), in William Morris, *Hopes and Fears for Art. Five lectures delivered in Birmingham, London, and Nottingham, 1878–1881* (London: Ellis & White, 1882).

Morris, William, *News from Nowhere* (London: Thames & Hudson, 2017 [1892]), facsimile of the 1892 edition.

Morris, William, *Gothic Architecture: A Lecture for the Arts and Crafts Exhibition by William Morris* (London: Kelmscott Press, 1893, first spoken as a lecture at the New Gallery, for the Arts and Crafts Exhibition Society, 1889).

Morris, William, *Some Hints on Pattern-Designing* (London: Longmans, 1899, lecture given at The Working Men's College, London, 10 December 1881).

Morris, William, 'The Lesser Arts of Life' (1878), in William Morris, *Architecture, Industry and Wealth* (London: Longmans, Green, 1902).

Morris, William, *The Earthly Paradise: A Poem* (London: Longmans, Green, 1907 [1868–70]).

Mowl, Timothy, *Stylistic Cold Wars: Betjeman versus Pevsner* (London: Faber & Faber, 2011).

Mulazzani, Marco and Federico Bucci, *Luigi Moretti: Works and Writings* (New York: Princeton Architectural Press, 2000).

Murray, Irena, and Julian Osley, *Le Corbusier and Britain: An Anthology* (Abingdon: Routledge, 2009).

Musson, Jeremy, *Romantics and Classics: Style in the English Country House*, photography by Hugo Rittson Thomas (New York: Rizzoli, 2021).

Muthesius, Hermann, *The English House*, 3 vols., ed. Dennis Sharp, trans. Janet Seligman and Stewart Spencer (London: Frances Lincoln, 2007, first complete English edition, first published as *Das Englische Haus*, Berlin: Wasmuth, 1904, 1905).

Muthesius, Stefan, 'Germanness, Englishness, Jewishness, scientificness, popularization', in Peter Draper (ed.), *Reassessing Nikolaus Pevsner* (Aldershot: Ashgate, 2004), pp. 57–69.

Nairn, Ian, *Nairn's London* (London: Penguin Books, 2014 [1966]).

Neiswander, Judith A., *The Cosmopolitan Interior: Liberalism and the British Home 1870–1914* (New Haven and London: Yale University Press, 2008).

Newman, John, *Glamorgan: The Buildings of Wales* (New Haven and London: Yale University Press, 1995).

Newman, Oscar, *CIAM '59 in Otterlo* (London: Alec Tiranti, 1961).

Norberg-Schulz, Christian, *Nightlands: Nordic Building* (Cambridge, MA: MIT Press, 1996).

Ozturk, Anthony, 'Geo-Aesthetics: Venice and the Architecture of the Alps', in K. Hanley and E. Sdegno (eds.), *Ruskin, Venice and Nineteenth-Century Cultural Travel* (Venice: Università Ca' Foscari Venezia, 2010), pp. 187–211.

Pallasmaa, Juhani, *The Eyes of the Skin: Architecture and the Senses* (Chichester: Wiley-Academy, 2005).

Pallasmaa, Juhani, *The Thinking Hand: Existential and Embodied Wisdom in Architecture* (Chichester: John Wiley, 2009).

Parry, Linda (ed.), *William Morris*, V & A exhibition catalogue (London: Philip Wilson, V & A Museum, 1996).

Parry, Linda (ed.), *William Morris* (London: Philip Wilson, 1996).

Parry, Linda, *William Morris Textiles* (London: V & A Publishing, 2013).

Payne, Alina, *From Ornament to Object: Genealogies of Architectural Modernism* (New Haven and London: Yale University Press, 2012).

Petherbridge, Deanna, *The Primacy of Drawing: Histories and Theories of Practice* (New Haven and London: Yale University Press, 2010).

Pevsner, Nikolaus, *The Leaves of Southwell* (Harmondsworth: Penguin Books, 1945).

Pevsner, Nikolaus, 'Reassessment 4: Three Oxford Colleges', *The Architectural Review*, vol. 106, no. 632 (1 August 1949), pp. 120–4.

Pevsner, Nikolaus, 'Obituary, C. H. Holden 1874–1960', *The Architectural Review*, vol. 128, no. 766 (1 December 1960), pp. 446–8.

Pevsner, Nikolaus, *Pioneers of Modern Design: from William Morris to Walter Gropius* (London: Pelican Books, 1960 [1936]).

Pevsner, Nikolaus, *An Outline of European Architecture* (Harmondsworth: Penguin Books, 1963 [1943], 7th edition).

Pevsner, Nikolaus, *The Englishness of English Art* (Harmondsworth: Penguin Books, 1964 [1956]).

Pevsner, Nikolaus, *The Buildings of England, London, 1 The Cities of London and Westminster* (Harmondsworth: Penguin Books, 1973, 3rd edition).

Pevsner, Nikolaus, 'The Modern Movement in Britain (Introduction by Bridget Cherry)', in S. Charlton (ed.), *British Modern: Architecture and Design in the 1930s* (London: The Twentieth Century Society, 2007), pp. 13–38.

Pevsner, Nikolaus, *Visual Planning and the Picturesque*, ed. Mathew Aitchison (Los Angeles, CA: Getty Publications, 2010).

Pevsner, Nikolaus, *Pevsner: The Complete Broadcast Talks: Architecture and Art on Radio and Television, 1945–1977*, ed. Stephen Games (Farnham: Ashgate, 2014).

Philipson, Garry, *Aycliffe and Peterlee New Towns 1946–1988: Swords into Ploughshares and Farewell Squalor* (Cambridge: Publications for Companies, 1988).

Piper, John, 'England's Early Sculptors', *The Architectural Review*, vol. 80, no. 479 (1 October 1936), pp. 157–62.

Piper, John, 'The Architecture of Destruction', *The Architectural Review*, vol. 535, no. 90 (1 July 1941), pp. 25–30.

Piper, John, 'Pleasing Decay', *The Architectural Review*, vol. 102, no. 609 (1 September 1947), pp. 85–94.

Posener, Julius, 'Knots in the Master's Carpet', *Architectural Design* (December 1951), pp. 353–7.

Powell, Kenneth, 'Richard Rogers Partnership: Lloyd's Building, London, 1978–86', in *Pioneering British 'High-Tech'* (London: Phaidon, 1999).

Powers, Alan, *Serge Chermayeff: Designer, Architect, Teacher* (London: RIBA Publications, 2001).

Powers, Alan, 'New Town Artistry', *The Architects' Journal*, vol. 24, no. 13 (11 October 2001), pp. 44–8.

Powers, Alan, *Britain: Modern Architectures in History* (London: Reaktion Books, 2007).

Prior, Edward S., *The Cathedral Builders in England* (London: Seeley, 1905).

Prior, Edward S., 'Architectural Modelling' (June 1895), in D. Valinsky (ed.), *An Architect Speaks: The Writings and Buildings of Edward Schröder Prior* (Exeter: Short Run Press, David Valinsky, 2014), pp. 80–3.

Prior, Edward S., 'Texture as a Quality of Art and a Condition of Architecture' (1889, pub. 1890), in D. Valinsky (ed.), *An Architect Speaks: The writings and Buildings of Edward Schröder Prior* (Exeter: Short Run Press, David Valinsky, 2014), pp. 44–56.

Quennell, Marjorie, and Quennell, C. H. B., *A History of Everyday Things in England: The Age of Production 1851–1934* (London: Batsford, 1934).

Randall, H. J., 'History in the Open Air', *Antiquity*, vol. 8, no. 29 (March 1934), pp. 5–23.

Read, Herbert (ed.), *Unit 1: The Modern Movement in English Architecture, Painting and Sculpture* (London: Cassell, 1934).

Read, Richard, 'Circling Each Other: Henry Moore and Adrian Stokes', http://www.tate.org.uk/art/research-publications/henry-moore/richard-read-circling-each-other-henry-moore-and-adrian-stokes-r1151308 [accessed 6 March 2018].

Richards, J. M., 'Black and White: An Introductory Study of a National Design Idiom', *The Architectural Review*, vol. 82, no. 492 (1 November 1937), pp. 165–76.

Richards, J. M., *An Introduction to Modern Architecture* (Aylesbury: Penguin Books, 1953 [1940]).

Robbins, David (ed.), *The Independent Group: Postwar Britain and the Aesthetics of Plenty* (Cambridge, MA: MIT Press, 1990).

Rowe, Colin, 'Mannerism and Modern Architecture', *The Architectural Review*, vol. 107, no. 641 (1 May 1950), pp. 289–99.

Rowe, Colin, 'James Stirling: A Highly Personal and Very Disjointed Memoir', in P. Arnell and T. Bickford (eds.), *James Stirling: Buildings and Projects, James Stirling, Michael Wilford and Associates* (London: The Architectural Press, 1984), pp. 10–27.

Rowe, Colin and Fred Koetter, 'Collage City', *The Architectural Review*, vol. 158, no. 942 (1 August 1975), pp. 66–92.

Rudofsky, Bernard, *Architecture without Architects: A Short Introduction to Non-pedigreed Architecture* (London: Academy Editions, 1964).

Sadler, Simon, *Archigram: Architecture without Architecture* (Cambridge, MA: MIT Press, 2005).

Saint, Andrew, *Architect and Engineer: A Study in Sibling Rivalry* (New Haven and London: Yale University Press, 2007).

Saint, Andrew, *Richard Norman Shaw* (New Haven and London: Yale University Press, 2010, revised edition).

Saxl, F. and Wittkower, R., *British Art and the Mediterranean* (London: Oxford University Press, 1969 [reprint of 1948]).

Schinkel, Karl Friedrich, *Collection of Architectural Designs* (Guildford: Butterworth Architecture, 1989, facsimile of 1866 edition of *Sammlung Architektonischer Entwürfe*).

Schmarzow, August, 'The Essence of Architectural Creation', in H. F. Mallgrave and Eleftherios Ikonomou (eds.), *Empathy, Form and Space: Problems in German Aesthetics 1873–1893* (Santa Monica, CA: Getty Center for the History of Art and the Humanities, 1994), pp. 281–97.

Schuller, Manfred, 'Le facciate dei palazzo medioevale di Venezia. Ricerche su singoli esempi architettonici', in Francesco Valcanover and Wolfgang Wolters (eds.), *L'Architettura Gotica Veneziana* (Venice: Instituto Veneto di Scienze, Lettere ed Arti, 2000), pp. 280–349.

Schulz, Juergen, *The New Palaces of Medieval Venice* (University Park, PA: Pennsylvania State University Press, 2004).

Segal, Hannah, 'A Psycho-Analytical Approach to Aesthetics', in M. Klein, P. Heimann, and R. E. Money-Kyrle (eds.), *New Directions in Psychoanalysis: The Significance of Infant Conflict in the Pattern of Adult Behaviour* (London: Tavistock, 1955), pp. 384–405.

Shapiro, Harold I. (ed.), *Ruskin in Italy: Letters to His Parents 1845* (Oxford: Clarendon Press, 1972).

Shimada, Takau, 'Is Sharawadgi Derived from the Japanese Word Sorowaji?', *The Review of English Studies*, vol. 48, no. 191 (August 1997), pp. 350–2.

Silver, Nathan, *The Making of Beaubourg: A Building Biography of the Centre Pompidou, Paris* (Cambridge, MA: MIT Press, 1994).

Sitwell, Sacheverell, *British Architects and Craftsmen* (London: Batsford, 1946–7, 3rd edition).

Sloan, Kim (ed.), *Places of the Mind: British Watercolour Landscapes 1850–1950* (London: British Museum and Thames & Hudson, 2017).

Smart, C. M., *Muscular Churches: Ecclesiastical Architecture of the High Victorian Period* (Fayetteville, AK: University of Arkansas Press, 1989).

Smith, Deborah (ed.), *The New Art Gallery Walsall* (London: Batsford, 2002).

Smithson, Alison, Peter Smithson, and Theo Crosby, 'The New Brutalism', *Architectural Design*, vol. 25, no. 1 (January 1955), p. 1. Reprinted in Banham, Reyner, *The New Brutalism: Ethic or Aesthetic?* (London: The Architectural Press, 1966), pp. 45–6.

Spalding, Frances, *John Piper, Myfanwy Piper: Lives in Art* (Oxford: Oxford University Press, 2009).

Stamp, Gavin, 'Introduction', in G. Stamp (ed.), 'Britain in the Thirties', *Architectural Design*, vol. 49, nos. 10/11 (1979), pp. 2–43.

Stamp, Gavin, *The Great Perspectivists* (London: Trefoil Books, 1982).

Stierli, Martino, 'Taking on Mies: Mimicry and Parody of Modernism in the Architecture of Alison and Peter Smithson and Venturi / Scott Brown', in Mark Crinson and Claire Zimmerman (eds.), *Neo-avant-garde and Postmodern: Postwar Architecture in Britain and Beyond* (New Haven, CT: The Yale Center for British Art, 2010), pp. 151–74.

Stirling, James, 'Garches to Jaoul', *The Architectural Review*, vol. 118, no. 705 (September 1955), pp. 145–51.

Stirling, James, 'Design Philosophy and Recent Work', *James Stirling Michael Wilford and Associates* (London: Academy Editions, 1990), pp. 7–13.

Stokes, Adrian, 'Form in Art', in M. Klein, P. Heimann, and R. E. Money-Kyrle (eds.), *New Directions in Psychoanalysis: The Significance of Infant Conflict in the Pattern of Adult Behaviour* (London: Tavistock, 1955), pp. 406–20.

Stokes, Adrian, 'An Influence of Buildings on the Graphic Arts in the West', typescript with handwritten amendments and additions by Stokes, Tate Archive TGA 8816/181. Given as a talk to the Institute of Contemporary Arts, February 1956: 'The Prime Influence of Buildings on the Graphic Arts of the West'. See http://www.helpmego.to/ica/OldWEBSITE/history/50years.pdf [accessed 31 October 2013].

Stokes, Adrian, *The Critical Writings of Adrian Stokes*, 3 vols., ed. Lawrence Gowing (London: Thames & Hudson, 1978).

Street, George Edmund, 'On the Proper Characteristics of a Town Church', *Ecclesiologist*, vol. 11 (1850), pp. 227–33.

Street, George Edmund, 'The True Principles of Architecture, and the Possibility of Development', *Ecclesiologist*, vol. 13 (1852), pp. 247–62.

Street, George Edmund, 'On Colour as Applied to Architecture', *Associated Architectural Societies, Reports and Papers*, vol. 3, part 2 (1855), pp. 348–66.

Street, George Edmund, 'Lecture on the Historic Architecture of Venice, Italy by G. E. Street', *Builder*, vol. 17 (26 February 1859), pp. 146–8 and (5 March 1859), pp. 170–1.

Street, Arthur Edmund, *Memoir of George Edmund Street, RA* (London: John Murray, 1888).

Street, George Edmund, *Brick and Marble in the Middle Ages: Notes of Tours in the North of Italy* (London: John Murray, 1874 [1855], 2nd edition).

Summerson, John, 'Act 3: Christian Gothic. Scene 1: William Butterfield', *The Architectural Review*, vol. 98, no. 588 (1 December 1945), pp. 166–75.

Summerson, John, *Architecture in Britain 1530 to 1830* (Harmondsworth: Penguin Books, 1970).

Summerson, John, 'Vitruvius Ludens', *The Architectural Review*, vol. 173, no. 1033 (March 1983), pp. 18–21.

Summerson, John, 'Vitruvius Ridens or Laughter at the Clore', *The Architectural Review*, vol. 181, no. 1034 (June 1987), pp. 45–6.

Temple, Sir William, *The Works of Sir William Temple in Two Volumes* (London: J. Round et al., 1731).

Thompson, Paul, 'All Saints' Church, Margaret Street, Reconsidered', *Architectural History*, vol. 8 (1965), pp. 73–94.

Thompson, Paul, *William Butterfield* (Cambridge, MA: MIT Press, 1971).

Truefitt, George, *Designs for Country Churches* (London: Joseph Masters, 1850).

Tunnard, Christopher, 'Colour and the Cottage Garden', *The Architectural Review*, vol. 83, no. 494 (1 January 1938), pp. 37–9.

Tunnard, Christopher, *Gardens in the Modern Landscape* (Philadelphia, PA: University of Pennsylvania Press, 2014 [1948, 2nd edition, originally published 1938]).

Ursprung, Philip, *Caruso St John: Almost Everything* (Barcelona: Ediciones Polígrafa, 2008).

Valinsky, David (ed.), *An Architect Speaks: The Writings and Buildings of Edward Schröder Prior* (Exeter: Short Run Press, David Valinsky, 2014).

Vall, Natasha, 'Social Engineering and Participation in Anglo-Swedish Housing 1945–1976: Ralph Erskine's Vernacular Plan', *Planning Perspectives*, vol. 28, no. 2 (2013), pp. 23–45.

Venturi, Robert, Denise Scott Brown, and Steven Izenour, *Learning from Las Vegas* (Cambridge, MA: MIT Press, 2017, facsimile of 1972 edition).

Verey, David, 'George Frederick Bodley: Climax of the Gothic Revival', in J. Fawcett (ed.), *Seven Victorian Architects* (London: Thames & Hudson, 1976), pp. 75–101.
Vidler, Anthony, *The Architectural Uncanny: Essays in the Modern Unhomely* (Cambridge, MA: MIT Press, 1992).
Vidler, Anthony, *James Frazer Stirling: Notes from the Archive* (Montreal: Canadian Center for Architecture, and Yale University, 2010).
Walsh, Victoria, *Nigel Henderson: Parallel of Life and Art* (London: Thames & Hudson, 2001).
Wardle, George, 'Morris Exhibit at The Foreign Fair Boston, 1883–84', www.burrows.com [accessed February 2017].
Wardleworth, Dennis, 'Passing By: Architectural Sculpture in Inter-War London', *Henry Moore Institute Essays on Sculpture*, no. 47 (Leeds: Henry Moore Institute, 2005).
Warren, Edward, 'The Life and Work of George Frederick Bodley', *Journal of the Royal Institute of British Architects*, vol. 17 (1910), pp. 305–40.
Watkin, David, *A History of Western Architecture* (London: Laurence King, 1992 [1986]).
Watkinson, Ray, *William Morris as Designer* (London: Studio Vista, 1967).
Weaver, Lawrence (attrib. signed 'W'), 'Country Homes Gardens Old and New: Home Place, Holt, The Residence of the Rev. F. M. Meyrick-Jones', *Country Life*, vol. 26, no. 670 (6 November 1909), pp. 634–42.
Webb, M. de [*sic*], 'Furniture Manufacturers Association Showrooms, High Wycombe', *The Architects' Journal*, vol. 129, no. 3342 (14 March 1959), pp. 451–4.
Weston, Richard, *Materials, Form and Architecture* (London: Laurence King, 2003).
White, Gleeson, 'An Epoch Making House', *The Studio*, vol. 14 (1898), pp. 102–12.
Whiteley, Nigel, *Reyner Banham: Historian of the Immediate Future* (Cambridge, MA: MIT Press, 2002).
Whyte, William, *Unlocking the Church: The Lost Secrets of Victorian Sacred Space* (Oxford: Oxford University Press, 2017).
Wigley, Mark, *White Walls, Designer Dresses* (Cambridge, MA: MIT Press, 1995).
Wild, Tessa, *William Morris and His Palace of Art* (London: Philip Wilson, 2018).
Wilford, Michael, 'An Evolving Design Philosophy', in *James Stirling and Michael Wilford: Architectural Monographs*, no. 32 (London: Academy Editions, 1993).
Wilhide, Elizabeth, *William Morris: Decor and Design* (London: Pavilion, 2014).
Wilkinson, Alan (ed.), *Henry Moore: Writings and Conversations* (Aldershot: Lund Humphries, 2002).
Williamson, Beth, *Between Art Practice and Psychoanalysis Mid-Twentieth Century: Anton Ehrenzweig in Context* (Farnham: Ashgate, 2015).
Wilson, Colin St John, 'The Vertical City', *The Observer* (17 February 1952), reproduced in Murray and Osley, *Le Corbusier and Britain*, pp. 170–2.
Wilson, Colin St John, 'Patterns in Living', *The Observer* (20 July 1952).
Wilson, Colin St John, 'The Natural Imagination: An Essay on the Experience of Architecture', *The Architectural Review*, vol. 185, no. 1103 (January 1989), pp. 64–70.
Wilson, Colin St John, 'Sandy Wilson: Living Dangerously' [James Frazer Stirling 1926–1992: in memoriam], *The Architectural Review*, vol. 191, no. 1150 (December 1992), p. 13.

Wilson, Colin St John, 'Brick', *Scroope: The Cambridge Architecture Journal*, no. 6 (1994–5).
Wilson, Colin St John, *Architectural Reflections: Studies in the Philosophy and Practice of Architecture* (Manchester: Manchester University Press, 2000).
Wolfe, Ivor de, 'Townscape: A Plea for an English Visual Philosophy Founded on the True Rock of Sir Uvedale Price', *The Architectural Review*, vol. 106, no. 636 (1 December 1949), pp. 354–62.
Wölfflin, Heinrich, *Principles of Art History: The Problem of the Development of Style in Later Art*, trans. M. D. Hottinger of the 7th edition of 1929 of *Kunstgeschichtliche Grunbegriffe*, originally published 1915 (Mineola, NY: Dover Publications, 1950).
Wood, Christopher, *The Pre-Raphaelites* (London: Weidenfeld & Nicolson, 1981).
Yorke, F. R. S., *The Modern House* (London: The Architectural Press, 1957 [1934]).
Zimmerman, Claire, 'Photography into Building in Post-war Architecture: The Smithsons and James Stirling', *Art History*, vol. 35, no. 2 (April 2012), pp. 270–87.

INDEX

Aalto, Alvar 155, 162, 215
    Baker House Senior Students' Dormitory, MIT, Cambridge, Mass. 163
    Paimio Sanatorium 136
    Säynätsalo Town Hall 163
Abbeville 17
Aben, Rob, and Saskia de Wit 49
Acland, Henry Wentworth 213
Adams, Holden and Pearson 111, Figs. 4.8–9
    see also Holden
Adams, Percy 106, 107, 274 n. 26
Adams, Robert 171
    Group 10, 'This is Tomorrow' exhibition (1956) 171, Fig. 6.11
    see also 'This is Tomorrow'
Addison, Joseph 149
African art 119
Alberti, Leon Battista 120, 173
    Tempio Malatestiano, Rimini 120, 173
Alexandria 25
    Anglican church of St Mark 25
Allan, John 131
Alloway, Lawrence 169
Alps 19, 20, 36
Amato, Joseph A.
    Surfaces: A History 2
Anglo-Saxon architecture 85, 94, 117, 158, 256
    All Saints, Earls Barton, Northamptonshire 94
    Jarrow monastery 85
    St Peter, Monkwearmouth 86
Appleyard, Bryan 230
Arabia 22, 24, 25, 63
Archer, Thomas 204
    St John's, Smith Square, Westminster, London 204

Archigram 151, 205, 223–35, 244, 254
    Archigram 1 224, 225, 226
    Archigram 2 226
    Archigram 3 226, 228
    Furniture Manufacturers Association Building 225, 226, Fig. 8.1
    Nottingham Shopping Viaduct 228, Fig. 8.3
    Piccadilly Circus competition 226
    plug-in city 151, 228
    see also Chalk, Cook, Webb
Architectural Review 5, 6, 7, 31, 32, 61, 63, 87, 100, 106, 118, 125, 127, 128, 129, 130, 132, 133, 134, 136, 140, 145, 147, 150, 153, 154, 156, 159, 171, 179, 181, 182, 187, 189, 190, 217, 235, 244, Figs. 5.2, 5.4, 5.5, 5.6, 5.7, 5.8, 5.9. 5.10, 5.11, 5.13, 7.1, 7.9, 7.10, 7.11
Arnheim, Rudolf 88, 198
    Art and Visual Perception 198
    The Dynamics of Architectural Form 88
Art-Brut 158
    see also As-Found, Brutalism
Art-Deco architecture 123
Art-Nouveau architecture 194
Arts and Crafts 3, 4, 5, 43, 69, 76, 83, 85, 87, 89, 96, 101, 102, 117, 123, 232, 245, 254, 255
    domestic interior Chapter 2 *passim*
    gardens 46–8, 55–6, 66, 96, Figs. 2.2, 2.3, 3.19
Arup, Ove, and Partners 167, 184, 229, 232, Fig. 6.9
    see also Jenkins, Ronald

as-found 88, Chapter 6 *passim*, 195, 201, 210, 213
  see also Art-Brut, Brutalism
Asplund, Gunnar 217, 221
  Göteborg Law Courts 217
Assyrian art 117, 119
Athens
  Tower of the Winds 114
Attenborough, Frederick Levi 147
Austria 245

Backström, Sven 236
Baird, George, and Charles Jencks
  Meaning in Architecture 194
Bakema, Jacob 189
Baker, Arthur 161
  Hereford Square flats, 161, Fig. 6.4
  see also Wilson
Bakewell, Robert
  Introduction to Geology 35
Banham, Reyner 99, 153, 154, 163, 169, 171, 174, 195, 211, 225, 226, 229, 235
  Age of the Masters 99
  'Façade' 181–2, 187
  'Italian Eclecticism' 190
  'Revaluation: Futurism' 174
  'Revenge of the Picturesque' 153, 154, 155, 156, 215
  'The great wall of Tyne' 235
  'The New Brutalism' 156, 158, 165, 167, 172
  The New Brutalism 158, 159, 209–10
  Theory and Design in the First Machine Age 153
Barjavel, René 232
Baroque architecture 31, 69, 89, 96, 101, 102, 110, 142, 143, 144, 181, 189, 204, 208, 209, 256
Barragán, Luis 176
Bath 128
  Bath stone 36, 104
  Circus 140, 158
  Royal Crescent 140
Bayes, Walter 118
Beatles, The 229
Beattie, Susan 104
  The New Sculpture 102

Beauvais 36
Belcher, John 102
  Institute of Chartered Accountants, City of London 102, Fig. 4.2
Beresford-Hope, Alexander 26
Beresford Pite, Arthur
  Institute of Chartered Accountants, City of London Fig. 4.2
  St. Bartholomew's Hospital, London 113
Berlin
  Altes Museum 215
  Gardener's House, Charlottenhof, Potsdam 215–16
  Haupstadt Competition 226, 240
  Textile Academy 184
Bernini, Gian Lorenzo 121
Betjeman, John 4, 5, 69, 125, 128
béton brut (raw concrete) 158, 159, 175, 255
Binski, Paul
  Gothic Wonder: Art, Artifice and the Decorated Style 1290–1350 2, 148, 257
Blake, William 127
Blashfield, John Marriott 28
Blomfield, Reginald 96
  'The Cult of Ugliness' 118
  The Quadrant, Regent Street, London 96
Blore, John
  Hereford Square, Kensington, London 161
Blundell Jones, Peter 219, 240
Bodley, George Frederick 1, 4, Chapter 3 *passim*
  All Saints, Jesus Lane, Cambridge 76, Fig. 3.10
  'Architecture: The Minster' 83
  'English Architecture in the Middle Ages' 73
  Holy Trinity, South Kensington, London 4, 69–73, 76, 80, 82, Figs. 3.1, 3.3
  St Augustine's, Pendlebury 73, 85, Figs. 3.4, 3.6
  St German's, Roath, Cardiff 81–2, Fig. 3.9

St John the Baptist, Tue Brook, Liverpool 83–5, Fig. 3.11
St Mary's, Eccleston, Cheshire 77–80, Figs. 3.7–8
St Michael and All Angels, Brighton 82
'Some Principles that may be Guides for the Applied Arts' 76–7
Bofill, Ricardo 245
Bone, James 118–20
Bone, Muirhead 112, 113
  55 Broadway, Westminster, London (perspective view) Fig. 4.8
Booth, Philip, and Nicholas Taylor
  Cambridge New Architecture 163
Boullée, Étienne-Louis 11
Bowellism 226, 232
Braque, Georges 136
Brazil 135
Brett, Lionel 184
Bricolage 8, 125, 136, 169, 235, 243, 244, 254
Brighton
  St Michael and All Angels 82
Bristol
  Abbey gatehouse 104–5
  Bristol Central Library 101, 104–7, Figs. 4.3–5
  Bristol Royal Infirmary 112
  Church of the Holy Innocents, Knowle 136, 138, Fig. 5.8
  St Andrew's, Clifton 138–9
British School of psychoanalysis 167, 174, 176
Britishness 1–3, 190, 244, 253–7
Bronte, Emily
  Wuthering Heights 32
Brooks, Michael
  John Ruskin and Victorian Architecture 12
Brunel, Isambard Kingdom 244
  The Great Eastern 215
Brutalism 1, 6, 7, 8, Chapter 6 *passim*, 179, 195, 209, 210, 223, 224, 226, 244, 253, 254, 255
  wallpaper 164–8, Figs. 6.7, 6.9
  see also Art-Brut, As-Found, Banham

Buckland, William
  Geology and Mineralogy Considered with Reference to Natural Theology 35, 38
Bulgaria 100
  Tŭrnovo 100
Burlington, Richard Boyle
  Chiswick House, Chiswick, London 208
Bullen, J. B. 93
Burckhardt, Jacob 16
Burges, William 53
Burne-Jones, Edward 4, 46, 48, 50, 53, 66, 257
  Broadwood piano case, 1 Holland Park 61, Fig. 2.7
  Oxford Union Society murals 50
  Pan and Psyche 61, Fig. 2.7
  'Sir Degrevaunt' mural 54
  The Backgammon Players 55
  The Green Dining Room, South Kensington Museum 57
  see also Morris, Webb
Burne-Jones, Georgiana 48
Burnet, John and Thomas Tait
  Adelaide House, London 123
Burri, Alberto 165, 167
Butterfield, William 1, 3, 6, 7, Chapter 1 *passim*, 69, 79, 159, 177, 203, 213, 222, 255
  All Saints, Margaret Street, London 25–33, 38, Figs. 1.7, 1.8
  Keble College, Oxford 213
  St Alban's, Holborn, London 32, 159
  St Matthias, Stoke Newington, London 32, 159
  St Paul's Cathedral, Melbourne, Australia 30
Byzantine architecture 13, 14, 15, 17, 24, 25, 69, 93, 94, 127, 254, Fig. 3.18

Cairo 25
California 176
Cambridge, UK 176, 216
  All Saints, Jesus Lane 76, 82, Fig. 3.10
  Churchill College 194

Grantchester Road house 176
Harvey Court, Gonville and Caius College 156, 163
King's College Chapel 254
Peterhouse College (William Stone Building) 176
School of Architecture extension 163, 176, Fig. 6.6
Sidgwick Avenue 150
Campbell, Colin 190
Cardiff
St German's, Roath 81–2. Fig. 3.10
Carpaccio, Vittore
Healing of the Possessed Man 15
Carpenter, Edward 59
Carpenter, Richard Cromwell
St Mary Magdalene, Munster Square, London 34, 41
Carter, Peter 126
Bentham Road Estate, Hackney, London 162, 187, Fig. 6.5
Coventry Cathedral competition 126
Group 10, 'This is Tomorrow' exhibition (1956) 171, Fig. 6.11
see also Wilson
Caruso, Adam, and Peter St John 1, 7–8, 244–53
Museum of Childhood, Bethnal Green, London 253
The New Art Gallery, Walsall 3, 247–53, Figs. 8.15–16
carving 1, 4–5, Chapter 4 *passim*, 125, 127, 169, 206, 245, 256, Figs. 4.11. 4.13
in contrast to modelling 102–4, 120–3, 163, 173–5
see also Epstein, Gill, Stokes, Moore
Casson, Hugh and Neville Conder
Sidgwick Avenue, Cambridge 150
Celle, Pierre de, Bishop of Chartres 148
Celtic art 127, 146
Cézanne, Paul 136
Chalk, Warren, Ron Herron, Dennis Crompton, and John Attenborough, for Group Leader Norman Engleback (Special Works Division, London County Council)

South Bank Arts Centre, London 226, Fig. 8.2
Chambers, Robert
Vestiges of Creation 35
Chamonix 19, 20
Chatterjee, Anuradha
John Ruskin and the Fabric of Architecture 2
Chaucer, Geoffrey
The Canterbury Tales 104
Cheetham, Mark A.
Artwriting, Nation, and Cosmopolitanism in Britain 3
Chermayeff, Serge 122, 132
Bentley Wood, E. Sussex 132–3, Figs. 4.14, Fig. 5.4
Chicago 6, 170, 195
Alumni Memorial Hall (IIT) 6, 157
Chemical Engineering and Metallurgy Building (IIT) 6, 157
Illinois Institute of Technology (IIT) 6, 170, 195
Lake Shore Drive Apartments 157, 187
Unity Temple, Oak Park 107
China 129
garden landscapes 129
CIAM (Congrès Internationaux d'Architecture Moderne) 239
Otterlo, Holland (1959) 239
CLASP, Hertfordshire schools programme 156
Clifton-Taylor, Alec 34
The Pattern of English Building 3
Coade stone 179, 187
Cockerell, Charles Robert 107
Westminster Insurance Company Offices, The Strand, London 107
Collymore, Peter 240
Cologne 82
Colquhoun, Alan 232–3
Bentham Road Estate, London 162, 187, Fig. 6.5
see also Wilson
Constable, John 136, 249
Constructed Abstract Art 195–203, 256
see also Pasmore

consumerism 8, 156, 169, 170, 177, 228, 235
constructivism 131, 196, 198, 203, 205, 213
Cook, Peter 8, 223–35, 244, 254
  see also Archigram
Cook, Peter, and David Greene
  Nottingham Shopping Viaduct 228, Fig. 8.3
Cook, Peter, David Greene, and Mike Webb
  Archigram 1 224–5
Cook, Peter, and Gordon Sainsbury
  Piccadilly Circus competition 226
Cordingley, Alan
  Sheffield University competition 203–8, Figs. 7.14–15
  see also Stirling
Cork, Richard 115
Cornish, Francis Warre 45–6
Coste, Pascal
  Architecture Arabe ou Monuments du Kaire 25
Cotman, John Sell 139
Cox, Anthony 131
Crane, Walter 60, 61
Crawford, O. G. S. (Osbert Guy Stanhope) 126
Crinson, Mark 161, 189, 205–6
Crosby, Theo 158–9, 196
Cross, Chris, Jeremy Dixon, Mike Gold, Ed Jones, Jim Muldrew, Don Ritson, Derek Walker, Philip Ware
  Netherfield housing, Milton Keynes, Buckinghamshire 237, Fig. 8.9
Cubism 100, 101, 107, 115, 127, 136, 191, 197, 202
Cubitt, James
  Church Design for Congregations 73, Fig. 3.5
Cullen, Gordon 5, 125, 128, 129, 132, 134, 136, 140, 150, 243
  'Bankside Regained' 136, Fig. 5.6
  'house and garden near Halland, Sussex' (Bentley Wood) 132–3, Fig. 5.4
  The Concise Townscape 136
  'The Wall' 134–5, Fig. 5.5
  Townscape 136, 235–6
  'Townscape Casebook' 134, 149
  see also Townscape
Cullinan, Edward
  Fountains Abbey Visitor Centre, Yorkshire 245
curtain-wall 12, 205, 225
Curtis, Penelope 116

Dadaism 196
Daguerre, Louis-Jacques-Mandé 23
daguerrotype 23–4, Fig. 1.6
Daniel, Peter 197, 200, Fig. 7.12
Darley, Gillian 244
Davey, Peter 96, 215, 244
Day, Lewis F. 60–1
De Morgan, William 60
De Stijl 196, 198, 213
Deane (Thomas) and Woodward (Benjamin)
  Oxford University Museum 213
Del Renzio, Toni 169, 174–5
Derbyshire
  Hardwick Hall 247, Fig. 8.14
development 3, 10, 11, 33, 35, 37–8, 41, 79
Devey, George 48
  Cottages, Penshurst, Kent 48
Devonshire 41
Dick, William Reid 123
Disney, Walt 240
Dixon, Frank 197
Dobson, Frank 123
Dodd, Francis 107
Doesburg, Theo van 196
Dresden 143
Du Cerceau 249
Dubuffet, Jean 158, 165
Duccio, Agostino di
  Madonna and Child with Angels 121–2
  Tempio Malatestiano reliefs, Rimini 120, 174
Duchamp, Marcel 210
Dudok, Willem Marinus 100
Dürer, Albrecht 249

Eames, Charles and Ray 177, 229, 240
earth-veil 12, 30, 254
  see also Ruskin
Eastlake, Charles 12, 24, 34, 84, 85
  A History of The Gothic Revival 83
  Hints on Household Taste in Furniture, Upholstery and other Details 59
ecclesiology 9–10, 11, 24, 26, 27, 34, 41, 77
  The Ecclesiologist 26, 32, 33, 34, 35, 38
Edis, Robert W.
  The Decoration and Furnishing of Town Houses 63, Fig. 2.8
  Upper Berkeley Street, London 63, 65, 67, Fig. 2.8
Edwardian architecture Chapter 4 *passim*, 208, 256
Egyptian architecture 25, 123
  Luxor 136
Ehrenzweig, Anton 6, 167, 168, 169, 174, 176
  The Hidden Order of Art 167
  The Psychoanalysis of Artistic Vision and Hearing 167
  'Unconscious form-creation in art' 167
Eickstedt, Egon Freiherr von 146
Einzig, Richard Fig. 7.16
Eisenmann, Peter 244
  'Real and English: The Destruction of the Box I' 213
Elgin marbles 110
Eliot, Thomas Stearns 209
Elizabethan and Jacobean architecture 1, 56, 59, 158, 247, 252, 254
  Hardwick Hall 158, 247, Fig. 8.14
Emberton, Joseph
  Empire Hall, Olympia, London 204
Engler, Mira 134
English Gothic architecture
  decorated 2, 4, 28, 69, 79, 80, 82, 85, 47–8, 257
  perpendicular 4, 69, 79, 80, 105, 145, 146, 147, 148, 158, 247, 254, 256
Englishness 4, 5, 6, 8, 17, 53, 69, 71–85, 101, 117–18, 123, 125–7, 128–39, 144–51, 153–4, 158, 170–1, 176–7, 183–4, 208–9, 244, 247–9, 253–7
Epstein, Jacob 1, 5, 101, 107–11, 113, 116–20, 123, 249, 257 Figs. 4.6–7, Fig. 4.13
  Autobiography 107
  Day, 55 Broadway, Westminster, London 111, 118
  Figures for British Medical Association, London 107–11, Figs. 4.6–7
  Night, 55 Broadway, Westminster, London 111, 118, Fig. 4.13
Ernst, Max 139, 167
Erskine, Ralph 1, 7–8, 235–44, 245
  Arctic Town project 239–40, Fig. 8.10
  Byker Wall, Newcastle upon Tyne 8, 235–44, 245, Figs. 8.11–12
  Drottningholm house 238–9
  Eaglestone housing Milton Keynes, Buckinghamshire 238, 243, Fig. 8.8
  Killingworth New Town housing 236
  Lissma house 239
Etchells, Frederick 208
Euston Road School 196
Exeter
  Exeter Cathedral 148
Expressionism 86, 94, 100, 117, 118, 194, 203, 213, 238, 240

Façadism 6, 179–90
FAT (Fashion Architecture Taste) 193
  Islington Square housing, New Islington, Manchester 193
Faulkner, Kate 61
Felton, Monica 192
Festival of Britain 1951 136, 154, 191, 226, 236
Florence 16, 189, 247
  Palazzo del Popolo 247, 253
  Piazza della Signoria 247
  S. Miniato al Monte 189
  Villa Medici, Poggio a Caiano 208
Forty, Adrian Forty 223, 226
  Concrete and Culture: A Material History 3

Foster, Norman 223, 229
   Willis Faber and Dumas Building, Ipswich 223
   see also Team 4
Frampton, Kenneth 163, 230, 245, 247
France 135, 136, 145, 149
   Abbeville 17
   see also Paris
French Gothic architecture 69, 83, 145, 146, 254
   Rheims Cathedral 147
Fretton, Tony 245, 247
   Lisson Gallery, London 245–7, Fig. 8.13
Frey, Dagobert 146
   The English Character as Reflected in English Art (*Englisches Wesenin der bildenden Kunst*) 145–6
Froebel, Friedrich 106, 229
Fry, Maxwell
   Church Street, Chelsea, London 101
Fuller, Buckminster 229
Futurism 174

Galilee 94, Fig. 3.18
Garden City 235
Garman, Kathleen 249, 252
Garner, Thomas 81, Fig. 3.9
   see also Bodley
Garnham, Trevor 85
geology 10, 13, 17, 19–24, 35, 38, 41, 255
   strata 38, 214
Geneva 77
Gerard, John
   Herball or General Historie of Plantes 57
Gerber, Heinrich 232, Fig. 8.6
Gernsheim, Helmut 140, Figs. 5.9–11
Gestalt theory 167, 169, 171, 173, 176
Gibberd, Frederick 149, 151, 154, 162
   Harlow New Town, Market Square 149, Fig. 5.12
   Lansbury Estate, Poplar, London 154, 162, Fig. 6.1
   Stevenage New Town, Town Square 149

Gilbert, Wallis
   Hoover Building, Great West Road, London 215
Gill, Eric 5, 104, 111, 114, 121, 123
   North Wind, South Wind, East Wind, 55 Broadway, Westminster, London 116–18, Fig. 4.12
   'The Future of Sculpture' 117
Giorgione 173
Girouard, Mark 32, 249
Glastonbury Abbey 214
Gloag, John
   The English Tradition in Design 146, 147
Godwin, E. W. 63
Goldfinger, Ernö
   Group 7, 'This is Tomorrow' exhibition 196
   Willow Road, Hampstead, London 145
Goldfinger, Ernö, Victor Pasmore and Helen Phillips
   Group 7, 'This is Tomorrow' exhibition 196
Gollins (Frank), Melvin (James), Ward (Edmund Fisher) Partnership 205
Gombrich, Ernst 167
Goodhart-Rendel, Harry Stuart 32, 77, 79, 81, 85
   St Olave's House, Hay's Wharf, London 123
Gothic Revival architecture 9, 83, 88, 209
Göttingen 125, 143, 145
Gowan, James 156
   Flats, Ham Common, London 159, 209, 210, Fig. 6.3
   Leicester University Engineering Building 156, 203, 210–15, Fig. 7.16
   see also Stirling
Grieve, Alastair 195
Greece 24, 30, 208
Greene, Charles and Henry 176
Grillet, Edward 87, 90
Gropius, Walter 218
   Bauhaus, Dessau 194

Church Street, Chelsea, London 101
Fagus Factory, Alfeld an der Leine 194
Weissenhof Exhibition (1927) Stuttgart 99
Grotesqueness 30, 31–2, 76, 118
see also Ruskin
Gutkind, Erwin Anton
Community and Environment 190

Hafod 126
Hall, Michael 73
Hamilton, Richard 169, 170, 171
Hanson, Brian 106, 111
Hardy, Alex
Cambridge School of Architecture extension 163, Fig. 6.6
see also Wilson
Häring, Hugo 240
Harlow New Town
Market Square 149, Fig. 5.12
Harris, Alexandra
Weatherland: Writers and Artists Under English Skies 3
Harwood, Elain 32
'Butterfield and Brutalism' 159
Space Hope and Brutalism 159
Hastings, Hubert de Cronin (Ivor de Wolfe) 139, 148
'Exterior Furnishing or sharawaggi: the art of making urban landscape' 128–30, 132, Fig. 5.2
'Townscape: A Plea for an English Visual Philosophy founded on the true rock of Sir Uvedale Price' 133
see also Cullen, Townscape
Hauser, Kitty
Shadow Sites: Photography, Archaeology, and the British Landscape 1927–1955 3, 126
Haussmann, Georges-Eugène 183
Hawksmoor, Nicholas 5, 110, 123, 204, 222, 233, 256
Orangery, Kensington Palace, London 96
St Anne's Church, Limehouse, London 209
St George's in the East, London 204, 211, 218
Helsinger, Elizabeth 10, 17
Henderson, Judith 165
Henderson, Nigel 6, 168, 169, 195, 257
Bethnal Green, London photographs 165–7
Hammer Prints 164–5
Head of a Man 169
'Patio and Pavilion' (Group 6), 'This is Tomorrow' exhibition 169–70, Fig. 6.10
photograph of Eduardo Paolozzi ceiling paper to Ronald Jenkins's office at Ove Arup and Partners 168, Fig. 6.9
'Sgraffiti on a Window' 165–7, Fig. 6.8
see also Paolozzi
Hepworth, Barbara 114, 120, 169, 174
Herron, Ron, Warren Chalk, and Dennis Crompton
Lillington Street Housing competition, Westminster 226
Herzog (Jacques) and de Meuron (Pierre) 247
High-Tech architecture 7, 8, 223–35, 237, 244, 250, 253, 254, Figs. 8.4. 8.6–7.
see also Foster, Piano, Rogers
High Victorian architecture 3, 4, 10, 33, 43, 69, 76, 79, 83, 213, 254
Hitchcock, Henry-Russell 28, 194
Hobbs, John ('George') 23
Hodgkinson, Patrick 156, 163
Harvey Court, Cambridge 163
see also Martin, Wilson
Hogarth, William 148
Holden, Charles 1, 3, 4, 5, Chapter 4 *passim*, 191, 249, 257
Bristol Central Library 104–7, Figs. 4.3–5
Bristol Royal Infirmary 112
British Medical Association building, London 107–11, Figs. 4.6–7

design of a provincial market hall 101–2, Fig. 4.1
55 Broadway, Westminster, London 111–20, 254, 256, Figs. 4.8–13
'If Whitman Had Been an Architect' 106
Law Society, Chancery Lane, London 104
Piccadilly Station, London 147
'Thoughts For the Strong' 106
War Graves Commission 101
Holden, Margaret 105
Holford, William
plan for the precinct of St Paul's, London 149, Fig. 5.13
Holkham Hall, Norfolk 209
Holland 100, 211, 239
Honnecourt, Villard de 147
Hoozee, Robert
British Vision: Observation and Imagination in British Art 1750–1950 3
Hope, Thomas 216
Hopper, Thomas 22
Horace 86
Hornby, Frank 229
hortus conclusus, hortus ludi 4, 45–55, 66, Fig. 2.3
Houghton Hall, Norfolk 209
Howard, Ebenezer 235
Hudnut, Joseph
'The Post-modern House' 194
Hugo, Victor
Notre Dame de Paris 11
Hussey, Christopher
The Picturesque: studies in a point of view 126, 128, 136, 139

Iceland 63
Imago Group 167
Impressionist Art 133, 174
Incrustation 3, 10, 12–13, 16, 20, 27, 28, 30, 38, 253
see also Ruskin
Independent Group 2, 167, 169, 176, 187, 189, 190, 195, 196, 203
Institute of Contemporary Arts (ICA) 167
Parallel of Life and Art 167

International Style 5, 99, 100, 125, 130, 153, 191, 192, 194, 203, 204, 209, 256
Ionides, Alexander (Alecco) 60, 63
Ionides, Alexander Constantine 60
Iran (Persia) 62
Irchester, Northamptonshire 35
Ireland 41
Islamic architecture 25
Iznik tiles 61

James, Henry 63
The Wings of the Dove 52
Japanese architecture 129, 159, 205
Jencks, Charles 194, 219
The Language of Post-Modern Architecture 219
Jenkins, Ronald 167, 168, 175, Fig. 6.9
Joass, John James
Holy Trinity, South Kensington, London (perspective) 71, 73, Fig. 3.1
Jones, Inigo 190, 204, 208
Queen's House, Greenwich, London 208
Jones, Owen 25, 65
The Grammar of Ornament 25, 253
Jones, Thomas 2
Judd, Donald 245

Kahn, Louis 233, 245
Kempe, C. E. 82, 85
Kennedy, John F. 224
Kent 33, 34, 41, 46, 48
Kenyon, George
Newcastle Civic Centre 236
Kilpeck Church, Herefordshire 11, 127
Klein, Melanie 167, 171, 173, 174, 176
Krier, Leon 245
Kunstgeographie (geography of art) 2, 144, 146, 183, 257

Lasdun, Denys
Royal College of Physicians, Regent's Park, London 194
Lasdun, Denys and Lindsey Drake 180, Fig. 7.2

Late Modernist architecture 7, 30, 38, 203, 222
Laugier, Marc-Antoine 11
Laurana, Luciano
  Palace of Urbino 173, Fig. 7.5
Le Corbusier 65, 99, 130, 153, 154, 156, 158, 159, 161, 163, 169, 172, 175, 183, 189, 194, 206, 213, 222
  Algiers city-planning 240
  Cité d'Affaires, Algiers 187
  Jaoul houses, Paris 156, 159, 162, 209, 210
  Journey to the East 100
  L'art decorative d'aujourd'hui (The Decorative Art of Today) 100
  La Chaux-de-Fonds, villa (1916) 206
  Le Modulor 156
  Maison de Weekend 161
  Mathés house 99
  Notre Dame du Haut, Ronchamp 156, 171, 172
  Salvation Army Refuge, Paris 206
  Towards a New Architecture 207–8
  Unité d'Habitation, Marseilles 155, 157, 159, 187, 204
  'vertical garden-city', (1937) Paris Exhibition 154
  Villa Stein de Monzie, Garches 101, 209, 210, 213
  Ville-Radieuse 149
  Weissenhof Exhibition (1927) Stuttgart 99
Leach, F. R. 82
Leatherbarrow, David, and Mohsen Mostofavi
  Surface Architecture 2, 157, 210
Lewerentz, Sigurd 247
  St Peter's church, Klippan, Sweden 252
Leipzig
  Old Stock Exchange (Alte Börse) 144
Lemere, Harry Bedford 60, 61, Fig. 2.7
Lenné, Peter Joseph 216
Lethaby, William 57, 85
  All Saints, Brockhampton 88
  Architecture, Mysticism and Myth 93, 94, Fig. 3.18

Lewis, G. F.
  Illustrations of Kilpeck Church, Herefordshire 11
Lisieux 28
Liverpool 229
  Liverpool School of Architecture 206
  St John the Baptist, Tue Brook 83–4, Fig. 3.11
Livesay, G. A. Bligh 94
Lloyd, Reverend Percy Robert 88
Lombardy 19, 63
London 32, 34, 107, 110, 111, 113, 123, 140, 145, 154, 224, 225, 256
  Adelaide House 123
  Agar Street 111
  Albert Hall 71
  All Saints, Margaret Street 25–33, 38, Figs. 1.7–8
  Architectural Association School of Architecture (AA), Bedford Square 195, 205, 224
  Bedford Square 179, 180
  Bentham Road Estate, Hackney 155, 162, 187, 190, Fig. 6.5
  Bethnal Green 164, 165, 253
  Blackheath, SPAN housing 191
  British Library 215
  British Medical Association (The Strand) 101, 107–11, Figs. 4.6–7
  British Museum 46, 110
  Central School of Arts and Crafts 167
  Chiswick House, Chiswick 208
  Christ Church, Streatham 24–5
  Church Street, Chelsea 101
  Churchill Gardens, Pimlico 190
  Clore Gallery, Tate Britain 7, 215–22, Figs. 7.18–20
  Crystal Palace 8, 12, 25, 33, 146, 224
  Economist Building, St James 3, 156, 171, 215
  Empire Hall, Olympia 204
  55 Broadway, Westminster 101, 111–20, Figs. 4.8–12

INDEX

Fitzrovia 167
Hallfield Estate, Paddington 179–82, Figs. 7.1–2, 7.4
Ham Common (Flats), Richmond 6, 159, 209, 210, 222, Fig. 6.3
Hayward Gallery 3, 226
Hereford Square 159, 161, Fig. 6.4
Highgate 130, 131, 132, 256
Highpoint I, Hampstead 130, 131, 132, 180, 183, 190, 256
Highpoint II, Hampstead 6, 130, 131, 132, 145, 179, 180, 183, 256, Fig. 5.3
Holland House 60
Holy Trinity, South Kensington 4, 69–72, 76, 80, 82, Figs. 3.1, 3.3
Hoover Building, Great West Road 215
Inns of Court 150
Institute of Chartered Accountants, City of London 102, Fig. 4.2
Institute of Contemporary Art (ICA) 167
Isokon building, Lawn Road, Hampstead 175
Kelmscott House, Hammersmith 54–5, 59, 60, 65, 67, Fig. 2.4
Kensington Palace, The Orangery 96
Lansbury Estate, Poplar 154, 162, Fig. 6.1
Law Society, Chancery Lane 104
Leicester Galleries 121
Lillington Street Housing, Westminster 226
Limerston Street 164, 255, Fig. 6.7
Lisson Gallery 245, 246, Fig. 8.13
Lloyds Building, City of London 8, 228, 233–5, Fig. 8.7
Museum of Childhood, Bethnal Green 253
1 Holland Park 59–67, Fig. 2.7
Paul Mellon Centre, Bloomsbury Square 36
Piccadilly Circus 226
Piccadilly Hotel, Piccadilly 96
Piccadilly Station 147

Priory Green Estate, Finsbury 7, 182
Purcell Room 226
Quadrant, Regent St 96
Queen Elizabeth Hall 3, 226
Queen's House, Greenwich 208
Regent Street Polytechnic 225, 235
Regent's Park 183, 187, 194
Robin Hood Gardens, Poplar 235
Royal Academy 32, 73, 89
Royal College of Physicians, Regent's Park 194
Royal Festival Hall 176, 226
St Albans, Holborn 32, 159
St Anne's Church, Limehouse 209
St Bartholomew's Hospital 113
St George's in the East 204
St James's Park 111
St James's Street 22
St John's, Smith Square, Westminster 204
St Mary Magdalene, Munster Square 34, 41
St Matthias, Stoke Newington 32, 159
St Olave's House, Hay's Wharf 123
St Paul's Cathedral 149, Fig. 5.13
St Stephen's, Hampstead 83
Soane Museum, Lincoln's Inn Fields 219
South Bank 226
South Bank Arts Centre 226, Fig. 8.2
Spa Green Estate, Finsbury 182–7, Figs. 7.3–5
Strand 107
Strawberry Hill, Twickenham 129, 209
Tate Britain, Westminster 1, 7, 203, 216, Fig. 7.18
Tate Modern 1
Thames 123, 136
Unilever House 123
University College Hospital 112
Upper Berkeley Street 63, Fig. 2.8
Victoria and Albert Museum 57, 121, Fig. 2.6
Victoria Street 111
Warburg Institute 208

Waterloo Bridge 136, 226
Westminster Insurance Company Offices, The Strand 107
Whitechapel Art Gallery 169, Figs. 6.10–11
London County Council (LCC) 112, 155
Long, M. J. (Mary Jane) 215
British Library, London 215
see also Wilson
Loos, Adolf 245, 247, 248
Müller House, Prague 247, 248
'The Principle of Cladding' 250–2
Loris, Guillaume de, and Jean de Meun
Roman de la Rose 46, 49, Fig. 2.1
Loudon, John Claudius 146
Lubbock, Percy 45
Shades of Eton 45
Lubetkin, Berthold 1, 6–7, 130–1, 145, 179–90, 191–5, 196, 234, 256
Hallfield Estate, Paddington 179–82, Figs. 7.1–2, 7.4
Highpoint I, Hampstead 130, 131, 132, 180, 183, 190, 256
Highpoint II, Hampstead 6, 130, 131, 132, 145, 179, 180, 183, 256, Fig. 5.3
'L'Architecture en Angleterre' 183–4
Peterlee New Town 191–5, Figs. 7.7–8
Priory Green Estate, Finsbury 7, 182
Spa Green Estate, Finsbury 182–7, Figs. 7.3–5
see also Tecton
Lutyens, Edwin 90, 96, 218
Hestercombe, Somerset 96–7, Fig. 3.19
Lyall, Sutherland 236, 237, 243, 245
The State of British Architecture 3, 236
Lyell, Charles 35, 38
Principles of Geology 35
Lyons, Eric
SPAN housing, Blackheath, London 191

Macarthur, John
The Picturesque 171
MacCarthy, Fiona 59
MacCormac (Richard), Jamieson (Peter) and Pritchard (David) 244
McGrath, Raymond 132
house, Cobham, Surrey 133
house, St Ann's Hill, Chertsey, Surrey 133
McHale, John 169, 170
Mackail, J. W. 46, 53, 54, 62, Fig. 2.4
McKean, John 211
Pioneering British 'High-Tech' 223
Mackintosh, Charles Rennie
Hill House, Helensburgh 105
Maki, Fumihiko 205
Malatesta, Sigismondo 120
Malevich, Kazimir 163
Malory, Sir Thomas
Le Morte d'Arthur 50
Manchester
Islington Square housing, New Islington 193
Mannerist architecture 97, 101, 187, 189, 190, 206, 213, 219, 222
Mansueti, Giovanni
Miracle of the Relic of the Holy Cross 15, 16, Fig. 1.2
MARS (Modern Architectural Research Group) 100
Martin, Leslie 163, 176, 257
Circle: International Survey of Constructive Art 203, 257
Harvey Court, Cambridge 156, 163
Manor Road Libraries, Oxford 163
Royal Festival Hall, London 176, 226
see also Wilson
Matisse, Henri 139
Matless, David
Landscape and Englishness 3
Maxwell, Robert 237
Mayan art 115, 117
Mediterranean 31, 100, 146, 183, 204, 208, 210
megastructure 205, 228, 229, 237
Melbourne
St Paul's Cathedral 30
Melnikov, Constantin
Moscow Worker's Club 211

Mendelsohn, Erich 194
Metabolism 205
Michelangelo 174
   Archers shooting at a herm 175
   Captives 111
   St Peter's, Rome 206
Mies van der Rohe 157, 158, 159, 177
   Alumni Memorial Hall (IIT), Chicago 157
   Chemical Engineering and Metallurgy Building (IIT), Chicago 157
   Illinois Institute of Technology (IIT), Chicago 6, 170, 195
   Lake Shore Drive Apartments, Chicago 157, 187
   Weissenhof Exhibition (1927), Stuttgart 99
Millais, Sir John Everett 32
   Christ in the House of his Parents 32
Milner, Marion 167, 174
Milton Keynes 236
   Eaglestone housing 237–8, Fig. 8.8
   Netherfield housing 237–8, Fig. 8.9
Minimalism 245
Mirô, Joan 126, 139
Mondrian, Piet 7, 100, 189, 201, 203, 206, 241, 256
   Composition with Red (1936) 189
   Pier and Ocean 201
Monet, Claude 249
Monroe, Marilyn 170
Mont Cervin (The Matterhorn) 19, 20
Monte Rosa 20
Monza
   Duomo 20, Fig. 1. 4
Moore, Charles 245
Moore, Henry 5, 111, 114–16, 120–2, 123, 132, 169, 174
   Composition, 1933 121
   Recumbent Figure, Bentley Wood, E. Sussex 122, 132, Fig. 4.14
   Unit One statement 114
   West Wind, 55 Broadway, Westminster, London 114–15, 120, Figs. 4.10–11

Moretti, Luigi 189, 190, 206, 207, 211, 222
   Casa del Girasole, Rome 187, Fig. 7.6
   Spazio 189
   'Structures and Sequences of Spaces' 206
Moro, Peter
   Royal Festival Hall, London 176
Morris and Company 56
Morris, May 51, 56, 65
Morris, William 1, 2, 4, 6, 11, 22, 43, Chapter 2 *passim*, 69, 86, 117, 126, 132, 147, 164, 255, 257
   Boston International Trade Fair 56
   'Chrysanthemum' wallpaper 61
   'Daisy' wallpaper 56
   Earthly Paradise 47, 55, 63
   'Forest' tapestry 65
   'Fruit' (Pomegranate) wallpaper 57, 63
   Gothic Architecture 51
   Green Dining Room 57–9, Fig. 2.6
   Hammersmith carpet 61
   Kelmscott House, Hammersmith, London 54–5, Fig. 2.4
   Kelmscott Manor, Oxfordshire 56
   'Making the Best of It' 48
   News from Nowhere 12, 45
   1 Holland Park, London 59–67, Fig. 2.7
   Oxford Union Society murals 50, 51
   Pimpernel wallpaper 55
   Red House 46–55, 66–7, Figs. 2.2, 2.3
   St George cabinet 49–50, 53, Fig. 2.3
   Some Hints on Pattern-Designing 51, 52, 56
   tapestry 51, 55, 60, 65, 67, 255
   'The Lesser Arts of Life' 53
   'Trellis' wallpaper 47, 56, 65, Fig. 2.5
   'Vine' wallpaper 65, Fig, 2.9
   wallpaper 55–7, Figs. 2.5, 2.8, 2.9
   see also Burne-Jones, Webb

Mowl, Timothy
    Stylistic Cold Wars: Betjeman versus Pevsner 5, 125
Munich 142
Muthesius, Hermann
    The English House 51, 53, 90

Nairn, Ian
    Nairn's London 32
Nash, John 161, 216
    Regent's Park, London 183, 187
Nash, Paul 126, 128
Nazism 143, 144, 146
Neo-Romanticism 5, 6, 125, 126, 128, 139
Neo-Vernacular 1, 7, 8, 191, 235–44, 253
Nervi, Luigi 225
New, F. H. 54, Fig. 2.4
New Materiality 1, 7, 8, 244–57
New Objectivity (*Neue Sachlichkeit*) 7, 154, 182
New Sculpture 5, 102, 104, 123
New York 107, 109, 113, 154, 225
    Central Park 110
    Coney Island 109
    Harlem 109
    Lever House 205
    Long Island 109
    Museum of Modern Art (MOMA) 237
Newby, Frank
    Group 10, 'This is Tomorrow' exhibition (1956) 171, 172, Fig. 6.11
Newcastle upon Tyne 240, 243, 244
    Byker Wall 8, 235–44, Figs. 8.11–12
    Cathedral 57
    Hadrian's Wall 241
    Jarrow monastery 85
    King's College, University of Durham 196
    Newcastle Civic Centre 236
Newman, Barnett 245
Newman, John Henry 11
Nicholson, Ben 114, 169, 174, 203, 245

Nitzchke, Oscar
    Maison de la Publicité project, Paris 230, Fig. 8.5
Norberg-Schulz, Christian 238, 239
    Nightlands 238

Olav V, King of Norway 236
'Old English' Vernacular Revival 76, 86
organic architecture 87, 129, 156, 172, 240
orientalism 25, 28, 63
Östberg, Ragnar
    Stockholm City Hall 236
Oud, Jacobus Johannes Pieter
    Weissenhof Exhibition (1927), Stuttgart 99
Oxford 77, 140, 149, 216
    Christ Church 140, Figs. 5.9–11
    Corpus Christi College 140
    Florey Building 32, 218
    Keble College 213
    Magdalen College 140
    Manor Road Libraries 163
    Merton Street 142
    Oxford University Museum 8, 213
    Pembroke College 140
    St Aldates's Church 140
    St Mary and St Nicholas, Littlemore 11
    SS Philip and James 36
    Union Society 50, 51
Oxford Movement 11

Palladian architecture 6, 131, 141, 158, 204
Palladio, Andrea 6, 158, 183, 249
    Villa Rotonda, Vicenza 206, 208
Pallasmaa, Juhani 90
    The Eyes of the Skin 176
Paolozzi, Eduardo 1, 6, 167, 169, 195, 210, 257
    ceiling paper to Ronald Jenkins's office at Ove Arup and Partners 168, Fig. 6.9
    Hammer Prints 164–5
    Head, 1953 167
    'Patio and Pavilion' (Group 6), 'This is Tomorrow' exhibition 169–70, Fig. 6.10

wallpaper, bathroom at Limerston Street, London 164, 255, Fig. 6.7
see also Henderson, Smithson
Paris 11, 107, 154 183, 229
   Boulevard Raspail 208
   Centre Pompidou 224, 228–33, Figs. 8.4, 8.6
   Champs Elysées 210, 230
   Jaoul houses 156, 210
   Maison de la Publicité 230–1, Fig. 8.5
   Rue de Renard 229
   Rue de Rivoli 208
   Salvation Army Refuge 206
Parry, Linda 61
Pasmore, Victor 1, 6–7, 256, 257
   Abstract in Black and White (1957) 201
   Apollo Pavilion, Peterlee New Town 202
   Line and Space No 23 (1964) 201
   Peterlee New Town 195–203, Figs. 7.9–13
   'What is Abstract Art?' 197
   'Where the Artist Comes In' 203
Paxton, Joseph 213, 244
   Chatsworth, conservatories 213
   Crystal Palace, London 224
Payne, Alina
   From Ornament to Object 52
Perret, Auguste 131
Peterlee New Town 7, 191–203, 256, 257, Figs. 7.7–13
   Apollo Pavilion 202
   Sunny Blunts housing 202
Petherbridge, Deanna 136
Pevsner, Nikolaus 5, 73, 94, 102, 107, 113, 128, 130, 139, 153, 183, 208, 213, 222, 247, 249, 254, 256, 257
   An Outline of European Architecture 144, 148
   Leipziger Barock. Die Baukunst der Barockzeit in Leipzig 143–4
   Pioneers of Modern Design (*Pioneers of the Modern Movement*) 46, 153
   'Reassessment 4: Three Oxford Colleges' 140–3, Figs. 5.9–11
   Reith Lectures (1955) *The Englishness of English Art* 6, 125, 145–51, 158, 209, 257
   'Sir William Temple and Sharawaggi' (with S. Lang) 140
   'The Anti-Pioneers' 194
   The Englishness of English Art 1, 2, 17, 127
   'The Genesis of the Picturesque' 140
   'The Geography of Art' 147
   The Leaves of Southwell 147
   'The Modern Movement in Britain' 145
   Visual Planning and the Picturesque 140
Philadelphia
   Vanna Venturi House, Chestnut Hill 189
Piano, Renzo 8, 255
   Centre Pompidou, Paris 8, 224, 228–33, Figs. 8.4, 8.6
   see also Rogers
Pibworth, Charles 5, 107, 123
   Bristol Central Library carvings 104, Fig. 4.3
   Law Society, Chancery Lane, London, carvings 104
Picasso, Pablo 126, 136, 139
Pick, Frank 120
Picturesque 1, 2, 5–6, 10, 22, 24, 31, 34, 35, 76, 100, Chapter 5 *passim*, 153–64, 171, 177, 179, 197, 204, 215, 216, 243, 253, 254, 255, 256, 257
   see also Banham, Pevsner, Ruskin, Sharawaggi
Piero della Francesca 173
Pinder, Wilhelm 143, 144
Piper, David 171
Piper, John 5, 125, 126, 128, 139, 204
   'Black and White' (with J. M. Richards) 147
   Church of the Holy Innocents, Knowle, Bristol 136, Fig. 5.8
   'England's Early Sculptors' 127
   'Pleasing Decay' 139

'Prehistory from the Air' 126
'The Architecture of Destruction' 136
'The Nautical Style' 147
Pisa 189
  Duomo 189
Pistoia 27, 189
  San Pietro 22, 23, Figs. 1.5, 1.6
Pite, Arthur Beresford
  Institute of Chartered Accountants, City of London Fig. 4.2
  St Bartholomew's Hospital, London 113
Poelzig, Hans 194
Pollock, Jackson 167
polychromy 16, 22, 24, 25, 26, 27, 28, 33, 35, 36, 38, 54, 69, 76, 82, 236, 213, 253, 254, 255
Pomeroy, Frederick 102
Pop-Art 169, 170, 171, 195
Pope, Alexander 156
Portland stone 3, 5, 107, 110, 112, 114, 123, 217, 233, 254, 256
Posener, Julius 187
Post-Modernism 1, 7, 8, 20, 30, 179, 189, 190, 193, 194, 195, 198, 203, 215, 219, 222, 234, 244, 245, 246, 249, 253, 254, 256
Powell, Philip, and John Hidalgo Moya
  Churchill Gardens, Pimlico, London 190
Powers, Alan
  Britain 3, 203
Pratt, Roger
  Coleshill House 208
Pre-Raphaelite art 46, 50, 65
Price, Uvedale 128, 133, 140, 154
Primitivity 85, 94, 110, 156, 159, 167, 195, 206, 209, 218, 224
Prior, Edward Schröder 1, 4, Chapter 3 *passim*, 256
  'Architectural Modelling' 90
  butterfly-plan cottage model 89–90, Fig. 3.12
  St Andrew, Roker 4, 69, 85–6, Fig. 3.2
  St Osmund, Poole, Dorset 93–5, Fig. 3.17

'Texture as a Quality of Art and a Condition for Architecture' 4, 86–8
The Barn, Exmouth 89–91, Figs. 3.13–14
The Cathedral Builders of England 88
Voewood House, Holt, Norfolk 88–97, Figs. 3.15–16
Proteus 9
Pückler-Muskau, Hermann Fürst von
  Hints on Landscape Gardening 216
Pugin, A. W. N. 1, 41, 56, 82
Purbeck marble 41, 61

Queen Anne architecture 69
Queen Elizabeth, The Queen Mother 221

Radford, Francis 60
Randall, H. J. 126
Rationalism 5, 85, 125, 128, 145, 148, 149, 153, 154, 156, 158, 172, 179, 187, 190, 209, 213, 217, 229, 237, 244
Read, Herbert 167, 169
  Art Now 169
Refinement 4, 76, 77, 79, 80, 85, 96
Regency Architecture 100, 132, 187, 191, 219, 237, 256
Reith, John 125, 145, 146, 147
Rembrandt 249
Renaissance Architecture 16, 17, 22, 31, 121, 156, 158, 161, 173, 184, 195, 204, 206, 207, 208
Repton, Humphrey 216
Reynolds, Edward
  Bristol warehouse project, Architectural Association, London 211
Rheims Cathedral 147
Rice, Peter 223, 232, 255
Richards, James Maude 100, 128, 139
  An Introduction to Modern Architecture 100
  'Black and White' (with John Piper) 147
Rietveld, Gerrit (Thomas) 100, 196

Rimini
    Tempio Malatestiano 120, 173
Robert Matthew, Johnson-Marshall (Andrew Darbyshire)
    Hillingdon Civic Centre, Middlesex 241
Robinson, William Heath 254
Rococo 56, 144
Rodin, Auguste 121
Rogers, Ernesto Nathan 190
Rogers, Richard 1, 7–8, 223–35, 255
    Centre Pompidou, Paris 224, 228–33, Figs. 8.4, 8.6
    Lloyds Building, City of London 8, 228, 233–5, Fig. 8.7
    see also High-Tech, Piano
Romanesque architecture 13, 20, 22, 31, 38, 41, 118, 127, 148, 189, 206
    Kilpeck Church, Herefordshire 127
    St Peter's, Rowlstone, Herefordshire 127, Fig. 5.1
Romano, Giulio
    Palazzo del Te, Mantua 219
Romantic Functionalism 8, 235–44
Romantic Pragmatism 8, 244
Rome 77, 154, 219
    Casa del Girasole 187–9, Fig. 7.6
    Palazzo Farnese 195
    St Peter's 206
    Temple of Antoninus and Faustina 31
Rossetti, Dante Gabriel 50
    Arthur's Tomb 50
    Oxford Union Society murals 50
Rowe, Colin 150, 151, 154, 213, 214, 215, 216, 253
    'Mannerism and Modern Architecture' 189–90, 206
    'The Mathematics of the Ideal Villa' 158
Rowe, Colin, and Fred Koetter
    'Collage City' 150–1
    Collage City 150
Rowntree, Kenneth
    Architectural Review (cover, January 1944) 136, Fig. 5.7
    urban panorama of 'sharawaggi' 129–30, 132, 164, Fig. 5.2
Royal Academy, London 32, 73, 89

Rudofsky, Bernard 8
    Architecture without Architects 237
Ruskin, John 1, 2, 3, 4, 6, 7, 8, Chapter 1 *passim*, 46, 49, 50, 52, 63, 76, 79, 86, 87, 88, 93, 126, 136, 139, 146, 179, 183, 184, 189, 190, 194, 213, 224, 232, 245, 253, 254, 255, 256, 257
    colour theory 24–5, 26–31
    'Influence of Imagination in Architecture' 224
    Linear Gothic 13, 17, 254, Fig. 1.3
    Modern Painters 12, 19, 20, 31
    Oxford University Museum 8, 213
    reading the wall-surface 1, 3, Chapter 1 *passim*, 88, 253
    St Mark's Rest 9
    Surface Gothic 17, Fig. 1.3
    The Poetry of Architecture 146
    The Seven Lamps of Architecture 3, 10, 17, 26, 27, 28, 34, 76
    The Stones of Venice 3, 9, 10, 12, 13, 15, 17, 19, 20, 24, 25, 27, 28, 30, 31, 49, Figs. 1.3, 1.5
    The Two Paths 63
    typology 19, 22, 93
    wall-veil 1, 2, 4, 12–24, 28, 30, 86, 87, 88, 184, 213, 254, Fig. 1.5
Ruskin, John James (father to John Ruskin) 23
Russell, John 120, 121
Russell, Vera 120, 121
Russian Orthodox art 131
Ryan, Sally 249
Rykwert, Joseph 136

Sadler, Simon 229
Saint, Andrew 232
St Cuthbert 9
Sandringham 89
Sansovino, Jacopo
    Library of St Mark's, Venice 208
Sant'Elia, Antonio 211
    La Città Nuovo 228
Saussure, Ferdinand de 194
Savageness 12, 30, 76, 86, 88
Scamozzi, Vincenzo
    Procuratie Nuove, Venice 208
    Villa Polini, Padua 208

Scarpa, Carlo 176
Scharoun, Hans 240
Scheerbart, Paul 224
Scheu, Andreas 65
Schinkel, Karl Friedrich
   Altes Museum, Berlin 215, 216
   Collection of Architectural Designs
     (*Sammlung Architektonischer*
     Entwürfe) 216
   Gardener's House, Charlottenhof,
     Potsdam 215–16, 219
Schmarsow, August
   The Essence of Architectural
     Creation 144
Scotland 2
   Skye 236
Scott, Geoffrey
   The National Character of English
     Architecture 146
sculpture and architecture 4–5, 10, 17,
   27, 31, 90, Chapter 4 *passim*,
   127, 132, 144, 145, 163, 174,
   196, 197, 202, 204, 210, 253
   see also Carving
Scott, Gilbert 79
Scott, Walter 254
Sedding, John D. 33
Segal, Hannah
   'A Psycho-analytical Approach to
     Aesthetics' 174
Semiology 194, 256
Semper, Gottfried 12, 13, 52, 144,
   251
Serlio, Sebastiano 249
Serra, Richard 252–3
Seurat, Georges
   The Bathers at Asnières 175
Sharawaggi 1, 5–6, Chapter 5 *passim*,
   164, 253, 255, Fig. 5.2
Shaw, Henry
   Encyclopaedia of Ornament 52
Shaw, Richard Norman 33, 89, 96,
   218, 241, 247
   Chesters, Northumberland 89
   Piccadilly Hotel, London 96
Shepard, Alan 224
Sheppard, Richard Herbert, Geoffrey
   Robson, and Partners
     Churchill College, Cambridge 194

Silbury Hill, Wiltshire 126
Simpson, J. Lomax
   Unilever House, London 123
Smithson, Alison and Peter 1, 2, 7, 126,
   154, 158, 159, 163, 167, 176,
   177, 189, 190, 195, 240, 247,
   257
   Coventry Cathedral competition
     156
   Economist Building, London 3, 6,
     156, 171, 215
   Haupstadt Berlin Competition 226,
     240
   Hunstanton School, Norfolk 6,
     156–8, 167, Fig. 6.2
   Limerston Street bathroom, London
     164–5, 255, Fig. 6.7
   'Patio and Pavilion' (Group 6), 'This
     is Tomorrow' exhibition 169–71,
     Fig. 6.10
   Robin Hood Gardens, Poplar,
     London 235
   Sheffield University project 226
   see also Brutalism
Sitte, Camillo 236
   Der Städtebau 140
Sitwell, Sacheverell 249
Skidmore (Louis), Owings (Nathaniel)
   and Merrill (John) (SOM)
   Lever House, New York 205
Smith, Sidney
   Tate Britain, Westminster 216
Smythson, Robert
   Hardwick Hall 158, 247, Fig. 8.14
Soane, John
   Soane Museum, Lincoln's Inn
     Fields, London 219
Socialist Realism 131
Soisson, Louis de 235
Southwell Minster 147
Spalding, Frances 126
Spence, Basil
   Coventry Cathedral 6, 125–6, 156
Stamp, Gavin 113, 123
Stevenage New Town 149
Stirling, James 1, 2, 6–7, 33, 154,
   155, 159, 169, 171, 187, 189,
   203–22, 244, 254, 255
   'Black Notebook' 189, 204

Center for the Performing Arts, Cornell University 216
Clore Gallery, Tate Britain, London 7, 203, 215–22, Figs. 7.18–20
Flats, Ham Common, London 6, 159, Fig. 6. 3
Florey Building, Oxford 32
Fogg Museum, Harvard University 218
'Garches to Jaoul' 209
Leicester University Engineering Building 6, 156, 209–15, Fig. 7.16
Sheffield University, competition design 203–8, Figs. 7.14–15
Staatsgalerie, Stuttgart 2, 245, 253, Fig. 7.17
see also Brutalism, Gowan, Post-Modernism
Stockholm
Stockholm City Hall 236
Stockholm Exhibition (1930) 235
Stourhead 126
Stokes, Adrian 1, 6, 120, 121, 163, 167, 171, 172–7, 210
 Art and Science 173
 'Form in Art' 174
 Inside Out 173
 Michelangelo 174
 Reflections on the Nude 174
 Smooth and Rough 173, 255
 'The Prime Influence of Building in the Graphic Arts' 174–5
 The Quattro Cento 173
 The Stones of Rimini 102, 120, 163
 Three Essays on The Painting of our Time 120
 see also Carving
Street, Arthur Edmund 36
Street, George Edmund 1, 3, 4, 10, 27, 33–43, 59, 69, 79
 All Saints, Boyne Hill, Berkshire 33–43, Figs. 1.9–12
 Brick and Marble in the Middle Ages 36, 38, 40–1
 'On Colour as Applied to Architecture' 41
 'On the Proper Characteristics of a Town Church' 34

SS Philip and James, Oxford 36
 'The True Principles in Architecture' 33–4, 37–8
Stuttgart
 Staatsgalerie 2, 245, 253, Fig. 7.17
 Weissenhof Exhibition (1927) 99
Sublime art 139, 206, 255
Summerson, John 4, 31, 32, 101, 218, 219
 'Christian Gothic' 159
 'Vitruvius Ludens' 217
 'Vitruvius Ridens or Laughter at the Clore' 217, 218
Suprematism 196
Surrealism 5, 128, 139, 196
Sunderland
 St Peter, Monkwearmouth 85
Swedish architecture
 'Million Dwellings Programme' 236
 'New Empiricism' 154, 156, 191, 236
 see also Erskine
Swiss architecture 245, 247

Taine, Hippolyte 63
Tapies, Antoni 165
Taut, Bruno 213
Team 4 (Su Brumwell, Wendy Cheesman, Norman Foster, Richard Rogers) 229
 Reliance Controls Factory 229, 230
Team 10 239, 240, 257
Tecton 6, 7, 130, 131
 Hallfield Estate, Paddington 179–82, Figs. 7.1–2, 7.4
 Highpoint I, Hampstead 130, 131, 132, 180, 183, 190, 256
 Highpoint II, Hampstead 6, 130, 131, 132, 145, 179, 180, 183, 256, Fig. 5.3
 Priory Green Estate, Finsbury 7, 182
 Spa Green Estate, Finsbury 182–7, Figs. 7.3–5
 see also Lubetkin
Temple, William 129, 140
Terragni, Giuseppe 189
 Casa del Fascio, Como 187
Terry, Quinlan 245

Teulon, Samuel Smiles 83, 85
  St Stephen's, Hampstead, London 83
'This is Tomorrow' exhibition (1956) 6, 7, 196, 203, 257
  Group 2 170, 171
  Group 7 196
  Group 10 169–72, 195, Fig. 6.11
  'Patio and Pavilion' (Group 6) 170, 171, Fig. 6.10
Thompson, Paul 27, 28
Thoreau, Henry David 69
Thorneycroft, William Hamo 102, 104
  Institute of Chartered Accountants frieze, City of London 102, Fig. 4.2
Tivoli 128
  Hadrian's Villa 151
Townscape 1, 5, 6, 125, 128–39, 140, 149, 150, 154, 156, 235, 236
  see also Cullen
Truefitt, George
  Designs for Country Churches 43
Tunnard, Christopher 128–9, 132–3
  Gardens in the Modern Landscape 128–9, Fig. 5.4
Turner, J M W 19, 216

Udine
  Palazzo Pubblico 36
Underwood, Eric
  Short History of English Sculpture 117–18
Underwood, Henry
  St Mary and St Nicholas, Littlemore, Oxford 11
Ursprung, Philip 253
Utrillo, Maurice 139

Van Eyck, Aldo 240
Vanbrugh, John 204, 209, 222
  Claremont House, Belvedere, Esher 209
  Seaton Delaval 170
Vantongerloo, Georges 163
Venice 3, 4, 9, 10, 12, 13, 15, 16, 17, 19, 20, 23–8, 30, 31, 49, 87, 93, 207, 253
  Accademia 15, Fig. 1.2
  Ca' Farsetti 13
  Ca' Loredan 13
  Calle di Rimedio 13, 15, 260 n35
  Campo Santa Maria Formosa 13
  Casa dell'Angelo 13–14, Fig. 1.1
  Doge's Palace (Ducal Palace) 17, 25, 28, 30, 93
  Library of Saint Mark's 208
  Murano 19
  Procuratie Nuove 208
  Rialto 13
  Rio de Palazzo 15
  St Mark's 9, 14, 24, 208
  Santa Maria Formosa 31
  Torcello 19
Venturi, Robert 189
  Complexity and Contradiction in Architecture 194, 222
  Vanna Venturi House, Chestnut Hill, Philadelphia 189, 194
Venturi, Robert, Denise Scott Brown, and Steven Izenour
  Learning from Las Vegas 194, 195
Verona 38
  Duomo 31
  marble 17, 24, 28
  San Zeno Maggiore 38
  Scala tomb 17
  Scaligeri Palace 36
Vicenza
  Casa di Palladio 206
  Villa Rotonda 206, 208
Victoria and Albert Museum 57, 121
  the Green Dining Room 57, Fig. 2.6
Vidler, Anthony
  'Losing Face' 215
Vitruvius 19, 217, 218
  The Ten Books of Architecture 215–16
Voelcker, John 169, 170

Wales
  Hafod 126
  Wye Valley 2
Walpole, Horace 129, 209
  Strawberry Hill, Twickenham 129, 209

Walsall 247, 249, 252
  The New Art Gallery 3, 8, 247, 249–53, Figs. 8.15–16
Warren, Edward 73, 80, 82
Wasmuth, Ernst 196
Waterhouse, Alfred
  University College Hospital, London 112, 113
Watkin, David
  History of Western Architecture 245
Watkinson, Ray 49, 51, 56
Watteau, Jean-Antoine
  The Music Party 175
Weaver, Lawrence 89, 92
Webb, Michael
  Furniture Manufacturers Association HQ, High Wycombe, England 225, 226, Fig. 8.1
Webb, Philip 1, 2, 4, 33, Chapter 2 *passim*, 247, 255, 257
  Green Dining Room 57–9, Fig. 2.6
  1 Holland Park, London 59–67, Fig. 2.7
  Red House 46–55, 66–7, Figs. 2.2, 2.3
  Red House, 'Palace of Art' design 4, 48–50, Figs. 2.2, 2.3
  St George Cabinet 49–50, 53, Fig. 2.3
  'Trellis' wallpaper 47, 56, 65, Fig. 2.5
  see also Burne-Jones, Morris
Weissenhof Exhibition (1927) 99
Wells, Randall 88
Wells Coates
  Isokon building, Lawn Road, Hampstead 175
Weston, Richard
  Materials, Form and Architecture 3
Whistler, James Abbott McNeill 60
white architecture 100
White, Gleeson 60, 61–2
Whitman, Walt 5, 101, 106, 107, 109, 123
  Leaves of Grass 105, 110
Wigley, Mark 99, 100
Wild, James
  Christ Church, Streatham, London 24–5
Wilford, Michael 216, 221, Figs. 7.17–20
  see also Stirling
Williams, Arthur Vivian 196
Wilson, Colin St John 154, 155, 163, 169, 173, 177, 189, 204, 210, 211, 215
  Bentham Road Estate, London 155, 162, 187, Fig. 6.5
  British Library, London 215
  Cambridge School of Architecture extension 163, Fig. 6.6
  Coventry Cathedral competition 126
  Grantchester Road house, Cambridge 176
  Group 10, 'This is Tomorrow' exhibition (1956) 169–72, 195, Fig. 6.11
  Harvey Court, Cambridge 156, 163
  Hereford Square flats, London 159, 161, Fig. 6.4
  Manor Road Libraries, Oxford 163
  'Patterns in Living' 190
  Peterhouse College, Cambridge (William Stone Building) 176
  'The Natural Imagination: an essay on the experience of architecture' 171, 173
  'The Vertical City' 154
  see also Long, Martin
Wilson, Richard 2
Wittkower, Rudolf 161, 172, 173, 190, 208, 209, 257
  Architectural Principles in the Age of Humanism 156, 208
Wittkower, Rudolf, and Fritz Saxl
  British Art and the Mediterranean 208
Wölfflin, Heinrich
  Kunstgeschichtliche Grunbegriffe (*Principles of Art History*) 144

Wollheim, Richard 167
Wood, John
   Circus, Bath 140, 158
Wren, Sir Christopher 5, 110, 123, 233
   Christ Church, Oxford 140
   plan for London 140
   St Paul's Cathedral, London 149, Fig. 5.13
Wright, Frank Lloyd 106, 159, 196, 229, 244
   Ernst Wasmuth portfolios 196
   Johnson Wax, Racine, Wisconsin 211
   Unity Temple, Oak Park, Chicago 107
Wyatt, Matthew Digby
   Specimens of the Geometrical Mosaics of the Middle Ages 28

Yorke, Francis Reginald Stevens
   The Modern House 100, 101

Zimmerman, Clare 209
Zuccheri, Federico 206